Understanding Fandom

Understanding Fandom

An introduction to the study of media fan culture

By
MARK DUFFETT

BLOOMSBURY
NEW YORK · LONDON · NEW DELHI · SYDNEY

Bloomsbury Academic
An imprint of Bloomsbury Publishing Plc

1385 Broadway	50 Bedford Square
New York	London
NY 10018	WC1B 3DP
USA	UK

www.bloomsbury.com

Bloomsbury is a registered trade mark of Bloomsbury Publishing Plc

First published 2013

ISBN HB: 978-1-4411-5855-0
PB: 978-1-4411-6693-7
e-PDF: 978-1-6235-6585-5
e-Pub: 978-1-6235-6086-7

Library of Congress Cataloging-in-Publication Data
Duffett, Mark.
Understanding fandom : an introduction to the study of
media fan culture / by Mark Duffett.
pages cm
Includes bibliographical references and index.
ISBN 978-1-4411-5855-0 (hardback) – ISBN 978-1-4411-6693-7 (paperback) –
ISBN 978-1-62356-086-7 (e-pub)   1. Fans (Persons)   2. Mass media–
Social aspects.   3. Mass media and culture.   I. Title.
HM646.D84 2013
302.23–dc23
2013020885

Design by Newgen Knowledge Works (P) Ltd., Chennai, India
Printed and bound in the United States of America

Contents

Foreword

What if? – reimagining fandom

Professor Matt Hills

*U*nderstanding Fandom sets out the key debates that have helped to shape fan studies. But it does more than that. Mark Duffett draws on his own prior research to illuminate discussions, and integrates work on media fandom – that is, fans of movie franchises and TV shows – with work on popular music fandom. Surprisingly, these areas have rarely been combined. Unusually, then, in the chapters that follow you will find Daniel Cavicchi's brilliant work on Bruce Springsteen fans (1998) quoted just as often as Henry Jenkins's seminal work from *Textual Poachers* (1992).

More than that, Duffett suggests new directions and intriguing critiques. Understanding fandom means recapping influential analyses and approaches, sure, but understanding cultural phenomena and their academic study can also mean identifying paths not taken, and returning to marginalized ideas or aspects of fandom. At its best and most worthwhile, understanding is not a passive repetition of received wisdom: it is also a *reimagining of the object of study*, a series of (realist) what-ifs. What if established theoretical frameworks have missed elements of fandom? What if fandom can be analysed in new ways? What-ifs enable us to perceive aspects of our cultural reality which common sense, or dominant systems of meaning and value, tend to set aside.

And to this extent, fandom and academia are curiously alike: both centrally involve processes of re-imagination. Academics strive to see things and theories anew, while fans often work on re-imagining their beloved objects, whether through fan fiction, commentary or projecting future versions of media texts and responding to imagined developments (*Star Wars* fans are currently busy pondering what a Disney-owned version of the franchise will look like, for instance). Both media scholarship and fandom – although, of course, these are not two hermetically sealed entities – work on re-thinking and challenging the popular culture that surrounds us.

How does *Understanding Fandom* start to reimagine fandom and fan studies? Well, it does the following: considers whether 'anti-fandom' (Gray 2003) can be invited under certain circumstances (Chapter 2); asks why work on celebrity has been separated from work on 'textual poaching' in Henry Jenkins's *oeuvre* (Chapter 3); argues that psychoanalytic theories may never be able to offer a wholly meaningful grasp on fandom (Chapter 4); devotes more attention to becoming-a-fan stories than is usually the case (Chapter 5); focuses on pleasures of connection as well as those of appropriation and performance (Chapter 6); considers fandom as a 'queering' of gender identities and performances alongside the reinforcing of gender norms (Chapter 7); sets out a novel theory of 'imagined memories' to think about multi-generational fandom (Chapter 8); suggests that fans' communal concerns may simply be 'tangential' to those of media producers, rather than in conflict or complicity with them (Chapter 9); and argues that there is 'now a crucial role for researchers who do not proclaim their own fandom' (Chapter 10).

These multiple, creative re-imaginings of fandom – and fan studies – carry many implications. Anti-fandom has become a burgeoning area of study: anti-fans are 'distant' readers who form an image of a text or genre without actually paying close attention to it, and who then viscerally define their identity against the disliked object. Anti-fandom can also shade into fandom, however, when fans rail against parts of their fan object, and profess to hate a new storyline, character or album. By suggesting that anti-fandom can be invited in certain circumstances, for example, by Bob Dylan's use of the electric guitar, or punk's DIY ethos, Duffett considers how significant changes can form part of a fan object's unfolding history, and how specific fan objects can carry codes of broadly 'anti-fan' rebelliousness. The fact that both Duffett's examples are from popular music fandom does seem to imply that 'invited anti-fandom' is linked to discourses of artistic risk-taking and revolt which may tend to be less present – or at least, less dominant – around some types of pop music as well as popular film and TV. For instance, does *Doctor Who* invite anti-fandom as it shifts from one production team to another? Arguably, quite the reverse: the 2010 move from Russell T. Davies's stewardship to Steven Moffat taking charge was marked by a strong sense of continuity and brand identity (showing all 11 Doctors in *The Eleventh Hour*), as if designed to reassure audiences that the show had not radically changed. Perhaps the possibility of 'invited anti-fandom' is feared rather than embraced in many media industry changes, where the threat of losing or alienating established fans becomes of paramount concern. If so, 'invited anti-fandom' may make more sense where art discourses are more strongly in place than the branding logics that are becoming typical of popular media.

Furthermore, do boybands invite anti-fandom if they attempt to re-orient their sound and target a new demographic and new audience? Take That seem to have made the leap from boyband to near-supergroup, but in this case they achieved such a transformation by disbanding and reforming, with the intervening period (of 'post-object' status: see Williams 2011) partly licensing their shift in cultural status, as well as marking a recognition that their original fan base had aged alongside them. Here, again, 'invited anti-fandom' is displaced by a sense of enduring fandom aligned with culturally appropriate discourses of age – upon reforming, Take That were no longer a 'boyband', and thus their own visible and culturally-meaningful ageing made sense of their altered industrial position. Invited anti-fandom may therefore hinge on sudden, unexpected and radical changes in the fan object – something which industrial processes of continuity (and franchising/branding) will frequently tend to oppose or smooth out. The concept cautions us to think carefully about the meanings that circulate around different fan objects, as well as how they are industrially positioned.

I will not defend psychoanalytic theories of fandom here; my own prior work offers a good enough sense of my likely position in the debate (Hills 2002). But having said that, Duffett's argument that fandom is always partly private and partly social – partly felt and partly performed – captures its hybridity extremely well. By refusing to view or define fandom as one thing, Duffett productively develops how we might best understand it. Readers looking for a handy, straightforward definition will be disappointed, of course, but those looking for a sense of fandom's different lives, and practices, and moments, will find much to savour.

Another of Mark Duffett's intriguing interventions arrives via the concept of 'imagined memories'. These are memories of key events in the fan object's history – the Beatles' early performances, or the campaign to bring back *Star Trek* after its initial TV run – that very few fans will possess themselves, but which nevertheless tend to circulate as lore within the given fan culture. As such, fans engage with reiterated, mediated narratives of production or performance which despite the fact that they may not have personally experienced these things, become so closely entwined with their sense of self (or are so greatly desired as experiences) that they become 'prosthetic' memories. Like invited anti-fandom, this concept appears more closely rooted in popular music fandom, although examples can no doubt be found for fans of long-running film and TV series. Despite Duffett pointing out that no memories are 'real' (they are all cultural and psychological productions based on cognitive processes and interpretations), there does remain a danger here: one of implying that something aberrant or psychologically distinctive happens to fans but not non-fans. If fandom is marked by 'imagined memories' but non-fandom lacks this dimension, then it may be hard to avoid a taint of psychological deviance or exceptionalism. Can fandom not be theorized in ways that articulate it with a wider range of enthusiasms and passions, rather than being locked into a notion of memory that seemingly does not cross its (sub)cultural boundaries? However, what imagined memory does usefully stress is, once again, the positive importance of imagination to fandom, with fans imagining what it might have been like to see Elvis perform live, or to watch the first ever episode of *Doctor Who* on its initial 1963 broadcast. As a concept, imagined memory will certainly provoke further work on fandom and the life course, as well as fandom and memory in general. Indeed, these areas are starting to come to the fore in fan studies (Harrington & Bielby 2010; Garde-Hansen 2011). *Understanding Fandom* thus very much forms an active part of, and crystallizes out, an emerging set of scholarly concerns.

I think the same is true of Duffett's argument that academics might no longer need to focus on their own personal fan engagements (see also Phillips 2010). This, too, helpfully captures a moment in current fan studies. I think Duffett is quite right: by forestalling discussion of personal fandoms, scholars may be better able to engage with a range of fan objects as equally deserving of theorization, something this book demonstrates very well. On the other hand, if the auto-ethnographic study of personal fandom remains absent while scholars continue to focus on 'their' personal, favoured fan cultures – rather than adopting more synthesizing and inclusive stances – then our accounts of fandom will remain highly partial, skewed towards cultural artefacts with certain values or appeals, and skewed away from investigating the fandoms surrounding 'regressive' texts, or texts at odds with academic politics, cultural identities and investments. To that degree, I think remaining reflexive about what we study, and why, and what goes missing along the way – potentially ending up outside the implicit 'canon' of much-studied fandoms – remains absolutely crucial. At the same time, academia's relationship to fandom may be structural as well as personal, as Deb Verhoeven points out in her (2009) analysis of film director Jane Campion's academic-fan following. Considering 'the preferences of academics as media consumers, in particular as a . . . market segment' (Verhoeven 2009, 155) could mean scholars tackling their fandoms not merely via auto-ethnographic 'confession,' but also via analysis of how scholarship itself is increasingly integrated into media paratexts, commodities and systems of value. If digital fandom can wittingly and unwittingly add value to media brands (De Kosnick 2013), then scholar-fandom might also find itself enmeshed in these media industry processes.

In his Conclusion, Duffett argues that fanaticism and fandom have typically been kept apart, conceptually, in contemporary culture. A common-sense cultural ideology thus depoliticizes fandom, condemning it to the realm of the 'trivial,' or treating it as mere personal taste. One can be 'fanatically' devoted to right-wing or left-wing belief systems – even to 'extreme' ideologies – but the language or discourse of fandom is not typically used in relation to public debates surrounding political systems and beliefs. In Duffett's terms: 'a person can be a fan of transgressive or taboo entertainment, say, the film *Cannibal Holocaust* . . . but they could only be "fanatical" about Adolf Hitler.' In fact, some writers have pushed at this common sense view of fandom, arguing that one can at least be a 'fan' of the news (Gray 2007b), or that political affiliations can be modelled using fan studies (Van Zoonen 2005; Sandvoss 2012), or indeed that fandom can be articulated with political activism (Jenkins & Shresthova 2012), even if being a 'Hitler fan' probably sounds very strange to our ears.

The conceptual distinction between fanaticism and fandom has also been played with in recent popular culture. *Osama: A Novel*, by science fiction fan and writer Lavie Tidhar, imagines an alternative world – unlike our own in a set of ways – where Osama Bin Laden is not a real person, but is instead the hero of a series of pulp action-adventure novels called the *Vigilante* books. In this Philip K. Dickian alternate universe, Osama fans gather together at OsamaCon, a convention celebrating the character, and Bin Laden's activities (identifiable as versions of our own news stories and our own recent history) are recounted as thrilling fiction. In one sense, *Osama* respects the cultural boundaries and ideologies which separate fandom from fanaticism. After all, it takes a re-imagined, counterfactual universe to reverse their polarity. But at the same time, Tidhar's novel subverts rigid categories of pop-cultural fandom versus political fanaticism, destabilizing them as imaginatively permeable. 'Osama fans': it is an audacious conceit, one which pushes readers to consider, and diegetically cross, the line between fandom and politics. *Osama* is a part detective novel, part counterfactual science fiction, demonstrating how our culture discursively polices the fandom/politics boundary, insistently compelling us to separate out 'serious' (or dangerous) belief systems from the allegedly banal frivolities of fandom and its meanings. Perhaps, whispers *Osama*'s reimagined universe, fandom is a serious belief system which (re)makes cultural worlds:

> There were other people in the hotel dining room and most of them also had Osama bin Laden paperbacks next to them, and many of them seemed to know each other and were talking, like friends who haven't seen each other in a while and were busy resuming an interrupted conversation . . .

'What's this *Osama Gazette*?'

The men exchanged glances. Clearly, their looks said, this was a stranger in their midst. 'It's a *fanzine* . . . a small publication dedicated to the scholarly *discourse* of the Osamaverse . . . You can find copies in the dealers' room'. (Tidhar 2012, 240, 242)

What *Osama* highlights is, again, the importance of *reimagining fandom*, and at the same time, the significance of practices of reimagining *within* fandom. Rather than creating 'AU' (alternate universe) fan fiction which casts familiar characters into a transformed narrative universe, or reworking an SF TV series to re-genrify or sexualize it, Tidhar's distinctive 'textual poaching' daringly appropriates news of terrorism as if it were the adventures of pulp fiction.

And Tidhar is not alone in his fantastical re-thinkings of fandom; Brandon Cronenberg's (2012) horror movie *Antiviral* also satirically trades on fandom, positing an imagined, alternative world where fans are so keen to feel connected to celebrities that they want to contract the same viruses as them. Here, the 'pathological tradition' interrogated by Mark Duffett and others, is re-imagined directly in relation to medical pathologies. In Cronenberg's fantasy world, fan-celebrity identification has tipped over into associations with, and experiences of, illness. Where Tidhar challenges readers to re-conceptualize 'the public sphere' and 'private' media consumption, Cronenberg seemingly reinforces negative images of fandom – albeit a particular type of fandom. This is not a fantasy-horror film mocking horror fans, but instead one seemingly looking down on fans of celebrity culture. Both Tidhar's and Cronenberg's counterfactual worlds depend, I would say, precisely on the ordinariness of contemporary fandom: an everyday lived experience can be transformed into a central premise of these SF/horror stories exactly because readers and viewers are counted on to recognize what it means to be a fan. But the cultural politics of these fannish what-ifs indicate that pop culture does not always just embrace media fandom; certain fandoms may look down on others, with *Antiviral* arguably reflecting this dynamic by assuming that horror fans will readily engage with satirical pathologizations of celebrity fandom. Perhaps we do not just need to challenge the lines between 'serious' politics and 'non-serious' fandom, but also the divisions and assumed cultural hierarchies between different types of (celebrity/cult media) fandom. Indeed, this takes us back to Duffett's observation that Henry Jenkins has had little to say about celebrity fandoms, focusing instead on the text-oriented fandoms engaging with fictional worlds. The separation would seem to residually reflect a strand of cultural common sense asserting that these are very different modes of being a fan. The fact/fiction binary perhaps structures differences in scholarship, whereby how one thinks about celebrity fans must be kept distinct from how one analyses media fans (and the controversies in fandom itself over real person fiction, especially real person slash, perhaps reflect these anxieties over blurring fact and fiction, given that these are immensely powerful cultural categories).

Whether or not a general theory of fandom remains possible, the fact that fans mock one another ('I'm not that crazy sort of fan stalker'), and mock other(ed) fandoms – for example, cult horror fandom symbolically attacking *Twilight* fandom – suggests that *scholarship still needs to reimagine fandom as a greater cultural collective*, where one's own fandoms are not celebrated while others' tastes are denigrated. Taking fandom seriously should mean *taking all fandoms seriously* rather than belittling soap fans while applauding *The Sopranos* fans, say, or belittling boyband fans while applauding Bowie fans. If *Osama*'s representations of fandom destabilize and transgress cultural categories, *Antiviral* perhaps problematically plays into subcultural categories of 'good' (body horror) and 'bad' (celeb glamour) fan objects.

The imagining of real world *what-ifs* has been key to fan studies' attempts to revalue fandom: Jenkins's *Textual Poachers* asked the question 'what if fandom was not negatively stereotyped and assumed to be trivial?' And what-ifs continue to be important to academic work introducing yet challenging prior theories and approaches, such as *Understanding Fandom*. What if the 'slippery slope' idea is wholly wrong, and fandom cannot be thought of as a potential gateway to pathological obsession, despite recurrent 'expert' narratives implying this within our culture? What if fandom cannot always be understood in relation to media producers and industries, but needs to be analysed at least in part on its own terms? What if fans possess 'imagined memories'? Vital universes of thought are generated by academia, fandom and sometimes popular culture itself, acting upon the world in new ways. This is an ongoing process of analysis and illumination that *Understanding Fandom* makes a thoughtful, valuable and, above all, *imaginative* contribution to.

Matt Hills
Professor of Film & TV Studies
Aberystwyth University
2013

Acknowledgements

While I take responsibility for the views in *Understanding Fandom*, I have many people to thank for the book's development. The first is Professor Matt Hills, who kindly agreed to be keynote speaker at an international symposium on music fandom that I organized in June 2010 at the University of Chester. It was his suggestion that I should create a new textbook on the subject and he kindly agreed to write the foreword. Without Matt, *Understanding Fandom* would not actually exist.

I would also like to thank my colleagues across the department and faculty at Chester for facilitating the symposium and giving me time in my professional life to develop this manuscript. Mention must also be made to the many cohorts of Chester students who have taken the module that I led on fan culture and challenged me with their questions.

Understanding Fandom's voluntary beta-testers, Lucy Bennett and Nancy Bruseker, also deserve credit for their help and enthusiastic support.

I would especially like to thank all the colleagues who have supported my academic career, including Tom Attah, Gary Burns, Claude Chastagner, Jon Hackett, Chris Hart, Paula Hearsum, Joli Jensen, Brian Machin, David Pattie, Tim Wall and the late David Sanjek, to name but a few.

I wish to express my deep gratitude to my partner Julie, and my parents, brothers and friends, for their continuing encouragement and inspiration.

Lastly, Katie Gallof at Bloomsbury deserves credit and thanks for helping me see this project through to completion.

1

Introduction

The first performer on stage was Sting. He walked out on stage with a group of black backing singers, who began to sing one of his hits, beginning as an acapella chorus of voices . . . By the end of the first line, the 70,000 or more voices present were all singing as one, sending a message to millions watching the television signals that were being broadcast around the world by satellite. My body reacted instinctively, and I can still remember the moment vividly. My body was filled with excitement, the hairs on my arms stood up, and the ones on the back of my neck prickled. I was washed with a wave of euphoria, my whole body tingled, filled with energy, with excitement, with the moment of Kairos, of time that stood still, that had quantity rather than pace. I experienced joy, elation, exhilaration, as well as passion, political motivation and conviction.

RUPERT TILL 2010, X

It seems as good a place as any to begin a book on media fandom with music researcher Rupert Till's account of the 1988 *Free Nelson Mandela* concert in London. Till's report seems to capture something about an overwhelming sense of emotional conviction that accompanies fandom. His identification with the music is unexpected, bodily and heartfelt and seemingly lacking input from his own conscious will. It is not approached in a calculating way or as an achievement. Closer inspection reveals greater complexity. Rupert Till's pleasure seems to spring unbidden from his experience of a live performance and yet it likely represents the culmination of an extended engagement with Sting's recorded and broadcast music. Till is in a leisure environment surrounded by a vast group of like-minded people, at an event that could well have resonated with his value system. It is unclear whether his connection is just about the music, what it said in the context of Mandela's incarceration or with Sting himself for making a statement. Moreover Till's recollection comes from an event that has, over two decades, become important as part of a generational memory. He can now speak about his experience using words like 'kairos' which act as reminders that he has, in the meantime, acquired the knowledge and vocabulary of an experienced academic.[1] These things are worth mentioning, not because Till's entry into fandom sounds in any way suspicious, but rather to highlight that fandom itself is a more complicated phenomenon than we might think.

Most of us can identify with Till's experience in some way. It supplies an example of the surprisingly commonplace moment where, as individuals, we discover something significant about our passion and identity. Many people attend concerts, collect recordings, enjoy the cinema and watch television. Almost everyone loves a particular star or TV show. Whether the fascination is with Sting or *Spiderman*, Marilyn or *Twilight*, almost everyone self-identifies as a fan in some sense. An estimated 90 per cent of American males have repeatedly played video games (Jenkins 2006, 201). CBS polls consistently find that over 40 per cent of all Americans consider themselves to be Elvis fans (Victor 2008, 152). One study of young adults found that over 75 per cent of the sample professed a strong attraction to a celebrity at some point in their lives, and over half claimed that a famous person had influenced their personal attitudes or beliefs (see Boon & Lomore 2001).

Media fandom is the recognition of a positive, personal, relatively deep, emotional connection with a mediated element of popular culture. I began researching the topic for a PhD in 1995 and still remain interested by the questions that it can raise. Fandom has intrigued a generation of scholars who are interested in the expression of social and personal identity in the context of media culture. One useful distinction to make here is between wider research fields and fan studies. **Fandom research** is a very broad, long-standing, multi-disciplinary body of scholarship that takes fandom as its primary focus. Interested scholars are either interdisciplinary in orientation or have come from academic traditions such as sociology, anthropology and psychology. **Fan studies** is a much narrower area which has emerged from cultural studies in the last two decades. Its practitioners aim to represent fandom in a positive light and tend to study fan communities and practices. A wide range of fan research still takes place, although fan studies currently attracts the most attention. Fandom remains a complex and challenging area of analysis worth studying for many reasons. As Western society shifts further into a digital, tertiary, service economy, its analysis can help to explain why individuals are increasingly constructing their personal identities around the media products that they enjoy. Given the continual mystery and ubiquity of the phenomenon, studying it can help us improve individual self-awareness. A focus on fandom uncovers social attitudes to class, gender and other shared dimensions of identity. In business, the analysis of fandom enables product development. Crucially, its study can expose the operation of *power* in the cultural field.

Understanding Fandom is based on the debated premise that its subject matter has enough coherence to warrant detailed analysis. Sports fandom remains the most accepted model for fandom in our society. Although a minority of researchers have studied both topics, in many ways sports fandom and media fandom are very different objects of study.[2] Sports fandom is ultimately tribal and based on a controlled, competitive mentality. It raises passionate instincts that are significantly different in both meaning and intensity to those associated with enjoying television, music or cinema. One example should suffice: in May 2008 when public video screen coverage of the UEFA cup final malfunctioned in Manchester's Piccadilly Square, a riot took place that involved 1,500 police officers trying to contain thousands of disappointed Glasgow Rangers fans. Some of the officers wore emergency riot gear as they were expecting trouble. Fifteen police officers were injured and 42 fans arrested. In contrast, although concerts, conventions, raves, festivals, film premiers and celebrity book signings can attract large numbers of people, they are not generally associated with the atmosphere of drunken bravado and mass violence that can spoil sporting fixtures. Media fandom is socially enacted through different sets of gender relationships, different styles of behaviour and types of feeling. Because sport has gradually been extended as mass spectacle and its elite players have increasingly taken up the associated trappings of stardom, the difference between sports fandom and media fandom has perhaps diminished. David Beckham, for example, arguably has fans who are media fans rather than sports enthusiasts (see Cashmore 2004) and of course many people follow both pursuits at once. That does not mean there is no difference between them. Discussion in the present volume will not address sports fandom.

Perhaps a more pressing question is whether media fandom is itself a coherent object. Concluding an important book-length study of television fandom, Henry Jenkins wondered:

> I am not sure that the types of fans I have discussed here, fans of a particular configuration of popular narratives, are necessarily identical with other varieties of fans, fans of specific media personalities, rock performers, sports teams or soap operas. These groups will have some

common experiences as well as display differences that arise from their specific placement within the cultural hierarchy and their interests in different forms of entertainment. (1992, 286)

Jenkins is right: different fandoms involve a range of experiences and occupy different places in the public imagination. **Telefantasy** is a broad genre of television programming that includes sci-fi and fantasy narratives. Jenkins' book was based on research with fans of several different telefantasy series. Two points are interesting here. He identified what we might loosely call 'celebrity followers' as unserved by his analysis. As a strain of media fandom, popular music is perhaps the most representative of this contingent. Studying the difference between different media, P. David Marshall (1997) argued that film, television and popular music performers are differently exposed in their respective mass media. Marshall suggested that the aura of film stars emerges from the *distanced* nature of their screen image; we, as an audience, only witness a tiny fraction of their actual personalities on-screen. Television constructs media celebrity in quite the opposite way: by an intimate, immediate over-abundance of imagery that habituates viewers on a daily basis to their familiar presence. Meanwhile, for Marshall, popular music performers are particularly associated with the image of the *live crowd*, the energetic group of admirers who have assembled in one place to see them. **Synergy** is the cross promotion of commercial products to different outlets. Marshall's differentiation argument may be breaking down in an era of multimedia synergy where film stars work on television and in theatre, and tweet messages directly to their fans online. Nevertheless, it remains useful for addressing Jenkins' concerns. The process of following mass mediated celebrities, which, taking Marshall's lead we might recognize as symbolized by pop fandom, is not so very different in kind from other types of media fandom. Instead it represents one pole in a process that can also include reading narratives (whether biographic or fictional) and creating new reference points such as fan fiction. Jenkins (1992) looks at fans who made music ('filk songs'), but rarely does he – for both political and intellectual reasons – directly address the 'cult of personality' that undergirds some prominent types of media fandom. If fan studies has mostly been a repository for writing about telefantasy fandom for rather too long, it has much to learn from an interchange with the much smaller body of research about the popular music audience. Media fandom *holds together* narrative and personality, criticism and emotion. Its different forms – represented at their *extremes*, perhaps, by sci-fi and popular music fandom – are associated with different theoretical perspectives, yet they are *not completely distinct*. Rather than claiming to be a comprehensive survey of fandom research, this book has a more modest aim of introducing some of the key writers from the field and drawing together commonalities between fandoms for a range of media.

A brief history of fandom

Fandom is a sociocultural phenomenon largely associated with modern capitalist societies, electronic media, mass culture and public performance. In most research there is a tendency to talk about the phenomenon as if it has always existed, fully formed, in society. Some scholars have called for more research that historicizes fandom. As that issue is increasingly being addressed, writers have begun to unearth a complex history which demonstrates Henry Jenkins' claim that 'Nobody functions entirely within fan culture, nor does fan culture maintain any claims to self-sufficiency. There is nothing timeless and unchanging about this culture; fandom originates as a response to specific historical conditions' (1992, 3). Those conditions stem from shifts in the media and their tendency to reconfigure everyday experience.

The term 'fan' first appeared in late seventeenth-century England, where it was a common abbreviation for 'fanatic' (a religious zealot). It became significant in the United States a century later, where it was used by journalists to describe the passion of baseball spectators (Abercrombie & Longhurst 1998, 122). This later usage was adopted to describe dedicated audiences for film and recorded music. It is easy to make swift generalizations and say that prototypical forms of fandom therefore never existed in earlier times. That would, however, mistake the invention of the label for the beginning of the phenomenon. As Leo Braudy (1987) has shown, fame is an ancient mechanism, a point that seems obvious when one thinks about institutions like royal, religious or political office and the circulation of human faces on coinage. Portrait painting was a longstanding way to keep a record of personal likeness. Shakespeare, who was a highly successful playwright in his own lifetime (1564–1616), became the centre of one of the most enduring cultural phenomena after his death. His birthplace in Stratford upon Avon – which still attracts around 400,000 visitors per year – has been open to the public since the mid-eighteenth century. By the Victorian era it had became fashionable for visitors – some of whom, such as Charles Dickens, were famous in their own right – to scratch their names on the window panes or scrawl them on the inner walls of the cottage. The Victorian visitors' engravings are not so different to the graffiti that is currently written by fans on the stone wall outside Graceland.[3]

In the early part of the nineteenth century romantic poets like Lord Byron established a new benchmark in literary popularity. Written reports and newspapers helped to spread the reputations of well known people. By this time there were multiple genres of stage performance. Long before the advent of cinema or recorded sound, performers like the singer Jenny Lind (1820–87) and actress Sarah Bernhardt (1844–1923) made international tours, complete with merchandise, on the basis of their reputations (see Waksman 2011 and Cavicchi 2011, 14–18). Newspaper reviews prepared prospective audiences for their arrival. In effect, some kind of publicity had always allowed performers' reputations to precede them. It now seems strange that audiences who had never actually seen or heard a star could be sent into paroxysms of glee primed only by press reports. Nevertheless, celebrity was mediated by such means.

A significant shift happened in the middle of the nineteenth century. The term 'celebrity', which had previously referred to the general *condition* of being famous, extended its meaning to encompass famous individuals. The development of photography catalysed and consolidated this meaning. Portrait photographers like Napoleon Sarony, who ran a studio in New York from 1867, took pictures of singers and actors. Publicity shots formed the basis of a merchandising industry of photos, cards and postcards that circulated the carefully-posed visual image of theatre performers in an era where followers could easily acquire visual referents. When the American showman Buffalo Bill (William Cody) came to London to display his travelling show in 1887, his apartment was, according to a local journalist, 'embarrassed by an overwhelming mass of flowers which come hourly from hosts of female admirers' (see Warren 2002). In the later part of the nineteenth century, audience appreciation was conferred not only on writers, heroes, singing stars, raconteurs and theatre actors. It extended to other public figures, including a coterie of dandies who combined an aristocratic sense of privilege with dapper styles of dress and a carefree approach to their personal finances.

Later in the nineteenth century, the invention of sound recording (Edison's phonograph in 1878), cinema (perforated celluloid in 1889) and airwave broadcasting (perhaps as early as 1906) laid the foundations for electronic media industries that would support the vast audiences and fan phenomena that dominated much of the twentieth century. As sociologists Ferris and Harris (2011, 13) explain, 'there would be no fame if there were no fans, and there would be no fans if there were no media, whether print or electronic'. By 1904 the Italian tenor Enrico Caruso had acquired contracts with the New York Metropolitan Opera and the Victor Talking Machine Company that consolidated his immensely popular career, though he died in 1921, four years before electrical recording enabled high-fidelity sound. Meanwhile, once film fans started writing to Hollywood, the studios began to use stars as in-house vehicles for audience engagement. Movie studios were deluged from 1908 onwards with letters for early film performers such as Florence Lawrence.[4] When Carl Laemmle Snr, the head of Independent Moving Picture Company, publicized the names of his actors due to public demand in 1910, the star system was born. *Motion Picture Story Magazine*, the first national film fan magazine in America, began that same year. Within five years it was joined by *Photoplay*, *Motion Picture* and *Shadowland*. Mainstream publications like the *New York Times* also began covering Hollywood stories. Some of the first fan clubs emerged around this time. By 1912, all the major film companies except for DW Griffith's Biograph revealed the names of leading studio actors.

Between the 1920s and 1950s, fan demands helped to shape Hollywood to some extent. The dominant studios initially aimed to reach a female audience and to provide young working women with figures of identification. Features such as George Melford's *The Sheik* and Rex Ingram's *The Four Horsemen of the Apocalypse* (both 1921) established Rudoph Valentino an early Hollywood heartthrob. When Valentino died of a perforated ulcer in 1926, a crowd of around 75,000 onlookers marched on his funeral home, creating a crush that shattered the glass windows and required a police charge. Reports of the event scandalized Hollywood and led to perceptions of film fandom as a form of dangerous, collective hysteria. Historian Samantha Barbas (2001, 172) suggests, however:

> Although many of the men and women in the crowd were true Valentino fans, many, perhaps even the majority, were not. Most of the rioters probably had never belonged to Valentino's fan clubs. Many never followed his career, and some may never have seen his films. In many ways, the Valentino riot was less a product of movie fan culture than of American celebrity culture. Fascinated and titillated by the possibility of seeing a famous figure in person, aggressive curiosity seekers descended on the Valentino funeral with remarkable ferocity.

At the end of the 1920s the Hollywood studios collectively received over 32 million fan letters per year for both male and female stars. By this point they had departments to monitor and respond to fan mail and were collectively spending over $2 million a year on photographs, postage and salary for fan mail department workers. The most loved stars, such as Clara Bow and Mary Pickford, received over 1,000 items of fan mail a day. The Great Depression brought even more audiences flocking to see *distraction movies*, including musicals, crime films and monster features. Universal began a particularly successful run of supernatural horror films with *Dracula* (Browning 1931) and *Frankenstein* (Whale 1931), films which made iconic figures of Bela Lugosi and Boris Karloff respectively. Lugosi's nefarious count was so successful with fans that he inspired various lines of merchandise and remained unrivalled until the Hammer studio recreated the story with Christopher Lee in 1958. *King Kong* (1933) was another early blockbuster feature that set new standards in cinematic fantasy and raised the profile of its heroine Fay Wray.[5] Actress Jeanette MacDonald had one of the strongest fan clubs of the era, founded in 1937. When one of her fans lost the use of his legs, club members rallied to start a therapy fund for him. They also circulated a quarterly journal called *The Golden Comet*. Other film fans began to lobby David Selznick to cast Clark Gable as Rhett Butler in *Gone with the Wind* (Fleming 1939). In the mid-1940s Guy Madison's fans also lobbied to get him meatier roles. Right from the start, then, ordinary devotees were a prominent voice in the industry.

Other media had prominent fan followings too. The adoption of radio in the 1920s led to programming that soon sparked loyal followings. The male announcers who led the dance marathons of the depression era had scores of female admirers. For a decade from the mid-1930s the sounds of the swing era prompted crowds of young people to dance to numbers performed by artists like Benny Goodman. Popular singers such as Bing Crosby quickly emerged to attract their own followings. The comic book genre, meanwhile – which had began as a supplement to newspapers and communal sales brochures for artists – exploded from around 150 titles in 1937 to nearly 700 in 1940. *Superman* comics were selling one and a quarter million copies a month that year (Hajdu 2008, 31), but within a decade the superhero boom had all but disappeared. With publications like *Tales from the Crypt*, EC Comics subsequently used controversial and macabre content to come up through the field.

As young people began to be a recognized population segment, fandom gradually became more identified as youth phenomenon. There were previous mass audience fads – like the jitterbug, popularized by Cab Calloway in 1935 – but it was Frank Sinatra's performance at New York's Paramount theatre in December 1942 that made female fans part of the spectacle in a way that set the template for Elvis, the Beatles and legions of other musicians who followed:

The solo singer stole the show and was retained for eight weeks, breaking the attendance record set by Rudy Vallée in 1924. 'Swoonatra'-ism began. Soon there were 'Sinatraddicts', adolescent bobby-soxers who wrote to him in lipstick: 'I love you so bad it hurts. Do you think I should see a doctor?' Fan fever: a bishop knocked down in a teen charge towards the singer; the singer almost strangled by two girls who pulled at opposite ends of his bow-tie. Fan fever for a popular singer, not a film star. Novel. His cigarette butts, his un-eaten cornflakes became highly prized items. So did locks of his hair, often plucked from his head. The hysteria was compared to the Children's Crusade of the Middle Ages. (Whitcomb 1972, 202)

In 1946 a group of 750 movie fans in San Francisco calling themselves 'The Senior League' started to denounce the bobbysoxers and rescue film fandom as a respectable pursuit. They were fighting against the tide. By the mid-1950s, rock'n'roll was taking over the music charts backed by a young audience who listened to the new wave of personality DJs like Alan Freed and Bill Randle.[6] According to Daniel Cavicchi, 'Fandom has always been part of rock'n'roll's myth, appeal, and strength' (1998, 3). Meanwhile, after television spread as a domestic medium (see Spigel 2001), Hollywood began to lose sections of the family audience. Teens and young adults then became a significant section of the film audience. As both a recording artist and movie star, Elvis Presley fostered a global fan following. Over three decades after his death, he still boasts one of the largest music fan clubs in the world, which is based in the United Kingdom and has had up to 20,000 members.[7] In the later decades of the twentieth century, young people were courted as a prominent demographic who were often the most visible section of the media audience (see Doherty 2002).

The products that inspire any genre can be distributed across a range of different media. Science fiction had grown as a literary and film genre by the 1930s. In 1939 the World Science Fiction Society created an ambitious global fan convention called 'Worldcon' that has survived to date. In the interwar years and beyond, the genre was publically championed by 'superfan' Forrest J. Ackerman, who is often credited with coining the term 'sci-fi'.[8] It bloomed through the 1950s and 1960s by playing on public interest in the Cold War and space race. The era led to a spate of monster, mad scientist and alien creature films that acquired dedicated followings and have become significant objects of nostalgia.

In the 1960s cultural entrepreneurs further penetrated the young end of the marketplace. Staple film and TV genres like the Western were repackaged for the matinee audience. Meanwhile, the most prominent strands of youth culture moved away from juvenile rebellion and integrated more with hedonism and leisure: teen angels, gentle folk, surf sounds and beach party movies entertained younger listeners. The film director Alfred Hitchcock adopted a celebrity persona to present his own television series and act as a one-man celebrity brand to market his acclaimed thrillers. On American regional TV networks, meanwhile, horror hosts – like Ghoulardi (Ernie Anderson) on WJW-TV in Cleveland – emerged to present reruns of old monster movies.

The 1960s were characterized by a continuation of the Cold War stalemate and the culmination of the space race. Popular culture became interested in the possibilities and problems of scientific technology and alien life forms. Beginning with *Dr No* (Young 1962), Eon Productions' James Bond films series (1962–) imagined a glamorous world of international espionage that has captured fans from each succeeding generation of viewers. Two new television series crystallized the concerns of the era and have since become landmarks for both sci-fi fan culture and academic writing on fandom. In England, *Doctor Who* (1963–89, then 2005–) portrayed a brilliant, foppish and eccentric time traveller who struggled against various monsters and ordeals. Three years later, *Star Trek* ran its first series (1966–9) on NBC in America. The show was originally conceived by its writer-producer Gene Roddenberry as a kind of Western set in space that would explore humanist themes of community, conflict and co-operation.[9] Both series became long-running franchises; *Star Trek* was remade in 2009 as a feature film by director Jeffrey Abrams. Maintaining its reputation for complex and exciting texts, the *Star Trek* franchise has continued to inspire prominent fan communities.

In the middle of the 1960s the astounding popularity of the Beatles sparked a new wave of debate that tended to characterize their phenomenon as fan hysteria. Two other intriguing episodes in the history of Beatles fandom happened in the summer of 1966 – when Americans learned that John Lennon had compared his group's popularity to that of Jesus – and October 1969 – when a false rumour took root that claimed Paul McCartney was dead.[10] Towards the end of the 1960s – partly in the wake of the band's influence – many young people 'dropped out' of society to form the counter-culture: a movement that mixed chemically-induced intoxication and enthusiasm for progressive rock with a commitment to civil rights and anti-war protest.[11] The 500,000 young music enthusiasts who attended the Woodstock festival in 1969 shared a generational love of rock songs and alternative social values. Within a few short years, however, arena rock bands were using spectacles of mass fandom to serve their own interests (see Waksman 2007).

In the 1970s, the rerunning of films on television sparked new fan interest in the highlights of past culture. At this point America was gripped by a nostalgia boom for the 1950s referenced in shows such as *Happy Days* (1974–84) and the film *American Graffiti* (Lucas 1973). In 1970 a cognoscenti of sci-fi fans in San Diego began a long-running annual fan convention which has survived to date as the San Diego Comic-Con International (see Jenkins 2012). In popular music, folk-inspired singer songwriters and serious rock performers separated from glam rock and prototypical boybands like the Monkees and the Osmonds who catered to younger fan bases.[12] In the years that then followed the Watergate scandal and end of the Vietnam war, popular culture was imbued with a more nihilistic strain of social criticism. The decadence of disco sounds and blandness of blockbuster movies like *Jaws* (Spielberg 1975) both, in effect, marked a high point of modernist society and exposed a feeling futility that stemmed from placing faith in an imperfect sociopolitical system. With its tagline 'A different set of jaws', *The Rocky Horror Picture Show* (Sharman 1975) caricatured alternative sexualities in the same year as Spielberg's ecological monster movie.[13] It gradually became a cult product when audiences at midnight screenings in New York's Waverley Theatre feigned interaction with the characters on-screen (see Rosenbaum 1980). As the decade progressed, Robert Stigwood's blockbuster musicals, *Saturday Night Fever* (Badham 1977) and *Grease* (Kleiser 1978), heralded popular phenomena with some longevity. Meanwhile, the punk explosion extended an ethic of 'do it yourself' which led to a wide range of bands and fanzines in the wake of the Sex Pistols' December 1976 *Today* show interview. Another blockbuster, George Lucas' 1977 space fable *Star Wars* entered the mainstream as a family science fiction hit and gradually became celebrated as a cult product. By this point, fan fiction writing had grown beyond sci-fi to include cop shows like *Starsky and Hutch* (1975–9) (Pugh 2005, 91). In 1978 the term 'graphic novel' was used to help extend the market for a comic book called *A Contract with God* (see Fingeroth 2008). This influential move helped give rise to a new depth of audience engagement in the comic genre.

The 1980s began in a tragic way when John Lennon was shot by Mark Chapman, a mentally ill security guard from Honolulu who posed as a fan to get near his target. Lennon's followers held memorial rallies in Central Park to remember their hero (Elliot 1998 and 1999). By this time another generation of pop fans was reading music magazines like *Smash Hits* (1978–2006) and listening to the gender-bending styles of the New Romantics, a movement that reinvented the posturing of the 1970s glam rock phenomenon (see Vermorel 1985 for a classic pop fan mail compilation). Their older siblings listened to more credible rock, metal, post-punk and later rave outfits.

The mass adoption of the video cassette recorder (VCR) and its placement in so many living rooms meant that viewers could choose from an archive of previous film and television products in an emerging culture of video shops. VCRs allowed film and TV fans to conveniently see what they wanted in a domestic context (Jenkins 1992, 71). In the United Kingdom this prompted concerns over 'video nasties': horror films accused of corrupting audiences with images of graphic violence. Video recording also allowed a different kind of fan engagement as shows were 'time shifted' and watched at their viewer's leisure (see Cubbitt 1991). Fans immediately began doing things with video. Since the 1970s they had created their own 'mash up' videos in a practice known as **vidding** and screened them at conventions.[14] After MTV started in the summer of 1981, fans were more widely inspired to create their own music videos. However, domestic technology soon reached its limit. In 1992 Jenkins reported that 'fan artists seek a level of technical perfection difficult to achieve on home video equipment' (239).

Throughout the 1980s and 1990s, television producers had been developing products with ever more complexity. Previous drama series tended to be shaped for syndication and have an episodic format, each show being organized around a self-contained, temporary crisis. Now shows like J. Michael Staczynski's *Babylon 5* (1994–8) contained both episodic drama and a coherent story arc (see Lancaster 2001). Together with reruns and niche broadcasting on private and public access channels, video helped to create an audience that was highly educated across a range of cultural traditions. Two comedy shows from the era, *Mystery Science Theatre 3000* in the United States (1988–99) and *The Royle Family* in the United Kingdom (1998–2000), commented on this media-savvy era by featuring TV viewers as their subject matter. Popular culture was also becoming globalized as an activity. The spread of satellite and cable TV across Europe, for instance, allowed fans to access foreign products. Video allowed American fans to dub and subtitle shows from Japanese language channels and to share them with friends (see Jenkins 2008, 161–2). Fan artists who might previously have drawn pictures or experimented with home cassette equipment now began to explore the special functions of their VCRs (Jenkins 1992, 244). Although fan communities inevitably shared cassettes, broadcasters and distribution companies still controlled the means for mass distributing and exhibiting films, so at that point access to video recording technology did not lead to an easily-accessible public sphere of 'homemade' movie presentation (Jenkins 2008, 146).

Educated by non-linear media such as video games, film goers began to expect a different entertainment experience. By 1999 a range of media began to provide it. **Transmedia** storytelling is the process of telling different parts of the same story through different electronic media. The success of *The Blair Witch Project* Website and horror film in 1999 encouraged Hollywood to further invest in the process (103). Directors Andy and Lana Wachowski released *The Matrix* that year as the first episode in a three-part franchise that told its story across many different media outlets. Their trilogy ambiguously mixed elements of sci-fi, anime, futurology, religious analogy, social history and morality tale. It also made unprecedented – and for some unwelcome – demands on consumers (96). As video games became more like movies, Hollywood therefore began to differentiate itself again by encouraging fans to engage with extended versions of the text before visiting the cinema (106). In parallel, television shifted to emphasize the excitement of live broadcasting. Reality shows became a way for broadcast networks to strike back against cable channels by creating and incorporating a fan buzz (60–4). They have offered the audience an illusion of collective action that has helped to build individual emotional investments, although fans can lose their trust if their votes are ignored. It would be a mistake to read all these changes in media production and use, however, as completely erasing the established, and often negative, ways in which fandom has been seen.

Computers had been a domestic fixture for around two decades by the end of the twentieth century and they were already integrated with the entertainment industry. Fans had been using the internet since its earliest days, playing interactive games in multi-user groups or debating their favourite shows on bulletin boards, chat rooms and forums. For years they had also created fan pages, posted fantasy fiction and set up virtual 'shrines' for their heroes. As early adopters, media fans rapidly shared information through new social media platforms. Indeed, fan writing – which achieved a semi-institutional status between the 1960s and 1990s (Jenkins 2006, 42) – has flourished in the internet era.

When internet share prices peaked and crashed, the dot-com bubble heralded a new phase in which the net took its full place alongside other media. A widespread adoption of the broadband services in the late 1990s and early 2000s signalled one of the most rapid and significant shifts in the history of communication technology. Different media – particularly television and the internet – gradually came into a kind of parallel alignment in the hands of an increasingly experienced audience. One dimension of this was that online fans could discuss film and television plotlines in real time as they were broadcast. Joss Whedon's series *Buffy The Vampire Slayer* (1997–2003) and *Angel* (1999–2004) exemplified the new breed of self-reflexive, intertextual television dramas that would became a staple for the new audiences (Jenkins 2008, 119).[15] The now warp-speed dissemination of information between ordinary members of the public meant that **spoiling** (advanced notification of plot or production details) began to change the practices of the media industry. For instance, *Scream 2* (Craven 1997), the second film of the postmodern horror franchise, was rewritten in production after its script was leaked on the internet. By the time *Scream 3* (Craven 2000) was released, its makers even decided against holding any audience-test screenings for fear that details of the movie would appear online ahead of its release.

With the networking of home computers, audiences had *increased access to vast catalogues of media products*. Digital archiving operated alongside a number of other trends, such as the rise of DVD and then blu-ray home playback systems, to make the consumption of television into a more sustained activity in which the audience could study each episode. Broadcasters shifted from 'appointment television' to 'engagement television' to take advantage by making their franchises available first as broadcast events and second as box-sets of recordings available for apprenticeship. Series like *Lost* (2004–10), *24* (2001–10) and HBO's *The Wire* (2002–8) have become staples for audiences who could gain a high level of literacy by sequentially watching all the episodes within a few days.[16] In 2006 Henry Jenkins could therefore report:

> The past decade has seen a marked increase in the serialization of American television, the emergence of more complex appeals to program history, and the development of more intricate story arcs and cliffhangers. To some degree, these aesthetic shifts can be linked to new reception practices enabled by the home archiving of videos, net distribution lists, and Web program guides. (2006, 145)

Alongside accessing news and information, many computer users also began to upload, download, stream and share digital audio and video files in the new era. 1999 marked a turning point in the development of fandom as a shared social experience. The recorded music industry was facing a gradual transformation and file sharing fans were not paying for music. The industry lobby group the Recording Industry Association of America (RIAA) unleashed a law suit against the peer-to-peer file sharing service Napster and branded fans as criminals for their capacity to enjoy free music. Although media piracy has flourished online, many fans have also paid for downloading and streaming services. Another result of the digital shift is that fans have sometimes had legitimate free and/or early access to cultural products online as part of their promotional process.[17]

Video uploading sites such as YouTube – which gained in mass popularity after 2005 – have allowed free instant access to vast archives of user-uploaded footage that included recycled programming, clips, footage of recent live events and amateur productions. In a trend that has been gathering pace for many years, access to digital archives has fostered an ongoing nostalgia culture in which past products have been rediscovered, and different generations shared the cultural interests (see Reynolds 2012). This democratization of pleasures from the past has characterized the consumption of a wide variety of cultural forms. Speaking about the BBC Wales post-2005 regeneration of the TV series *Doctor Who*, Matt Hills (2010b, 87) explained, 'In the here-and-now in which the show is made, we are all everyday time-travellers; we borrow styles from the past (nostalgia for the 1980s has been popular recently), watch digitized "archive" TV shows and recombine these tastes into a new pattern of newness'. Video sites have facilitated fandom for independent, lost and obscure cultural phenomenon that might formerly have gone undiscovered. New artists, meanwhile, can now find fame and fan followings quicker than ever. Amateur producers and prominent fans have developed followings in their own right. Novel cultural forms have appeared, such as 'machinima': 3D digital animation created in real time by game engines (Jenkins 2008, 156). Bloggers have claimed their place as 'citizen journalists', commentators and reviewers. Coteries of professional broadcasters and critics are no longer the only group with a voice in the media. Consumers have a much wider range of sources from which to choose.

Summarizing the first decade of the new millennium, popular music commentators discussed key 'performers' not so much as particular stars – though some like Lady Gaga did appear – but by celebrating *platforms* like Facebook along with personalized gadgets and *mobile devices* like the iPod and Blackberry. For fan researcher, Henry Jenkins (2006, 138), 'In many ways, cyberspace is fandom writ large'. He means that fandom has become more visible, more mainstream and more normal:

> Across the past decade the web has brought these consumers from the margins of the media industry into the spotlight; research into fandom has been embraced by important thinkers in the legal and business communities. What might once have been seen as 'rogue readers' are now Kevin Robertson's 'inspirational consumers'. (Jenkins 2008, 257)

In this environment 'fan ownership' has became a rhetorical claim within the media industry (Hills 2002a, 37). In the contemporary era, fan phenomena, then, are as likely to be measured in tweets as they are in box office figures (see Sanderson & Cheong 2010; Barfoot Christian & Givens-Caroll 2011). However, the narrowing gap between fans and the rest of the media audience heralded by the stereotype of the chic 'techno geek' does not mean that fans have escaped all stereotyping. Much of the fan culture of the *Harry Potter* era and beyond has been associated with comic book heroes and franchises for younger viewers; products such as the *Twilight* film series (2008–) and *Glee* television show (2009–) (see Click et al. 2010; Hills 2012). Recent tabloids news stories about 'Bieber Fever' – supposed hysteria for young singer Justin Bieber – suggest that some types of fandom still carry a social stigma.

Finally, here I want to introduce and contextualize some shifts in the place of university education in society in the past two decades and how they have impacted upon fan studies. I will examine the content of some of the academic thinking about fandom in Chapter 3, but for now I wish to chart the changing historical context of the academic field. In 1992, Henry Jenkins wrote a book called *Textual Poachers* that challenged existing stereotypes and represented fans as thoughtful, productive and creative people. Jenkins showed that fandom was similar to but also different from the standards of ordinary middle-class culture. He aimed to go beyond notions of fandom as simple-minded obsession and to reveal the complexity and diversity of fan cultures (Jenkins 1992, 277). The quest led him to explain:

> In the late 1980s and early 1990s, cultural scholars, myself included, depicted media fandom as an important test site for ideas about active consumption and grassroots creativity. We were drawn toward the idea of 'fan culture' as operating in the shadows of, in response to, as well as an alternative to commercial culture. Fan culture was defined through the appropriation and transformation of materials borrowed from mass culture; it was the application of folk cultural practices to mass cultural content. (Jenkins 2006, 257)

Textual Poachers became a bible for fan researchers, a 'how to' book that showed ways to respectfully talk about fandom. The book even developed its own fan following (15). It came at a time when universities were increasingly looking to outside sources of funding in exchange for prestige and expertise. Academics had to play to a wider public (34). As the electronic media shifted they facilitated the co-optation of fandom as a marketing device, and business became increasingly interested in fan phenomena. **Crowd sourcing** (collective problem solving over the net) and **fanagement** (fan-focused online marketing) are some of the new concepts that have emerged in this new era. Jenkins' ideas have been adopted by business schools (Jenkins 2008, 12). Older ideas about the authority of an elite minority of qualified critics have given way to more seemingly democratic ideals of audience sovereignty.[18] In a parallel set of developments, the gradual replacement of student grants with loans in the United Kingdom has helped to change higher education from the province of an intellectual elite to a consumer business offering education as an advanced form of vocational training. Some writers have seen the university itself as a place designed to accommodate young people's media passions (Hills 2002a, 4). Since the 1990s it has become possible for scholars to be *both* fans *and* academics at the same time (Jenkins 2006, 4). In this environment claiming the mantle of fandom – at a time when a variety of social leaders (politicians, celebrities, university vice chancellors and others) were increasingly doing the same – was not so much a rebellious stance against social censorship as a shrewd acknowledgement that times were changing. Academics had to re-orientate their public role and closed the gap with fandom. Fan researcher Matt Hills noted that Jenkins' work allowed other researchers to 'come out' as fans (see 35). In 2002 Hills explained:

> The battle to place fandom on the cultural studies agenda has long since been won. In that sense, Henry Jenkins's 'tactical' portrayal of fandom in

Textual Poachers has been eminently successful, but in its wake it leaves new battles and questions, which focus on the roles of 'rationality' and 'religiosity' in both fan and academic activities. (2002a, 183)

Objectivity is the idea that universally valid knowledge can be built from impartial investigation. No history can be completely objective; it is necessarily a limited and partial explanation. Francesca Coppa's (2007) otherwise excellent history of media fandom in relation to fan art, for example, tends to focus on US television shows. Every act of storytelling means not only making choices about what to keep in and leave out but also how to slant the evidence. Since no narrative can include every perspective at the same time, there is no such thing as a perfect overview. We should therefore ask, 'History for who, for what purpose?' My short history of fandom has, to an extent, masked the politics of its own construction. One issue is that it has crammed in too many topics and said too little about most of them. Much of the account is focused on the United States or United Kingdom, missing out the cultures and traditions of many other countries. It views fandom as a shared phenomenon rather than a personal experience. The story focuses on mainstream media phenomenon and marginalizes gay or lesbian fans (though see, for instance, DeAngelis 2001, Dyer 2004 and Lipton 2008). It is told through shifts in media technology, form or genre, as if they offer the primary context for dialectical changes in fan activity – a point which neglects changes wrought by many ongoing, living cultures of fandom, including fan fiction writing communities. What any half comprehensive history of fandom must show is that new each development in media culture has brought new public figures and fan practices with it that have become incorporated and important in their own right. Fandoms therefore create social structures, ecologies, rituals and traditions of their own.

The term 'fan' now covers a wide range of ordinary people who positive emotional engagement with popular culture. That engagement may take the form of a connection with the text, image, performance or creative signature of a public figure. It might include love for a particular cultural form or genre. Given such complexity, we must now consider how to define the central idea guiding our discussion.

Defining fandom

Everyone knows what a 'fan' is. It's somebody who is obsessed with a particular star, celebrity, film, TV programme, band; somebody who can produce reams of information on the object of their fandom, can quote their favoured lines or lyrics, chapter and verse. Fans are highly articulate. Fans interpret media texts in a variety of interesting and perhaps unexpected ways. And fans participate in communal activities – they are not 'socially atomised' or isolated viewers/readers . . . So, how have 'fandom' and the media 'cult' been defined academically? To date, defining 'fandom' has been no easy task, despite (or perhaps because of) the 'everydayness' of the term.

MATT HILLS 2002A, IX

The definition of fandom has some easy answers at first sight. Discussions have focused not just on the *degree* of audience involvement, but also on its *quality* (Cavicchi 1998, 39). A fan is a person with a relatively deep, positive emotional conviction about someone or something famous, usually expressed through a recognition of style or creativity. He/she is also a person driven to explore and participate in fannish practices. Fans find their identities wrapped up with the pleasures connected to popular culture. They inhabit social roles marked out as fandom. Both academic and fan theory emerges from local contextual norms and interpretive disputes (Hills 2002a, 16). Each of these definition of fandom has its own implied explanations, exclusions, consequences and counter-arguments: 'We are, perhaps, all "stuck" on something, whether academic theory or fan object' (112). Unlike some sociologists and philosophers suggest, however, fans create their attentions through a process of subjective exploration. Fandom can therefore be seen as a form of cultural creativity, as play (90). An **object** of study is simply the thing being studied. Scholars in this area may have been guilty of 'reifying' their object: stopping the process of fandom and artificially trying to pin it down. Maybe fandom is a functional operation enacted by each individual: 'It might be useful to think about the work rather than the worth of fandom, *what it does*, not what it is, for various people in particular historical and social moments' (Cavicchi 1998, 9; emphasis mine). The 'work' of fandom includes the ways it can heighten our sense of excitement, prompt our self-reflexivity, encourage us to discuss shared values and ethics, and supply us with a significant source of meaning that extends into our daily lives.

Is fandom a coherent object?

Perhaps fandom is such an interesting object to study because it remains so elusive when subjected to analysis. Even *Textual Poachers* author Henry Jenkins claimed, 'My task here is not to signal the fluidity of cultural communities but rather to make a case for fandom as having any degree of coherence and stability at all' (1992, 3). His admission is significant because

Jenkins had, by then, studied fans for several years. Like Jenkins, Matt Hills claimed that fandom is not just one site or 'thing' (Hills 2002a, 7). *Star Wars* fandom researcher Will Brooker (2002, 32) has also noted there is no such thing as a typical group of fans. **Discourse**, loosely defined, means a socially shared way of talking about a particular issue or object. Different fandoms are associated with different kinds of discourse (Jenkins 2006, 24). This means that the label 'fan' can mean very different things in different contexts:

> On the whole, it is used both descriptively and prescriptively to refer to diverse individuals and groups, including fanatics, spectators, groupies, enthusiasts, celebrity stalkers, collectors, consumers, members of subcultures, and entire audiences, and, depending on the context, to refer to complex relationships involving affinity, enthusiasm, identification, desire, obsession, possession, neurosis, hysteria, consumerism, political resistance, or a combination. (Cavicchi 1998, 39)

Does this diversity mean that we should just give up studying fandom? Giving up may not be useful, so the question becomes as to how we can *refine* our understanding. For some researchers, fan cultures have to be treated separately and individually. No universal theory can be constructed:

> It is impossible, and perhaps even dangerous, to speak of a single fandom, because fandoms revolving around the TV program *Due South* have rules different from those of fandoms revolving around the *Lord of the Rings* books and movies, and fandoms that are centered around face-to-face meetings, exchange of round-robin-style letters, or a generation of hard-copy fan fiction magazines (say, the experience described by Camille Bacon-Smith in *Enterprizing Women* [1992]) are each different from the kind of online fandom that is the primary focus here. (Busse & Hellekson 2006, 6)

Fandom can indeed involve different experiences, concern different practices and mean different things in various contexts. Even if we share identity as fans of the same media object, my fandom may be experienced as something very different from yours. If fandom is not a singular entity, though, why do fans of the same object have the same interests? Also, why do fans of different objects behave in such *similar* ways? An ideal theory would be calibrated to shared experiences, sufficiently simple and internally consistent. There may be much to gain from exploring fan theory as a kind of template: not a way to generalize about all fandom, but to act as a yardstick against which to measure interest in particular objects or in particular contexts. Matt Hills therefore makes a valid point when he argues, 'Perhaps unfashionably, I will suggest that a general theory of media fandom is not only possible but also important; too many previous works have focused on single TV series, singular fan cultures, or singular media ("TV fans" versus "cinephiles")' (2002a, 2).

More than consumers

In a sense, fandom is sometimes seen as an umbrella term for various potentials: elements like fascination, celebrity following, group behaviour and exuberant declarations of conviction. 'Consumption' is one such element. While each may be part of the phenomenon, they do not encompass its whole meaning. To make the accusation of **reductionism** means to challenge an otherwise elegant theory by suggesting that it focuses on only part of a phenomenon when attempting to explain all of it. As this sections shows, to confuse fandom with its various components is to take a reductionist stance. The word 'consumption' indicates participation in a commercial process, but since 'to consume' means to digest and to exhaust it also implies a kind of *using up*. We can therefore separate two intricate meanings for the same word: to be part of 'economic' consumption means to participate in a financial transaction as a buyer, while to 'culturally' consume is to *meaningfully examine* a particular media product. Discussions about media consumption often confuse those two distinct meanings, not least because commercial culture does as well. Sometimes wider society uses the term 'fan' to indicate an impassioned economic consumer. The chocolate manufacturer Cadbury, for instance, celebrated 'fans' of its Whisper chocolate bars. It seems odd to label chocolate buyers as fans, but in our role as consumers we colloquially use the term all the time, saying things like, 'I was a real fan of their end of season sales'. Consumer movements are not limited to fandom. For instance, Christians used their clout as a collective audience to support Mel Gibson's *The Passion of the Christ* at the box office (Jenkins 2008, 211). Coca Cola lovers also campaigned when the corporation tried to change the recipe for its flagship soft drink in the mid-1980s. While we cannot describe these groups as media fan communities, the gap is perhaps narrowing. Stars and brands have mutually learned from each other and now celebrities are also, in effect, corporately organized and protected as consumer brands. They segment the market place (see Garde-Hansen 2011, 132; Cashmore 2004; Barfoot Christian 2011). Furthermore, fans can also seem like consumer groups in their collective vocal advocacy for certain media products. Nevertheless, in human terms a meaningful difference remains between, say, following an actor and campaigning to save your favourite soft drink or chocolate bar.

In some senses, media fans resemble ideal brand consumers: they snap up the latest thing, buy extra merchandise, participate in promotions, join official fan clubs and build collections (Cavicchi 1998, 62). They form a particularly stable market. If fans are the target consumers for new products and franchises, they are also niche markets that represent the residue of a culture first facilitated by mass marketing (Hills 2002a, 45). The 80–20 rule says that 20 per cent of the audience (i.e. fans) create 80 per cent of the profits (Jenkins 2008, 72). Indeed, their acceptance is seen to be an organic measure of the triumph of many media products and is integral to promotion: 'Fan consumers are no longer viewed as eccentric irritants, but rather as loyal consumers to be created, where possible, or otherwise to be courted through scheduling practices' (Hills 2002a, 36). Fandom does not escape or resist commodity culture. Instead consumption facilitates fans' contact with media products. For some writers this almost means, however, that fandom is primarily *about* consumption: 'Given that fandom at its core remains a form of spectatorship, fan places are places of consumption' (Sandvoss 2005a, 53). Specialist retail has not often been examined in media studies, yet shops like *Forbidden Planet* offer a space in which fans can socialize and discover more objects of interest (Hills 2002a, 28). However, to see fandom as primarily about consumption is to forget, first, that fans often like things for free, and, second, that they are always *more than* consumers. They are more than buyers and their transactions are pursued with a cultural interest that goes beyond merely practicing the process of buying. An interesting example of this is provided by Tom McCourt and Patrick Burkart (2007) who show how music fans need online discussion spaces that are greater than anything that customer relationship management systems can provide. Fans are more than consumers because they have especially strong emotional attachments to their objects and they use them to create relationships with both their heroes and with each other (Ferris & Harris 2011, 13). They can be distinguished by their off-by-heart knowledge of their text and their expertise both about it and any associated material (see Brooker 2002, 31; Gray 2010). They are *always already* consumers – as we all are – but they necessarily have more roles than that (Hills 2002a, 27). Fans are networkers, collectors, tourists, archivists, curators, producers and more.

In political and economic theories, consumption is a stage of economic circulation that is neatly separated from production. Consumers are alienated recipients who profitably complete the chain of economic circulation by spending money in exchange for goods or services. Marxist ideas separate the value that users find in their personal consumption of a product (use value) from the way that production, marketing and marketplace can socially facilitate another level of perceived value (exchange value). Both use value and exchange value comes from fans' processes of valuation (35). Yet in relation to the cultural processes of the media industry, the split between producer and consumer cannot be mapped neatly on to star and fan. Many texts allow their audiences to enter particular realms of imagination and fans often role-play (Sandvoss 2005a, 46). This play can also mean that they make tangible things – like art prints, self-published books, soft toys – that can then be sold to other fans as part of a cottage industry. Their play may also be part of their own training process as participants at various levels of media culture, both amateur and professional. If things move in and out of commodity status, where is the line drawn? (Hills 2002a, 35). In an internet age, businesses rely on fans' social exchanges and amateur production to create the content that attracts audiences for the advertisers who sponsor Websites. Fans also make attempts – sometimes welcome or invited – to directly intervene in the production process of broadcast media. Personally and collectively, they are used as part of many cultural events, for example, as crowds at rock concerts or film premiers, so they have become an essential part of the show: in effect, part of the symbolic apparatus of production.

At worst, commerce is often associated with exploitation. If fans represent a predictable marketplace, they can also articulate and meaningfully pursue *anti-commercial* beliefs (Hills 2002a, 29). Jenkins takes this a stage further:

> Fandom's very existence represents a critique of conventional forms of consumer culture. Yet fandom also provides a space in which fans may articulate their specific concerns about sexuality, gender, racism, colonialism, militarism, and forced conformity. These themes regularly surface with fan discussions and fan artworks. Fandom contains both negative and positive forms of empowerment. (1992, 283)

At first sight, Jenkins' statement seems extreme since fans evidently participate in the economic process of consumption on a regular basis: they buy tickets, merchandise, recordings. Discussing fandom in a digital age, Paul Booth explains:

> When producers release DVDs for a fan's favourite TV show, many fans will buy them even if they have already seen them when the show aired, and the sales can be staggering. Fandom, however, can also be perceived as a non-monetary environment online: highlighting instead the social standing of the individual. (2010, 26)

He then elaborates that 'while media producers in the market economy function by selling texts, fans often bypass this economy by *sharing* texts'

(42; emphasis mine). If there have been times when fans have explicitly organized themselves *against* economic consumption, these have been incidental to the social environments in which they have found themselves: the counter-culture, the new digital technosphere; places and moments where whole publics – not just fans – have seized an opportunity, not so much to opt out of cultural consumption, but just not to *pay* for it. **Agency** is the ability of individual people to act and behave in ways that make a difference to wider society. Booth's idea that fans operate a parallel economy of sharing when they can is useful because it shows a *moment of agency* when fans are motivated to help others to experience their favourite texts, not necessarily for anyone's financial gain. What we can therefore say, perhaps, is that fans will *often talk* about their connections to mediated phenomena, but – at least in speech if not in practice – they are rarely enthusiastic advocates of *economic* consumption per se. They may have discovered their interests through it. They may sometimes accept it as a necessary means of acquiring the experiences, making the connections or providing the benefits of media resource ownership that they desire. Yet they do not enact the process for its own sake or enter into it with an innate passion for it alone. Rather, the non-commercial nature of fan culture is, for many fans, one of its key characteristics: they are engaged in a labour of love (Jenkins 2008, 180) and if they produce or promote media culture, it is often on a not-for-profit basis. For this reason, several researchers have understood fan exchange as a *gift economy*.[19]

Even as they proclaim their passions and share access to their favourite texts, media fans are wary of being manipulated by the imperatives of the media industries into the roles of billboards or funding sources, tricked into perpetuating an economic process that could ultimately prove unrewarding and socially disadvantageous. *American Idol*'s most loyal fans, for instance, questioned the way that their television show manipulated ordinary viewers into consumption activity (90). Such fans portray themselves as the opposite of mindless, undiscriminating, 'bad' consumers (Hills 2002a, 21). Both fans and academics have therefore rejected 'the consumer' as a shameful identity.

Variations on a definition

Pastime

The Oxford English Dictionary defines a fan as 'a devotee of a particular activity or performer'. The dictionary separates fans from 'fanatics', who are filled with excessive and often misguided enthusiasm, and also from 'fanciers', who are really connoisseurs or enthusiasts. Whether a line can be drawn between these is open to debate. More seriously, the label 'devotee' also implies a kind of submission or giving up of identity. Do people who find they are fans give something up, or get something extra, or both? Dictionary definitions also imply that a fan can follow a performance *or just an interest* like clubbing or gardening. Yet fans form very different sorts of relationship to the object of their interest than do other hobbyists like bowlers or gardeners (Ferris & Harris 2011, 12). Perhaps the researchers who have distinguished fandom from similar identities with most discrimination are Abercrombie and Longhurst (1998). They treat both fans and enthusiasts as 'a form of skilled audience' (121), but are then careful to make finer distinctions:

> First, enthusiast's activities are not based around media images and stars in the way that fans' activities are. Second, the enthusiasts can be hypothesized to be relatively light media users, particularly, perhaps of the broadcast media, though they may be heavy users of specialist publications which are directed toward the enthusiasm itself. Third, the enthusiasm would appear to be rather more organized than the fan activity. (132)

This distinction allows the two researchers to distinguish people like custom car drivers from media enthusiasts, though their argument about organization seems rather odd. On and offline, fans can focus on particular practices in an organized way. They can also be socially organized in communities, whether those are fan clubs, ticket exchanges, discussion groups, spoiling teams or tourist parties. What the distinction allows Abercrombie and Longhurst to do is to separate fans on a 'skills continuum' from, on one side, consumers, and on the other, 'cultists', enthusiasts and petty producers (see Abercrombie & Longhurst 1998, 144). The skills in question are technical, analytical and interpretive, the researchers' point being not that consumers are any less skilled than producers, but rather that that each identity involves a different skill set. Perhaps the main problem with this idea is that the same individuals can be fans, consumers, cultists, enthusiasts and petty producers *at the same time,* and each of those roles intersects with and supports the others. The identities of fans and cultists are particularly hard to differentiate as cultists are basically located as more dedicated and specialist fans. What we can say is that fandom is often pursued as a hobby, but it has elements of passionate identification that take it beyond a mere pastime and make it part of the identity of the individual. I call this **personal fandom**: the fannish identity and experience of an individual person. Furthermore, in contrast to Abercrombie and Longhurst (1998), this book uses the term 'enthusiast' more loosely as a synonym for 'fan'.

Identification

According to Henry Jenkins, 'Fandom celebrates not exceptional texts but rather exceptional readings (though its interpretive practice makes it impossible to maintain a clear or precise distinction between the two)' (1992, 284). With this he shifts focus from the media products that supposedly trigger fan followings to consider the way that fans engage with appropriate media. That approach takes us beyond the idea of fandom as pastime. Cultural studies writer Lawrence Grossberg (1992, 56) has argued that fans have 'a different sensibility' and relationship with their favourite media products. For Grossberg the fan relationship is positive, immediate and based on an emotional process of identifying or investing. Like the Oxford Dictionary definition, Grossberg's one carefully distinguishes fandom from ideological mass persuasion like politics or organized religion. Nobody likes to believe that they are ideologically manipulated. Fans say that they 'love' their heroes. While they may have experiences and feelings that are different from non-fans, they are not fundamentalists or zealots. They seem enjoyably fascinated with their own passions. Yet, upon closer inspection the idea of fandom as a *particular type* of identification or connection has more issues than one may think. Cornel Sandvoss (2005a, 6) has argued that definitions of fandom centred around emotional intensity are poor because fans do not always self-classify based on their emotional intensity. Because media genres like horror conventionally celebrate knowledge over emotion, some dedicated fans may fail to self-identify as they *do not* display the required intensity of commitment (Hills 2002a, xv). Some forms of genre-based and collecting-orientated forms of fandom are associated with an early peak of emotion that tends to change and give way to different, more intellectual and 'cooler' forms of passion.[20] Also emotional intensity cannot be scientifically measured. Just as there are floating audience members who lack dedication but nevertheless self-identify as fans, so there are emotionally engaged consumers who can shun the label. Rather than isolating an objective category, perhaps we need to see *identifying* as *one* of the central personal and cultural processes of fandom. At some initial point the fan has to deeply connect with, and love – or at least be fascinated by – the object of their interest.

Practice

If the strength of identification is a rather inexact measure of fandom, another possible alternative is that it is really a matter of practice: a frequent and regular process of watching or listening. At the start of his book on pilgrimages, Roger Aden explains, '"I'm a big fan!" . . . one summer I checked out every Alfred

Hitchcock movie owned by the local library' (1999, 1). On the surface Aden's dedication seems like a fan's quest, but taken alone it is merely an effort to explore Hitchcock's output. Aden's Hitchcock fandom could only be verified if he mentioned viewing those films more than once and *repeatedly returning* to them. Cornel Sandvoss sees fandom as the 'regular, emotionally involved consumption of a given popular narrative or text' (2005a, 8). Similarly Henry Jenkins has noted that television fandom does not mean watching a series, but becoming interested enough to make a regular commitment to watching it (Jenkins 1992, 56). What issues do such definitions raise? First, despite the myth of 100 per cent dedication, most fans are fascinated with a variety of different artists or media products. Daniel Cavicchi noted that most of the fans who self-identified as Bruce Springsteen followers listen to Springsteen's music 30–50 per cent of the time, between two and four hours a day (1998, 113–14). More significantly, genre fans may watch or hear a particular text just once and still claim to be dedicated. Maybe we should therefore examine other practices. Fans are theorists and expert critics (Jenkins 1992, 86). They tend to be **auto-didacts**: self-taught experts. In the 1980s, for instance, 'fan video' makers usually learned by experimenting with their VCRs rather than going through any formal training (247). Nevertheless, there is still a crucial problem: any focus on fandom as practice misses a crucial dimension. According to soap fandom researchers Cheryl Harrington and Denise Bielby:

> We believe that this conceptualization of fan as doer obscures an important dimension of fanship, the acceptance and maintenance of a fan identity. One can do fan activity without being a fan, and vice versa. Fanship is not merely about activity; it involves parallel processes of activity and identity. (1995, 86–7)

In other words, those who enact different practices of fandom – whether going to see films, reading comics, collecting or some other activity – may, for various reasons, not describe themselves as fans. Performing a practice does not construct an identity unless we suggest it in language by changing verbs to their noun form (e.g. 'film-goer', 'comic reader' or 'collector') and even those names do not *completely* describe any fan. There is no universal and definitive practice which guarantees that a person's fannish identity, except perhaps 'loving' a specific performer or his or her work, but equally fans can be critical some of the time too. According to Harrington and Bielby, 'Being a fan requires not only participation in activities but the adoption of a particular identity that is shaped through subjective and affective experiences' (97). Perhaps this is, however, the wrong way round. Surely, initial experiences *lead* to practices and forms of self-identifying that ultimately mean one defines oneself as a fan. The question becomes what has to be in place for such initial experiences to occur.

Community and performance

> This ability to transform personal reaction into social interaction, spectatorial culture into participatory culture, is one of the central characteristics of fandom. One becomes a 'fan' not by being a regular viewer of a particular program but by translating that viewing into some kind of cultural activity, by sharing feelings and thoughts about program content with friends, by joining a 'community' of other fans who share common interests.
>
> HENRY JENKINS 2006, 41

Identities are often clarified through comparisons or contrasts with other people. This leads us in two directions: to think about community and to consider performance. Henry Jenkins has defined fandom as social. While Jenkins identifies an important dimension of activity for many fans, critical interrogation of that definition can also isolate what it seems to miss: the possibility that some fans *do not* translate their viewing into shared communication. Matt Hills has suggested that an emphasis on the communal dimensions of fandom is a result of the way scholars approach their shared focus of attention: 'Viewing fandom as a "thing" or "object of study" has led previous studies of fandom to treat the ways in which fan identities are legitimated as authentic "expressions" of a group commitment' (2002a, xii). Face to face or online, social networking is a central part of the continuation of fandom for many millions of people, and there is therefore a circular relationship involved: fandom facilitates networking, so those looking for friends with a common interest will utilize the fan community for support. While fans proclaim and compare their identities in the group environments – whether online forums or face to face meetings (at conventions, for example) – their initial identifications do not always (or therefore necessarily) appear to begin as an immediate result of shared experiences.

The performance of identity is another direction to consider. While fandom is an identity that can feel innate, it is also often publically adopted. In her classic edited volume in media fandom, Lisa Lewis provided one of the most simple definitions of fandom, that fans are 'the most visible and identifiable of audiences' (1992, 1). Dressing in t-shirts or wearing badges, and sometimes gathering en masse, fans can appear highly visible *at times*, but what are the benefits and limitations of this definition? Performance is a complex term that combines implications of repeated doing and theatrical artificiality – or at least self-consciousness – with measurable success or failure. The sociologist Ervin Goffman (1959/1990) provides a classic and useful definition. For Goffman, performance is broadly defined as human behaviour that functions to create an emotional reaction in another person. Goffman's definition implies that all the world is a stage and that everyone is performing all the time, whether they do so with conscious intent *or do not*. However, performance is a rather slippery term in relation to both daily life and to fandom. Fans can be seen as performers only when others acknowledge their identities (Sandvoss 2005a, 45).

The first question to ask of a performance-based definition of fandom is for whom exactly are the fans visually performing? Music enthusiasts collectively and exuberantly represent themselves at rock concerts. One way to align fandom with performance is therefore to consider stage performance (or its mediated equivalents) as a power relationship between stars and their fans. Traditional views here posit fans as non-performers, but the power relations that characterize these encounters *do* manifest performances from the fans, even if they are not always exactly replicas of those displayed on stage: 'In many ways, fans see themselves as performers along with Springsteen. They sing along with him, yell out his name and other messages between songs, and even act out some of the lyrics' (Cavicchi 1998, 93).[21] Crucially, as another example from Cavicchi suggests, fans do, in effect, *counter-perform*:

> Indeed the crowd was performing as much as the band on stage; at one point, when Springsteen said, 'When they told me to sit down, I stood up', one fan in the balcony to my right stood up and gestured with open hands to the crowd to do the same. (29)

While such people express themselves on a visual level, to reduce fandom to a visual phenomenon is to confuse a common *consequence* with an innate *cause*. Lisa Lewis' visibility dictum ignores 'hidden' fans: those who are less visible at any particular moment. It also provides a description of fandom guided by channels of visual media, outlets that – for various reasons, as we shall investigate – tend to visually construct fandom as *different* to 'normal' behaviour. While the social value of fandom has fluctuated as society has changed, not everyone is happy with the label. Performative definitions tend to measure fandom primarily as an activity in public life. There are fans who never 'come out', however; closet fans who pursue their passions in private and sometimes in secret. For various reasons, such media enthusiasts may be ashamed to admit the direction or depth of their interest. They may love an object that is considered taboo (like porn), 'uncool' (like *Star Trek*) or just not usually seen by others as appropriate for their particular gender or peer group – often sex symbols of the same sex, boybands or soaps stars – or they may just be concerned about the label 'fan' itself. Fans who do not talk about their passions may, furthermore, not be closeted, just quiet: isolated, unsociable, anti-social, ex-communicated from (or disappointed with) the fellowship of like-minded fans.

Though it relates to fascination with a socially-shared mediated product, each individual's fandom can begin as a personal and sometimes relatively private experience. To locate fans as defined by their public performance is to progress in a way that implies the centrality of either community, theatricality or perhaps even contagion, none of which seem to offer a firm foundation for defining fandom. Matt Hills has therefore drawn attention to the way that self-declarative behaviour is always *political* for fans:

> I want to suggest that fandom is not simply a 'thing' that can be picked over analytically. It is also always performative; by which I mean that it is an identity which is (dis-)claimed, and which performs cultural work . . . Fandom, then, is never a neutral 'expression' or singular 'referent'; its status and its performance shift across cultural sites. (2002a, xi–xii)

In other words, each person adopts or disowns his or her status – though not, I would argue, identity – as a fan depending on an estimation of the immediate social context. Given that fandom is a socially recognized role or label, those who harbour the intense forms of identification usually described as fandom may or may not want to publicly align as a fan or describe themselves by using the label.

While adoption of the internet has made the social side of fandom much more prominent and convenient, isolated fandom has always been a possibility for some individuals. On a personal level, though, perhaps a kind of *internal* performance is necessary as a way to make sense of the process for anyone who finds himself or herself in a fan's role. Here fandom becomes part of our own inner dialogue. Some researchers have begun to consider fans *as individuals* rather than examine fandom as a shared social phenomenon. Academic accounts have historically tended to emphasize singular fandoms, as if rock fans are not also *Doctor Who* fans, for example (Hills 2002a, 86). Though we know that they can engage with various objects and phenomenon at the same time, fans' interests have often been understood singularly and their communities falsely bounded. For Nick Couldry (2000, 73), individuals each have a 'textual field' of multiple fan interests. As they pursue these pleasures, their interests can either multiply at the same time or emerge serially as they continue to meander (see Hills 2002a, xiv).[22] Similarly, Karen Hellekson (2006, 1) uses the term 'monofannish' to describe her dedication to one specific media product while her co-editor Kristina Busse describes herself, in contrast, as a 'fannish butterfly'. Jenkins again takes this further: '[Julia] Ecklar sings not as a Trekker but *as a fan*, a category defined less by specific cultural preferences than by nomadic raids on the full range of mass culture. The intertextual dimension of fan culture has surfaced repeatedly throughout this book' (1992, 251; emphasis mine). Performances therefore help to form each fan's sense of a socially-situated self (Sandvoss 2005a, 47). Yet if we focus on the individual rather than the media product, the change of perspective acts to 'individualize' each person's fandom, implying that it can be defined as a kind of disposition that is projected on to specific media interests.

Existence

What all the definitions of fandom discussed so far have missed out is its highly personal, experiential, inner dimension. To become a fan is to find yourself with an emotional conviction about a specific object. As a fan himself, Daniel Cavicchi has emphasized this dimension in his own definitions. He explains, 'Fandom is not a bounded entity to be discovered and commented on, or a problem to be questioned and answered; it is a complex, private yet shared, ongoing experience' (1998, 18). This is important to Cavicchi, because many – perhaps most – popular academic theories have seen the self as a set of social relationships and denied the validity of the autonomous individual. To put it another way, fans' heartfelt convictions are missing in action from cultural theory, relegated as unimportant compared to processes of economic or sociological interaction. For Cavicchi, 'On the whole, fandom is not some particular thing one has or does. Fandom is a process of being; it is the way one is' (1998, 59). If the first part of his statement suggests movement (a 'process'), then the second part is an existential claim that it locates fandom as a type of human condition felt by fans as *the way they are* in the world, something at the core of their being. What this definition captures is that fandom does not feel like something conferred from the outside or rationally achieved, but instead represents a realization of personal identity that is beyond rational explanation and yet emotionally *come home*.[23] While Cavicchi's claim sensitively registers the strong feelings of personal conviction that are common to fandom, it remains limited in other ways. Existential categories usually have a notion of inevitability or destiny attached to them. Cavicchi's notion cannot quite explain how people find this particular category of existence or why they might find themselves leaving it. Perhaps it even implies that we are all – or are *potentially* all – born as fans and just need to realize it. The idea therefore elevates an interest in media culture to the level of the soul and forgets that common (shared) processes – perhaps operating unconsciously – might help shape an individual's emotional convictions.

Inconclusive definitions

What an extended analysis of definitions shows is that the term 'fan' is used by a variety of people and does not have a precise definition. Any definition of the term is also an act of persuasion about who fans are and who they are not. Some thinkers have tried to create master descriptions of the phenomenon that address all of its dimensions. Harrington and Bielby offer a four part model of fandom as a mode of reception, shared practice of interpretation, an 'art world' of cultural activities and an 'alternative social community' (1995, 96). In their model individual fans are visible, involved, knowledgable about their media franchise, aiming to support the continuity of their chosen interest and having a tendency to associate with other fans. Collectively such people adopt a particular mode of reception, organize themselves around shared interpretations and form an alternative, consumption-based community. Equally, Henry Jenkins has suggested that fandom encompasses at least five levels of activity: a particular mode of reception, a set of critical interpretive practices, a base for consumer activism, a form of cultural production and an alternative social community (1992, 277–80). Although we might contest some of these particular points, a multidimensional approach to fandom seems much more sophisticated that reducing it to individual components. Yet in encompassing everything there is a sense in which even these definitions miss out on something. Since they are hard to apply with any clarity, a satisfying definition of fandom necessarily remains somewhat partial and elusive. Words like 'fan' and 'cult' form part of a social struggle over meaning (Hills 2002a, xi). Fixing timeless distinctions may actually be a mistake in academic discussions. Perhaps we can therefore agree with Daniel Cavicchi when he suggests, 'Ultimately, the definition of music fandom lies not in any terse phrase or single image but rather in the tension between all of these relationships at any given moment. That is why fandom is so difficult to grasp' (1998, 107).

What follows . . .

The rest of this book interrogates fandom from a variety of different perspectives.

The second chapter examines how popular representations of fandom draw on stereotypes that normalize non-fan audiences. Because not all objects of fandom are socially perceived as of equal value, it also considers how perceptions of various forms of fandom shape discussions of the subject. Finally, through a series of case examples, it examines how media representations negotiate between various audience factions in order to define how fandom should be perceived.

Chapter 3 goes beyond the text to explore a classic tradition of work from communications research, audience analysis and cultural studies that locates the production of meaning in relation to the practice of reading media texts. It considers the limits of textual analysis as a method of approach in the study of fan culture and looks carefully at how fans engage with the process of reading their chosen texts. After traversing a long history of media reception scholarship, the chapter examines an era academic of work defined in more detail by the *textual poaching* metaphor. After digesting that section those interested should understand why fans were so often identified as 'resistant readers' and why that description was useful in establishing a base line for discussion in fan studies.

The fourth chapter looks at a long-running, deep-rooted research tradition mostly outside of cultural studies that tends to pathologize fandom as a form of personality disorder or social hysteria. In the first part I consider how and why psychologists and others have located extreme fandom as something on the dark side of human nature. I consider the 'slippery slope' model, a scale of supposed deviance that connects normal cultural engagement with dangerous and abnormal behaviour. The second part of the chapter addresses a series of claims from fan studies that suggest some attention to normal everyday psychological processes might help us to understand much about how individual people operate as fans.

Chapter 5 tackles the thorny and often ignored issue of how people actually become fans. In this chapter I examine ideas about contagion, affect and the recurring comparison between fandom and religion. My argument here is that the metaphor of sacred religiosity is an inadequate tool with which to interrogate fandom. I nevertheless suggest that because fans so often show that getting closer to their favourite public figure gives them a special thrill, Durkheim's concept of effervescence *is* useful in exploring their intensity of emotion. Furthermore, I suggest marrying that explanation with a metaphor borrowed from Hellinger's family constellations therapy, the idea of the 'knowing field'. Individuals who become fans are *in process*: they therefore enter and leave a terrain of emotional conviction as described in the chapter.

The next chapter analyses fan practices to examine why ordinary people who have very different objects often behave in similar ways. In this section I separate three categories of fan practice, each denoting an associated type of pleasure. First, there are practices associated with *pleasures of connection* that operate when fans seek greater intimacy with their celebrated heroes.

These practices include staging encounters and collecting autographs. Second, there are practices such as spoiling and fiction writing that stem from *pleasures of appropriation*. In these, fans take a textual phenomenon as a form of raw material that they adapt to their own needs. Fan studies has shown a high degree of interest in such practices because they demonstrate that fans are creative people. Finally, there are *pleasures of (fan) performance* that stem from practices such as conference participation and impersonation.

Do male and female fans really behave differently? The seventh chapter considers the degree of difference between male and female fans in terms of gender expectation. Media fandom has traditionally been relegated as a feminized pursuit. Moreover, specific forms and fields of fandom are associated with some quite strong and specific expectations. If 'real men' find it hard to express their fandom there are also ways in which fandom itself acts as a forum for shared desires and can provoke 'gender trouble'.

Drawing on Elvis Presley as a case study, Chapter 8 looks at myths, cults and places. Fandom often involves dreams of far-off destinations or personal engagement with whole worlds of meaning. This chapter considers how those realms are structured and realized. It also introduces the idea of iconicity as well as considering what the increasingly used 'cult' label means and whether 'cult fandom' should be separated as a distinct concept.

The internet era has meant that fans can encounter like-minded enthusiasts with as little effort as switching on their home computers. Both online and offline communities can help their participants sustain their fandom as part of a shared social experience. Chapter 9 looks first at how the internet has shaped fan communities. It also adopts a sociological perspective to examine how those communities are structured and what functions they can fulfil. The chapter also begins to explore a concept that Henry Jenkins has used to examine the activities of online fan communities, the notion of participatory culture.

The tenth chapter considers the protocols and pitfalls of directly examining fandom as an object of academic scrutiny, the first of which is simply how the investigators position themselves in relation to the 'two hats' of fan and researcher. A whole series of ethnographers have investigated fans in the past. What can we learn from how they have done things? Does having 'insider' status in a fan community guarantee that a better study will be produced? Fan research is, in some senses, a distinct field. The chapter therefore attempts to explore issues specific to fandom as an object of study.

Fans are people whose role has consistently been misdiagnosed and misrepresented in both academic study and in wider society. In order to challenge the negative stereotypes of fandom found in the media, fan studies itself has sometimes contained competing impulses that alternately seek to *understand* the object and to *change* its representation. *Understanding*

Fandom's concluding chapter offers a summary of some of its main contributions and suggests some avenues for further research.

Understanding Fandom aims to treat its subject with dignity and respect. While adopting a critical and logical approach remains an appropriate aim, no scholarly activity is ever completely impartial. My approach translates to *not saying anything about fans that I would not say about myself*, not least because I am also a media fan.[24] Rather than claiming to be a comprehensive survey of the field, this book has a more modest aim: introducing some key themes and thinkers and exploring commonalities that connect the different kinds of fandom for various media objects.

2

Fan stereotypes and representations

Starting points

- What are the social functions of fan stereotypes?
- To what extent does it make sense to talk about different degrees of fandom?
- Why aren't all forms of media fandom valued equally by society?

In 1947, Ellen Roufs came up with an idea that thrilled film fans throughout the nation. As president of the International Fan Club League, an umbrella organization that co-ordinated the activities of over 500 different movie star fan clubs, she decided to revive the idea of the national fan club convention, a meeting that had been held annually in the 1930s. In June, she proposed that over 250,000 fan club members meet in Hollywood, learn about each other's activities, go on studio tours, and meet their favourite stars. According to Movieland magazine, it promised 'to be the biggest thing that ever happened to fan clubs'. But when news of the proposed convention reached the studios and press, Roufs's hopes began to dim.

SAMANTHA BARBAS 2001, 159

In a useful account of movie audiences, Samatha Barbas showed the strength of feeling amassed against the first post-war incursions of fandom. Discussing Ellen Roufs's efforts to create a Hollywood fan convention she reports that the *New York Times* urged fans to keep their 'half-neurotic, half-idiotic hero worship' at home. Roufs ignored the naysayers and held the convention without the addition of studio tours. Why were the industry, press and public so against what she represented? In the 1940s film fandom acquired a social stigma for representing what respectable critics aimed to repress: a widely accepted, passionate, collective expression of fondness for Hollywood icons. To the critics, movie stars were inauthentic industrial products who distracted audiences from more worthwhile cultural pursuits and turned them into subservient and addicted worshippers. Such views came from a tradition that said that high culture – epitomized in traditional but elite events like opera and ballet – represented the most graceful and lyrical flights of the human spirit and if those events were not immediately accessible, it was a critic's place to help cultivate appreciation for them. In an era where electronic mass media had socially marginalized such activities, fandom became perceived as a byword for the public's supposed gullibility. Representations of collective fandom located individual fans as members of irrational mobs liable to exceed the constraints of civility at a moment's notice. This elitist view of culture was exemplified in the arguments of English scholar F. R. Leavis, who claimed that only a minority in society were appropriate custodians of culture, able to discern the finest human achievements in an era of general decline (for a good summary see Storey 2009, 22–8). The growing centrality of mass-produced culture throughout the twentieth century reduced general interest in Leavis' claims. Yet, according to Cavicchi, 'Unfortunately, fandom's origin in the reorganization of public performance by capitalism and technology has meant that fandom has often come to epitomize those changes, particularly for critics' (1998, 3). To question fandom, those critics drew on dominant discourses about the deplorable state of mass culture.

Even in the mid-1990s, fans were still seen as a marginal group. As Harrington and Bielby explained at the time, 'A staff member of the National Association of Fan Clubs says that one of the group's explicit goals is to improve the public image of fans and fan clubs' (1995, 105). If recent years have seen some change, traces of the critique of fandom still remain: 'Historically fans have been known to act a bit odd . . . But the so-called cult fan is more myth than reality, a definition based on a skewed understanding of audience behavior that is largely outdated' (Robson in Abbot 2010, 209). Although the failure of the Leavisite project has gradually become more apparent, public perceptions of fandom have, nevertheless, survived as a kind of after image. Even in 2002, Matt Hills reported:

To claim the identity of a 'fan' remains, in some sense, to claim an 'improper' identity, a cultural identity based on one's commitment to something as seemingly unimportant and 'trivial' as a film or TV series. Even in cultural sites where the claiming of a fan identity may seem to be unproblematically secure – within fan cultures, at a fan convention, say, or on a fan newsgroup – a sense of cultural defensiveness remains, along with a felt need to justify fan attachments. (2002a, xii)

Othering

Much of cultural studies devotes itself to the political study of popular culture. The academic term **othering** is used by scholars to describe processes in which one group of people label another as different, an embodiment of everything that they are not. For the group in control of media representation, the other becomes a terrain on which to project anxieties and desires. A classic example of this comes from the work of Edward Said. In his book *Orientalism* (1978), Said showed how the Western world used othering as a pretext to legitimize its colonization of far-away countries. Western adventurers, ambassadors and governors interpreted the Orient as everything that the West was not, or rather everything that they *did not want* the West to be: erotic, barbaric, uncivilized, dangerous and exciting. This construction of an imagined space of potential was a way to both excuse the creation of the Empire and to define Western society *through contrast* as a superior, civilizing culture: a move that in turn naturalized the invasion and rule of foreign countries. The concept of othering is extremely useful because social groups of different identities continue to differentiate themselves in our society in ways that are based on mistaken perceptions and claims to superiority. Fans have long been othered by their critics, academics, mainstream audiences and even each other.

Fan stereotypes

Henry Jenkins has presented a more nuanced description of how othering operates to create stereotypes of fandom. For Jenkins, 'Public attacks on media fans keep other viewers in line, making it uncomfortable for readers to adapt such "inappropriate" strategies of making sense of popular texts' (2006, 40). Jenkins carefully described how this happens. Analysing a comedy sketch on *Star Trek* fandom from the American TV series *Saturday Night Live*, he found a series of stereotypes which suggest that *Trek* fans:

a　Are brainless consumers who will buy anything associated with the program or its cast (DeForst Kelly albums).

b　Devote their lives to the cultivation of worthless knowledge (the combination to Kirk's safe, the number of Yoeman Rand's cabin, the numerical order of episodes);

c　Place inappropriate importance on devalued cultural material ('It's just a television show');

d　Are social misfits who have become so obsessed with the show that it forecloses other types of social experience ('Get a Life');

e　Are feminized and/or desexualized through their intimate engagement with mass culture ('Have you ever kissed a girl?');

f　Are infantile, emotionally and intellectually immature (the suggestion that they should move out of their parents' basement, their pouting and befuddled responses to Shatner's criticism, the mixture of small children and overweight adults);

g　Are unable to separate fantasy from reality ('Are you saying we should pay more attention to the movies?'). (Jenkins 1992, 10)

Jenkins's list of stereotypes remains a useful tool for interrogating representations of fandom. Some of its items are explicable in terms of the Leavisite project, particularly charges (b), (c) and (f). Fans are, for example, often stereotyped as 'a group insistent on making meaning from materials others have characterized as trivial and worthless' (Jenkins 1992, 3). An example of this is mentioned in Stephan Elliot's 1994 film *The Adventures of Priscilla, Queen of the Desert*. In the famous ABBA turd scene, Adam Whitely (who performs as 'Felicia Jollygoodfellow' and is played by Guy Pearce), looks through his wardrobe and explains his trinket collection to Ralph (who performs as 'Bernadette Bassinger' and is played by Terence Stamp):

Ralph:　(holding up jar)　What's this?
Adam:　That my darling is my most treasured possession in the whole wide world.
Ralph:　But what is it?

Adam: Well, a few years ago I went on a pilgrimage backstage to an ABBA concert, hoping to grab an audience with her Royal Highness Agneta. Well – when I saw her ducking into the ladies loo, naturally I followed her in, and after she had finished her business I ducked into the cubicle only to find she had left me a little gift, sitting in the toilet bowl.

Ralph: What are you telling me, this is an ABBA turd?

Adam: (looking at dress) I know what we can do with this.

In a movie about cross-dressing stage performance as camp parody, the ABBA turd scene lambasts fandom as a tasteless pursuit. How many ways to degrade fandom can you spot in Adam's explanation of his interest? The scene marks Adam out as a fan in denial of his own lack of taste: by looking at his dresses after Ralph's final question, he changes the subject. The choice of ABBA as a cultural interest is a comment on both the group's place in the cultural hierarchy – as a *pop* (not rock) act subjected to endless parodies – and their particular role in relation to the more macho elements of Australian culture. While it operates as a scatological denigration of fandom, what is perhaps more worrying is that at least one serious researcher has taken it as a *realistic* example of fan behaviour:

Fandom in general thrives on stuff that bears some trace (literally) of the figure that the fans adore: the pap smear from Madonna that is treasured by one of the kids in the movie *Slackers*; the reliquary-like 'Abba Turd' that is the prized possession of one of the characters in *Priscilla, Queen of the Desert*; the black leather jacket worn by Elvis that is lovingly highlighted at Graceland Too. Like many fans, the MacLeods [proprietors of exhibition/home Graceland Too] rely on visual, touchable stuff to signal Elvis's special status and stake their claims on him. (Doss 1999, 59–60)

If examples framing fandom as a tasteless pursuit are easy to dismiss, stereotypes of mass cultural consumption still hold that fans have an appetite for what seems to be trivia. When 'trivia' is defined in particular ways, such charges can appear right. The question then becomes a political one: who is in control of deciding what 'trivia' means and what seems trivial? This issue is evident when we consider the UK's fortnightly music magazine *Smash Hits*, which ran from its inception in 1978 into the middle of the last decade and offered a glossy and wonderfully irreverent celebration of pop for the teenage market. In its 1980s heyday, *Smash Hits'* journalists would treat New Romantic pop stars as celebrities rather than musicians, gleefully asking them questions about what they had for breakfast. The magazine arguably contributed to a process of trivialization which, allied to an increasingly intrusive media, helped to change the status of celebrities from icons of privilege to victimized opportunists. Yet those 'trivial' questions also helped pop celebrities to seem ordinary and brought them within reach of the imagined worlds of their fans. Part of fan interest in 'trivia', therefore, is that it provides a certain feeling of intimacy with each chosen celebrity (see Barbas 2001, 126).

It is important to realize that all stereotypes contain a grain of truth, but it is the generalization and misinterpretation of that kernel that creates the problem. The first aspect of stereotyping challenged by Jenkins dealt with the idea of fans as consumers discussed in the last chapter. In particular, the angle here was that fans are undiscriminating followers of mass culture. This locates fandom as a kind of tool of the media industry and denies fans *agency* as end products of its marketing process. In reality, fans often make untutored choices about what or who to follow and how to relate to them. Indeed, fans do not just follow whatever is popular: some popular shows have no *real* fan base and some rare ones have thriving, extended fan communities (Jenkins 1992, 90). Equally, to casual observers, specialist fan knowledge *can* seem like a questionable voyage into obscurity (Brooker 2002, 129). Yet, as Harrington and Bielby (1995, 91) found in their study of soap audiences, fan expertise actually represents a highly developed form of *literacy*: 'They are keenly aware of the constructedness of the genre, are savvy about production details, and often believe that they know the show better than those who create it.' Sharing such information also means that dedicated fans exhibit 'epistemophilia' – a pleasure in exchanging knowledge (Jenkins 2006, 139).

Media representations of fictional fans often amplify the notion of the fan as immature or infantile (see Jensen 1992).[1] The term **groupie** arose in the 1960s and was usually given to female fans who aimed to create a real sexual or romantic liaison with their favourite rock or pop musician. Portrayals of groupies have epitomized this perception of fandom. Jody Long, a schoolgirl played by Jessica Barden in the recent comedy drama *Tamara Drewe* (Frears 2010), provides a classic example. Long is infatuated with boy-band drummer Ben (played by Dominic Cooper). She unsuccessfully attempts pursue her crush by combining a break-and-entry of the house where he is staying with a clumsy attempt at planned seduction. While it is true that a fraction of fans have found all sorts of ways to enter the real lives of their objects and the locales in which they live, Jody's belief that Ben will easily fall for her ordinary and underage charms positions her fandom as a central part of her naïve and innocent persona. This theme is pushed to its limits in the British exploitation feature, *Groupie Girl* (Ford 1970), in which Esme Johns plays Sally, a fan who is sexually interested in members of the rock band Opal Butterfly. The feature's American poster read, 'I am a groupie! . . . A rock group freak all the way – but what I collect *ain't* autographs. All I own is this suitcase and all I want is this pad for tonight'. While Sally hopes to find the reflected glamour of being *with* the band, she becomes increasingly *used* by members of their entourage to a point where she realizes that her dreams have been exploited to her own detriment, compromising her reputation and sense of self-respect. She is not portrayed as in control, collaborating or establishing a relationship. Instead she appears naïve, low in self-esteem and manipulated by the very people she hoped would rescue her. *Groupie Girl* therefore does cultural work by presenting a cautionary tale about female vulnerability and simultaneously exploiting it as a thrilling moment of lascivious titillation. Real life 'groupies' – who were both lauded and exploited by music magazines like *Rolling Stone* as the epitome of young, sexually liberated womanhood – were represented as a stereotype of late 1960s and early 1970s rock fandom in a process that clearly showed how anxiety and desire could be projected on to fans as a seduced other (see Rhodes 2005).

Perhaps the most important charge on the list of stereotypes unearthed by Jenkins was (g) that fans could not tell their fantasies from reality. A pair of terms from the philosophy of knowledge are worth introducing here: **ontology** and epistemology. Ontologists examine systems of knowledge to see how they conceptualize *what there is to know* about the world. **Epistemology** is the study of *how* people form acceptable knowledge. In relation to fandom, the stereotype of fans as fantasists suggests that they have got it wrong ontologically (in believing that they can fully 'know' a celebrity, if, for example, they find out what he/she ate for breakfast). It suggests that they have also made an *epistemological* mistake in gathering their knowledge about stars, because they cling to a grave falsehood (the celebrity image) and perceive commercially mediated encounters as reliable sources. The critique of fandom therefore suggests that fans cannot tell fantasy from reality and are on the road to trouble. Harrington and Bielby (1995) reported that on the Lifetime Channel's *Jane Pratt Show* four daytime soap actors said they were regularly greeted in public by their character names. When the actors wondered whether their fans could tell the difference, 'A male audience member shouted, "But that's all we know you as". He felt that calling actors by their own names would be presumptuous given that he is familiar with the characters only' (Harrington & Bielby 1995, 103). Addressing soap characters by their real names was therefore conceived as an overly familiar invasion of privacy. In this situation, it was evident that the fan *could* tell the difference between the actor and his character, but focused on the latter image. The researchers assessed this by asking about fan mail and related that 'only 2% of our respondents report having written fan letters to the character rather than the actor, and many more were amazed (if not insulted) by the question'

(105). Likewise, music fans recognize that they do not actually *know* Bruce Springsteen; they are highly aware that the image is not always the same as its bearer (Cavicchi 1998, 54). They understand that their idol is an industrial participant and not simply a folk singer who can bring his message straight to the people (60). Fans realize that they are watching a sort of fiction, but find that approaching the characters *as if* they are real adds to their pleasures.

What is going on is not that media fans are epistemologically mistaken, or that they do not care about the difference between people and the screen roles they play. Instead many fans deeply enjoy playing with the line between the fictional and the real. As one soap fan told Harrington and Bielby, 'Sometimes the actors and the characters blend into a believability so strong that you almost feel you're eavesdropping on real lives and it is fascinating' (1995, 91). The pair of researchers concluded that most fans, far from being fooled, *consciously* played with the boundary between fiction and reality. This play is also part of a process of self-investigation. For Cavicchi,

> In addition, Springsteen fans' conscious discussions of self making do not indicate that popular culture is shaping their identity but rather that they are shaping their identity with popular culture . . . Identification with characters in the music, for instance, raises questions for some fans about how to define identity itself. But in the end, for fans, participating in the world of popular music serves rather than destroys, enhances rather than diminishes, their perception of themselves as unique individuals. (1998, 157)

A further point here is that fans are cognizant of their image and may work to avoid the possibility of being stereotyped. Harrington and Bielby (1995, 95) found that some fans do things to emphasize that they are not stupid people divorced from reality, but they instead have political concerns, for example. Many fan clubs raise money for charity. It is almost as if they are compensating for a public perception that they know is mistaken, but one that inevitably affects their daily lives. In that sense, as we discussed in the last chapter, fans are performers too, aware of the ways in which wider society can greet and stereotype them.

What is the function of stereotyping? The list of supposed characteristics that Jenkins discovered through his perceptive analysis of mainstream television primarily functions to *normalize* the rest of the media audience. In constructing fandom as an other, it locates 'ordinary' viewers as a hidden, idealized opposite to the fans: (a) discriminating, in control; (b) and (c) pursuing worthwhile cultural projects; (d) and (e) socially adept; (f) mature and (g) able to fully differentiate the real world from the imagined. Behind this superior portrayal is a kind of fear that fans inevitably identify in ways that suggest they experience an alien set of feelings and operate on different assumptions to other people. If this appears like it might be true, it is crucial to note that fans *come from* the ordinary population and the existence of their fandom does not automatically make them into the grotesques sometimes presented by the media.

Fandom and the ordinary audience

While mainstream media producers often present fandom as an other in order to normalize mainstream audiences, *fans also consider ordinary audiences in different ways as their counter-parts*. Considering what separates them from the ordinary audience, Cavicchi describes the perspective of Springsteen's fans: 'This distinction, from the point of view of fans, is clear enough: Fans have a connection to Bruce Springsteen that nonfans do not. However, in reality, the distinction is far more ambiguous and difficult to pin down' (1998, 87).

The first thing to notice here is that the unified audience is partly a fiction of the media industries. Cavicchi observed that the rock audience for Springsteen was diverse: 'During these songs, I noticed a clear division between people in the audience. In particular, while many older fans sang along to "The River", many other people got out of their seats and moved into the aisles to get another beer or some food' (30). Industrially, fans are therefore not so much opposites as *intermediaries* between producers and ordinary audiences (Jenkins 2008, 73). They have a capacity to scout out and enthusiastically discuss particular new series and products. Yet as these series continue, fan communities can also be disappointed that programme-makers have pandered to more casual audience factions – the 'commodity audience' – and not specifically fannish interests (Jenkins 1992, 30).

There are also qualitative differences of approach and experience separating fans from other audience members. Devotees build knowledge from a different starting point: 'For fans, a Springsteen concert is not a single theatrical event but rather a ritual in which they regularly participate over time' (Cavicchi 1998, 92). Unlike the ordinary audience, fans also stay 'in frame' after the performance ends.

Typical/Minimal fans?

One way to think about the distinctions between fans and other audience members is to consider whether we can talk about 'typical' or 'minimal' fans. If fandom for less hip cultural forms like soaps is an 'abnormal' practice, then the question becomes how we can determine and understand 'normal' fandom. When critics use ideas about rationality and 'staying in control' to define normal fandom, what they are often doing is actually attempting to isolate excessive, 'extreme' or 'obsessive' fandom as an other. The division of roles between fan and non-fan has made it hard to see quite where normal fandom exists, especially as those attempts to other extreme fandom can actually locate it as fandom's most representative form. Also, to different degrees, everyone participates in the practices that are used to define fandom, including the use of the media to define identity, so perhaps – as Harrington and Bielby (1995, 112–16) suggest – we should really be thinking about a kind of *continuum* that stretches between the least committed fans and the most dedicated ones. This notion of a continuum allows empirical results to be interrogated in several ways: breadth (genre) versus depth (single show) fandom, the way that fandom emerges from different points of access (like storyline or character) and also other matters like fan self-identification, community participation, consumption of publicity material and archiving. However, debating the line between fan and non-fan is not a scientific matter undertaken by neutral observers. It is part of the way that fans negotiate their identities, especially during periods when the audience for an icon is dramatically changing. Making a firm distinction between minimal, typical and extreme fans is an idea that has significant limitations. Daniel Cavicchi (1998, 30 and 87–96) examined this issue in more detail, noting that the distinctions allow people to distance themselves from others in elitist ways. It can also mean that fans who *do not* follow practices to obsessive lengths feel that they do not measure up. While the notion of the minimal or 'casual' fan is debated in fan communities, if we adopt that idea then it is much harder to isolate fans from other audience members. This may be flowing with the tide of the media industry, however, as we are living in an era when ordinary audiences are being invited into subject positions that increasingly resemble fandom. Indeed, back in 1998 Abercrombie and Longhust argued:

> Our view is that 'ordinary' audience members are more like fans and enthusiasts than might initially be thought and that, given the increased contemporary salience of media fan-like and enthusiast-like qualities, sociation patterns are increasingly likely to resemble some of the relationships identified in the fan literature. (122)

Over a decade later their statement seems prophetic, because the combined forces of celebrity culture, box set product lines and accessible social media have conspired to make the former practices of fans more easily enacted by a much wider public. One response to this is to say that we are *all* fans now as media audience members and that the distinction no longer matters. An associated perception is that fans were the pioneers who spearheaded the current age of audience participation. Yet if cult film and TV series are increasingly organized as elaborate franchises, if media products are orchestrated to provide a greater depth of cultural stimulation, if box sets and streaming Websites allow any of us to watch our favourite episodes again – and if viewers are encouraged to leave comments online (see Gorton 2009, 40–1) – does that not automatically make everyone a fan? The distance between *media consumption practices* may be narrowing, but contemporary culture still marks out an emotional and rhetorical divide between the identities of the fan and the ordinary audience member. Owning a box set does not make one a fan. Neither does watching every episode. There has to be a peaking of fascination inside the individual that is expressed in some way. Furthermore, while fans may have become the talkative poster-children of an era of new media, beyond academia they are still framed as inadequate by significant sections of society, especially when they pursue particular kinds of interest and objects of attention.

Marginalized fandoms

The incident [of encountering a male Philadephia Eagles fan] reminded me that a sort-of social hierarchy still existed when it came to 'fandoms', and within the hierarchy sports would always be at the top of the pile while media fandom would be regarded as slightly suspect by the mainstream. There's nothing odd at all about flying your team flag in front of your house, but can you imagine your neighbours reaction if you hoisted up the iconic *Doctor Who* logo?

DEBORAH STANISH 2010, 31

Suggestions by some scholars that we no longer need to challenge pop culture stereotypes of fandom may be premature. Deborah Stanish's recent discussion as a *Doctor Who* fan marks out a social distinction between sports fandom – which is shown on TV and in the press as socially acceptable – and media fandom, which has arguably been marginalized. In other words, although sports fans are *normalized* as a prime embodiment of acceptable spectatorship, media fans are sometimes represented as an eccentric faction with interests beyond the comprehension of the ordinary media audience. Furthermore, there are subtle processes of othering going on *between* quite similar media fan phenomena and also *within* some types of media fandom.

The development of perceived cultural hierarchies can occur between different objects of fan interest. This section will not so much theorize them, but
simply note that for many observers, they are there.

Within sci-fi, for instance, there is a spectrum of fan objects that – especially
for adolescents interested in peer approval – depart from the respectable into
the eccentric, from *Star Wars*, through *Star Trek*, on in to minor objects like
Battlestar Galactica and *Buck Rogers*, and finally through to *Doctor Who*: 'It
wasn't cool Brit like the Sex Pistols or vintage Bowie, but weird Brit with bad
teeth and laughable special effects' (Stanish 2010, 33). Similarly, we know
that liking certain kinds of music can place a person as relatively highbrow or
low brow, cool or uncool.

Attacks on fans can make it uncomfortable to speak publically as a fan
(Jenkins 1992, 19). Partly for this reason, hierarchies of acceptability are
sometimes reproduced within fan communities. On one level, this appears
to be a re-enactment of external processes of labelling designed to ward off
what are seen as the 'worst' elements of cultural excess from more 'cool'
areas. For example, in analyzing gendered responces from his sample of *Star
Wars* fans, Will Brooker found that 'obsessive fandom is acceptable as long
as it avoids the unacceptable social types of perpetually single misfit and
homosexual' (2002, 3). Another instance of this internal marginalization is the
use of the term 'squeeing' in sci-fi fan communities to caution against emotional
exuberance when fans discuss shows or meet well-known participants. Using
a metaphor from addiction, Lynne Thomas explains that when visiting fan
conventions, 'I was hooked on the "getting to meet celebrities on my show"
experience. A "squee" girl was born – despite my not having yet heard of
the term' (2010, 81). Thomas simultaneously acknowledges her response as
enthusiastic yet somehow unwelcome and abject in game of sci-fi fandom.
The term 'squeeing', however, makes little or no sense in relation to forms of
fandom that are premised on emotional enthusiasm, such as rock fandom. To
shout out loud at a rock concert is to participate as a fan in the spectacular
experience of music being expressed as a form of social energy. Here the
musical medium becomes a space in which people can let themselves go
as full participants in what is, ultimately, also a form of collective culture. For
this reason, we might say that the process is usually one of *collusion* rather
than mutual distancing – or rather that processes of communality and social
distancing often go on *at the same time*. Another point here is that desire
for emotional intimacy has traditionally been socially coded as feminine, so
spaces of community in popular culture may conceivably liberate fans who
might otherwise have trouble in letting themselves go.

To help them ward off the taint of overzealous enthusiasm, fans of certain
genres use discourses from art appreciation that imply a kind of emotional

distancing from the maker of the cultural product. Art discourses register critical separation rather than emotional connection (see Jenkins 2006, 23). Discourses supporting traditional criticism champion the idea that viewers should keep a certain distance from the object of their passion to allow them to make up their own minds *after* standing in judgement. While fans cannot be fully distanced from their object, some do aim for this kind of critical distance. One way it is expressed is by putting a focus on the work itself – on the media product, not its maker. In effect this evokes a literary approach to popular culture. *Backstreets*, for instance, is a professional fan magazine for Bruce Springsteen followers and has an editorial policy not to discuss Bruce's personal life, even though some fans are interested (Cavicchi 1998, 54). Editorial policies that focus on a creative work, not its maker, indirectly promote the maker's agency *as an author* and therefore attempt to move their object up the cultural hierarchy. This approach is limited, however, because celebrity-following is a dimension of most fandom, and some icons – such as Elvis Presley in his 1960s Hollywood phase – rode out whole periods where their releases were universally criticized by the entire audience: critics, fans and star alike. Such moments go to show that we understand icons as larger than their media output. When their releases fail to reach an appropriate standard, fans either support them by using an estimation of what they are capable of, or by empathizing with their struggle. Both factors suggest that fans are not literary critics who marginalize everything except for the finished product.

Furthermore, there are occasions when fans realize that their own goals may be in conflict with how they want their object portrayed to the whole of the audience. Samantha Barbas (2001, 116–23) describes one function of individual and collective fan behaviour. **Boosting** means lobbying industrial agents to raise the profiles and float the careers of new stars. Once people realized it was best done collectively, boosting became a shared practice that helped to generate many fan phenomena of the classic Hollywood era. If marginalizing their own fandom aids the boosting process, some fans will make the sacrifice. For instance, while *Doctor Who* was off air in the 1980s and 1990s its fan community was criticized for their inability to move on. When it was regenerated from the inside by media professionals who described themselves as remaining fans, the insider term 'fanwank' was repeatedly mentioned to police 'excessive' demands for the use of obscure continuity material that might push away fresh viewers. This view assumed, perhaps unhelpfully, that long-term fans and wider audiences wanted different things (Hills 2010b, 60–1). The idea of 'fanwank', which was premised on opposing fans and non-fans, stereotyped particular sections of the fan community as infantile.[2]

Anti-fans

The plethora of cultural options online and a reduction in the power of professional critics may have *appeared* to create the ultimate in audience choice, yet the critic's abdicated chair has sometimes been filled by other audience members who rail against specific cultural tastes. Jonathan Gray describes these **anti-fans** by saying, 'Opposed and yet in some ways similar to the fan is the anti-fan: he/she who actively and vocally hates or dislikes a given text, personality, or genre' (2005, 840). The idea has been taken up by other researchers. Discussing audiences for the reality TV series *Survivor* (1992–), Derek Forster (2004) separated ordinary viewers, 'official fandom' (fans who do not play with the world of the text), guerrilla fans (who seek to spoil the text) and anti-fans (those who find pleasure knocking the show rather than enjoying it). Such typologies have a degree of *logical* coherence, but they arguably tend to taint fandom by lumping it together with unconnected modes of audiencehood. What, then, is the difference between an anti-fan and a critic? We might usefully distinguish ordinary and loving cultural critics here. Ordinary critics, whether amateur or professional, make it their business to trawl through the whole range of products in order to decide the best and worst of the crop. To do this they must separate themselves from what they see, internalize a set of artistic criteria and use them to stand in judgement. A loving critic cultivates no such critical distance. Instead they become so bound up with their particular text or genre that they become disappointed if new products do not reach standards achieved elsewhere in the franchise or canon. They may not even be able to articulate *why* the product has failed. Ordinary criticism has traditionally come with an embargo against emotional passion. Fans can be loving critics, but they have to put their fannish identity aside if they wish to play the role of the ordinary critic. Meanwhile, anti-fans, in Gray's sense, are neither fans nor ordinary critics. Instead they are the inverse of loving critics; as hating critics they are bound up with the text and vehemently complain about it. They have dropped the ordinary critic's embargo against passion because they passionately dislike or even detest the object of their attention. Consequently, rather like the idea of 'anti-matter' in physics, although Gray's label *is* illuminative – insofar that it points to something formerly invisible in a sociocultural sense – it does not quite grasp its own subject. *Anti-fans are not inverse fans, but are inverse loving critics.*

There are many examples of anti-fandom and many reasons why anti-fans might appear. One reason is a wish to revel in critique or contradict mass sentiment.[3] Sanderson and Cheong (2010, 336) mention how some writers on the online platform Twitter used condemnatory language to emphasize their contempt for a recently deceased Michael Jackson. These anti-fans may well have disliked the wave of support for Jackson in light of the allegations of child abuse that haunted his career. The comments of anti-fans often contain what Sheffield and Merlo (2010) have called a 'rhetoric of superiority', a phrase implying the display of 'elite' status.[4] Anti-fans often take a moral or ideological stance too. Diane Alters described how one family that she studied was particularly upset by television series like *Ellen* because, in contradiction to their evangelical Christian religious values, the show casually portrayed a lesbian lead character (2007, 348). Anti-fans can emerge on a more parochial level if they believe that a new media franchise will usurp the fan base of their favourite show. This can set up mutual antagonisms between different fan bases, because fans of populist phenomena can believe that if their community loses size then it might be in danger of being forgotten. *Doctor Who,* for example, had run on British television from 1963 onwards while *Star Trek* came later in 1968. In *Who* fan lore, if you like *Doctor Who* you are likely to be an anti-fan of *Star Trek* (Hills 2010b, 55). Similarly, in popular music, press stories often set artists up against each other in supposed battles. Examples here include Elvis Presley against Pat Boone in the 1950s, the Stones against the Beatles in the 1960s, Guns N' Roses against Bon Jovi in the 1980s, and Blur against Oasis in the 1990s. While such oppositional pairings create news copy by highlighting important distinctions in the masculinity or cultural orientation of each pair of contenders, what such music battle stories – or sci-fi contests, for that matter – forget is that ordinary fans frequently like *both* contenders and may well be dedicated fans of both of them.

Elaborating on the anti-fan idea, we might say that the stance of certain artists (and consequent expectations of their fan base) actually *include* an element of *invited anti-fandom*. On one level, certain stars seem to invite criticism by *not* engaging with their audiences. Some are famous for avoiding their fans. Greta Garbo, for example, refused even to offer her signature so that the fan mail department at MGM studios could fake it on replies to well wishers. Other stars have complained about the way that media fans follow them as celebrities rather than for their professional output. One argument is that as a cultural worker, each successful actor or musician is simply doing a job, like a plumber, and why would anyone want to visit their plumber's house? In his book *Toxic Fame,* Joey Berlin recalled that the film actor John Malcovich told him, 'I don't have any desire to be popular. It's humiliating, I think' (1996, xv). A critic of mass culture might agree that popularity is not the measure of great art, then point out that Malcovich's fans are doubly duped: first for following a person who is ungrateful to his fans, and second for following a person who is deliberately being naïve about the operation of his profession. Apart from those who claim to find interest only in enjoying Malcovich's film output and therefore see him as a cultural worker, there is also the idea that what he says *may not matter* to his fans because they primarily interpret him as a figure of ego-identification (an outspoken role model), rather like a group leader. It is one thing if such individualists have loyal fans, but quite another when stars *purposefully provoke* their audiences. A good example here is Bob Dylan. Dylan's distinct combination of creativity and rebelliousness locates him as a bohemian hero, particularly for scholarly or lower middle-class fans. He is famous for playing electric guitar in the face of expectations from a folk audience, and is therefore associated with both a sense of literary or artistic creativity and outspoken social rebelliousness. In his heyday, Dylan was loyal to his first cohort of fans, but he also very much enjoyed the vitriolic energy of his anti-fans. As the singer's interviewers, Nora Ephron and Susan Edmiston, recalled, he asked his secretary to save two kinds of fan mail:

> [Dylan saved] either violent put-downs (the ones that called him a sell-out, fink, fascist or Red), to which he said, 'I really dig those', and the ones from old friends: 'These are letters from people who knew me in New York five, six years ago. My first fans. Not the people who call themselves my first fans. They came in three years ago, two years ago. They aren't really my first fans'. (Eisen 1970, 68)

That Dylan might be involved in a game with his critics implies that he actively provoked his own anti-fandom. The notion of his loyalty to his 'first fans' is also interesting here. Tied to a shared sense of locality, early fans can often claim that a performer is one of their own and form an ambiguously critical connection once he/she outgrows the locality. Those first fans can actually become *anti-fans* of new members of the fan community. The pattern is similar when artists change direction and pull a large number of new recruits into their fan base. Under such conditions old and new fans can be antagonistic towards each other.

Finally, there are whole genres where a kind of anti-fandom, or at least critical distance, is written into the contract that fans have with their heroes. Punk rock, for example, was founded on a 'Do It Yourself' ethos that linked a sense of social nihilism to an attack on the institution of music stardom. Audiences who understood the punk ethos were expected to be vocal. They were expected to spit and heckle at live events as part of the ritual (see Duffett 2009). Johnny Rotten's incendiary attitude was therefore a kind of test case which ignited a whole generation of fans who were conflicted about how to proceed. In fan mail, they either expressed a conflicted sense of critical distance or identified with their heroes by expressing shared individualism and rebelliousness (see Duffett 2009 and 2010c).

Polysemic representations

The last chapter showed that the place of fandom in society has gradually shifted. As part of this a range of media producers have used fandom as part of their public image. Fan passions have been part of the story for a range of celebrities, many of whom have used their fandom to distinguish their own celebrity brands and genres of media output. **Auteur** theory is the idea that certain individuals stamp their creative signatures on the process of cultural production. Consider some of the following individuals and how their own fandom has been represented as part of their image: Andy Warhol, Steven Spielberg, David Bowie, Princess Diana, Quentin Tarantino, Lady Gaga. In the image of each of these characters, fandom can indicate a disarmingly common touch ('she's just like me') or mark out a moment of dedication to craft. Here, to be seen as fan is to reveal your credentials as an ordinary person. High-profile fans also help to regenerate the image of fandom itself as an acceptable form of cultural identity.

In a media environment that is polarized between fans and their critics, producers can sometimes find themselves having to face a compromise in order to encompass the whole of the audience, both the mainstream and fan population alike. They have used irony and parody as tools to help. **Polysemy** is the capability of an artwork or media product to leave itself open to diverse interpretations. Modern representations of fandom are often strategically polysemic as a way to encourage the collective interest of a fragmented audience. Whether these products stereotype or support fandom depends on the perspective of the viewer and is therefore open to debate. Discussing the television documentary *Wacko About Jacko* (IWC Media, 2005), Matt Hills found:

> Jackson fans do not monolithically approve or disapprove of *Wacko About Jacko*, and that a range of fan readings are made from its structured polysemy, some being almost wholly oppositional to the programme's stereotyping of Jackson fandom, and others choosing to read selectively in order to ''rescue'' parts of the documentary. Despite these differential readings, it is difficult to argue that any one reading would or could be 'preferred', as the structure of the documentary seems to deliberately enact a semiotic splitting between extremely pathologised 'wacko' fandom and

less obviously demonized 'good' fandom while still representing Jackson fans within specific ideological limits thereby enabling 'positive' and 'negative' fan readings even while continuing to cater for, and reproduce, a common-sense ideology of 'irrational', emotivist fandom. (2007b, 475)

It is possible that fans who participate in one way and are then portrayed in quite another might sympathetically read such a documentary as an excuse to defend their own participation. Nevertheless, Hills' work reminds us that portrayals of fandom often both operate within the remit of social stereo-typing, but unpick the stereotypes by helping us to find points of identifica-tion with the subject. In other words, while films about *extreme* fandom almost always tend to other and dismiss it as a socially inappropriate activity – see, for instance, Kirstyn Gorton's (2009, 37) discussion of the Stephen King film *Misery* (Reiner 1990) – many comedies, dramas and documentaries about fandom contain moments when we, as an audience, are at least asked to acknowledge that the fans portrayed are more than their role and just like us.[5]

3

Beyond the text

Starting points

- In what ways have academics traditionally understood fandom?
- How might we understand how fans make meaningful use of media texts?
- Why has it been useful to conceptualize fans as textual poachers?

All that The Waverly [cinema] produced was a minor amount of ballyhoo [in readiness to screen The Rocky Horror Picture Show]: *a few balloons, and the practice of playing the soundtrack recording in the auditorium a few minutes before the film came on. The remaining impetus came from a few isolated individuals who met and became friends in the process of starting a cult, which quickly spread to other theatres and cities. . . . There is first of all an established speech by Piro who welcomes 'virgins' (i.e. newcomers) to the cult, introduces out-of-town guest performers . . . and offers a few local rules and guidelines ('We don't call Brad an "asshole" every time he appears'). After this the assembled costumed performers (usually more than a dozen) dance the 'Time Warp' to the soundtrack before the lights dim.*

JONATHAN ROSENBAUM 1980, 78–9

So far in this book I have held off describing media products and franchises as **texts**, though this is the dominant metaphor used in media studies and cultural studies. The idea of the text (and also the canon) came to these disciplines from a long tradition of biblical and then literary scholarship. As a notion, textuality operates to fix its object of study, bounding and locating a definitive portion of content in each media product. It also introduces the ideas of *meaning, reading, interpretation* and *literacy* (the cultivated ability to read). American film writer Jonathan Rosenbaum's report on the early history of audience responses to *The Rocky Horror Picture Show* (Sharman 1975), however, exposes a kind of 'living textuality' where fans have turned their viewing practice into a lively, ritual activity. The film became the focus of their 'cult' in a way that its makers never anticipated. Its fans practiced it in a way that included their own performance and participation. Reporting all this, Rosenbaum also notes that other audiences behaved in very different ways when watching the same film. This chapter takes a historical approach and examines how media scholars have understood the ways that audiences interpret their texts. How might we productively conceive fans' relationships with the many texts that fascinate them? What follows will review the literature to trace an early trajectory in audience research from the idea that fans passively absorb their texts right through to recent advances in the field. Looking at the history of theory is rather like travelling back in a time machine: many of the ideas in this chapter are not in tune with the current discussions in fan research, but there are still lessons to be learned from their perspectives and limitations.

Early history of audience research

Qualitative research takes language and meaning as its concern. This section provides a whistle-stop tour of qualitative research on audiences. To make rather a gross – but often accurate – generalization, we might say that European scholars have tended towards more pessimistic and economy-driven approaches, while scholars working in America have taken a more liberal and celebratory stance. The history of audience research reflects an oscillation between the two approaches.

One of the earliest approaches to textual meaning, at least in the social sciences, was contributed in Claude Elwood Shannon and Warren Weaver's 1948 book *A Mathematical Theory of Communication*. The Shannon-Weaver model suggested that meaning was conveyed *from* the maker of the message through the message itself *to* the receiver, rather like a relay baton. This model, which broadly emerged from the application of probability theory to wartime telecommunications, introduced the notion of coding and decoding.

It understood the text purely as a delivery system for the message, and positioned the receiver as a kind of end point in the relay of meaning. On the surface the Shannon-Weaver model might sound like common sense, but its elegant simplicity hides a number of problems. One is that it gives no agency to the receivers and sees them as passive, absorbent receptacles for the message. If the message is unclear to the receiver, the model suggests that its maker has failed in his/her duty to clearly convey the content. In a sense, the Shannon-Weaver model therefore lends itself to unilateralism, because the responses of listeners who reinterpret the text based on their different cultural background are merely seen as a pretext for clarifying the message. The schema therefore offers a model of communication that forgets the politics of reception. For that reason, later researchers used the term 'hypodermic model' to question way that ideas like those by Shannon and Weaver presupposed that the receiver would naturally just *absorb* the message. **Textual determinism** is the idea that the text determines its own meaning and can therefore automatically influence its readers. If the Shannon-Weaver model makes textual determinism into a central premise, it is also true that the idea has underwritten whole fields of theory that articulate anxieties about the social 'dangers' of particular media texts from horror films to video games.

On the other side of the Atlantic, a few years before Shannon and Weaver's research was published, in an essay called *On the Fetish-Character in Music and the Regression of Listening,* Theodor Adorno (1938/2001) began crystallizing his concerns about fandom and the perceived dangers of the popular music. Adorno was a central member of the Frankfurt School, a group of research intellectuals initially based at the Institute for Social Research in the University of Frankfurt am Main who developed a series of interdisciplinary, neo-Marxist ideas suggesting that mass culture was a means of controlling the public. He worked at a time when fascist political movements were co-opting strategies from art and swaying public opinion through propaganda. As a Marxist scholar, Adorno saw the culture industries as an ancillary form of social control: a way to keep the masses distracted in trivial pursuits. His specific concerns about popular music also developed out of his personal interest in the revolutionary potential of 'serious' musical composition. As such, he combined a Marxist position with a distinct brand of cultural elitism (being, in effect, a snob on behalf of the people). His conceptual toolkit was also Freudian: referencing the idea that individuals harbour innate instinctual drives that are channelled or repressed by society. Furthermore, Adorno's writing strategy was **polemic**. Polemicists are essayists who forward controversial ideas, often by abdicating objectivity in favour of reasoned persuasion. Adorno's work cannot therefore be dismissed as lacking objectivity because it questions that stance by declaring its bias from the start. When Marxists discuss the economics of material goods, they usually distinguish each commodity's use value and exchange value. Use value is the product's worth as a basic utility, whereas exchange value is its market price (determined by factors such as rarity and demand). Use value and exchange value cannot be fully separated (Hills 2002a, 33–4). Ordinary logic cannot fully capture a contradictory reality – one of exchange value *and* use value – so, for Adorno, an oscillating, *dialectic approach* is needed to move between opposing viewpoints.

Adorno tends to associate commodity culture with social control. He argues that a small army of business agents, songwriters and performers create music that is both relatively standardized and emotionally appealing. Its intoxicating sounds and melodies lull listeners into a passive state of distraction. Fans are therefore, he argues, the manipulated end product of this process. In this schema they fit into the totality of a much broader argument about the power relations of commercial culture; to focus on them alone, as I do here, is therefore somewhat problematic. In *On the Fetish Character*, Adorno differentiates between two broad types of fan:

> Whenever they attempt to break away from the passive status of compulsory consumers and 'activate' themselves, they succumb to pseudo-activity. Types rise up from the mass of the retarded who differentiate themselves by pseudo-activity and nevertheless make the regression more strikingly visible. They are, first, the enthusiasts who write fan letters to radio stations and orchestras and, at well-managed jazz festivals, produce their own enthusiasm as an advertisement for the wares they consume. They call themselves jitterbugs, as if they simultaneously wanted to affirm and mock their loss of individuality, their transformation into beetles whirring around in fascination . . . The opposite type appears to be the eager person who leaves the factory and 'occupies' himself with music in the quiet of his bedroom. He is shy and inhibited, perhaps has had no luck with girls, and wants in any case to preserve his own special sphere. He seeks this as a radio ham. At twenty, he is still at the stage of a boy scout working on complicated knots to please his parents. (Adorno 1938/2001, 52–3)

Adorno's discussion of fans here closely matches more recent definitions of *enthusiasts* (Abercrombie & Longhurst 1998, 132). Although the fans that Adorno mentions here enjoy pastimes rather than follow celebrities, his depiction is clearly designed to other them. Adorno's rhetoric attacks any trace of decency or nobility evident in their public image by articulating stereotypes similar to those discussed in the last chapter. Pointedly deploying a stereotype later exposed by Henry Jenkins – that fans devote their lives to the cultivation of worthless knowledge – he adds mention on the same page of 'the listening expert who can identify every band and immerses himself in the history of jazz as if it were a Holy Writ' (54). Media commentators such as Adorno have often used fandom to critique modern life, when they could have studied fan behaviour instead (Cavicchi 1998, 8). However, Adorno did not advocate conducting field research with fans: 'if someone tried to "verify" the fetish character of music by investigating the reactions of listeners with interviews and questionnaires, he might meet with unexpected puzzles . . . [because] every answer that one receives conforms in advance to the surface of that music business which is being attacked by the theory being "verified"' (1938/2001, 45). In other words, according to Adorno fans are so steeped in the rhetoric of the industry that they will say nothing meaningful about the value of their objects; they are consumerist 'temple slaves' of the music industry (39).

Nevertheless, Adorno sees fans as epitomizing the tendency of recorded popular music to turn people into 'regressive' listeners, in effect drugging and distracting them with sounds that are easy to hear and will never shake them out of their political sleepwalking. The Frankfurt school leader was therefore largely pessimistic in his stress on popular culture's tendency to become a form of social control (by naturalizing the social order) rather than on its potential to encourage social change, either as a repository of rebellious tactics, laboratory-type play space or temporary utopia (Hills 2002a, 31). When Adorno complained that consumption reduced creative culture to sentimental mass-marketed clutter, he had no conception of the dialogic, folk reworking of cultural material (Jenkins 1992, 51).

According to Matt Hills, 'The work of Theodor Adorno is regularly criticized and dispensed with in academic and academic-fan accounts of fan culture' (2002a, 31). For a long time, Adorno became a kind of tackling dummy in media studies because his arguments could provoke students who believed in the 'soul' of commercial music. Critics have dismissed the Frankfurt school leader's seemingly arrogant and elitist conception of the 'passive' mass audience (31). Rather than simply rejecting him as a curmudgeon elistist who used Marx and Freud as alibis to attack the fannish masses and their agency, it is worth returning to his work to salvage what insights it offers. All too often Adorno's work has been selectively read in ways that have missed its useful points (31). Although his dismissive attack on fandom exploited the lowest stereotypes, to an extent his broader argument about the industrial production of culture remains relevant: in various ways media producers do wield considerable power and constantly encourage us to collude with their agenda. Fans, particularly as a collective, can be power brokers who engage in more than 'pseudo-activity' to please media business. The inspirations behind their interests are nevertheless arguably social and industrial, even as they are championed through natural and personal experience.

In some ways, although mass culture critics on both sides of the Atlantic, notably Dwight Macdonald (1957) in the United States of America and Richard Hoggart (1957) in Britain, held quite similar views to Adorno, his relentless pessimism about popular music was not entirely borne out by the way that musical shifts reflected social turmoil key moments of the post-war period. In different ways, rock'n'roll, late 1960s rock and 1970s punk were all infused by an air of counter-cultural rebellion. As we saw in the introduction, other forms of media culture shifted too.

At the start of the 1970s a new wave of American researchers offered a more optimistic perspective on media consumption. For example in 1972, in their chapter in *The Sociology of the Mass Communications*, Dennis McQuail, Jay Blumler and J. R. Brown posed four main needs that the media gratify: *diversion* (easing our worries by looking at the problems of others), *personal relationships* (developing imaginary relationships with celebrities), *personal identity and growth* (learning from others in the same predicament) and *surveillance* (using the media to gather information about the world). Work like this became known as *uses and gratifications theory*, an American trend in audience analysis that inspired further research – such as that by Elihu Katz, Jay Blumler and Michael Gurevitch (1973) – which argued that broadcast televison squarely met audience needs. Uses and gratifications research was an advance on previous ideas because it analysed actual media audiences. **Empirical** *research* in media or cultural studies means field analysis conducted by actually talking to producers or consumers. Researchers like Blumler and Katz escaped from the 'mass audience' paradigm, allowing their readers to begin to see the activity and individuality of ordinary viewers. No longer the passive dupes of the mass culture critique, audience members were now understood as ordinary people who chose to turn on their TV sets, had needs and could change channels. From that perspective, fans who consumed media products were simply getting their own needs met.

Although uses and gratifications appeared a 'common sense' theory, rather like the Shannon-Weaver model, its self-contained facade hid a multitude of problems. The theory prompted criticism on several scores for being too simplistic. First, uses and gratifications posits an audience that is harmonious and never in conflict with broadcasting networks. Yet audiences have sometimes complained that television shows are *not* meeting their needs and expectations. Second, by artificially bounding an isolated viewer and a media message, the theory socially isolated and decontextualized mass communication. Key aspects of the text were ignored, including its content, changing popularity and multiple interpretations. The theory ignored social interactions in the viewer's life and could not explain the frequency of his or her media use. A third problem was that it posited human needs as innate, universal and transhistorical, when in reality they are different in different places, societies, philosophies and eras. Contemporary theories occasionally reproduce this thinking: evolutionary psychologists, for example, sometimes say that humans are 'hardwired' to reproduce and parlay their genes into the next generation. However, feminists and queer theorists have questioned the basis of such theories, exposing reproductivism as a political construct (see, for instance, Edelman 2004). Humanity got on fine without television until its widespread adoption in the 1950s. If there are any innate human needs, it is therefore doubtful that television meets them. Indeed, it could be argued that the 'needs' met by the media are circular, a product of its own marketing and rhetoric. The broadness of these categories of need posited by uses and gratifications is also problematic because it means that media researchers can escape the necessity of creating empirical questions open to refutation by audience comments. Finally, the uses and gratifications idea is open to charges of conservatism insofar that it overplays the freedom of audience and forgets the media corporations can function as political interest groups. In that respect it has supported the status quo by becoming another mouthpiece for the ideological supposition that the media does not require any improvement because audiences always get what they most need. Despite later efforts to resurrect it (see Ruggiero 2000), because of the simplistic way that uses and gratifications theory understands the sociological context of the media audience, it has been widely challenged in media and cultural studies. In a sense, the theory's academic reception acts as a cautionary tale reminding us not to posit universal human needs. Whether they are the need to grieve for a dead star or to express a religious impulse, such needs can be perceived as social constructions.

In Britain, a separate tradition of research emerged from the writings of Richard Hoggart and Raymond Williams and took shape at the Birmingham Centre for Contemporary Cultural Studies (BCCS). Members of the Birmingham School, as it was called, were widely known for their broadly Marxist interpretations of subcultures as spectacular examples of working class youth resistance. In 1973 the BCCS's long-term leader, Stuart Hall, contributed a theory of media communication that considerably opened up the field (reprinted in Hall 1980).

An **ideology** is a set of ideas circulating in society that can be challenged and operates to uphold inequalities between different groups of people. Othering, for instance, is an ideological process because it locates 'them' as inferior to 'us'. The notion of ideology was popularized by Karl Marx.

Acknowledging Marxism's relatively unfashionable status, recent writers in cultural studies have tended to jettison the word 'ideology' and still keep the idea. When they talk about the 'cultural work' of media texts, they usually mean the way that those texts attempt to persuade us to adopt a particular ideological position. Stuart Hall was interested in the ideological role of the media. In effect, Hall combined an interest in the politically persuasive nature of texts with an advance on the Shannon-Weaver model of communication. He saw texts as carriers of dominant ideologies that were encoded by their makers and decoded by audiences. However, unlike Shannon and Weaver, Hall suggested that particular audiences could read the text *against its grain*. Even though authors may not consciously adopt the dominant ideology, they are prioritized in Hall's model as instruments of it. In relation to this ideology supposedly expressed in the text, Hall presented three types of audience reading: *preferred* readings (in which the dominant ideology was uncritically accepted), *oppositional* readings (in which the audience challenged the ideology conveyed by the text) and *negotiated* readings (compromised interpretations that ended up being somewhere between the preferred and oppositional versions).

By positing potentially rebellious viewers, the encoding-decoding idea broke audience research out of the reductive trap of **textual determinism**: the idea that texts determine their meanings regardless of *who* reads them. Nevertheless, one of the problems of Hall's idea was that it presented a kind of theoretical estimate that was untested on real audiences. To address this David Morley constructed a series of focus groups that examined the news magazine TV show *Nationwide*. **Focus group** research means asking a small, temporarily-assembled group of people about their opinions, concerns or habits. In his study of the *Nationwide* audience, Morley (1980) showed screenings of the programme to various focus groups that represented constituencies of British society. His results confirmed that certain sections of society, such as university arts students and trades unionists did not follow the preferred reading but made negotiated or oppositional readings instead. Morley's confirmation of Hall's ideas, however, came a little too soon, as other researchers challenged the artificial nature of the audiences that Morley constructed. Many of his research subjects (the people being researched) had never seen *Nationwide* before he exposed them to the show in the screening room. There was another issue too, in that the preferred reading was an analytical construct made by the researcher, not something that could automatically be read from the surface of the text. To address these issues a new generation of reception scholars ventured out to meet real audience members and aimed to understand how they used the text.

Ethnography is the deep study of human cultures in the places where they happen. Often equipped with a theoretical background that prioritized feminism, the next generation of reception scholars met media audience members in their own homes and took notes of how they consumed their favourite texts. Researchers such as Joke Hermes (1993), who examined the consumption of women's magazines and soaps, were intrigued to discover that ordinary people had things to say about their interests. Sometimes, however, the researchers noted a sense of personal disappointment that media consumers were not pursuing their practices with a more resistant or oppositional frame of mind. Their academic responses were, in a sense, evidence of how far off the mark cultural studies had begun to drift.

The most famous of this new generation of reception studies was Janice Radway's book *Reading the Romance.* Originally published in 1984, Radway's work was empathetic to her research subjects. Her book had such a good reputation that Helen Wood reported 20 years later, '*Reading the Romance* continues to sell as many copies now as it did in its first year of publication' (2004, 147). Radway began to shift attention from how people were *reading* texts to what they were *doing* with them, although in fact she looked at both elements. She examined how women in a small American used romance novels to enhance their daily lives. Romance fans, she concluded, created their own spaces and short breaks from family life by reading short chapters from paperback novels.

It is interesting to compare audience ethnographies like Radway's to work going on in other research fields, because by this point cultural studies was on a very different track. Film studies, for instance, had tended to focus on authorial intent (the director as auteur) and remain mired in textual determinism (by analysing the symbolic structure of cinematic texts). Film scholars who came in the wake of discussions in the journal *Screen* and Laura Mulvey's (1975) seminal article on the male gaze, tended to see their medium as embodying gendered ideologies. A **subject position** is a role offered by the text that acts to restrictively orientate and position the individual reader. Film texts were seen as offering their viewers particular subject positions within given ideological or psychoanalytic parameters. In other words, feature film characterizations were understood as stitching audiences into them and into their seats. There was no understanding that fans might read films in 'aberrant' ways and make interpretations that suited them. Instead, film audiences were viewed as manipulated by the text: guided and constrained by what each film visually and audibly presented. Academic understandings of the text had been highly politicized, but theories of its reception contained little room for contested readings or unexpected uses.

Partly because fans were so prominent as dedicated members of the media audience, scholars who were part of the second generation of reception studies sometimes became interested in conducting audience ethnographies of fan cultures. **Telefantasy** is a broad genre of TV programming that spans from sci-fi and fantasy to horror. Two women in particular came to prominence at this point for discussing telefantasy fandom, both looking at *Star Trek*. The first was Camille Bacon-Smith who, in her book *Enterprizing Women* (1991), examined how female fans used their interests to create communities and pursue practices. Although Bacon-Smith positioned herself as an outsider, her ethnographic research contested many stereotypes and still offers a valuable portrait of a media fan community in the pre-internet era. It contains sections on dressing up, fanzine writing, and even on the 'Welcommittee': a team of female fans dedicated to instructing newcomers (1991, 82). For Bacon-Smith, fans make their media text meaningful partly by rewriting it: 'Accordingly the group produces narratives vigorously and activates them in a wide variety of uses. I have observed that community members use fictional narratives to discuss personal, real-life situations' (303). The second important researcher at this point was Constance Penley. Taking a psychoanalytic approach, her research on *Star Trek* erotica created by fans explored how they used the series to play with gender relationships (see Penley 1991, 1992 and 1997). By drawing attention to the way that the text was creatively used as a resource by fan audiences, Bacon-Smith and Penley both, in effect, established a foundation for what was to follow.

From Fiske to Jenkins

At this point it is useful to separate two different terms. **Mass culture** broadly refers to products in the media market place designed to satisfy the widest possible audience, but which seem to deserve little cultural merit. **Popular culture**, on the other hand, tends to be seen as the fraction of commercial culture that the audience takes to their hearts, usually because it contains aspects that resonate with their own world or attitude. Both terms have complex histories and trajectories (see, for example, Storey 2009, 5–6 and 21–2). Alongside, but somewhat separate to, the ferment of second generation reception studies, John Fiske emerged as a prolific writer and prominent media scholar. His reputation was consolidated by two key books: *Reading the Popular* (1989) and *Understanding Popular Culture* (1989). Unlike the approach of many of the second generation reception scholars, Fiske tended to take a more theoretical and interpretive perspective, often using his own interpretations of the media as a starting point. Semiotics is the study of signs. Fiske described the audience's approach to meaning as cruising the 'semiotic supermarket', a metaphor that suggested that audiences mixed and matched items from what was available in the text. Fiske began to champion the agency of individual audience members to remake media products in their own image. In chapter 5a of *Reading the Popular*, he looked specifically at Madonna fans and argued that they had agency in choosing to adopt similar styles to their heroine. As part of his philosophy, he proposed a very specific interpretation of the term 'popular culture'. In Fiske's eyes, mass culture could only become popular culture when it was appropriated by ordinary people. He described that appropriation as a process of *excorporation*. In order words, if ordinary people use the signs and meanings of cultural products in ways unintended by media producers, then those people participate in popular culture. On the other hand, if the audience members accept the signs and meanings offered by the industry, then they participate only in mass culture. When a popular cultural phenomenon happens, it is not long before the culture industries co-opt the impulse by making their own version of it once again; Fiske describes this process of absorption of the impulse as *incorporation*. This leads him to explain the relationship between mass culture and popular culture as *circular and dialectical*; each kind of cultural activity mutually inspires the other. A good example of this was the trend for people to wear ripped jeans. In their original formulation, jeans were designed to be hardwearing garments fit for use in manual labour. They later became a universal uniform. When fashionable people began to wear older, *fraying* pairs of jeans, others took up the style and ripped denim became a spontaneous street trend. With their teams of market researchers and scouts, jeans manufacturers were soon aware of the change. They began to sell jeans that were already frayed, ripped and distressed. The wheel of cultural innovation had turned full circle between industrial and everyday production: mass culture had become popular culture, which in turn had again become mass culture.

In Fiske's model, fans are celebrated because they do things of their own accord that are tangential to the media's place for them. He describes them as an 'active audience'. Fiske went further than this, too, however, and posited that some texts lay themselves more open to audience appropriation than others. He called these **producerly** texts. Equally, some audiences can be more seen as more 'active' or 'producerly' than others. Fiske's work leads to a model of the consumer *as a* producer – the rather awkward term 'prosumer' has sometimes been used for this. He emphasized the capacity of audience to redeem texts that had been marginalized or discarded by the media industry.

Academics like Fiske theoretically relocated fandom by reducing its connection to consumerism and talking about fan productivity (Hills 2002a, 30). Inspired by a departmental visit by John Fiske, Henry Jenkins, who was then at the graduate school in the University of Iowa, began to formulate his own ideas on fandom. One of the things that marked Jenkins out from other scholars at this time was his history as a fan and his personal willingness, despite criticism, to speak as an 'insider' about fandom. Cultural studies orthodoxy had previously encouraged researchers to disengage from their fandom and maintain sufficient emotional distance in order to treat their subject matter critically. Fiske bucked the trend by talking about his own fandom as a resistant stance *within* the culture offered by capitalism. Jenkins took this further by positioning his personal identity as part of a fan collective and speaking from within the fan community. His 1988 essay *Star Trek: Rerun, Reread, Rewritten*, contained residual traces of existing thinking that stereotyped fans, but used those stereotypes (of fans as undisciplined children and trash scavengers) in a supportive mode:

> The fan constitutes a scandalous category in contemporary American culture, one that calls into question the logic by which others order their aesthetic experiences, one that provokes an excessive response from those committed to the interests of textual poachers. Fans appear to be frighteningly 'out of control', undisciplined and unrepentant, rogue readers. Rejecting 'aesthetic distance', fans passionately embrace favoured texts and attempt to integrate media representation within their own social experience. Like cultural scavengers, fans reclaim works that others regard as 'worthless' trash, finding them a source of popular capital. Like rebellious children, fans refuse to read by the rules imposed by their schoolmasters. For the fan, reading becomes a kind of play, responsive only to its own loosely structured rules and generating its own kinds of pleasure. (Jenkins 1988 in Jenkins 2006, 39)

This early formulation foreshadowed his later writing and began to show the way that Jenkins' research was marked by a tendency to adopt a politically utopian conception of fandom – expressed here as the return of the socially repressed – in effect a kind of *queering* of mass culture:

> Fandom is a vehicle for marginalized subcultural groups (women, the young, gays, and so on) to pry open space for their cultural concerns within dominant representations; fandom is a way of appropriating media texts and rereading them in a fashion that serves different interests, a way of transforming mass culture into popular culture . . . For these fans, *Star Trek*

is not simply something that can be reread; it is something that can and must be rewritten to make it more responsive to their needs, to make it a better producer of personal meanings and pleasures. (Jenkins 1988 in Jenkins 2006, 40)

Fan studies was already beginning to turn a corner when Jenkins wrote, as Penley and Bacon-Smith were writing too (Jenkins 2006, 3). It was Jenkins' 1992 book *Textual Poachers* that fully heralded a new era in fan studies. *Textual Poachers* intelligently countered the negative stereotypes of media fandom by supplying ethnographic evidence about the creativity of fans who watched shows like *Star Trek* and *Beauty and the Beast*. Jenkins described, for example, how television fans made a music video that combined footage of Crockett and Tubbs – the main characters from the television series *Miami Vice* (1984–9) – with an audio track by the sentimental soft rock band Air Supply: 'Unlike the program's linkage of consumption and male potency, the video focuses on issues of intimacy and trust, the pressures that push the two men apart and the feelings that draw them back together' (1992, 235).

Jenkins' book was in some ways an extension of the Fiskean approach. While Radway had recognized that women used romance paperbacks to momentarily escape their daily lives, Jenkins argued that researchers needed to think about *how* fans were using media texts and *what* new meanings they were creating (Jenkins 1992, 60). He demonstrated that fans are not just audiences but active participants in media culture: 'Fandom does not prove that all audiences are active; it does, however, prove that not all audiences are passive' (287). Textual poaching countered the claim that fans were 'dupes', but it also masked and distorted specific aspects of the phenomenon, focused on fan frustrations, encouraged heavily politicized academic readings of fanfic and pitted consumers and producers against each other (Jenkins 2006, 37). Fiske's distrust of 'bourgeois' culture was used as a point of departure in the book too, as Jenkins argued that fan objects and identifications were different to those prescribed by educational traditions and the established cultural hierarchies (Jenkins 1992, 18).

A foundational element that Fiske contributed to Jenkin's work was his conception of popular culture. In the Fiskean schema popular culture is the product of audiences who appropriate, transform and 'redeem' the fruits of commercial mass production for a their own purposes. Prefiguring a central concept in his later research, Jenkins explained in *Textual Poachers*, 'Fandom here becomes a participatory culture which transforms the experience of media consumption into the production of new texts, indeed of a new culture and a new community' (46). This approach countered much of the history of critical theory to suggest that fans were able to question and rework the ideologies that dominated the mass culture. Jenkins explained, 'My goal, then, is neither to see fans as totally outside the mainstream nor as emblematic of all popular reading' (54).

Changing the mainstream

Jenkins' work formed a crossroads between various positions. Supposedly embodying traditions that stretched back to the era before modern capitalist social relations, **folk culture** is the non-commercial (or at least cottage) activity of the ordinary people. It references pastimes like bee keeping and country dancing. The Fiskean version of popular culture places it as *a contemporary form of folk culture* in which raw materials from media franchises are recontextualized and practiced in unsanctioned ways. As Jenkins put it later, in this research tradition popular culture is what happens when mass culture gets pulled back into folk culture (2008, 140). In *Textual Poachers* he qualifies this by saying, 'fan culture is not "pure" or "authentic" folk culture, but it is vitally connected to [a history of appropriation and] folk culture traditions' (Jenkins 1992, 272). This folk cultural reading of fandom became quite common in the 1990s. For example, Heather Joseph-Witham's *Star Trek, Fans and Costume Art* (1997) was released as part of the University Press of Mississippi's Folk Art and Artists series.

For Jenkins, 'Unlike classical ethnographers, my project is already concerned with a subculture that exists in the "borderlands" between mass culture and everyday life and that constructs its own identity and artifacts from resources borrowed from already circulating texts' (1992, 3). When fandom is defined through this borrowing and it is labelled a 'folk' activity, perhaps we should be suspicious of the way that it frames fandom as a populist activity: quaint, outside modernity and of the people. The danger here is that the very process of championing fans could itself again be othering them.

Within the politicized tradition of cultural studies, Jenkins combined an ethnographic approach from second generation scholars with a conception of the popular and active audience from Fiske's work. To these he added the self-appointed role of insider champion to the fan community. *Textual Poachers* was also charged with the central metaphor carried in its title, which came from the rather literary philosophical writing of the French thinker Michel de Certeau. De Certeau's book *The Practice of Everyday Life* had been translated into English in 1986 and featured a series of discussions on the way that ordinary people escaped the guidelines and boundaries set by modern planners. In one chapter de Certeau pondered the border between life and death. In another he talked about how people walked their own paths through the city, taking shortcuts and ignoring those created for them. In a third he portrayed readers as poets and poachers; people pursuing their own interests and understandings tangentially to the intentions of the author, but nevertheless remaining on the terrain of his or her text. Michel de Certeau therefore characterized reading as an impertinent 'raid' on the literary 'preserve' that took away only those things that seem useful or pleasurable to the reader. This was the exact theory that Jenkins needed to talk about fandom. The poaching metaphor offered a reminder that fans and producers *both*, to a different extent, have power over the social construction of meaning and their interests can sometimes conflict with no easy victory in sight. However, De Certeau hypothesized isolated readers who were separated from the practice of writing; Jenkins (1992, 45) realized that fans operated communally and could make their own fanzines, novels, art or music. Unlike de Certeau, he believed he should not just theorize readers' activities but also *document* them.

The notion of fans as poachers emerged in a particular way. By the time Jenkins wrote *Textual Poachers* an array of satellite channels and home video technologies helped to make the media audience's nomadic tendencies more apparent. In Jenkins' account, fan readers were both drifters and poachers, always moving across and between texts, delightedly creating new intertextual connections and juxapositions. In this environment, audience members can meander between progressive and reactionary ways of thinking in the same conversation (35–7). Their appropriation is not set by adherence to textual values, but is instead limited by them. To explain this, Jenkins drew on the Russian scholar Mikhail Bakhtin's work on 'heteroglossia' (multi-vocality) to emphasize that if any cultural agent wants to specify a term's meaning in a particular context, they must struggle against existing conditions. Bakhtin suggested that words were already charged with the taint of the former context in which they were used. Speakers necessarily borrowed what they said and only began to really inhabit their words once they infused them with *their own* intentions and accents (see 224). In an example of such poaching, fan novel writer Jane Land called her work 'an attempt to rescue one of *Star Trek's* female characters [like Christine Chapel] from an artificially imposed case of foolishness' (Jenkins 2006, 47).

Countering the notion that fans were manipulated cultural dupes, Jenkins' work saw them as model poachers who recycled media culture *because they had to*: they were inevitably torn between fascination and frustration with texts that the media industry offered (1992, 23). Three years later Jenkins elaborated:

Resistant reading is an important survival skill in a hostile atmosphere where most of us can do little to alter the social conditions and where many of the important stories that matter to us can't be told on network television. It is, however, no substitute for other forms of media criticism and activism. (Jenkins 1995b/2006, 112)

In 2008 Henry Jenkins restated the position: 'Fandom, after all, is born out of a balance between fascination and frustration: if media content didn't fascinate us, there would be no desire to engage with it; but if it didn't frustrate us on some level, there would be no drive to rewrite or remake it' (258) What is interesting here is Jenkins' conception of agency. On one hand fans seem to be free agents, gleefully transforming commercial culture to suit their own ends. On the other, it appears that they are forced to develop this skill because of the inability of media producers to meet their needs: 'Fans are not unique in their status as textual poachers, yet they have developed poaching to an art form' (Jenkins 1992, 27). This conception of fans as the artful dodgers of media culture offers them at least an active and intelligent role. However, as Jenkins (34) has said himself, fan readings do not *have to* be resistant or made in the absence of other contextual conditions.

Textual Poachers emerged from the philosophical stance that Jenkins, in later years, came to recognize as 'critical utopian' in orientation: 'As a utopian, I want to identify possibilities within our culture that might lead to a better, more just society' (2008, 258). He has argued that 'critical pessimists', like the famous radical political historian Noam Chomsky, focus on obstacles to achieving a more democratic society. This is unfortunate because 'the way they frame the debate is self-defeating insofar as it disempowers consumers even as it seeks to mobilize them' (258). When Jenkins wrote *Textual Poachers*, his utopian ideals posited fandom as a *seemingly* criminal (but in fact rightful) challenge to the domination of the media industries.[1] He later wrote, 'Undaunted by the barking dogs, the "no trespassing" signs, and the threats of prosecution, the fans have already poached those texts from under proprietors' noses' (Jenkins 2006, 60).

In Jenkins' writing, fans have it their way. One described his/her media text as being treated like 'silly putty' by peers: its boundaries stretched to accommodate a range of desires (Jenkins 1992, 156). By emphasizing this the textual poaching idea positions the fan community as a utopian space that represents the return of the repressed: 'an alternative sphere of cultural experience that restores the excitement and freedom that must be repressed to function in ordinary life' (Jenkins 2006, 42). *Textual Poachers* therefore marked a new era in which reception studies merged with fandom research to create *fan studies*. In the introduction to his 2006 compilation volume *Fans, Bloggers, Gamers*, Jenkins suggested that in less than two decades the field of fan studies had included three generations of scholars: active audience ethnographers who operated as outside critics (second generation reception studies), critical insiders (who were criticized for being fans) and new researchers who were comfortable with declaring their status as *both* fans *and* academics. He put his *Textual Poachers* era work in the middle category (12). At the time of its release the book had a mixed reception. *Textual Poachers* was critically assessed by some reviewers through the very stereotypes of fandom that it sought to dispel. In one news story Jenkins was later called 'perhaps the most prominent scholar in the country devoted to examining pastimes often deemed profoundly frivolous' (188). Yet the dignity and respect with which *Textual Poachers* treated fandom meant that Jenkins in effect gathered his own fans. In 2001 he explained to Matt Hills, 'now I get people quoting my words as if they were biblical and as if they had this enormous authority and certainty behind them, as if things that I tentatively put forward were well-established and proven once and for all' (quoted in Jenkins 2006, 35).

While the idea of poaching was useful in shifting perceptions of fandom away from the stereotypes of passivity and manipulation evident in earlier approaches like those of Thedor Adorno, it was, at the same time, arguably something of an *interpretive imposition* on fan culture. As early as 1988 Jenkins noted that fans did not see themselves as poachers: 'the fans often cast themselves not as poachers but as loyalists, rescuing essential elements of the primary text "misused" by those who maintain copyright control over program materials' (Jenkins 1998 in Jenkins 2006, 41). In *Textual Poachers* he suggested that the idea of 'misreading' preserves the traditional hierarchy, suggesting that objective scholars, not fans, are in the right place to decide what constitutes the appropriate meaning of the text (1992, 33). The poaching idea got some way beyond that, but not all the way since its conception of criminality tied it back to issues of authorial intent. Fans saw themselves as 'rescuing' characters or shows that were mishandled by studios, keeping programmes like *Star Trek* 'alive' – in the sense of being living cultures – in the face of studio or network indifference or incompetence (55). To the idea that the 'official' reading is essentially an analytical construct, we might also add that fans themselves can police those who 'poach' the established meanings of their texts.[2] After quoting Jenkins' claim to have accented the positive in *Textual Poachers*, Matt Hills explained, 'Jenkins's work therefore needs to be viewed not simply as an example of academic-fan hybridity, but also as a rhetorical tailoring of fandom in order to act upon particular institutional spaces and agendas' (2002a, 10). Some writers questioned Jenkins for using the fan community to further his own political agenda but of course many studies legitimately do exactly that. He stood accused of projecting the values of the academic community on to fandom, of rationalizing fans, of making fans out to be academics in miniature (10). To this list I would add that his work took attention away from some of the *usual* practices associated with fandom – collecting and autograph hunting, for instance – and focused on a different set of activities in order to interpret fandom as a kind of *counter-culture*; something partial, alternative, pleasure-seeking and rebellious.

In *Textual Poachers*, Jenkins noted that previous accounts of fandom had been sensationalistic and fostered misunderstandings, and that those misconceptions had consequences (1992, 7). In effect, his book gave fandom a publicity make-over by revealing the startling creativity of fans as ordinary people, but it failed to fully develop the idea that they might be something more than aberrant consumers. De Certeau saw consumption within a frame of appropriation whereby consumers had no 'proper' space of their own. The problem with his approach was that media consumers had, historically, also literally *been or become* official producers. In the 1990s, fan studies got caught up in an unhelpful binary that opposed relatively powerless poachers against powerful producers (Hills 2010b, 61). Yet fandom is a training ground for those developing professional skills. Role-playing games offer people ethical laboratories, spaces of play for discovering themselves and reconsidering the culture around them.[3] Because the industry needs fans as producers, *in some cases their play is a prototypical form of work* and their activities are eventually absorbed when they personally become professionalized (Hills 2002a, 40). One way out of the fan/producer dilemma is to consider the career paths of fans into the media industry (Hills 2010b, 57). A good example of this relates to Britain's most popular sci-fi telefantasy show, *Doctor Who*, which started in 1963. In to the 1980s and 1990s, a generation of *Who* fans moved into professional journalism and TV production (10). After the show was revived by BBC Wales in 2005, fan 'poachers' became its official producers, or 'textual game-keepers'. In the production team for the new *Doctor Who*:

> Executive producer Russell T. Davies and producer Phill Collinson were card-carrying fans; the actor playing the tenth Doctor was a fan; writers such as Paul Cornell, Mark Gatiss, Steven Moffat, Gareth Roberts and Rob Shearman were all fans; even Radio Times writer Nick Griffiths had grown up as a *Doctor Who* fan. (56)

As Matt Hills has noted, seeing fans either as duped, rebellious or somewhere in between still locates them primarily in relation to the demands of the industry. Perhaps there is more to fandom than media industry agenda. Perhaps, too, then, if we are to understand the full scope of fandom our theoretical approaches should begin to include conceptions that allow fans to be *indifferent*, or even better to give them opportunities to *collude* with their favourite texts.

Resistant readers

Textual Poachers resonated with existing concerns in cultural studies and looked out among the media audience for signs of resistant reading. With Jenkins at the centre of the debate, it led to an avalanche of fan studies that examined fandom as a place of resistant reading and cultural production where ordinary people struggled against constraints placed on their creative expression by the culture industry. This section will explore some of that work in more detail.

One view of media producers is that they see the most active fans as a nuisance and aim to constrain and crack down on them for infringing on their textual properties. Current copyright law has no clause for creative expression from the audience. Amateur producers have often been seen as copyright abusers without an additional case to make, so no civil liberties unions have stepped in to protect them (Jenkins 2008, 197). Because fans have never really been able to challenge the legal power of the studio system, there is no body of case law concerning the legitimacy of fan fiction. What usually happens is that fans back down when studios challenge them. Small Websites, for instance, have been sent cease and desist letters by media companies when they were interpreted as infringing copyright. If similar fan productivity – things like making online video parodies and t-shirts – is rarely in *direct* competition with producers, it can still shape how people think about a franchise. Sometimes producers challenge fans over what are, in effect, ideological judgements. In the early 1980s, for instance, Lucasfilms was generally perceived as cracking down on *Star Wars* fanzines in ways that propagated its particular notion of the 'family values' portrayed in the original films (Brooker 2002, 165). Jim Ward, the vice-president of marketing explained:

> We love our fans. We want them to have fun. But if in fact someone is using our characters to create a story unto itself, that's not in the spirit of what we think fandom is about. Fandom is about celebrating the story the way it is. (Murray 2004, 11)

Sometimes media producers can be hostile to fans' attempts to steer their work. Rather disingenuously, *Doctor Who* producer Russell T. Davies argued that 'once a script has been made and transmitted, I honestly believe it belongs equally to those who watch it . . . I've got no more authority over the text than you!' As Hills explains, however, Davies does have authority in designating particular 'facts' as 'official' and endorsing particular information (2010b, 63–4). When the most dedicated 'Whovarians' became critical of his version of the show, the Doctor Who producer described them as 'mosquitoes' and 'not real fandom' because they had a tendency to dissect and complain about the series. He also called more dedicated Who fans 'ming-mongs', a term that dates back to a 1987 Victoria Wood sketch which lampooned Doctor Who fans for their 'technobabble'. Who writer Steven Moffat attempted to rescue the term by saying 'It's only us ming-mongs that care' about leaked storylines (212–3).

In reality, corporations often want audiences to 'look but not touch' their intellectual properties (Jenkins 2008, 142). Professional media producers and their parent corporations therefore have a necessarily mixed view of fandom and can simultaneously pursue conflicting policies within the same organization. Studios cannot fully recognize fan creativity as they want to say that all creativity resides in the franchise property (142). They therefore oscillate between collaborating with fans and prohibiting their activities (Hills 2010b, 68). Whether fans and producers share common ground or disagree can depend on which discourse is being used; there is no simple collaboration or antipathy between them (79). The issue also depends on the particular type or genre of fan creativity in contention. According to Brooker (2002, 175), Lucasfilm's approach to fan films, for example, seemed more generous than to fan writing. Fans therefore occupy a 'powerless duality': sometimes cared for by programme's producers and sometimes positioned as a threat or annoyance by them (Hills 2010b, 214). In this context, fan communities have evolved strategies to outwit online censorship from the 'official' guardians of their texts (see Brooker 2002, 124).

Fans can sometimes feel concerned they are being manipulated by production processes and conventions into serving as fodder for the desires of media producers. In such situations, media fans may organize themselves directly in opposition to commerce. Jimmy Buffett has grossed around $50 million a year from his fans. As Mihelich and Papineau discovered, 'A segment of Buffett fans offer an explicit critique of Buffett commercialism and, by extension, capitalism and consumption' (2005, 179). Similar fannish 'rebellion' can either be prompted as a critique of exploitation or as a way to ameliorate the worst excesses of commerce. For instance, Cavicchi (1998, 63) found that some rock fan practices – like ticket trading and romanticizing celebrities as 'outside of the industry' – effectively reduced the impact of the industrial on what they did (63). Harrington and Bielby reported that in daytime soap fandom, 'Ambivalence also results from viewers' convictions that they are manipulated by the soap format' (1995, 91). It is interesting here to compare fans to a different group of media consumers: 'culture jammers' want to opt out of media consumption, challenge its ideology and promote a negative stance on popular culture. In contrast, rather than simply confronting or dismissing media producers (see Jenkins 2006, 150), fans are generally more interested in pursuing emotions, creating dialogues and collaborating to release unrealized potentials. Nevertheless there have been occasions when they have staged backlashes again shows which seem too exploitative.[4]

Beyond unadulterated resistance to commercial exploitation there are a number of other reasons why devotees can organize themselves into resistant or protesting groupings. Fans can be resistant when shows are cancelled or when the established tenets of their particular narrative or character are ignored. Hills calls this a 'textual conservationist' stance (2002a, 28). *Starman* fans collectively organized and lobbied network executives to keep the 1986–7 show on the air when ABC cancelled it before the end of its first season, but they found themselves powerless to alter its fate (Jenkins 1992, 29). Such lobby groups have often approached studios and TV channels requesting them to keep their favourite shows in production and on the air. Recycling Francesco Alberoni's (1960/2007) term from star studies, John Tulloch has consequently described fans as a *powerless elite* that hovers 'between the power of the industry that makes the show, [and] the general public on whose "votes" its future depends' (1995, 144).

In the formulation of fan culture that emerged in the wake of *Textual Poachers*, fans were seen as rebels. Fandom was thought of as essentially different from – and frequently opposed to – 'official' media production. And it was resistant 'poaching' that provided the key metaphor for this fan/producer difference. Fans were creative but relatively powerless; producers had power over 'official' media texts (Hills 2010b, 56). Indeed, producers could strategically use or ignore the voice of the fan community as a way to maintain their interests (Jenkins 1992, 29). For Brooker, fans 'are faced with a situation where someone else still owns the story, is pitching for a wider audience than their dedicated group, cares not at all for their interpretation of the sage, and will attempt to shut down their sites forcibly if they contradict his version of the characters and plot' (2002, xvi). This results in what he calls 'an unhappy conflict' (xvi) in which fans celebrate George Lucas's creative contribution and decry his uncharitable approach to the myth that he created for them. The problem connects to censorship. Writing fan fiction has offered marginalized social groups – especially women – a tool for social criticism (see Derecho 2006, 26). While some fan communities have banded together to protect their right to express themselves in writing, others have crusaded to prevent the censorship of the texts that they love. *Harry Potter* fans organized themselves against Christian censors by creating the group Muggles for Harry Potter. They were joined by publishers, book sellers, librarians, teachers, writers, civil libertarians and consumers (Jenkins 2008, 204). Their plight suggests that those who love the text sometimes have organized themselves to fend off both commercial and moral censorship challenges that come from opposite directions.

A problem with seeing fans as rebels is that they also form a significant section of marketplace to which media texts are promoted, a fact that can make them both courted and contested. To see fans as collectively ranked against the strength of the media corporations would be to both selectively and romantically perceive their orientation. Fandom contains 'a dialectic of value' insofar that it tends to oscillate between resisting and intensifying commodification, between religiosity and reflexivity, between private attachments and communal interpretations and between community and hierarchical social structures (Hills 2002a, 182). This means that fans can be seen as conflicted too. Those who tried to find key information in advance of the airing of shows like *Survivor*, for example, demonstrate that producers and consumers do not always have the same interests; on one level the fans are allies, on another they can be enemies (Jenkins 2008, 58). Will Brooker (2002, 77) has noted that instead of assenting to the 'official' status of Lucas creations, fans treat George Lucas with a mixture of admiration and scorn. Some – like Chris Albrecht who runs an official *Star Wars* film competition at AtomFilms – have become double agents encouraging fan production from within the corporate machine (Jenkins 2008, 143). The presence of fans in the professional hierarchy of media organizations has helped change corporate perceptions of fan activity.

At one extreme, some cultural producers take a charitable approach to fan creativity. Will Wright, who created *The Sims* game in 2000, did not assert copyright over an unofficial Website called 'The Mall of the Sims'. Instead he just let it happen and even courted the fans, by saying, 'We are competing with other properties for these creative individuals'. This is significant as *The Sims* became one of the most successful games franchises ever (171). Other producers have aimed to bring fan creativity under their wing, as Lucasfilm did with *Star Wars* (Jenkins 1992, 30–1). After the media controversy over Warner's quashing of *Harry Potter* fan creativity, the corporation decided to *collaborate with* and *deputize* fans (Jenkins 2008, 196). Aided by shifts in digital technology, media producers are therefore increasingly recognizing that fan cultures represent an *alternative* rather than oppositional community (Mihelich & Papineau 2005, 184).

Much of the writing on resistant fan cultures has come from organized fandom for film and television narratives. While there is evidence that the management of living stars and the estates of dead ones have also tried to quash fan creativity, much less has been written about creative antagonisms between fans of individual celebrities and their idols.[5] In popular music, the reappropriation of star sounds and images is just as vigorous (see, for instance,

Marcus 1999), but only fans who participate in particular music genres and discourses – notably punk and indie – concern themselves with the role of the industry. Rock fans see a person rather than a marketed commodity and can become irritated but relatively indifferent to the strictures of industry:

> In fact, fans' general stance toward the music business could be better characterized as a kind of indifference or disregard . . . they saw the business as incidental to their connection with Springsteen. For one thing, many fans saw Springsteen as existing outside the business and its routine production of pop stars . . . On the whole, Springsteen fans do not sit around and wait for what the record company is going to do next or scheme to come up with ways to subvert its intentions. They see Columbia Records as rather a bothersome nuisance, simply part of the way the music world works. What's important to fans is Bruce's music, not how one gets it. (Cavicchi 1998, 61–3)

Since Cavicchi wrote this passage, however, times and distribution technologies have changed significantly. In the early days, the mass wave of illegal downloading and 'leaking' of material from new albums online suggested that fans were infuriating the music industry and depleting one of its key revenue streams. From that perspective, rather than 'poaching' established meanings, fans were poaching the whole text (as intellectual property). However, the designation of music fans as pirates may be confusing a new practice with a much older identity. Lucy Bennett's recent work on REM fans, for example, shows that at least one subset of one fan community has resisted the temptation of hearing leaked material, not so much as a means to financially support their band, but instead as a way to nostalgically evoke the thrill of virginal listening (see Bennett 2011). In the wake of new albums being immediately redistributed for free, companies such as Web Sheriff now share one or two promotional tracks per new album with bloggers as a kind of free sample. The success of this approach suggests that online music fans are rarely pirates determined to sabotage the industry. They are simply scouting for more songs to hear from artists that they love: 'The only thing most fans are guilty of', according to music industry lawyer John Giancobbi (in Lewis 2011), 'is over-exuberance'.

Meaning and identificantion

Chapter 9 will deal with the more recent incarnations of Henry Jenkins' research, in particular his efforts to understand the fan community as a power-broking entity in its own right. One of the central issues with Jenkins' research has remained his critical silence over celebrity. Researchers sympathetic to fandom were pleased that *Textual Poachers* changed the image of fandom from servile devotion to resourceful appropriation. Cultural studies writers did not want a return to the dismissive Adornoesque conceptions that sometimes still circulate in the mainstream media. Neither did they desire to return to the days when their work was either out of touch with fans or out of alignment with the political direction of the field. No writer that I know of has mentioned that Jenkins so rarely deals with celebrity, yet for many – perhaps most – media fans an interest in the life or work of a famous person is at the generative heart of their fandom. Indeed, Jenkins has rarely examined celebrity figures, except for when he has talked about himself as a public academic. In *Fans, Bloggers, Gamers*, in particular, readers learn something about the followers who supported *Textual Poachers*, and its author's public role as 'Professor Jenkins'. Support for celebrity icons is associated with issues of power, distance, intimacy and fantasy which position fans not just as readers who collectively organize themselves, but as individuals who identify and follow stars. To end this chapter, what follows will consider some work across the humanities that addresses *how* people identify with famous figures.

In the first chapter, a simplistic distinction was made between an interest in genre or narrative and an interest in *celebrity*, whether a 'real person' or simply a fictional character. This distinction is not, of course, definitive: narratives operate to foreground particular figures of identification, and celebrities prompt ongoing media coverage that places them at the centre of narratives about their lives. *Doctor Who* provides a good example of the first process. Viewers seek affinity in characters in terms of parallels with how the character thinks (see Bradford 2010, 169). According to Mary Kowal:

> The real hooks to the show, though I didn't realize it [at] the time, were the Doctor's companions. For the most part, they were ordinary people, not just super-gifted or bizarre aliens. Discounting the odd robotic dog, a companion could be someone like me. You understand the allure, don't you? I don't think there's a single teen who gets through high school without feeling like a misfit at some point. . . . (2010, 165)

If the media offers us figures for identification, one way it does so is by using particular character types. At the deepest level it could be argued that these are archetypes or reflections of the human condition. Sometimes, for example, in film noir, such figures become the foundation of an entire genre. Researchers have confused *industrial conventions* that imply identification – whether through character types or genre conventions – with the actual ways that audiences have identified. In their 1978 article 'Rock and Sexuality', for example, Simon Frith and Angela McRobbie argued that pop stars fitted various types of sexual personae (see Frith & McRobbie 1978 in Frith & Goodwin 1990). Frith and McRobbie distinguished 'teenyboppers' (heart throbs, teen angels and boyband members) from 'cock rockers' (graphically thrusting, macho rock singers). Their work was soon criticized for conflating the image of the artists with identifications made by different audiences. In a sense, music research paralleled the textual determinism in film studies, where the notion of subject-positioning offered spectators little or no agency – it suggested that the text itself automatically positioned audiences and happened to them (Jenkins 1992, 62). **Essentialism** is the idea that the essence or meaning of an object is located within the object itself. A key problem with essentialism is that it forgets the role of external attribution in the creation of meaning. Ideas suggesting that a text's adherence to generic conventions or its content are what creates its meaning are problematic because they are essentialist. They forget that the same text – or here the same celebrity image – can be read in very different ways in different contexts.

A further development came when researchers began to realize that the same character type or icon could be read in different ways by different *fractions* of the audience. In an interesting 1988 study, for instance, music researcher Alan Wells showed that male and female students regularly perceived images of the same stars in very different ways. Wells showed his class some slides of the cover of *Rolling Stone* magazines featuring artists like Madonna and Cyndi Lauper. He asked each of his students to choose words from a pool that he left on the blackboard. Madonna was controversial at the time for the way that she combined a sexually alluring 'pop tart' image with a sense of savvy, independent womanhood. Wells discovered that male and female students used different words for the same picture of her, and the result was repeated with several other artists. Although Wells' use of students was a convenient but limited methodology, by indicating that audience members of different genders sometimes think differently about the same stars his findings resonate with common sense. This is also borne out in the gendering of audiences and fan mail. Sophie Aldred, who played Ace, a companion to Sylvester McCoy's eighth incarnation of *Doctor Who*, once said, 'I started getting letters from young girls who were so relieved to see a realistic, strong female character on British TV' (Aldred 2010, 71). To generalize about how the sexes differently understand and receive media culture is questionable from some perspectives, not least because it marginalizes the possibility of *shared* interpretations. In effect it essentializes the production of meaning to each sex, leaving little room for the myriad of other factors in reception – from place and era to morality, politics and personality – that can frame the way individual fans might identify.

The trend towards segmenting the audience and claiming a different identification motive in each segment perhaps reached its height with Cathy Schwichtenberg's edited volume, *The Madonna Connection* (1993). Schwichtenberg's book understood Madonna's popularity as a combination of her ability to speak to discrete (sub)cultural constituencies, including black audiences and gay men. In effect, for Schwichtenberg, aspects of social identity – race, gender, age, sexual orientation – were prime indicators of differences in reception. At first sight, Schwichtenberg's willingness to differentiate different elements of the audience seems like a useful act of discrimination. Yet it also homogenizes each of these social groupings and forgets that they may be internally divided. Some reviewers questioned *The Madonna Connection*'s compartmentalized understanding of Madonna's audience and suggested that Schwichtenberg had forgotten the gravitational pull of stardom. Was it that Madonna spoke to various constituencies, or was it that her celebrity created a stake that attracted the attention of a wide public?

Against the idea that audience segments defined around existing social identities would necessarily create different readings, a minority of researchers in the 1980s began to focus on the notion of shared perceptions. They contended that a star's images were interpreted in ways shared by large numbers of audience members, but *not necessarily determined* by the identities of those audience members. A perception, then, is simply a common interpretation of a celebrity. Even if perceptions originate with specific fractions of the audience, there is no sense in which audience members of a specific social identity can 'own' them. Perceptions can float around as discursive resources, open to appropriation by a wide variety of audience members for a variety of reasons. Richard Dyer's discussion of Judy Garland in his 1986 book *Heavenly Bodies* describes one such perception, that Garland was a camp performer. **Camp** means taking delight in artificiality and frivolity (see Sontag 2001). Although camp identities and performance styles are sometimes associated with gay men, they are not inherently camp since it is really a perceived and performative style of behaviour. For Dyer, Judy Garland was perceived as camp for several reasons. She had struggled to fit into marriage and family life, and in that sense she was a survivor. Garland also had a sense of 'unintentional' campness about her, a certain gawkiness. The idea of unintentional campness is interesting, as it reminds us that performances can be unintentional and are interpreted in the mind of their beholder.

The problem with the approaches discussed so far in this section is that they assume that people who share the same social identities will inevitably make the same readings. This opens up the issue of how to theorize fan reading practices in a meaningful way without making such generalizations. Sue Wise (1984/1990) offered a different example that connected her experiences as a fan to her perception of Elvis Presley. Wise began her account autobiographically, describing her childhood as a fan of Elvis and explaining that she lost her fandom when her friends in university rejected the icon for his aggressively seductive behaviour. They saw Elvis as a chauvinistic seducer bent on conquering women. However, when the star died in 1977, Wise reconsidered her childhood interest and returned to the pages of her Elvis fan magazines. She discovered that Elvis enthusiasts who wrote stories in the magazines made two readings of the star. One affirmed that he was a 'butch God' whose hallmark was his sexual prowess. The other positioned him more as a 'teddy bear': a benign and affectionate sort of person that anyone might like as friend. Wise's fellow students had seen Elvis as a 'butch God' but as a child she had seen him as a 'teddy bear'. What was interesting about these two perceptions, however, was that they were *not* restricted to any particular gender or other social grouping. Sometimes adult female fans revelled in the 'butch God' reading, rather than seeing it as marginalizing their interests. Instead of being fixed to particular groups, the two interpretations functioned as social resources, vehicles that fans could use for different reasons at their own convenience.

The idea that stars, in effect, offer up potential discursive resources to their fan bases begins to both suggest that interpretations of their images are tied neither to particular identity constituencies in the audience (say, gay men), nor that the analysis of meaning must be limited to questions of a preferred or 'poached' reading. The question then arises: how can we conceptualize the context of these particular interpretations? In literary studies, work on *interpretive communities* by Stanley Fish (1980) and others provided an answer: when people – here fans and media consumers – build up their interpretations in the act of reading, they do so in the context of being *part of communities of readers*. This model suggests that the individual activity of reading enacts shared concerns. Tony Bennett and Janet Wollacott drew on the approach in their study *Bond and Beyond* (1987). For Bennett and Wollacott, sections of the James Bond audience viewed their object through two different prisms. Reading is never a neutral act, but as Peter Rabinowitz has suggested is 'reading as' (as in 'reading as romance' or 'reading as horror'). Genres set expectations that help to guide our reading practices and the questions we bring to the text (see Jenkins 1992, 133). Each **reading formation** represented a whole constituency who came to the text with a different set of genre expectations prompted by a particular 'diet' of media consumption. On one hand, those audience members who liked to read romance novels understood James Bond primarily as a romance hero. On the other, those who read novels about Cold War espionage understood Bond as a glamorous British spy. While genre is based on a set of conventions shared by the audience and producers alike, the notion of reading formation locates any expectations firmly in the minds of audience members and suggests that they *guide* interpretations, even for products that are ambiguous in relation to genre categories. The result is that our personal journeys of media consumption frame readings which then translate into communities that share similar interpretations of the texts.

The problem with notions of interpretive community and reading formation is that they take us back to the idea that fans are isolated, at least save for their personal histories of media consumption. What they forget is that fans often form communities – whether online or offline – which share interpretations through discursive means. Consequently, rather than thinking about each reader's understandings being *set by* such things as his/her social identity, the text itself (as in hypodermic models, semiotics or auteurism), previous texts (as in reading formations), or shared understandings or the reader's social identity, it may be valuable to consider ways that wider forms of discussion help to guide our understandings of meaning. **Discourses** are widely shared and socially legitimated ways of talking about specific things. To pay attention to them means to look at the history of discussion. Academic research is itself a discourse with very specific rules of engagement that specify who can say things and what can be said. The exact approach or focus of a discourse may change over time, but its focus on managing its object does not. For example, although this chapter has shown the history of a number of disciplines – like film studies, cultural studies and media research – they have all been relevant to the social process of understanding fans as an audience. Researchers who study reception have paid much attention in recent years to the way that discourses can give us the cognitive resources to organize our understandings of what we see in the media. These discourses can relate to social identity (gender, age or class, for example) or be about particular media forms, genres or texts (as in 'the popular discourse on sci-fi'), but they can also be about viewing itself (such as the discourse on the morality of watching violence on-screen). If discourses help to structure how fans perceive and understand their objects, then issues of *literacy* become relevant. **Media literacy** is the idea that as citizens, viewers can be equipped with particular discursive resources to help them understand the media and use those understandings in a socially responsible way. Attention to media literacy means thinking about what discourses readers are schooled in and how having or not having them might determine interpretations of the viewing experience. Henry Jenkins has argued, 'As we move into the classroom, teachers can play a vital role in helping students to become more conscious about assumptions shaping their simulations' (2006, 214). Fans can also be considered as having high levels of literacy for their own media forms, communal qualifications that strongly shape how they understand the nuanced complexities of their texts. Paul Booth's (2012) recent work on the way that horror fans make video trailers for the *Saw* franchise is interesting here. High levels of 'cineliteracy' amongst horror fans can act to normalize their interpretation of what outsiders see as a sadistic and transgressive 'torture porn', yet the sheer excess of their object challenges fans to creatively re-imagine it.

Attention to discourses and notions of literacy remind us that the world of experience informing each of our interpretations is both complex and changing. In the actuality of history, the nature of the medium, text, audience and reading continually changes as technology, news, experience and other informational resources grow and shift around each of us. The most radical, but perhaps most astute ideas about sense-making therefore dissolve the text into the constant process of reinterpretation that each new reading brings. In some understandings, the notion of an original (perhaps intentional) meaning of the text then disappears. Hence, 'There is, in fact, no "book" other than these ever-different repetitions [of reading]' (Spivak in Derrida 1976, xii). How can we theorize a series of reiterations that create different meanings each time? Drawing on another idea from literary studies by Gérard Gennette (1997), Jonathan Gray (2010) has drawn attention beyond the traditional boundaries of media textuality. **Paratexts** are items which are beyond the edges of the text and yet still connected to its interpretation. Génette views them as extras inside each published work such as the title, author's name and preface, whereas Gray extends the idea to talk about media products and their trailers, reviews and other secondary materials. A good example of this is the 'lurid' cassette cases of the video nasty era that pre-sold horror films to those who wanted to rent or buy them: your interpretation of a film might differ quite radically depending on whether you *only* saw its cassette case, *only* watched the film or (as was usual) watched the film straight after seeing its cover. Paratexts 'hype' the products to which they refer, sometimes changing their meanings quite radically. Knowing this opens up another interesting issue: each member of the audience may have seen a different set of paratexts. Aware of this problem, Cornel Sandvoss has argued that the issue of fan interpretation should be considered not in terms of *polysemy* – the text's openness to different readings – but instead through what he calls **neutrosemy**: 'the far reaching elimination of meaning inherent in fan texts' (2005b, 824). He adds that, 'Different meanings in fan texts are not reflexive of readers' engagements with textual blanks as Iser conceptualized them, but, instead *of fans' ability to define boundaries*' (832; emphasis mine). In other words, unless we can instil an essential core of meaning or social relevance in a text, its resonance may relate to its *inability* to definitively signify anything, and attention should therefore be shifted more radically from the text to a field account of its readers.

If we focus on the way that readers actually make meaning, new issues emerge and draw us back towards some of the fandom research previously presented in the chapter. Kurt Lancaster's (2001) work is relevant here. Lancaster examined the constellation of texts, products and paratexts that surrounded the series *Babylon 5* and argued that they allowed fans to 'immerse' themselves in a world of role-playing where meanings and identities were forged and expressed in a mutual process of performance. In Lancaster's study, fans are *textual performers* rather than textual poachers. They are not pursuing creative activities or interpretations that are at odds with the text, but instead actively using it as *a social resource* in a variety of different ways. Lancaster's work is useful in escaping both the passive view of readership offered by the mass culture critique and the text-reader model inherent in much of the cultural studies tradition. It encompasses the possibility that audience members might draw on the text for emotional self-expression, but his work has no strong model of the individual subject and why he/she connects so enthusiastically with *Babylon 5* in particular (see Hills 2002a, 41–2). For Lancaster the fan's relation to the world of the text inherently involves *social performance* (Sandvoss 2005a, 45). This raises the possibility that there might be fans who make meanings but *do not* perform them socially in the spectacular ways that capture the attention of fan studies researchers. After discussing fans listening to a CD, for instance, Daniel Cavicchi explained that 'any discussion of the interpretation of music must include what happens when a listener hears a piece of music, in the case of fans, it must also include *what that hearing makes happen*' (1998, 126; emphasis mine). If performance is *one* answer to the question of how meanings that get made are used in a social setting, then another is that fans may create and draw on specific meanings of the text in order simply to help them enjoy it more or to cope with difficult situations in their lives. Laura Vroomen (2004, 243), for example, described Kate Bush fandom as a way of coping with everyday life. Finally, in relation to this it must be said that theory is a way of coping too. Researchers are intertextual readers who use their existing stock of theory and creative imagination to advance their understandings of why fans make meaning. To an extent, for better or worse, it is always *our* interpretation of *their* interpretation, even when we count ourselves among them.

It is evident from this chapter that meanings are social and yet (re)made inside the heads of fans as participants in media cultures. Many of the theories discussed are not completely incompatible; meanings may be inspired from multiple nodes in the network or constellation of elements that surround the reader. What all of these theories are limited by is the guiding metaphor of textuality itself and the way that it prioritizes meaning-making as a cultural activity. Fandom is a meaningful experience, but that does not mean that we must locate it only in relation to its objects and texts. The notion of textual poaching attempted to relate the process of meaning-making to the wider power relations of fandom, *while staying on an agenda of concerns set by the idea of textuality*. There may be milage, however, in jettisoning the academic hunt for understanding semiotic meaning in favour of seeing other, equally important, dimensions of fandom.

4

The pathological tradition

Starting points

- Is there a natural progression from normal fan behaviour to obsessive behaviours like stalking?
- Do cases like the assassination of John Lennon prove that extreme fandom can lead to dangerous behaviour?
- Can universal psychological processes account for the motivation behind fan behaviour?

The literature on fandom is haunted by images of deviance. The fan is constantly characterized (referencing the term's origins) as a potential fanatic. This means that fandom is seen as excessive, bordering on deranged behaviour. This essay explores how and why the concept of the fan involves images of social and psychological pathology.

In the following pages I describe two fan types – the obsessed individual and the hysterical crowd. I show how these types appear in popular as well as scholarly accounts of fans and fandom . . . Once fans are characterized as deviant, they can be treated as disreputable, even dangerous 'others'.

JOLI JENSEN 1992, 9

Despite its nature as a socially harmless form of engaging in popular culture, fandom has often been distrusted and at worst portrayed as a kind of evil force, a disturbance in the fabric of the self and society. The dystopian sci-fi film *Children of Men* (2006) starts in 2027 with a strange 'future shock' scenario: literally no one in the world can have children. The youngest person alive is an 18-year-old boy who has become a media celebrity. His name is Baby Diego. The film begins in a London café. A crowd of stunned onlookers watches the news unfold on television: Baby Diego has been stabbed to death. The anchor explains, 'Witnesses say that Diego spat in the face of a fan who asked for an autograph. He was killed in the ensuing brawl. The fan was later beaten to death by the angry crowd'. *Children of Men*'s portrayal of fandom is, to follow its own trope, pregnant with meaning. Our society rests on a Descartian split between the mind and the body, prioritizing the clear mind of a reasonable and rational individual. Fandom has often been associated with what this represses: old dangers of emotional excess and the collective irrationality of mob behaviour. In this model fandom articulates a Dionysian force – a disease of the social body expressed as the beast within or grasping collective – that can supposedly seduce 'vulnerable' adolescents or otherwise healthy humans to take leave of their senses. In the most uncharitable of Freudian terms, fandom is therefore represented as a social mania: a frenzied and cathartic outpouring of dammed up sexual repression or perhaps even a kind of death drive which can turn ordinary citizens 'queer'. Twenty years ago, Joli Jensen defined and challenged two negative stereotypes of fandom. These stereotypes generally perceived female fans (collectively) and male fans (individually) as cultural deviants. This chapter will show how much has happened since Jensen's commentary was published.

Before the emergence of fan studies, the traditional way to introduce any academic discussion about fandom was to touch on established notions of deviance and extremity (see Jensen 1992, 9). Discussions charted how much research departed from positing fans as collectively falling for mass hysteria or as individuals having socially dangerous obsessions. Cultural studies in general and fan studies in particular rehabilitated the image of fans as creative, engaged and sometimes resistant individuals – just normal people. By representing them as creative rogue readers, fan studies created a fresh analytic perspective on the subject, but other cultural spheres – including some quarters of psychology and sections of the tabloid press – continued to ignore the new reading. Despite this sustained assault on the stereotype of the fan as an inadequate member of society, 'extreme' fandom is still seen in some quarters as a form of abnormal deviance. Portrayals of fandom therefore almost inevitably encompass *both* normality *and* monstrosity, self and other.

What follows will proceed in three parts. In the first I present the logic of the 'slippery slope' argument and then challenge it piece by piece. In the second, I focus on the case of Mark Chapman to explore why stereotypes of 'deranged' fandom continue to circulate in public life. In the final section I examine arguments that have been made in fan studies which suggest fans' minds operate through normal psychological processes. My argument in the chapter is simple. Although in reality there is no necessary *causal* relationship between fandom and personality disorders like stalking, monstrous depictions of fans as divided subjects and deviant others have served to both normalize mainstream audiences and offer a popular critique of the dangers of the media. Extreme fandom has been used to continually signify the monstrous precisely because it encapsulates social anxieties about the perils of celebrity culture.

The slippery slope

Pathology is the study of medical problems. This tradition implies that ordinary fandom shades into insanity, social deviance and extreme behaviour. Given the existence of intense forms of audience identification with the media, one response in psychology has been to posit measurement scales of social deviance. Psychologists like James Houran and John Maltby have therefore attempted to explore celebrity attachment in relation to scales of abnormality (see, for instance, McCutcheon et al. 2002; Giles & Maltby 2003). Their work uses fandom to explore the borderline between sanity and insanity. Quoted on a BBC news Website, Maltby explains, 'Worshipping a celebrity does not make you dysfunctional, but it does put you at risk of being so. There is this progression of behaviours, and if you start, we don't know what's going to stop you'.[1] Writers who say fandom is dangerous often argue that particular individuals in fan cultures are vulnerable since each fan can develop intense personal feelings of obsession to a point where he/she experiences something strong and irrational. Obsessed fans *supposedly* retreat into social isolation, have 'narcissistic linking fantasies' and become overly fixated on their star. If the fan's attempts to communicate with the celebrity go unrequited – or if the celebrity challenges the image that has been constructed of them – the obsessed follower's immense emotional investment can supposedly cause them to enter a resentful rage and to release their anger by attacking or murdering their hero. Is this *really* about warding off the beast within, or is it about celebrity psychiatrists courting the media by pathologizing fandom? Gayle Steever has recently contested the use of ideas about the use of celebrity worship scales in relation to fandom by saying that they are undefined and untested on 'normal' fan populations:

> If significant numbers of fan-club members do not meet the criteria on these scales as celebrity worshipers, then it would follow that the validity of the claim that fan clubs are made up of celebrity worshipers is questionable. In addition, the assertion that membership in a fan club is the first step on the

road to more pathological celebrity worship is unsupported by data from real fan clubs. To infer that a person is a fan based on their score on the CAS [Celebrity Attitude Scale] and then to claim that all fans are celebrity worshipers because the scale says so is circular reasoning. (2011, 1357)

Concerns like these do not seem to have dawned on a significant tradition of psychological scholarship that draws its research subjects from *outside* of established fan communities, assuming, perhaps, that media fans occur so frequently in the general population that they will inevitably figure in the sample. In the journal *Applied Psychology in Criminal Justice*, for instance, Karl Roberts (2007, 59) applied John Bowlby's famous schema of attachment to think about fan encounters. Bowlby's work uses dimensions of self-anxiety and other-avoidance to demarcate four distinct styles of attachment based on experiences in infancy: *secure* (love of self, love of other), *fearful* (fear of self, fear of other), *pre-occupied* (fear of self, love of other) and *dismissive* (love of self, fear of other).[2] From this Roberts hypothesizes that potential stalkers are more likely to be anxious about themselves, but also able to approach (low on the avoidance scale). In other words, he surmised they would be 'pre-occupied' in attachment style: basically, sociable but dependent as people. Using a mixed sample of 200 undergraduates, Roberts (2007) found that around half his sample had approached a celebrity in some way (mostly by sending fanmail) (62). While *none had harassed anybody*, the fans that made approaches *did* fit the suspected profile (66). In the journal *Applied Psychology in Criminal Justice*, Roberts then reported:

It has been argued that parasocial relationships are a normal part of social development during childhood and adolescence . . . a romantic parasocial relationship with a pop star may enable a young person to practice a relationship at a safe distance as preparation for an adult relationship . . . however, for some individuals the relationship with a celebrity may become highly significant and even come to dominate their lives. . . . (56)

He concluded that he had discovered a link between pre-occupied attachment styles and approach behaviours, possibly suggesting that pre-occupied attachment *could* also be an element in celebrity stalking. The crucial thing here is the jump from students to fans to stalkers is made by the logic of the study rather than evidence of any empirical process.

Social theorists outside of fan studies have traditionally been uncomfortable with fandom because in their view it is based on imagined intimacy with distant heroes and therefore smacks of alienation and deception. In 1956, Donald Horton and Richard Wohl contributed a seminal piece of research on the subject of how viewers connected with media personalities called 'Mass Communication and Parasocial Interaction: Observations on Intimacy at a Distance'. Drawing on their knowledge of 'personality' disk jockeys on radio, Horton and Wohl suggested that we know more about celebrities than we know about our neighbours. In their view, celebrity performances offer gestural cues (such as folksy humour) that invite responses from the media audience. They argue that the mediated performance of a personality can broadcast cues which give each audience member the illusion they know and are interacting with him/her. Horton and Wohl called this condition **parasocial interaction**. Audience responses are unhealthy because they are one-way (para-social) and not a real exchange: '[Mass media] give the illusion of face-to-face relationship . . . In time, the devotee – the "fan" – comes to believe that he "knows" the persona more intimately and profoundly than others do' (Horton & Wohl 1956, 216).

Half a century after Horton and Wohl's piece was published, parasocial interaction has been examined in wider fandom research, especially by psychologists, but is much less discussed in fan studies.[3] Nevertheless, it has a wider purchase in the academic world. Slavoj Žižek, in his eponymous film documentary *Žižek*, discussed his discomfort with the image of Jacques Lacan as a media celebrity:

> The central idea of ideology . . . is precisely that ideological propositions do not determine us totally. 'We cannot be reduced to our public image; there is a warm human being behind'. *This* is ideology at its purest. The most horrible anti-ideological act for me – and really horrible, terrifying – is to fully identify with the ideological image.

Žižek is suggesting that the media is not to be trusted in its claim that by engaging we are meeting people and getting to know their personalities. This is one of the more recent versions of the idea that electronic mediation is a sleight of hand trick which levers our capacity for human empathy in order to draw us more deeply into alienated and inhuman processes of media consumption. If the possibility of identifying with the celebrity image could leave a thinker like Žižek cold, as a researcher he is not alone.[4] Outside of media and cultural studies, both academics and the wider media have traditionally seen something wrong with fandom because for them it symbolizes addiction to a screen image. Addiction is defined clinically as a problem that a person has when he/she is out of control and taking more of a substance than is healthy. Heavy and prolonged use impairs participation in normal activities to a point where withdrawal starts to occur if the substance is given up (Harrington & Bielby 1995, 108). Any fan's supposed addiction is therefore read as a kind of social impairment. In the rest of this section we will explore this 'slippery slope' argument point by point.

After two decades of participation in various fan communities and documentary evidence from 150 fans, Gayle Stevers (2009) found that although many fans had very intense interests in celebrities, a large subgroup contained a less obsessive and more socially motivated category of fan, one propelled by an interest in the work of the celebrity and in the potential for networking with other fans. However, the slippery slope idea is never decided by looking at what the mass of ordinary fans are doing. According to Jenkins:

> Building on the word's traditional links to madness and demonic possession, news reports frequently characterize fans as psychopaths whose frustrated fantasies of intimate relationships with stars or unsatisfied desires to achieve their own stardom take violent and antisocial forms. (1992, 13)

Having an affective interest in popular culture is often used as a form of shorthand to express individual humanity. Yet variations in the way that fandom has been defined can act as alibis for pathologizing judgements. There is a degree of variation inherent in fandom itself that can act as a kind of excuse for this pathologizing: to be a fan is often to admire something about another person (whether creativity, talent, looks or style) or to participate in an emotional world that they have helped to create. In some cases – rock concerts as mass spectacles, for example – the emotional aspect of that relationship is publically performed as part of the phenomenon itself. There is a line, however, between admiration and subservience, participation and manipulation. The latter terms imply that the fan has no agency or has at least relinquished it in pursuit of a greater reward.

Academic projections have sometimes located the idea of obsessive fandom as a potential descent into savagery. In the drama of the slippery slope model, the steps move forward something like this: a subset of fans is vulnerable to the progressive deterioration of their minds. Social isolation, parasocial interaction and unhealthy fantasizing lead them towards the dark side. This is spelled out by Meloy et al. in their own chapter of their edited collection on the subject:

> On the periphery [of fame], however, resides a much smaller group of individuals who lack the ability to discriminate between their own private fantasies and the figure's public behaviour, believe they are entitled to pursue the person and may present a risk of violence. They may feel personally insulted by perceived betrayal, or fanatically in love because

of a perceived affectionate or sexual invitation, or simply be pre-occupied with the daily life of the public figure. Such individuals may fixate on the public figure and do nothing more. Others communicate or approach in a disturbing way. A few will threaten. And on rare occasions, one will breach the public figure's perimeter and attack. (2008, 3)

Beyond addiction to a screen image, in this schema the earliest stage happens when a minority of obsessed fans supposedly lose their social compass to the extent that they become removed from real relationships in their ordinary lives. In effect, their fandom isolates them. Insofar as it assumes that fans make 'real' responses to the 'false' signals coming from the media, the idea is an extension both of Horton and Wohl's and Žižek's argument. In other words, fans' supposed confusion is both epistemological (they no longer know how to differentiate between 'real' and 'fake' interpersonal relations) and social (they refuse the overtures of 'real' but comparatively unglamorous people). Meloy et al. explain that 'there is no demarcation between internal and external for a psychotic individual. Fantasy is reality' (2008, 19). While all fans respond to performance and some evidently fantasize, we can still tell the difference between fantasy and reality. It is, of course, the parasocial stereotype that labels ordinary fans *as* psychotics and, more importantly, somehow positions psychotics who also happen to be fans as typical representatives of 'extreme' fandom. So, for example, while Spitzberg and Cupach remain careful to say that most stalking cases *do not* involve fans who stalk celebrities (2008, 292), they also explain, 'Fans who do engage in campaigns of pursuit risk crossing the (rope) line and the "spectre of staking" arises . . . This crossing-over may occur in escalating stages . . .' (293). Such comments suggest an intriguing dual standard when contrasted with Meloy et al.'s claim that 'What appears at first to be an issue-driven and politically-motivated pursuit of a public figure can hide a severe psychiatric disturbance' (2008, 16). In other words, while it might be *possible* to see fandom, too, as a place where particular individuals 'can hide a severe psychiatric disturbance', there is instead a tendency among many to view it as an escalating temptation to approach the 'rope line' that separates ordinary people from stalking behaviours.[5] As part of this, the idea of 'fallen fans' suggests that they constitute a *dangerously isolated subset* of the whole population – a micro-sample of the fan base – that is both atypical and yet somehow representative of fandom itself. A stock character in films like *King of Comedy* (Scorsese 1983) and *Misery* (Reiner 1990), is what journalist Julie Burchill has called the 'fan in the attic': someone isolated, who is socially and emotionally immature, given over to media-inspired fantasies and unable to find a respected place in society.

The next stage in the slippery slope schema, it is argued, suggests that some fans start to pursue mediated relationships *in preference* to real ones. In effect, their fandom insulates them to the extent that they become isolated from ordinary relationships; they supposedly lose their moral compass. Without considering whether *the reverse* is true – that mediated relationships offer *consolation* when real ones are not available – the slippery slope schema suggests that we actually come to *prefer* alienated interactions, hiding ourselves from intimacy in solitude and settling for unrequited love. A consequent step in the slippery slope hypothesis is to suggest that fandom is most essentially *about fantasizing* because stars are out of reach. However, my own research has suggested that fan fantasies often revolve around fulfilling the individual's role *as a fan*. For example, fans can dream about being on the front row of an amazing live event or by acquiring a rare recording (see Duffett 1998).

A further stage in the slippery slope schema supposedly happens when isolated, alienated, socially inadequate fans then attempt to make personal contact with their celebrity heroes. For example, psychologist Karl Roberts claims:

> First of all, it is known that a subset of fans may develop pathological interests in favoured celebrities that often involved repeated attempts to approach and/or contact them (Giles & Maltby, 2003; McCutcheon, Lange, & Houran, 2002). Knowledge of such psychological characteristics associated with such behavior might be helpful in designing treatment interventions for these individuals. Secondly, approach behavior that becomes sinister and provokes fear in a celebrity may be of interest to law enforcement. (2007, 55)

If they are unwelcome, the 'repeated attempts to approach' that Roberts refers to here are known as stalking. Stalking implies not simply following a person, but crossing a spatial or mental boundary, entering a place of intrusion or harassment. In order to make a connection, fandom has to be aligned to the common motives for such behaviour. One example is a personality disorder called erotomania. Erotomania is a rare disorder in which the patient has a delusional belief that a particular person is falling in love and making amorous advances towards him/her. Erotomaniacs mistakenly believe that their object is actively signalling a dance of courtship with them. Since it has a parasocial dimension, erotomania *seems* to fit descriptions of twisted fandom. Is there really a link between fandom and stalking that can be described by this disorder? Harrington and Bielby looked at Meloy's existing studies of celebrity stalking and noted he concluded that only 5 per cent of diagnosed erotomaniacs ever become violent, only 16 per cent of 214 stalking cases actually had erotomaniac delusions, only 5 per cent of erotomaniacs believed they were actually married to a star (1995, 109). In another study for the journal *Comprehensive Psychiatry*, Kennedy et al. reported:

> Fifteen erotomanic subjects (11 female, four male) were identified. Most were isolated, without a partner or full-time occupation . . . Less than half of the objects of their affection, mainly non-celebrities, were subject to harassment . . . In this series, erotomanic symptoms largely occurred in the context of other psychiatric disorders . . . Subjects were less dangerous and engaged in less harassment of victims than the literature suggests. Subjects were often isolated, unemployed, and with few social contacts. Strong family psychiatric histories were seen particularly with regard to mono-delusional disorders raising the possibility of genetic inheritance. (2002, 1)

There are some important points here. First, erotomania is pathology that primarily emerges from social inequality, insofar that the erotomaniacs are often socially marginalized (unemployed) while their objects are of high status. Second, most erotomania is non-violent and does not involve stalking behaviours. Third, erotomania has many causes and is more likely to occur after a physical injury – like an accidental bang on the head – than as the culmination of a fan's supposed descent into social isolation. Finally, celebrity following is rarely correlated with erotomania. Of course, to a star who feels threatened, a 1 per cent chance is still too large. Are celebrity stalkers really resentful ex-fans? As Karl Roberts found in his study:

> The motives for contacting or approaching celebrities in the present study also appear to be different to the most common motives for stalking another individual. Stalking behavior is most commonly associated by a desire to start or rekindle a romantic relationship (e.g. Meloy, 1998; Mullen, et al., 2000); however, the self-reports of participants in this study indicate no such motivation. (2007, 56)

Despite problems with framing erotomania as a motivation, some psychologists remain certain that extreme fandom is potentially dangerous, because fixated fans who are ignored by their heroes *are predicted* to react angrily in the face of disappointed expectations. In rare but significant cases their high degree of emotional investment is then supposed to go sour and manifest as resentment, rage, harassment and even murder. In the drama of the slippery slope model, the steps are therefore connected by a *logic* that moves forward something like this: a subset of fans is vulnerable to a descent in which parasocial interaction, social isolation and fantasizing gradually lead them down to intrusive, obsessive, stalking behaviours that act out the darker side of their mental constitution. At any point, the performer may choose *not* to acknowledge them and accidentally trigger an angry and potentially murderous flash of resentment. Psychological researchers have suggested that the slippery slope is important because it can end up not simply in mild harassment or intrusion, but in serious violence and occasionally in murder. Anthony Elliot suggested:

> [In] the process of identifying with a celebrity, the fan unleashes a range of fantasies and desires and, through projective identification, transfers hopes and dreams onto the celebrity . . . In psychoanalytic terms, this is a kind of splitting: the *good or desired parts of the self are put into the other* in order to protect this imagined goodness from bad or destructive parts of the self. There is, then, a curious sort of violence intrinsic to fandom . . . The relation of fan and celebrity is troubled because violence is built into it. (1999, 139; emphasis mine)

For Matt Hills, Elliot's account moves from psychoanalytic reasoning to stereotypes of 'deranged' fandom (2002a, 97). After quoting the passage, he goes straight to the end part of the argument:

> Elliot draws on Melanie Klein's work on the paranoid-schizoid position, as well as referring to 'projective identification'. The latter, as Elliott's account demonstrates, is a psychical process whereby *dangerous or disavowed aspects of the self are projected onto somebody else*. But this attempt at 'getting rid' of part of the self is not entirely successful . . . (96; emphasis in original)

What is interesting about comparing Elliot's and Hills' quotations is that they switch the psychic material that is purportedly disavowed. The Elliot quote says that the 'good' parts of the self are projected on to the heroic celebrity, whereas Hills talks about the 'dangerous' aspects of self being projected (the celebrity being seen as in some way othered or engendering hate). There must be a middle term in the process where the imagined fan – *and they are only imagined here* – switches from loving the celebrity to hating them. In many accounts this moment comes if the celebrity inadvertently breaks the fans' imagined social contract. In part the slippery slope *seems* based on solid generalizations: fans *can* become very dedicated in their quests to meet heroes and no celebrity *wants* to lose control of their space or privacy.[6] Does that mean that the slippery slope idea is correct?

Beyond the slippery slope

The slippery slope idea assumes that fandom feeds a twisted journey into murderous obsession that can draw an otherwise sane individual from normality to violent insanity through their engagement with popular culture. It therefore posits a kind of continuum that artificially converts a variety of cases of normal, moderately deviant and dangerous behaviour into a *scale* of psychological progression *which is then imagined as the journey of one idealized individual.* While the slope sounds logical, it invites us to commit the fallacy of generalizing from small parts of isolated cases and using them to fabricate a hypothetical example that then dominates the discussion. In doing so it seriously misinterprets and misrepresents fandom, confusing it with psychotic disorder.

As Joli Jensen explained, 'The fan-as-pathology model implies that there is a thin line between "normal" and excessive fandom' (1992, 18). There are therefore methodological issues in slippery slope studies. Karl Roberts' 2007 research, for example, claimed to discuss fans when the research subjects were ordinary students and faced the issue that harassing behaviour was unlikely to be self-reported. Beyond those two issues, it is precisely his apriori adoption of the slippery slope idea which means he can make an inferential leap from saying *people who contact stars are more likely to like others but dislike themselves* to claiming that *because they approach more often these same fans are more likely to be stalkers.* This fairly recent study shows traces of fan stereotypes still loom large. Although fans assert their desire to get closer to their heroes, psychologists often position fandom as a childish phase which revolves around a 'safe,' distanced rehearsal for real life (i.e. the parasocial relationship); when combined with the slippery slope model, dedicated fans therefore seem – paradoxically – immature, vulnerable and potentially dangerous. Roberts goes on to imply that approaching a celebrity is one stage on the road to harassing them. What follows will challenge the slippery slope's logic point by point while exploring why it has become so entrenched in the public imagination.

A fair place to begin interrogating the logic of the slippery slope is the idea that it begins with the tendency to indulge in repeated behaviour. Certain forms of popular culture, from slasher films to dance music, have repetition built into their structure (see Middleton 2006, 15). For example, recording artists often play carefully cloned versions of their existing records to live audiences. Fans are viewers that like to engage repeatedly with the same particular text. Much of their pleasure comes from repeatedly encountering the same material and trying to anticipate its structure (Jenkins 1992, 69). Discussing repetition back in 1914, Sigmund Freud explained:

> The patient does not remember anything of what he has forgotten and repressed, but acts it out. He produces it not as a memory but as an action; he repeats it, without, of course, knowing that he is repeating it . . . not as an event of the past, but as a present-day force. (1914/2001, 150–1)

The process of repetition, at least in this Freudian incarnation, is not so much a case of repeatedly pursuing pleasure, but rather of exorcizing a repressed trauma by acting it out. Locating fandom in relation to this is difficult because fans have not shared any obvious trauma which they have in common. Nevertheless, notions of other repeated behaviour such as fascination and fixation tend to imply an abnormal psychological interest. To describe fandom as the acting out of a 'repetition compulsion' in the Freudian sense would seem questionable because fans are not trying to quell anxieties by repeatedly restaging traumatic moments. Instead they are interested in exploring their connections and rediscovering joys they have found in the text as they let its structures, themes and values resonate with their concerns. Repetition extends this pleasure by reviving the stuff of pleasant memories. Take one recent comment from Tim Robey about Hitchcock's 1958 film *Vertigo*:

> What I hadn't realized is that *Vertigo* is the ultimate grower . . . [it] makes more sense the more we see it repeated: it's an experience that gets correspondingly more deep and dreamlike with every viewing, echoing further back into the reaches of the subconscious. There's something quasi-religious about returning to it, knowing all the mistakes that [lead actor James] Stewart's Scottie Ferguson is going to make all over again, and recognizing every facet of Kim Novak, from ethereally seductive to seemingly guiless to manipulative and doomed. (2012, P1)

While Robey's comment suggest that pleasures can come from new details every time, they can also come from being able to rerun engaging scenes or from being able to predict what will happen as the text unfolds. In the context of pleasurable cultural consumption, the process itself is enchanting and intoxicating.

The slippery slope model suggests that fans lose their grip on reality as they fantasize. In fact their pleasure can come from playing with the notion of 'the real' itself. It is no suprise that because their media representations populate our waking life, stars appear in virtually everyone's dreams, daydreams and fantasies (for example, see Vermorel & Vermorel 1985; Turner 1993). Fantasy matters in the slippery slope idea because it supposedly allows fans to make a further epistemological mistake: that they cannot tell what is real any more. Swayed by television narratives, for example, they often start to call actors by their character names. According to Harrington and Bielby (1995, 110), while such fans *do* appear to play with the boundary between reality and fiction, they do *not* ever seem to *confuse their own identity* with that of the actor. For example, I might playfully shout 'Hello James!' at Bond actor Daniel Craig, but I do not believe that I actually *am* him. This is true even of impersonators who are caught in the double bind of maintaining their own identities while soliciting social recognition for approximating the style of a different person. We might *desire* to get inside the text or star's private world, or to have a famous or fictional character become part of our daily lives; each route equalizes an imbalance of social power demarcated by glamour. No normal fan believes, however, that this rebalancing has already happened and that they are now living inside the dream.

Fandom is not *fully* premised on 'touching at a distance', the existential fallacy that we are vicariously meeting stars when we watch them on-screen. Instead the star's mediated behaviour can be understood on its own terms as a set of gestures that *performs* identity, *accrues* fame and *lets audience members decide* if they want to get closer or know more. It is from such motivations that fandom springs, making do with commodities and objects that fill the fans' needs only secondarily, as substitutes for a closeness that – especially in the case of a fictional or dead star – can never be fully realized. Most fans know that they cannot meet their heroes, but they are not deterred from aiming to communicate with them if possible. Critics of this process see it as a turning away from the reality and responsibilities of ordinary social life. While fandom, evidently, has a social and psychological purposes for each individual in daily life, moral entrepreneurs portray it as possession and fantasizing that poisons the social body. Fan practices are frequently more about comfort, relaxation and pleasure than they are about frustration with unavailable intimacy. Of course, admirers may wish to communicate their feelings or to meet their star – just for the thrill – but it is important to realize that they *already* feel boosted by their engagement. As Cavicchi reported:

> Media critics consider fans abnormal or dangerous; however, I have found that my fandom for various musical performers has, instead, gotten me through many tough times over the years and has been the source of many friendships, including my relationship with my wife. (1998, 8)

According to sociologists Kerry Ferris and Scott Harris, 'Fans differ from ordinary consumers of fame because they form especially strong emotional attachments to the objects of their interest, and they can use those attachments as the stepping-stone both to relationships with other fans and to relationships with the famous themselves' (2011, 13). Yet media fans are, no doubt, not really in love with specific objects or people (though it usually feels that way). Rather, they are in love with their own pleasures: *Beauty and the Beast* fans, for instance, used the romance as a formula for judging their chosen text. When the show's producers refused to deliver increased intimacy between its two main characters, the fans felt betrayed (Jenkins 1992, 143–5). This example is typical insofar that fan audiences can be critical *based on* their strong investments. Their enthusiastic interest in the continuity of the text – or the idea that its maker will live up to his or her creative reputation – can leave them disappointed if the media release does not rise to the occasion. Fandom, then, implicitly involves an unwritten set of expectations between performers and their followers, expectations that can extend beyond the primary performance itself to include how the audience is treated. However, such expectations never form a solid charter or written social contract. At any point the performer may choose to reject or not acknowledge them. Rather than descend into a murderous resentment rage, the characteristic response of fans on such occasions is to feel a degree of disappointment and nostalgia for past performances, or to search for another performer who will provide fresh pleasure.

Some theorists have caricatured the fan audience by its persistent tendency to overstep boundaries. Professor Daniel Hertitz has produced a carefully considered discussion of audience complicity in the problematic excesses of media culture. Writing on the case of Princess Diana, Hertitz in effect likened the audience to *looters*:

> The more she was hounded, the more obvious her contempt, the more the voracious British public wanted more. Their sympathy ever profound, they also felt themselves entitled to ongoing royal action: this was a prerogative of their sense of public ownership of the monarchy, of their sense that it is theirs (even if they can't join in). (2008, 123)

He extended this in his conclusion:

> And the cult around her conceals blood lust for her pain under explicit admiration for her stardom. It is a whopping paean to voyeurism in all its aspects . . . The very media that are called upon to narrate these celebrity and star lives levitate them, hunt them, curdle them and turn them into the stuff of silver screen and soap opera. (142)

Hertitz's comments are typical of the kind of discussion that takes place over issues of celebrity and privacy. They unquestioningly imply that the press operates – intrusively and unethically – on behalf of an over-reaching fan 'cult'. In fact, the function of the tabloid press is to secure a mass readership for its advertisers; fans are only a minority of potential readers. They are, furthermore, an audience fraction that would, more often, step back to protect the stars that they love. News and gossip reporters who demonstrate invasive cruelty are now *less* ethical in their actions than *any* true fan: their tone panders to an audience that is *not* part of the star's 'cult' following at all, but instead a less supportive cross section of the public who do not think that the person really deserves his or her privacy or fame. Ethical dilemmas over press intrusion are thus displaced on to fans as an audience faction because they appear to be more eager than others to know the 'real' performer. Their interest, however, is about affirming their own fancies (asking, 'What is he really like?'), not in degrading and disparaging an idol.

Separating fandom from 'celebrity following' is also crucial here. Rather like press photographers, there are also ordinary individuals who make it their business to meet as many celebrities as possible and bask in the reflected glory. Indeed, what they usually do is lever the fame of others to create their own *niche* fame. One set of people who seem to wear the garb of fandom but operate as celebrity-followers are amateur photographers. Starting in 1965 with a Brownie Bullseye camera when he was just 15 years old, Gary Boas took around 60,000 photographs of himself over the next 15 years with a range of celebrities in New York City. Eventually his extensive collection became the raw material for an art exhibition and book called *Starstruck* (Boas 2006). While he was marketed as a 'fan's fan' and 'superhero to fans everywhere', Boas was *different* to a typical media fan, not just in the depth of his dedication but because of the way he converted fame into pure exchange value. If he had any kind of engagement with the performance and creative personae of any of those he photographed, it was incidental to his collecting pursuit. He was simply after evidence that they endorsed him. Since he briefly entrapped hundreds of celebrities, one must conclude that *what Boas was collecting was fame itself.*[7] He was literally putting himself in the picture with New York's glitterati to accumulate their collective social value: a very different (and perhaps more pathological) venture than discovering and pursuing a personal connection with a particular famous person.

Boas was an exception, but not an isolated case. In 1989, Richard Simpkin began taking celebrity photos in Australia starting with the lead singer of the group INXS. Simpkin (2007) also created a book featuring pictures and stories about his encounters with a vast range of famous people from Elton John to Martin Scorcese. In the introduction he explained:

> For me getting a photo with a celebrity is far more important than getting their autograph because anyone can buy an autograph but how do you put a price on actually meeting someone that is going to be remembered in history? . . . I got to thinking, if people were so fascinated with celebrities then I should start to get my photo taken with every celebrity that I met . . . The photos that I have taken represent a moment where the celebrity transcends into the world of reality. Am I the reality or am I simply just trying to escape my world into the world of celebrity? It's something that I do question from time to time. (10–11)

As if to form part of an answer, Simpkins added, 'Security, public relations girls, doormen and limousine drives all look at you in disbelief as you casually walk over to the celebrity . . . All that waiting is quickly forgotten; the battle was won and you feel the highest high' (13). Simpkins' words imply that he created the photo encounters mainly for the challenge, not just the reflected glory.

A further example of someone who levered celebrity for its *exchange* value – and who was perhaps the greatest master at that – is Andy Warhol. Warhol has an exceedingly complex relation to fandom. On one level he was the ultimate fan, bringing dedication to his creative life and levering his influence to become part of New York's celebrity jet set.[8] On another level, he exploited the exchange value of celebrity in his life and art to the point where his work was a commentary on its vacuity. It was evident from the pages of his magazine *Interview* that Andy got a thrill out of meeting particular famous people. His occupational roles as an artist, film maker, magazine editor and manager of recording artists all allowed him to direct the creative process in a way that self-consciously commented on the mass-produced nature of fame and celebrity itself. It is no wonder, then, that Warhol's observations on the subject have been widely circulated.

Given the limited explanatory capacity of the slippery slope argument, it is fair to say that stalking has been significantly misinterpreted by the popular media as a form of fan activity. Why, then, do these stories persist? In the 1980s Fred Vermorel placed the blame on the media for inviting John Lennon's murder:

> It is hardly surprising, when stars offer themselves so lavishly for consumption, that some fans will take the invitation literally. Like Mark Chapman. After all, one plausible way to 'consume' people is to annihilate

them. And in this light, the grisly episode of Lennon's killing (and its publicity aftermath) appears less an aberration that the following through of a cultural logic implicit in showbiz itself. There is a kind of violence about the fan/star relationship not adequately explained by the psychologistic maxims of, say, Bob Randall's *The Fan* or Peter Gabriel's 'Family Snapshot' which reduce the problem to individual psychosis while ignoring the massive and systematic social and cultural provocation. (1985, 250)

Designed to cause controversy, Vermorel's argument fails when one realizes that 'consuming' is not actually the same as killing. In 1984, the anthropologist John Caughey presented a different argument in his book *Imaginary Social Worlds*. He suggested that everyone, both sane and insane, has a terrain of imagination populated by celebrities. We all see stars in our dreams. However, as Caughey noted, the insane can sometimes use celebrities as vehicles for their own dangerous pathologies. He cited three examples to demonstrate his case: John Lennon's killer Mark Chapman; Ruth Steinhagen (a woman who shot baseball player Eddie Waitkus in June 1949) and John Hinckley (who in 1981 tried to shoot President Reagan in a bizarre bid to impress Jody Foster). Caughey's conclusion was that the media needs to take more responsibility for the strong emotional attachments it helps to arouse. By suggesting that stalkers start as disturbed individuals, not fans, Caughey's work begins to contest the pathological tradition. The way that he raises the issue of media responsibility is, as we shall see, a point of connection with the more familiar version of slippery slope thinking.

Behind the pathological fan argument is a fear about the power of the media itself. **Media effects** arguments suggest that rather than simply informing or inspiring audience members, the media *makes* them do things. Because academic work on the supposed dangers of parasocial interaction suggests that popular shows create addicts and unrequited obsessives as a characteristic (mal)function of the 'fan factory', it really offers a variant of the media effects argument. There are crucial problems with the notion that the media directly *makes* us do anything, however. Education is not the same as indoctrination: we cannot be brainwashed (Jenkins 2006, 212). Futhermore, we often use our cultural passions as a reason to greet other people in our everyday world. Stars and fictional characters are not just fodder for fantasy encounters. They help to sustain further social relationships since they enable fans to befriend *each other* (45).

Because the process of becoming a fan can involve being emotionally overwhelmed by the discovery of a powerful inner conviction, it can feel pleasantly unsettling. Fandom is often actually defined by this process and associated with significant change in the individual's life. Fans become fascinated by realms of meaning developed by other people. Many discover emotive attachments to famous individuals. Such behaviour implies an impulsive loss – or instinctive rejection – of rationality and emotional distance, and is therefore framed by outsiders as a potential loss of agency or type of addiction. In his provocative pop fan mail compilation, *Starlust,* Fred Vermoral wrote, 'Fanhood can be a quite frightening kind of possession' (1985, 248). One anxiety associated with fannish pursuits is therefore that they seem to lead people into whole realms of deep, non-rational emotion. Henry Jenkins elaborates:

> 'Fan' as an abbreviation of 'fananticus' ('a temple servant, a devotee') and while the term became applied to media culture, 'it never fully escaped its earlier connotations of religious and political zealotry, false beliefs, orgiastic excess, possession, madness'. . . . (1992, 12).

Portrayals of fandom have often been associated with youthful naivety, childishness or immaturity (see 12). Lady Gaga – whose music uses monstrosity as a metaphor to explore the perils of stardom – parodies this by calling herself 'Mother Monster' and her fans 'Little Monsters'. According to Hills (2002a, 160), to locate fans entirely as addicts – 'Little Monsters' – is to remove all of their agency, yet to understand them as entirely logical and autonomous agents is to ignore their inability to rationally explain their shift in personal identity. In slippery slope portrayals, talking about obsession is therefore a way to *socially emphasize* a supposed lack of agency.

Obsession is a psychiatric term specifying the state when an individual's mind is fixated on one particular person or topic to the point that they become blinkered and neglectful. Perhaps because fandom can be represented through displays of emotional conviction, it is often described – sometimes by fans themselves who have internalized elements of a popular vocabulary – as being or being about obsession: 'Several fans even told me about the necessity of having an "obsession" with Springsteen; anyone without that obsession is somehow not quite a "real" fan yet' (Cavicchi 1998, 102). Jensen, notes that 'obsession' is a value-loaded term with cultural and class connotations that implies an irrational and potentially pathological form of abnormality: fans of popular culture are 'obsessed' while high cultural aficionados simply become 'impassioned'. Equally, rather than 'obsessed' eccentrics, others in society, such as athletes and research academics, are described as 'dedicated' to their fields (1992, 20).

Fandom begins when we identify something of great interest to us. It is driven by personal connection and fascination and it can become a kind of quest for intimacy with a famous person. It is also a process where personal passion and energy are productively focused. This does not mean that fandom is inherently *about* obsession, however. Instead, the term exploits fascination as a way to pathologize fandom as always vulnerable to imbalance and excess, always potentially tipping over into something inappropriate and dangerous. Commentators who see fandom as excessive implicitly contrast it to more restricted and 'civilized' forms of behaviour. They confuse a social role with a personal predisposition; perhaps we can say that *individuals* can be obsessive, but *roles are just roles* and do not have the agency to obsess. To attribute that agency to roles is, in this case, to say that fandom marks out our pervasive social anxiety about losing our individuality and independence. In some ways, obsession is therefore really another way to discuss *possession*. Taking this a step further, since fan dedication sometimes boils down to trumping others' knowledge, media collections, or tales of intimacy with a highly-valued star, we can say that the obsession/possession discourse may well reflect the external assumption that extreme fandom is a trap in which individuals fall when they attempt to elevate their low self-esteem by competing against others.[9]

The word 'obsession' encompasses a vast conceptual territory that extends between dedication, fascination, emotional connection and deviancy. Diagnosed as potentially pathological, 'obsessive fandom' therefore holds open a space that connects normality and insanity. In books such as Joey Berlin's 1996 compilation of quotes from star interviews, *Toxic Fame*, fans are portrayed as a graceless rabble who brazenly pursue their own interests, overstepping the mark at a moment's notice. The book contains a whole section called 'Close Encounters with Fans' that begins, 'Remember Rebecca Shaeffer, Selena or John Lennon? They were murdered by deranged fans. These are extreme cases, but there isn't a celebrity in the world who doesn't entertain that fear at some point. Some are haunted by it every day' (51).[10] The result of deductively connecting various elements of the slippery slope schema is to position fandom as, at best, a subservient activity that is the product of mass manipulation, and at worst as an urge tempting us to harass the famous. Love is not harassment, participation not manipulation, admiration not subservience, conviction not possession, and dedication not addiction. The latter terms imply that fans have no agency or ethics. Overly intrusive, threatening and harassing behaviour departs from the category of fandom altogether; the media's repeated use of terms like 'obsessive' or 'deranged' is designed to mark out the extreme fan as a potentially monstrous individual. Researchers are not isolated from the public sphere so a final point here is that the slippery slope is part of the cultural noise in Western society. The theories and assumptions that they already hold can play a major role in perceptions of fan activity. For example, Nick Stevenson (2009) reflected:

> Returning to the fans perhaps many men find it easier to receive emotional support from a relationship based on distance than they do from relationships based on proximity (94) . . . I noticed how depressed I would start to feel on the journey home from the interview . . . After only a period of a few years since the interviews took place, I can recognize that these intense feelings of depression were connected to deep feelings of loneliness that many of the interviewees engendered within me . . . It is undoubtedly the case that many of the men I was interviewing unknowingly to them, had reminded me of times in my own life when I had felt deeply alone and anxious about what the future might hold. (95)

This issue of researcher projection is especially important when it comes to process of othering where certain groups are marked out as deviant by those who are in control of making representations. Extreme deviants are often perceived in ways that articulate widespread social anxieties. Depending on how the term 'monster' is defined, it can mean an inhumanly cruel individual or a phantom object of shared fears. Steven Schneider argued that 'the metaphorical nature of horror film monsters has facilitated their entrance into our collective consciousness' (1999, 181). Through their repeated cinematic appearances, monsters like Frankenstein and Dracula have become part of the cultural furniture. For Schneider, these perennial bogeymen recur primarily because they contradict widely shared beliefs that the dead cannot return to life. Having earned their place in the dark patheon of monstrosity, at different times they can then be reorientated to express more specific, contemporary fears. Horrifying monsters therefore represent convenient and cautionary metaphors selected time and again to act as signposts on the road to damnation. They form a repertoire of archetypes that can be summoned to articulate the deepest fears of a changing society. At first sight, fandom seems an unlikely candidate for such a role. It is simply an invested response in commercial culture, a response in that it reflects an appreciation of a famous person or work. Fans feel an ongoing connection with their heroes. Their phenomenon has sometimes been seen as a part of mass culture or connected with youth, perhaps even relegated to a lifestyle choice. Nevertheless, fandom circulates in both fictional and news media as an identity of monstrous potential.

On 25 October 2011, England's national free newspaper *The Metro* carried a front page headline which read, 'Madonna: My Fear of Stalker in My Home'. Its tagline added, 'Obsessive Fan Locked Up Indefinitely'. The story explained that Madonna's home intruder and burglar Grzegorz Matlok suffered from two serious mental disorders: schizophrenia and erotomania. He believed that Madonna was in love with him and claimed that she had invited him to her house. An analysis of other press reports suggests that Matlok, a visitor from Poland, was homeless, but – except for the hysterical headlines – there is no factual indication that he has ever been a Madonna fan. The Madonna stalker case is the latest in a long line of stories about the celebrity stalking phenomena that portray fandom, at worst, as a monstrous activity. The monstrosity stereotype persists because it normalizes non-fans and reflects the anxieties of contemporary culture. Key cases like this fall apart on closer inspection for a simple reason: there is no inexorable logic of fandom that can lead an otherwise sane person into stalking behaviour. Fame monsters are therefore fantasy cultural constructs assembled from the body parts of the audience in order to express deeper anxieties. Ordinary fans are not potential fame monsters.

Fans become fodder for wider social fantasizing because they make emotional connections through the alienated realm of electronic media. Looking at the way in which viewers understood the truth of what they found in the electronic media, Horton and Wohl said:

> But unlike a similar exemplification of happy sociability in a play or a novel, the television or radio programme is real; that is to say, it is enveloped in the continuing reassurances and gratifications of objective responses. For instance there may be telephone calls to 'outside' contestants. . . . (1956, 223)

This research emerged in an interesting historical context as it was published in the same year that Elvis Presley's controversial performances exploded across the American media. As television took its place alongside cinema and radio, the media landscape was changing rapidly. New kinds of performers and styles of presentation indicated that previously undercapitalized demographic segments (African-Americans, the lower classes, the youth market) now had enough spending power to enter the media market place. Folksy disk jockeys like Dewey Phillips were evidence of a major shift and they started to oust more staid announcers. Each similar reconfiguration of the national mediascape in the last century spawned an army of critics suggesting that society was being hurled into an even more alienated and dystopian future (e.g. Meyrowitz 1985). Seen this way, Horton and Wohl represent the psychological wing of mass cultural criticism, researchers who exploited the mimetic qualities of the mass media to indirectly question the preferences and behaviour of less educated audiences. In more recent years, other critics have warned of the 'dangers' of transmedia worlds as webs of diversion that draw people away from reality (Jenkins 2008, 202). The anxiety beneath the parasocial interaction hypothesis is that 'unreal' celebrities and strangers are actually equal to 'real' family and friends *insofar that they are all ideas in our heads*. We build up a stock of knowledge of *everyone*, from our own parents, partners and children, to global figures like Lady Gaga. If everyone represents a stock of knowledge to us, then one horror is that distant media phantoms can *in theory* become as meaningful and important to us as our nearest and dearest. For most people this remains a theory; indeed, many deepen and extend their connections with those around them by talking about the antics of celebrities. In that respect the exploits of the famous can form a kind of social currency.

Times and ideas have changed a great deal in the last half-century. Some have argued that parasocial relationships are a *normal* part of childhood and adolescence (see Roberts 2007, 56). Furthermore, the digital era promotes **virtual co-presence**: the idea that instant, two way electronic communication lets us *experience togetherness* with geographically separated loved ones. While some have suggested that virtual co-presence destroys real intimacy, in reality it *transforms* daily life (Jenkins 2008, 17). We now live in an era where not only stars but our own family and friends are mediated through e-mail, mobile phones, web cams and other devices (see Garde-Hansen 2011). Contemporary culture has accepted the notion that although mediation may degrade interaction with those around us in the here and now, it also enables us to extend rather than destroy intimacy and to connect with people in places that were previously inaccessible. We actively choose those in our social circle and accept mediation as a dimension of our interaction with them. In Horton and Wohl's world, famous personalities levering the mass broadcast media created their own ideational spaces into which the real audience members were lured. Critics might argue that the process has gone so far that we now take it as second nature. The use of social media, however, also suggests that we are, to an extent, *co-creators* of the media realm, going public and entering into communicative exchange ourselves. What the widespread acceptance of social media shows is that most of us readily accept mediation when physical closeness is impossible. The slippery slope idea suggests that we actually come to *prefer* those kinds of interactions, either as unrequited moments (in the broadcast era) or as a form of hiding ourselves (in the internet age). In that sense, the slope points to the perils of heavy media usage, not fandom per se.

Because society feared female promiscuity, obsessive fans were portrayed as groupies back in the 1960s. The stalker became an important archetype after that because society increasingly came to lament the undeserved ubiquity of celebrity. As Robert Fein and Bryan Vossekuil said in their foreword to the book *Stalking, Threatening and Attacking Public Figures*, 'It may fairly be said that "stalking" became *the crime "celeb"* of the early 1990s' (2008, x; emphasis mine). In their relentless pursuit of a (supposed) course of action, stalkers represent something more symbolic: the sacrifice of privacy symbolized by celebrity itself. If Gzregorz Matlok's supposed 'obsessive fandom' for Madonna was constructed as part of a media discourse that linked normality to celebrity stalking, the anxieties behind it did not come entirely from normal fandom, but instead from a slightly different place. In *The Sun*'s version of Madonna's story:

> The huge home in Marylebone has an array of CCTV cameras and a state-of-the-art alarm. But a senior police source told *The Sun*: 'Something dreadful has happened here. The security around the world's most famous pop star should be impregnable'. (France, 2011)

As an element in a media discourse, the deviant figure of the 'extreme' fan marks out the possibility that celebrity privacy is fully breached, that there is no privacy or dignity left for stars who, as individuals, already have the least private occupations in society. Obsessive fandom therefore gets used to mark out the ever-shrinking and already transgressed boundary that attempts to separate the celebrity's private self from their ever-more public persona. In other words, the popular obsession about celebrity stalking may represent social anxiety, not so much about fandom itself – although it is a convenient scapegoat – but privacy. It dramatizes a *loss of privacy*; an issue that more and more of us face in a digital age where most of the population discloses some form of personal information.

Scary monsters? Mark Chapman and the spectre of 'deranged' fandom

In December 1980, after posing as a fan in front of the Dakota building in New York, Mark David Chapman shot dead John Lennon. Chapman's case is frequently cited as an example of how defective or 'deranged' fandom can find its expression in violent monstrosity. It remains important because it is often used as a touchstone in slippery slope arguments. Laura Wood's 2004 book *Famous Last Words*, described Lennon's killer as a 'deranged fan' (41). Wood's description is typical. Yet Chapman's case was much more complex. The murder holds a fascination precisely because it can so easily – but nevertheless poetically – be read as a fan's revenge, a return of the parasocially repressed: *a fan now exploitatively performing an illusion of intimacy* instead of their star. However, the motivations for Chapman's actions were far more complex than those of a supposedly normal fan who gradually concluded that his idol had failed to deliver. Chapman's journey into murderous madness can only be connected to his previous Beatles fandom if we posit a slippery slope that culminated in his failure to achieve equality with his object. Indeed, *despite* Lennon's willingness to pay him attention – albeit momentarily – by signing his copy of the album *Double Fantasy*, Chapman still killed the singer. Mark Chapman *had* been a Beatles fan a decade before he shot John Lennon. Since then he had become a fan of Todd Rundgren, who actually had a feud with Lennon at one point. Chapman suffered from a major personality disorder which did not spring from his fandom. He heard voices inside his head and took counsel from an internal committee of imagined figures he called the 'Little People'. He dabbled heavily in psychedelics and other drugs, flirted with alcoholism and went through phases of intense desperation. By the time he began to think about killing John Lennon, Chapman had been sectioned in a psychiatric hospital, prayed to Satan in the nude, tormented his wife and engaged in a range of other troubling activities. He was *already* seriously ill. At his trial, the first mental health professional to meet Chapman said he had suffered from confusion and agitation about himself, depression, mood fluctuations, paranoid tendencies, suicidal thinking and rage (see Duffett 2004c). When Chapman became fixated on the singer he then *posed* as fan in order to get close. By that time he was therefore *not* a fan driven insane, but an insane man *pretending* to be a fan in order to meet John Lennon.

If slippery slope thinking cannot offer an adequate explanation for Chapman's actions, there may be other reasons why his case continues to resonate in the popular imagination. Chapman's myth is not so much about fandom as about *the cultural politics of celebrity itself*, and it never quite seems to go away for that reason:

> Cases like the killing of John Lennon fall apart on close examination for a simple reason: there is no inexorable logic of fandom that can lead an otherwise sane person into stalking behaviour. The stereotypes persist because they normalize non-fans and reflect the anxieties of contemporary culture. Back in the 1960s obsessive fans were portrayed as groupies because society feared female promiscuity. The stalker has become a central archetype because we lament the ubiquity of celebrity, the easiness of stardom, and the growing significance of the media in controlling our view of the world. (Duffett 2004c, online)

The idea that psychotic identity could find an outlet in fandom was portrayed elsewhere in popular culture both before and after Lennon's assassination. It is relevant here to say that stereotypical portrayals of the dangers of extreme fandom have often been gendered. Dedicated female fans have been misrepresented in an eroticized way, as groupies (Jenkins 1992, 15). Extreme male fans are often portrayed as comically inadequate or frighteningly disturbed. In a number of *fictional* representations, fans have been portrayed as inhumanly cruel or wicked people, monsters who perhaps use their fandom to grotesquely reference something about themselves.[11] In a classic intertextual scene from *Nil by Mouth* (Oldman 1997), for instance, the drug-taking Danny (played by Steve Sweeny) is stripped to the waist and covered in grotesque tattoos and piercings. As he watches *Apocalypse Now* (Ford Coppola 1979), Danny simultaneously enacts the frenzied monologue uttered by a manic freelance photographer played by Dennis Hopper:

> You know something man, I know something that you don't know. That's right Jack. The man is clear in his mind, but his soul is mad. Oh yeah – He's dying I think. He hates all this. He hates it, but, err, the man's err –Nobody's going to call Jack loud, alright. And a voice, a voice. He likes you because you're still alive. He's got plans for you. Nah – I'm not going to help you. You're going help him, man. You're going to help him. I mean, *what are they going to say when he's gone? He died when it dies, man. What it dies, he dies. What are they going to say about him, what? Are they going to say he was* a kind man, *he was* a wise man? *He had plans, he had wisdom. Bullshit, man! Am I going to be the one who set him straight? Look at me: Wrong!* . . . You . . . Haha haha haha.

It is hard to convey the changes in volume, tone and urgency that characterize this scene, which ends with creepy music, maniacal laughter and Danny pointing at young Billy, who laughs uncomfortably at the performance. As one commentator explained: 'The camera lingers, too, with stubborn patience on the scene where a tattooed low-lifer picks fleas from a puppy while mimicking line-by-line, as he watches Dennis Hopper's spaced-out stichomythia in *Apocalypse Now*'.[12] It is evident that Danny is using his recital of the Vietnam film as a vehicle for his own psychotic anger and aggression. His acting out is also an indication of his fandom, because he has evidently watched *Apocalypse Now* enough to be able to effortlessly repeat every line. Feature films often associate male fandom with 'wimpish' masculinity; *Nil By Mouth* is therefore quite unusual in its portrayal. Nevertheless, popular representations have sometimes drawn on the slippery slope model to connect the portrayal of male fandom with a potential for psychosis. Indeed, *perceptions of stars' anxieties* often inspire these fictional representations: TV shows, films and books that manifest stalking as the result of a social fantasy. In Bob Randall's *The Fan* (1978), for example, Douglas is an admirer of Sally Ross, an ex-movie star who acts in a Broadway musical. The book uses various correspondence between its main characters as a device to follow Douglas's descent into murderous resentment. His letters start in January 1976 with a simple request for a photograph. By the end of May he has defecated and urinated all over her dressing room, asked to borrow a Luger pistol and written, 'Dear Bitch, Well it's all been too tiring. What has? Why, deciding how to kill you, my dear' (1978, 197). *The Fan* seems rather misnamed because to be a fan means *loving* the performer and understanding where the lines are drawn. However, coming two years before Mark Chapman's notorious actions, the book suggests that Chapman realized a fantasy that was *already circulating in the popular imagination.*[13] Because Chapman's retrospectively self-acknowledged, twisted motivations offer a moral perspective on fame and celebrity – rather than just because he had previously been a Beatles fan – he is seen as an archetypal case of monstrous fandom.

Given the frequent discussion of cases like John Lennon's death, we have to ask why readers might want to hear about celebrities being stalked. The murder was loaded with symbolic resonance for many reasons. By turning Lennon into a martyr, the murder aligned his star myth with an iconic, selflessness message. That the ex-Beatle's killer justified his actions by saying he felt betrayed by the star's 'phoney' social utopianism is particularly interesting insofar that it comments on the idea of stardom as a false promise. When Lennon was shot it meant that the 1960s died: the assassination marked a turning point between naïve countercultural optimism and a new era of materialism. While Chapman said that he felt justified – at least superficially – by Lennon's hypocritical materialism, he also realized that he had, in retrospect, became a 'somebody' by shooting a much-loved public figure. Chapman's quest can therefore be seen as exploring the notion of fame as a universal currency: there for the taking no matter what the means. In that sense the phantom behind Lennon's killing represents an archetypally large, ugly and frightening *imaginary* creature whose role in the public imagination is to associate monstrosity, celebrity and 'deranged' fandom.

Twenty five years after he shot Lennon, fictionalized images of Mark Chapman made an appearance in Anglo-American popular culture when two feature films, *Chapter 27* (Schaefer 2006) and *The Killing of John Lennon* (Piddington, 2006) were created to explore the case. Starring Jared Leto and Lindsay Lohan, *Chapter 27* billed itself as 'an illuminating descent into the mind of a deranged fan'. The other film starred Jonas Ball in the lead role and described its protagonist as a narcissistic celebrity stalker. Its DVD cover read, '*The Killing of John Lennon* . . . does not set out to condone or exonerate the shooting of Lennon or his killer's desire for fame'. Both movies recounted the same scenes and attempted to tell Chapman's story from his own perspective. They used his interviews as a basis for the character narrating in his own voice; indeed, much of Chapman's personality is conveyed in *Chapter 27* by Leto's creepy, spaced-out whisper. In both films we follow Chapman fighting with his impulse *not* to shoot Lennon. By adopting this approach both *Chapter 27* and *The Killing of John Lennon* encourage us to explore how far we can empathize with Chapman in his alienation, opposition to hypocrisy and internal struggle. Since they were based on Chapman's own interviews, both films had to jettison the slippery slope idea, though each highlighted a supposed residue of Beatles fandom inside the protagonist to lament the sheer inexplicability of his actions. In *Chapter 27*, the Chapman character says, 'I used to love the Beatles. I still love the Beatles. I swear to God, I really do. Sometimes I felt like the Beatles music was made just for me'. Meanwhile, in *The Killing of John Lennon* when a police man asks, 'So, why'd ya do it?' he explains vacantly, 'I like John Lennon'. In a moment of great pathos, the now even more vacant officer replies, 'So do I'.

Rather than directly referencing the idea of the deranged fan, the two assassination dramas express their concerns about extreme fandom *through* an analysis of elements of Chapman's personality and the popular reaction to him. Both films oppose Chapman to the more normal female fans who linger outside the Dakota building, fans not inclined to unpredicable and psychotic over-reactions. In *Chapter 27*, Chapman's conversation in a diner with Lindsay Lohan's 'normal' fan character references his advocacy of determination, self-help and the power of emotional conviction; it is as if his personality is given to a form of *fundamentalism*. This sense of emotional conviction conjoins 'extreme' fandom with fundamentalism by making *both* seem problematic from a rational viewpoint. Meanwhile, in the other film, Chapman's mood touches a kind of fundamentalism after he explains that the murder had been fated to advertise Salinger's book: 'I became europhic, knowing that there was a reason beyond myself for what I had done'. Cultural conviction (whether fannish or religious) supposedly evokes questions about where to place personal agency and individual responsibility here, in a parallel way to portrayals of fandom as addicted or possessed. Indeed, the inner conflict that plays out in each film is referenced by Chapman's alienated struggle with his own agency. In *Chapter 27* he explains:

It was like this crazy stage had been set up and all the actors were coming and going. I was merely an image, a tin man playing a Beatles fan, playing an autograph seeker. And underneath I was a boiling cauldron of rage, but no one could tell a God damned thing.

In *The Killing of John Lennon,* the protagonist explains similarly, 'It felt like I was in a movie'. His statement to the police leaves more clues: 'I didn't want to kill anybody and I really don't know why I did it. I asked God to help me, but we are all responsible for our own actions'. Before finally undergoing Christian exorcism, he explains, 'I was not mad. I was blessed'.

In *The Killing of John Lennon* we learn that Chapman's first defence lawyer resigned in a hail storm of threats from irate Beatles fans. After showing rough television footage of mourning fans, the film includes a voiceover from a newscaster who says, 'The feeling is of tremendous loss and these people feel very personally'. Other reporters later add, 'The threat of a lynching is almost too much for the police,' and, 'they fear the fans might decide to storm the hospital'. In that respect, although Chapman's actions were evidently atypical for a fan, and at least partially explained by his disturbed personality, the film's final gambit is to suggest that the fans' emotional response to his heinous act comes from the same register of base emotion that motivated the murder in the first place. Fandom thus becomes visible as a manifestation of the same destructive, Dionysian force that compels the lynch mob; the film thus achieves the elision between normal fandom and its deranged other which Chapman's own inner conflict can never quite manage. As the lead actor, Jonas Ball, explains, 'normal kids don't grow up to kill ex-Beatles'. The implication is instead that they grow up to love the Beatles and become so invested that they lash out in hate at anyone who disturbs their dream. As a crowd, here and elsewhere, fan masses have been portrayed as a collective beast that is daunting in size: an irrational mob, baying to rip its quarry apart. According to sociologist Kerry Ferris 'in a contemporary culture in which celebrity stalking is a ubiquitous part of the zeitgeist' (2011, 29), outsiders – including celebrities themselves – can see the fans' acts of collective and individual enthusiasm as strange, obsessive, invasive and threatening.

Mark Chapman is a real person whose ugly and pointless crime meant that he has been denied parole for over a decade. The monstrous 'deranged fan' role is something he has never fully inhabited, however, because, upon inspection it works primarily as a myth about celebrity. If Lennon's murder found its symbolic resonance in marking a shift from the anti-materialist 1960s to the ultra-materialist 1980s, by the mid-noughties its cinematic representation offered evidence of a social fascination with stalking that indirectly critiqued the vacuity of contemporary celebrity culture. In an era where seemingly undeserving glitterati from Paris Hilton to Victoria Beckham found fame just for being themselves, and where *Celebrity Big Brother* (2001–) and its variants made the rejection of celebrities into a spectator sport, stalking was symbolically refurbished as a fulfilment of collective fantasy. Capitalizing on the sixth occasion that Chapman was denied parole for his crime, echoing Lady Gaga's album, the Salon journalist Mary Elizabeth Williams (2010) called Chapman a 'fame monster'.

Fandom as normal psychology

Pyschoanalysis is an intellectual and therapeutic approach that aims to help people by making them aware of their repressed fears and conflicts. Academic opposition to it suggests that the method dehistoricizes and universalizes individual subjectivity. Insofar that psychoanalysis can be framed as a mode of enquiry with a more historically specific aim (describing how *Western* society has shaped its inhabitants to fit its requirements) the charge of ahistoricism is somewhat unfair. More fundamentally, each psychoanalytic school potentially remakes what it sees in its own image. There is a danger that any tendency to see all phenomena through a psychoanalytic frame *imposes* precisely the psychic structures that pyschoanalysis claims to unearth. Given these issues one might ask why psychoanalysis has been useful to fan theorists. If popular representations have often taken delight in locating fans as a dangerously irrational other, academic accounts have been much more mixed. Several fandom scholars have turned to psychoanalysis, not as a way to pathologize fandom but as an explanation of ordinary mental processes that might account for the phenomenon. Psychoanalysis remains a powerful and controversial mode of explanation and has promted debates over whether it can convincingly account for the processes that create fan phenomena. Ethical opposition against the practice suggests that it is an elitist form of criticism that 'reads' the unconscious of the other, allowing 'us' academics to read 'them' but not vice versa. More bluntly, it is associated with the troubled psyche and therefore arguably pathologizes fandom, suggesting that it springs from a kind of inner unhappiness. A psychoanalytic approach might elevate fandom beyond any specific objects and social contexts, but fails to account for it as an everyday process, a normal activity (Sandvoss 2005a, 94).

Fans themselves sometimes use psychological and even pathological language; one TV science-fiction fan said online, 'I am insanely obsessed. I hope to NEVER be cured' (quoted in Hills 2002a, 180). Another television show enthusiast explained to Harrington and Bielby, 'I am painfully aware of [soaps'] faults . . . yet I still get hooked from time to time' (1995, 93). Other fans like fiction writer M. Fae Glasgow have used an even more elaborate psychoanalytic vocabulary to describe their practices (see Sandvoss 2005a,

69). Yet many fans are openly hostile to the prospect of their interests being dissected by psychoanalytic researchers. Fandom is, however, often experienced as an emotional activity. Emotions are not just physical disturbances of the body: they follow from beliefs and thoughts. In theory, psychoanalysis may help to create a more emotionally engaged depiction of individual fans. Therefore to talk about fandom we may need to keep both individual psychology and its cultural context in motion. According to Matt Hills:

> Any 'single-lensed' theoretical approach (i.e. 'sociological' or 'psychoanalytic') to fandom remains incapable of accounting for the social and cultural regularities of fan cultures, and for fan cultures' dialectic of value, and thus for fans' intensely felt 'possession' and 'ownership' of their fan object. (2002a, 63)

Although, for a number of reasons, interpreting the fantasies, motivations and desires can leave researchers uncomfortable – defining whether their results are 'true' if they are also unique and unreproducible, for instance – psychoanalysis may still be a useful investigative tool because ideas about the social may not be alone enough to explain an individual's continuous engagement with his or her object. Fan theorist Cornel Sandvoss avers, 'To fully understand fandom and the relationships between fan and object of fandom, we thus have to understand the psychological foundations of the self' (2005a, 68). If that is a given, the question then becomes one of how to understand *the fannish self*. As Matt Hills suggests 'There are probably as many schools of pyschoanalysis as there are fan cultures' (2002a, 95). Most of these have emerged directly or indirectly from Freud's seminal studies. Freud argued that individuals repressed their sexual instincts in order to fit in with social and familial structures. Sandvoss has suggested that attention to Freud allows researchers to see fans' searches for pleasure – even of a sexual kind – as a reflection of the universal human condition (2005a, 71). Since Freud's fascination with disorders like hysteria might pathologize fandom, fan studies researchers have usually chosen *not* to focus on his work, or that of his famous disciple, Jacques Lacan. Instead they have primarily looked at ideas from later psychoanalysts such as Melanie Klein and Donald Winnicott. For Sandvoss the benefit of these theorists is that their work enables us to see fans as subjects who have a dynamic sense of self and use their cultural interests as tools (2005a, 79). In comparison, the Freudian conception of the adult self tends to be relatively static.

Cornel Sandvoss (2005a) has, so far, been the main cultural studies writer to apply Klein's work to media fandom. For Sandvoss, fandom is based on objective physical, social and economic distance *combined with an experience of intimacy*: a contradiction that generates much of his discussion. A controversial aspect of psychoanalysis, then, is the way that it contextually frames personal fandom:

> There is a second form of narcissism in fandom, more closely linked to forms of self-reflection, which does not presuppose that fan texts are performed in front of an actual audience . . . the first and foremost audience for the performance of fans is the fan him- or herself. I am thus proposing a model of fandom as a form of narcissist self-reflection not between fans and their social environment but between the fan and his or her object of fandom. (98)

Sandvoss appears partially right here: it is important to understand that fans recognize their own fandom as an aspect of their personal identities, and that they can engage with stars or auteurs in ways that feel intensely personal. Fan researchers have tended to focus on agency and activity, and neglected structure and object (93). Is there something inside each fan, then, that organizes his or her connection to a hero? Back in the 1920s, Freud posited that the ego of each individual is partly motivated by an impulse towards death. In the Kleinian model, the death drive causes such extreme anxiety that the individual's ego splits and enters a paranoid-schizoid state from where it starts engaging with other human objects. In other words, for Klein we are all in denial of our own natural anxieties: to have a paranoid-schizoid mind is not so much a disorder as a normal condition. Two important mechanisms then allow us to cope: each child can channel 'bad' internal feelings through **projection**, and integrate 'good' aspects of external objects with their own split self through **introjection** (see 80).

As a psychological phenomenon, the process of projection involves seeing the world through learned presuppositions. It is an inevitable process that happens when individuals perceive reality through the filter of their own understanding, in effect exporting their mental structures on to a perceived world that then seems to affirm those assumptions. For Klein, 'bad' parts are dissociated from the self and projected on to an object outside. Since the boundary between the self and object gets blurred, it becomes a site of anxiety and perceived as requiring control. Projection therefore is a prototypical form of paranoid-schizoid behaviour. Although we all have an internal dialogue and capacity for self-consciousness, the idea of two inner selves only emerges if the self is under stress (Hills 2002a, 96). For Sandvoss, fan objects are 'not simply points of identification – they are extensions of the fan's very self' (2005a, 102). At an extreme, this idea is associated with the notion of the **blank slate**: that stars are essentially devoid of meaning and function as empty vessels upon which the audience can *project* desire on the basis of its own need. The theory draws on correct assumptions (that stars can be read in different ways, that meaning-making happens in the heads of audience members, that projection is a crucial psychological phenomenon) but it forgets that stars are not endlessly polysemic, already have personal and social identities and that shared interpretations of star images circulate as discursive resources which help to guide interpretation. According to Sandvoss, (2005a) 'However, it is not only the fan who shapes her object of fandom, but the object of fandom which shapes its fans' (81). Moreover, although stars are predominantly 'good' objects, they can also function as 'bad' ones who absorb negative projections. Under a section marked *Fan Violence* Sandvoss explains, 'processes of projection and introjections in fandom cannot only manifest a bond between the fan and object world (and its dominant social system), but can equally function to construct a hated "other"' (82). Anthony Elliot uses the notoriously scathing critical music biographer Albert Goldman as an example of someone practicing projection, since Goldman's quest to 'know' his celebrity subjects – notably Elvis and John Lennon – became the premise for him to project his own fantasies on to them (1999, 26). Equally, Mark Chapman's incomprehensible motivation for assassinating Lennon can only be understood if we see it as the result of Chapman's inner fantasies. As Sandvoss notes, Elliot does not distinguish Chapman's *processes* of projection from those of normal fans, even though the contents are vastly different (2005a, 84). If projection is a process that everyone undertakes, however, the real question is why theorists would want to talk about it specifically in relation to *fans*, rather than any other groups or individuals. A focus on projection continually returns us to the issue of parasocial interaction. Since fans may never have personally met their object of interest, in this view it is not so much whether they project – we all do – as whether their own processes of projection have then been exploited, somehow, to manipulate them.

A second Kleinian process is that of introjection, or 'role modelling' as it is more widely known. 'Introjection' sounds like ingestion, a process of taking in, but it really examines how fans *use* their heroes as idealized guides and mentors. In other words, rather than becoming complete replicas of a hero, followers may potentially want just to *do what he/she does* (see Cavicchi 1998, 140–2). The interesting thing about this is that it puts a focus on how fans might *do* things with their connections, not simply why they hold them. We can see a form of everyday introjection in the way that people adopt catch phrases, quirks, hair styles and other elements from leads set by famous people. To perform like – or counterperform to – a star is to participate in a social world that they create. Fans can also role model themselves on idealized forms of identity conveyed in specific star images (Sandvoss 2005a, 82). Film studies theorist Jackie Stacy (1994) talks about four extra-cinematic identification fantasies: pretending, resembling, imitating and copying. Stacey found that despite the 'other worldly' nature of stars, spectators regularly aim to adopt aspects of their gender identities. An intense relationship with a particular star may offer fantasies of personal transformation. By bringing the star or stars into the self, many report that they were able to take on their attributes and characteristics. Women said that they are able to gain personal confidence or fashion a more edgy or rebellious form of femininity. Like anyone else in the modern world, fans can certainly be involved in processes of self-fashioning which can involve using stars as resources. **Cosplay** means 'costume play': dressing up as famous characters. While introjection might result in a range of practices right up to impersonation and cosplay, its more common and subtle associated processes can involve an admiration and recognition of shared values. A good example of this comes from Nick Stevenson's work on Bowie fans. As Stevenson explains:

> There was a growing awareness throughout the interviews that, for many of the male fans, Bowie operated as a kind of father figure . . . We might explore these questions from the viewpoint of the often derided men's movement . . . By choosing David Bowie as their 'guide' it might be argued that many of the men are responding creatively to the so-called crisis in masculinity without seeking recourse in more overtly patriarchal images or simply denying their maleness. (2009, 90)

In this view, Bowie becomes a kind of inspirational resource available for consultation during difficult times much like a teacher or guide. In the language of self-help, the star becomes a member of the fan's 'mastermind group', perhaps especially relevant because he/she has been personally chosen by the fan. While generalization is rarely of value – undoubtedly *not all* fans use Bowie as a father figure – the idea suggests that he might demonstrate some success strategies to male fans that are otherwise less obvious. That notion echoes a classic but largely discredited paradigm of media research from the 1970s – uses and gratifications – the difference being that Stevenson is not saying that patriarchal guidance is a natural reason for Bowie to exist. He goes as far, though, as saying that Bowie's image corresponds to the crisis in masculinity which makes him a figure towards whom male fans gravitate. Listening to someone for advice is not the same as emulating them. A theoretical emphasis on introjection can lead us to assume, perhaps wrongly, that fans want to *become* their idols. My own research found that fans often actually want to occupy the role of a *friend* or simply that of *a much more recognizably successful fan*: say, backstage or on the front row when the star walks on the red carpet. Those dreams may seem pedestrian to outsiders, but they show that fans have an interest in maintaining their roles and can get an immense thrill from the way fan-star relations are currently organized. Attention to introjection focuses us on the way that fans can collectively *idealize* their heroes: 'Fan criticisms involve shaping an image of "ideal" [Doctor] Who, a kind of Platonic essence of the series (which may never have been realized fully in any one story)' (Hills 2010b, 5). In tune with Hills' theory, *Doctor Who* fan Elizabeth Bear has said of her television hero, 'I prefer to think that we can learn from him, grow up, take responsibility for ourselves . . . when we are our best selves we're very much like him: ingenious, adventurous, lucky, energetic, damn-the-torpedoes, humane. And aspiring to be more' (Bear 2010, 16–17).

Some scholars have been reluctant to engage in psychoanalysis for fear that it could pathologize fandom and focus too much on individual motivations. Fans also operate socially, of course, but their passions do, however, function as *intermediate spaces*, not just between the individual's self and outer reality but also between that self and the star as other (Sandvoss 2005a, 90). Beyond the mechanisms outlined by Klein, some researchers have explored the ideas of Donald Woods Winnicott. Rather than conceptualizing the self as split and struggling, Winnicott instead shows it engaged in a natural process of self development. He argues that when children play they enter into a state akin to concentration. They then focus on one physical object that has inter-subjective status. This play thing is *transitional*, taking up the role of their first 'me and not me' object. For Winnicott, the self's 'lack' of wholeness is therefore mediated by the use of an object as an intermediate space where inner life and external reality merge together. The transitional object is *acknowledged* as belonging to an external reality but *experienced* as a safe object of attachment.

Winnicott's ideas, if selectively adopted, suggest that we continually form emotional attachments as a way of maintaining our psychological health, a reading that escapes the idea of fandom as deficient or pathological. As Matt Hills argues, 'All of us, throughout our lives, draw on cultural artifacts as "transitional objects"' (2002a, 106). He takes this further by then *defining* fandom as attachment:

A fan culture is formed around any given text when this text has functioned as a *pto* (proper transitional object) in the biography of a number of individuals; individuals who remain attached to this text by virtue of the fact that it continues to exist as an element in their cultural experience. (108)

The idea of fandom as play with transitional objects is interesting as it enables us to escape from unrealistic stereotypes that focus on fandom as something that comes from either being duped, passive or deranged. Harrington and Bielby (1995) claim that theory has often explained away or over-rationalized fan experiences. They employ the notion of the transitional object to examine soap fan culture. According to Hills:

> Fan cultures, that is to say, are neither rooted in an 'objective' interpretive community or an 'objective' set of texts, but nor are they atomized collections of individuals whose 'subjective' passions and interests happen to overlap. Fan cultures are both found and created, and it is this inescapable tension which supports my use of Winnicott's work, as well as supporting what I have termed the 'dialectic of value' that is enacted by fan cultures. (2002a, 113)

Winnicott recognizes a natural vulnerability felt by all human beings. His notion allows us to see how fans might address this natural anxiety and build social networks around shared interests. It also resonates with accounts by those fans who claim to like celebrities that are approachable, passionate and sincere. Because the idea of the transitional object is associated with a specific stage in the development of childhood, however, it implies a state of regression and cannot fully account for fan interests found later than in childhood (see Sandvoss 2005a, 87–91). Neither does Winnicott's schema fully explain how people transfer from their proper transitional object to an objective outer world of social organization (Hills 2002a, 107). One avenue opened by the idea is to see fandom as a kind of safe haven for the knocks that life can throw at each of us. Some fans recognize that fractions of the fan base find vicarious comfort and escape in following a star. As Sandvoss explains:

> Fandom provides one of most stable eggs in the [self-esteem] basket . . . in this sense fandom is not an articulation of inner needs and drives, but is itself constitutive of the self. Being a fan in this sense reflects and constructs the self. (2005a, 48)

This is an interesting idea, but it does not quite show what separates fandom from any other type of relationship or field of cultural activity such as work, love or religion. It also implies that fans are *lacking*, in the sense that they choose to return to fandom as a kind of refuge. There may be other, very different ways to conceptualize what fandom means to the individual.

According to Sandvoss (2005a), psychoanalytic studies of popular culture *focus too often on the text*, locating meaning within its structure and ignoring the psychology of specific readers (73). Without such perspectives, however, media texts structured on a symbolic level might otherwise be hard to understand. Psychoanalysis may also help us investigate *individual fandom* as a reflection of each individual's personal psychology. If the paradigm *can* often produce compelling explanations, what are its limits in relation to the study of fan culture? Matt Hills has argued psychoanalysis has some significant limitations as a method. By focusing on fandom *purely as fantasizing* there is a danger that psychoanalytic researchers have artificially isolated individual fans and discounted other aspects of the phenomenon of fandom, like social communications, practices and discourses. As Hills suggests, 'Kleinian accounts of fandom seem unable to recognize fan culture as anything other than a confirmation of key Kleinian terms' (2002a, 97). Such frames locate fandom as a compensation for personal lack generated by psychological processes like anxiety. There may be scope however to view the emotions manifest in fans' lives as more of a *boost* that a lack, something *productively added* rather than intrinsically needed. Hills notes:

> Psychoanalytic accounts have generally been tailored to the cut of (ideological) academic arguments and moral dualisms, constantly placing fans as deficient, and constantly decrying the possibilities of fan 'knowledge' in favour of an emphasis on fan affects, emotions or fantasies (which of course, do not possess the status of [academic] 'knowledge'). (2002a, 104)[14]

As soon as we move beyond each individual to talk about either followings for specific objects or media fandom in general *as collective process*, something is, nevertheless, lost in making psychological generalizations. Interestingly, as Hills notes 'Psychoanalyses of fandom have been thin on the ground' (95). The leading fan studies scholar, Henry Jenkins, for example, carefully avoids a psychological approach to fandom in his work. According to Hills, Jenkins has seen non-fans in psychological terms – projecting their anxieties on to fandom, for instance – while he has generally avoided any examination of the individual or collective psychology of fans themselves (9).

Whether or not we agree with the charges of circularity and imposition, psychoanalysis *has* formed a widespread mode of explanation, socially shared in a way that has paralleled the historical existence of fandom itself. Freudian ideas were 'in the air' throughout the twentieth century, circulating and becoming a kind of touchstone for theorists in public life. Attention to them *as a discursive resource* may help to explain a great deal about why fandom has been interpreted in this particular way.

As well emphasizing questionable ideas such as the slippery slope, celebrity worship and media effects, one of the problems of the pathological tradition is that it posits a *singular type* of identification. The Weberian notion of **ideal type** suggests that sometimes a common feature can be misrecognized as a definitive one: in this case, a range of *different* fan interests in a star or franchise can be hidden in one generalization. Used to theorize star phenomena, psychoanalysis never escapes this drive towards inappropriate generalization. The real challenge to fan researchers may be to see how far they can go in conceptualizing their object *without* recourse to psychoanalytic explanations, not because those explanations cannot grasp the symbolic dimension of chosen *texts* or represent a limited assessment of the minds of *individuals*, but because they can easily be misused to *generalize* individual psychology in a way that forgets fandom is a sociocultural phenomenon mediating between wider elements that are only connected indirectly to the depths of the mind. These elements, whether discourses, practices or social identities, frequently *make connections between* the private and public, the individual and collective.

5

How do people become fans?

Starting points

- What can we learn from ideas like contagion, taste and emotional affect about the way that people become fans?
- Is fandom a substitute for religion?
- When it comes to personal identity, how can we combine ideas that say fandom is both a journey and a destination?

Gregory Peck: Hello there. You came all the way from London [to America] for this evening, did you now?

Peck's fan: Absolutely. I'm speechless – I don't know quite what to say.

Gregory Peck: So tell me about yourself?

Peck's fan: Well, I've admired you for many years. I wanted to see for myself whether you really are what you appear to be on-screen. Tonight has proved to me that you are what you appear to be.

Gregory Peck: (chuckling) Well I hope so. I hope it isn't a put on for all these years.

Peck's fan: No. That's what I wanted to find out for myself. I thought, 'The hell with it: I'm going to blow all my savings and I'm going to going to come here and see for myself what you are like'. And I'm so glad I did; it's been the experience of a lifetime.

Gregory Peck: (shaking hands) God bless you. Thank you for coming.

A Conversation with Gregory Peck (KOPPLE, 2001)

Media fans are just people. Like anyone else, they can be rational, biased, stubborn, critical, tired, liberal or open-minded. One of the central differences between fans and other people, however, is that they have experienced a meaningfully different *feeling* to others and cannot always rationally explain *why*. Researchers have described this as a kind of self-absent quality. A feature-length documentary called *A Conversation with Gregory Peck* (Kopple 2001) was made using footage of the classic screen icon's retirement tour of America. In the documentary, Peck recounted his tales about life in Hollywood to live audiences of his now-middle-aged fans. One lady, who came all the way from England, met her idol backstage and entered into a friendly conversation with him. What is evident from the conversation was that Peck's fan was achieving a lifelong dream and discovering whether he actually fulfilled his own media image. She was not just emotionally excited by the encounter, but *seemed* self-absent too. In the midst of the contradictory – but I am sure much anticipated – moment when her dream came true, she neither knew quite what to say nor did she begin the process of trying to relate to Peck as one ordinary person to another, even though she finally got a chance. Peck's invitation for her to talk about her own life was met with her restating her role as his fan. From one perspective this seems like irrational subservience. From another, it can be seen as a logical attempt to maintain the thrilling *consented inequality* that is an essential part of the star-fan divide. In that sense her fandom functioned as much *for her* as it did for him. Their mutual encounter also opens up questions: Why she was a Peck fan? What role did emotion play in her fandom in the first place? Had she set Peck up as a religious idol? And, central to this chapter, how do people like her – that is, people like us – become fans?

Any discussion of how anyone becomes a fan has to contain a theory of why fans *are who they are* and why they *do what they do*. Most researchers examine the fan community or its representative individuals, as if personal fandom had always existed and was a timeless, all-encompassing identity. The origins of each individual's fandom therefore represent an 'elephant in the room' in fan research. One perspective on this is to say that real life is much more complex than any theory, so our time might be better spent in situ examining the meanings and politics of real historical moments experienced by actual audience members rather than trying to devise a master plan. However, popular theories proliferate in the absence of any convincing explanatory framework that accounts for new personal fandom as a biographic transition. In other words researchers are failing to fill a popular demand and leave their object wide open to crude stereotyping. What follows will draw on academic arguments from media research about taste, contagion, affect and religion. My aim is partly to clear a path for two additional contributions to the field. The first suggests that researchers could productively examine one element from the influential sociologist Emile Durkheim's notion of religion to explain the emotional 'buzz' when fans meet their heroes. The second contribution suggests that when people become fans they enter a 'knowing field,' (i.e. a field of emotional knowing): a terrain of conviction that defines their fannish identity. Both these ideas aim to avoid the reductionist view that fandom is primarily about fascination/ obsession (*entirely* personal) or about contagion/hysteria (*entirely* social). If we understand it as *both* personal and social, where each dimension is experienced *through* the other, then the real question becomes how to bring the personal and social together in a productive way that unravels the mysteries of the phenomena.

Beyond contagion

In his book-length discussion of fan cultures, one of the questions asked by Matt Hills (2002a, 88) was how personal fandom starts. How does one from any number of mine texts become *mine* and start *my* fandom? Why do only particular performances light my fire? There have been many answers to that question. In his classic research on music listening, Theodor Adorno (1938/2001) suggested that jitterbug enthusiasts produced their own fannish enthusiasm as an advertisement for the wares they consumed and thus aimed to 'infect' those around them. Common sense suggests there may be something in what he is saying. Indeed, one of the useful things about the idea of contagion is that it implies a significant *experiential* difference between the individual's state before and after the start of their fandom. Contagion is a common colloquial explanation of fandom, but how useful is it in explaining *precisely* how people become fans?

Contagion-based arguments are deceptive as they smuggle a series of assumptions into the discussion that may not be helpful. By suggesting that individuals are vulnerable victims they associate fandom with pathology. They also imply that fandom is merely about being in the right place at the right time. If the idea of contagion suggests that a fan can be 'contaminated' by each new interest then it appears to strip them of their agency. Yet it is also true that the beginning of any fannish attachment can feel *overwhelming*. Contagion seems impersonal in implying that *any* individual can be 'bitten' by the bug of a fan interest. Unless we accept the metaphor of immunity as something more than a blunt figure of speech, it fails to explain why some individuals *do not* become fans. Contagion also arguably implies that fandom is 'contracted' with relative speed primarily due to 'exposure' to an outside source. Sometimes media genres such as melodrama are described as having a contagious tendency in that they seem to be able to convey emotion from the screen to the audience by staging a compelling series of dramatic events (for a critical discussion see Hills 2010b, 101). More crudely, such ideas point down a path that leads to the notion that heavy metal songs, violent films or other contentious media products are to blame for *making* people commit terrifying acts of evil. **Media effects arguments** like these place causation in to the hands of products themselves. We should be wary of making such claims: they fail to see that audience members have a degree of choice and responsibility when it comes to their own actions, even when they are informed by the media or use products as an inspirational resource (see Barker & Brooks 1998 for an extended discussion). Also, ideas about contagion – as Sarah Ahmed points out – see emotion merely as an unchanging social property able to be passed unproblematically from one body to the next (2004, 10). For Ahmed, emotion creates the very surfaces and boundaries that allow all kinds of objects to be delineated (10). In other words, it is not a relay baton so much as tool for understanding what matters. In light of these general warning signs, it may be possible to start analysing key moments to mark out the role of 'contagion' in interpersonal encounters that have led to people finding their fandom.

In this section I will draw on Thomas and O'Shea's 2010 book *Chicks Dig Timelords* because the first person essays are by *non-academic* contributors describing various experiences of fan initiation. A first example suggests that potential fans sometimes feel moved when they realize the sheer *numeric* size of a particular fan base:

> *Star Trek* fandom lured me in for a time, mostly by simple fact that most of my friends were active in it . . . But *Trek* palled – for which I'm relieved, given how it's all turned out – and I found myself in a rather strange position. *I was a fan without fandom.* Fortunately that didn't last long. PBS lured me back to *Doctor Who* with Sunday night reruns. The show's charms prevailed against half a decade of entrenched cynicism, and I shamefacedly admitted that I had treated it unkindly. Then a friend convinced me to visit Gallifrey One, a *Doctor Who* convention in Los Angeles, whereupon I learned that the fandom still thrived. Hello, thought I. Maybe there's still some fun to be had here. And, unlike other fandoms, the fact that I was female seemed quite incidental. . . . (Mead 2010, 56; emphasis mine)

If Johanna Mead's use of terms like 'lured' and 'charms' implies seduction and contagion, there is also something more at work here. Her idea of being 'a fan without fandom' is fascinating because it suggests that telefantasy fandom (at least) might be more of a *learned predisposition* towards media consumption than a personal epiphany. However, one can never recognize oneself as 'a fan without fandom' *before* the first time one is a fan; the first episode seems to come quite out of the blue. What Mead is therefore talking about is actually that she had *previously* experienced fannish pleasures from her engagement with a particular media genre, and she wanted to *rediscover* those pleasures with a new object of interest.

As Adorno has suggested, the dedication of existing fans – if they are like us or what we aspire to be – can at least act as an indication that something is *worthy of closer attention*. For instance, eventual *Doctor Who* fan Tara O'Shea was intrigued when she met an alluring stranger named Fred who dressed in a home-knitted scarf at a sci-fi convention: 'I decided afterward that a show that inspired such loyalty and passion had to have something going for it. Intrigued, I started watching on my local PBS broadcasts of the show, and peppered Fred with questions . . .' (2010, 98). On one level this might seem like a classic case of contagion, but Tara did not say that Fred's fandom *caused* her own; he only *prompted* her to investigate the material. The process extends across close relationships too. Helen Kang recalled, 'I wanted to be part of [my friend] Robert's fandom, too' (2010, 41). As part of the Music in Daily Life Project at SUNY in Buffalo, Daniel Cavicchi also found listeners who discovered artists in parallel with their siblings. One woman, for instance, discussed how she discovered several artists such as Joni Mitchell at the same time as her sister, and she felt a sense of 'female camaraderie' about them (1998, 180). This kind of camaraderie inspires people to explore their siblings' record collections as a form of peer identification, whether at the time or later in nostalgic reverie.

Another relevant example is that parental or romantic relations can trigger what appear to be processes of contagion. Couples often look for, and find, shared objects. As Lynne Thomas explained:

And then I fell in love with a *Doctor Who* fan. Michael had his work cut out for him – I didn't even know what that mean, to be a fan, in the active fandom sense of the word. He slowly introduced me into media properties that had fandoms we could enjoy together, like *Xena: Warrior Princess*. Later, we added *Buffy*, *Angel*, *Firefly* and *The Avengers*, along with *Doctor Who* (2010, 81).

What is interesting here is that Lynne and Michael's relationship is the pretext for investigating a common object. They both assume that finding something appealing in the same series would deepen the bond between them. Indeed, many couples meet and marry through fan communities. Their shared fandom is taken as an indicator of compatibility. A common focus also helps to establish intimacy by providing something that they can both enjoy. More work needs to be done on the way that individuals explore media culture on self-motivated quests to understand their nearest and dearest, or dearly departed. Equally, parents can try to hand down fannish passions as gifts for their children. Kate Bush scholar Laura Vroomen noted that fans who passed on their musical taste to their children or stepchildren were not just securing the ongoing existence of the fan base; they were establishing a bond and a teaching relationship that allowed them to share knowledge within their family environment (see 2004, 244). Vroomen's analysis is interesting here because it focuses on fans' motives for socially declaring their interests. It raises the issue of how fandom functions and is used within an immediate social environment, in this case the family. Liz Myles has discussed how her mother had been an avid *Doctor Who* fan since the series began in 1963:

> She made sure that my sister and I were brought up on a steady stream of nineties VHS releases. It wasn't a complete success: my sister thought all this space and time adventuring was a lot of daft nonsense (though that didn't stop her flailing in terror at Haemovores in 'The Curse of Fenric'), but I was convinced that *Doctor Who* was surely the most brilliant and exciting story ever told. (2010, 137)

Myles' story shows that because each instance depends on the personality of the would-be fan, contagion is not a fully adequate explanation. If it were universally the case, everyone exposed to a product would become interested. Such accounts begin to raise significant issues for the contagion theory.

There are also many subtle problems with the contagion idea that collectively create a major case against it. First, fans' efforts to encourage those around them to join with their interests often fail. In their homes and workplaces many are separated from others of a similar passion, which is why they may seek out like-minded friends in fan clubs or online: 'Almost all fans to whom I spoke felt misunderstood or unwelcome in the eyes of those around them. Such isolation ranged from toleration to downright hostility' (Cavicchi 1998, 161). Second, one of the key problems with the contagion idea is that people can be familiar with media products as audience members for many years *before* discovering that they harbour a fannish interest. Lynn Thomas explained how she became a *Doctor Who* fan:

> As Michael's collection grew, so did my affection for the series. But I didn't become a real fan, not really, until I saw Ace take on a Dalek with a souped-up baseball bat in 'Rememberance of the Daleks'. Because traveling with the Doctor may be hard, frustrating, and dangerous, but it sure beats the hell out of being a waitress in an intergalactic malt shop. At that moment, something clicked in my brain, saying, YES. THIS. I get it. Ace became my companion, and Sylvester McCoy became my favourite

Doctor. I was ready for a Who convention. . . . (2010, 82; emphasis in original)

In this case, the individual's recognition of something in the text and how it related to her identity led her to declare she were a fan, as if she found part of themselves in the text. While many such 'becoming a fan' stories contain elements of social initiation, contagion can be seen as a post hoc rationalization of a more complex process. Specifically, while Adorno's living advertisements for the text can have a role to play in the genesis of fandom, more often than not they simply provide an invitation or motivation to evaluate the text and explore more of the catalogue. They do not constitute a full explanation because they do not offer a full account of causative. Contagion replaces a comprehensive theory of the origins of personal fandom with a simplistic figure of speech that both neglects the agency of the would-be fan and can play into other questionable ideas.[1]

Taste

One position on fandom is that it is purely a matter of personal passion and individual taste. In his 1984 book *Distinction*, the late French sociologist Pierre Bourdieu argued that taste is a social system rather than a purely personal choice: 'Taste classifies and it classifies the classifier' (1984, 6). Bourdieu came to his diagnosis by studying subtle differences in the lifestyles and cultural preferences of French citizens at different places in the class hierarchy. **Induction** is the idea that researchers who are relatively unencumbered by theory can go out and study the world then observe patterns from which they build new ideas. Bourdieu's relatively inductive, monumental study of French society and its cultural life exposed many subtle distinctions in the ways that ordinary people lived. One field of activity that he described was cinema, where he noticed that working-class spectators tended to be more interested in particular actors and Hollywood films, while more middle-class spectators talked about directors and European films. In effect, these class-based audiences had slightly different objects of interest. Bourdieu's analysis covered similar distinctions in a range of cultural repertoires including food, wine and interior decoration. His conclusion was that people used taste to separate themselves from the others who were *closest* to them in social space. Most of us can spot the cultural difference between individuals who are far apart on the class spectrum, but it is really the subtle distinctions and more arcane forms of knowledge – like knowing whether a good bottle of Beaujolais should ever be served chilled – that distinguishes those 'in the know' from the uninitiated. From this, Bourdieu created a functional schema that showed how these distinctions were reproduced. Offering the idea that individuals accumulate **cultural capital** (and therefore using an economic metaphor for a sociocultural process), he proposed that each person claimed their place in society by acquiring a stock of knowledge that reflected their particular social position. The sociologist discovered that upbringing and formal education both constituted central channels through which people learned about these fine gradations. As they unconsciously strived to locate themselves in social space, each individual cultivated (mentally stored up) a personal stock of learned predispositions in what that Bourdieu called his or her 'habitus'. To successfully exploit this stored knowledge is to display your cultural capital and therefore align yourself with a very particular social grouping. Each individual lets his/her habitus accumulate a stock of cultural capital that can then be displayed to an advantage. The acquisition of taste is thus a subtle game of one-upmanship that each of us (perhaps unknowingly) plays with our closest neighbours in order to climb, or at least keep our place in, the social system. Taste is therefore a means we use to competitively classify ourselves as social beings.

How useful is Bourdieu's work in understanding fandom? After its publication, the theory started to become an orthodoxy in the social sciences and was examined by media, film and music scholars. His ideas have a ring of common sense about them, especially when one considers words like 'hip' and 'cool' or popular expressions like, 'Keeping up with the Jones's'. There are also subtle intersections between Bourdieu's notion of taste and ideas about fandom. His work also enables us to examine fandom's relation to social status and the social hierarchy, dimensions sometimes missing from utopian accounts of the subject. It allows us to see how fans play with social rules (Hills 2002a, 46). On one level, a straight reading of this research might relate fannish distinctions to slight differences in social status. This means that fans can, in theory, reveal their class positions by investing in particular cultural objects. An example might be the 'underground indie' trash cinema fans who despise 'archivist' trash cinema fans, when less discriminating outsiders would place them both in the same category (see Hills 2002a, 61). However, fans can struggle over issues that Bourdieu could never have predicted.

John Fiske drew on Bourdieu's work for his chapter in Lisa Lewis' 1992 book *The Adoring Audience*. He argued that fans displayed cultural capital in their regular exchanges of knowledge. Fiske adapted Bourdieu's work by talking about an unclassed 'popular habitus' that supported fandom. As part of his project to show fans as an active audience, he used Bourdieu's conception of taste to suggest that unlike the existing stereotypes suggested, fans were neither passive nor culturally duped. When Simon Frith (1996, 19) suggested that popular music fans were a highly discriminating audience, he also found common ground with Bourdieu. Perhaps Bourdieu's ideas are therefore best used to examine how fans take up their roles *within* the institutions of the fan community (56).

There is no doubt that after steeping themselves in the conventions of their genres, fans display levels of knowledge and create bonds within their peer groups. They constantly make distinctions that are lost on outsiders. Horror fan Mark Kermode provided a good example of this:

> For a horror fan, the recognition of these recycled elements is a crucial part of the enjoyment and appreciation of the movies. At its most basic, this is merely a rarified form of 'getting the joke', of feeling 'in the know', of understanding that a knife is never just a knife. Produce a chainsaw on-screen in a horror film, and the devoted fan will automatically click into a celluloid history dating back to Tobe Hooper's ground-breaking *Texas Chainsaw Massacre*, and the marauding to the present day via the parodic excesses of *Motel Hell*, *Hollywood Chainsaw Hookers*, *Bad Taste*, *The Evil Dead* and, of course, *Texas 2, 3* and *4*. To a genre fan, a chainsaw is not a threatening weapon – it's a magic talisman, conjuring up a heritage of horror. (1997, 61)

Comments like Kermode's help us to understand the way that genre appreciation – here knowing the local meaning of genre symbols – can be both a display of cultural capital and badge of membership within a specific fan community. Another way in which this works is through knowledge of cultural producers who are not well known to mainstream audiences. For instance, if you live outside Italy but know who Dario Argento is then you are probably a fan of horror cinema.[2] The distinction between fans and ordinary audience members is also signified when media fans sometimes adopt a language of aesthetics to distance themselves from less knowledgeable listeners. Bruce Springsteen, for example, has been read by his fans through an aesthetic framework similar to that used for high culture – emphasizing complexity, clarity, novelty and seriousness – which helped his fans separate themselves from ordinary music consumers (see Cavicchi 1998, 122).

There are, however, some fundamental problems with applying Bourdieu's ideas about cultural taste to fandom. Matt Hills argued that Bourdieu's theories have caught on because they resonated with the concerns of cultural critics (2002, 56). How useful is it to examine fandom as an indirect cultural function of class distinctions? To adapt the French sociologist's work wholesale to fandom is to misread it in the context of its time: 'Strictly speaking, Bourdieu does not attach the label of "fandom" to the dominant bourgeoisie; there is something always culturally "improper" about fandom in his account' (Hills 2002a, 48). To an extent I think Hills is right here. One of the most crucial passages in Bourdieu's work was actually a footnote on popular music stardom that has been ignored or forgotten by subsequent writers. When he did his fieldwork, he noted:

> Thus the [hit] song, as a cultural property which (like photography) is almost universally accessible and genuinely common (since hardly anyone is not exposed at one particular moment or another to the 'successes' of the day) calls for particular vigilance from those who intend to mark their difference. (1984, 60)

To work efficiently, cultural texts therefore have to lend themselves to distinctions that are *esoteric and visible only to a suitably select fraction of the players*. In other words, numerically popular mass culture – like, say, James Bond, *The Exorcist* (Friedkin, 1973), *Harry Potter* or 'Hey Jude' by the Beatles – is enjoyed by all class fractions, so it cannot lend itself to the game of taste and is exempt from the process. Also, the media, society and popular culture have changed significantly since Bourdieu conducted his field work. Although people still make cultural distinctions, what has changed significantly is the clarity of class as a sociocultural grouping, and the type and predictability of many of the formerly telling alignments between class position and taste. Bourdieu's work suggests that moral evaluations stem from the cultural struggles *between classes* (Hills 2002a, 49). This origin had to be transcended to understand it in relation to fandom. In some ways cultural distinctions perhaps seem to be even more refined than before and are less about class. The concept of taste as social classification has therefore been subjected to considerable criticism, as it appears rather monolithic and generalizing. Some cultural objects are *multivalent* in terms of their cultural caché: they have very different connotations for different audiences. For example, in America, *Doctor Who* fandom was 'hip' but only in certain social circles. On the one hand the show represented an Anglophile pleasure from the exotic United Kingdom (Nye 2010, 103). On the other, being a *Doctor Who* fan was 'social suicide' in school for American girls, because, unlike *Star Wars*, nobody had heard of the show (McGuire 2010, 118). Fan cultural capital is often, therefore, of limited value outside the fan community; it is precisely because it cannot easily be converted into economic or academic status that its 'purity' may matter (Hills 2002a, 52).[3]

Another problem is the extent to which application of Bourdieu's ideas presupposes that fans prioritize their interests *in a calculating and rational process*. The theory closes down alternative interpretations of fandom by returning us to the figure of the logical and socially competitive individual. Ultimately, Bourdieu-style readings locate fandom as a compensation for social powerlessness. Ideas about cultural capital paint fans in the making as 'committed utilitarians, assessing the options that are open to them before deciding' yet becoming-a-fan stories show us that fandom does not work like that: fans seem more pleasantly overwhelmed than calculating (55). An interesting example here comes from *Bye Bye Baby*, a memoire written by the American author Caroline Sullivan, a rock fan who eventually became a music journalist on the other side of the Atlantic for one of Britain's quality national newspapers, *The Guardian*. As Sullivan explained:

> Credibility was all about the music you liked, and our town wasn't like urban Newark or Jersey City, where kids listened to trendy disco music. Millburn's affluence took its toll in a surprising way. Kids could afford to buy as much dope as they could smoke, and with dope came the desire not to listen to hip disco but to Led Zepplin, Pink Floyd and, pain me though it does to recall, Emerson, Lake and Palmer. (1999, 9)

She added, 'we were getting into Yes and Zep' (10), but another interest emerged to take over from her fascination with the music of these 'credible' rock bands when, as part of the audience for *The Howard Cosell TV Show*, she witnessed a satellite link-up with young pop band The Bay City Rollers:

> After they finished 'Saturday Night,' there was a stage invasion that resulted in [lead singer] Leslie briefly being knocked unconscious. This was after the satellite link-up had ended so we didn't see it, but I knew how those girls felt. I wanted to invade that stage myself. The moment the show ended my bud Sue rang. 'My God,' she breathed, 'Eric'. When she said that, I knew something weird was happening to us. Sue, who was five voluptuous years older and even more of a music fan than me, wasn't a girl who fell in live with teenybopper groups. We'd met six months before at a Queen gig, and had taken to going to shows together, she always with her camera in tow. (35)

Sullivan was highly aware that identifying as a fan with tartan teenyboppers Bay City Rollers would seem tacky and was not what anyone of her age and status should do. She explained, 'My entire Rollermaniac career was a struggle between knowing they were no Led Zep and loving them anyway' (20). It was as if her romantic attachment to the Rollers gave her a fannish motivation that thoroughly trumped the game of taste played among the older teens in her native Millburn. While Caroline Sullivan 'came out' as a Rollers fan, those who admire 'inappropriate' objects often struggle to keep their identities hidden. Ultimately, *Distinction* can help us understand the *social licensing* of particular fannish objects. We can say that the game of taste occurs *alongside* fan activities, delineating socially acceptable objects.

In her book on playlists, haircuts and record collections, Sarah Thornton (1995) extended Bourdieu's ideas about taste to discuss the sociology of electronic dance music. She described forms of club culture in which 'subcultural capital' was not correlated to class. For Thorton, the *habitus* (cultivated stock of cultural distinctions) is not primarily located in each individual's head but exists instead in fashionable *niche media*. Clubbers contrast their participation to those who settle for a supposedly feminized and lower class clubbing 'mainstream'. Rejecting the chains of provincial drinking parlours and mainstream clubs who play 'handbag house,' they perceive a hierarchy of different clubs to visit and use access to relatively obscure social networks and niche media to seek out the ones with an underground reputation. Being 'in the know' therefore allows interested clubbers to visit hip and underground places that have a cultural caché recognized most widely *within* their own subculture. In theory, therefore, if we update Bourdieu's ideas for contemporary society (and hold its social structure relatively rigid), *Distinction* can help us explore the cultural wavelength in which an individual fan might feel comfortable choosing their object. It can provide a working guess at the causes of debates within and between fan communities. Yet it cannot fully explain *why* each of us picks *our own* particular cultural object or why we invest quite so much emotion in it.

Affect

What had she been waiting for so stubbornly all her life? What had she expected? . . . 'He is holy'. For the first time ever she hears a man being described as 'holy' during his lifetime. She herself would have described him as 'unusual,' as very unusual, for otherwise she would not have become seriously ill from all those years of thinking about him. She did not even think that it had anything to do with 'love'. Rather a deep, unhealable fright from her meeting with him, which had been carefully prepared by the vision of 'The Man of Jasmine'.

UNICA ZURN (1994, 73)

The poet Utica Zurn's vivid and creative surrealist story *The Man of Jasmine* is about one woman's journey to find a man who has so intensely haunted her life. Zurn's story simultaneously reflects how Zurn is overwhelmed and empowered, rendered frustratingly desperate by her fascination with a mysterious face (who in real life was the artist and photographer Hans Bellmer). The story was subtitled 'Impressions from a mental illness' indicating that Zurn's particular interest was pathological: an infatuation and obsession that was damaging to herself. Her 'Man of Jasmine' was a seductive projection based on everything that Zurn could wish for. His aura affirmed her own worth and creativity, and yet he was always a lost object, a step away from her grasp. While there are important differences between ordinary fandom and Zurn's narrative and while the comparison is highly problematic in some respects – and the last two decades of fan studies have aimed to escape from it – there is also *something* about Zurn's description that chimes with some forms of fandom: the idea that iconic figures might be 'holy' in their own lifetime, the unrequited fascination with a stranger's face, the projection of expectations on to someone who is not there. The experience of emotion is central or at least initiatory to many forms of fandom. Theorizing involves a process of emotional estrangement that is challenged, in some ways, when emotion and fandom are the research objects. Most academic traditions aim to preserve an aura of impartiality and emotional neutrality in the research process. The metaphor of textuality tends to focus on semiotic meaning rather than emotional experience. Matt Hills has questioned a focus on meaning at the expense of emotion and encouraged other researchers to focus on the emotive rather than cognitive dimensions of fandom (see Hills in Jenkins 2006, 5 and 139). Screen icons, pop stars, boybands, comic book heroes are all too often Men of Jamine, and socially celebrated as such. How can we discuss the emotional aspect of fandom as a personal and shared activity, *without* resorting to psychological models like the ideas of hysteria or parasocial interaction? How, then, can we study our emotionally charged connections?

Academics need a plausible language through which to talk about emotion (Jenkins 2006, 26). One way of thinking about it in cultural studies has been to use American scholar Lawrence Grossberg's idea of affect. Grossberg emerged as one of the most important thinkers in cultural studies during the 1990s. His career has followed a trajectory from writing about popular music and the evocation of collective emotion to considering issues of cultural policy and civic governance (see Grossberg 1992 and 2011). Furthermore, Grossberg's ideas built on a much older tradition. Early in the twentieth century one of the key questions for Marxists was why socialist revolutions had never actually happened in modern societies. Antonio Gramsci formulated a concept called hegemony to answer that question. **Hegemony** is the idea that an alliances of elite groups maintain their status in a process of cultural leadership in which ordinary people are given what they want. My own work has applied this idea to the way that the British Royal family used popular music to create a national celebration (see Duffett 2004a). Royal spectacles like the Diamond Jubilee Concert in June 2012 attempted to attract a broad cross section of the public by offering a wide range of musical performances. The Royals have therefore traded off a little of their traditional privilege for endorsement from 'rock royalty'. It does not matter whether the Queen actually likes popular music; what matters is that most of the general public *cannot* say that they *do not* like it. Hegemonic formations therefore use undisputed premises to further political goals. In the wake Diana's tragic death in 1997, events like the Diamond Jubilee Concert have helped to rescue and revamp the Royals.

Hegemonic incidents happen in history and they must be placed in their temporal dimension. Grossberg's particular concern was how, as times changed in the shift from the 1960s to the 1980s, communitarian radicalism had lost its bedrock of political support, and how its central emblem – rock music – had shifted meaning to become a part of right-wing hegemony. He was fascinated by the way that music of one generation had been drained of all its meaning and edge, but still sounded the same and could then be used to sell the *opposite* set of values. To explain why the social meaning of cultural forms could shift so radically, Grossberg began to consider the collective experience of emotion. To discuss it he used the term 'affect'. **Affect**, for Grossberg, is not something inherent in the text itself (supposed meaning) nor something that individuals invest in the text (emotions, desires); instead it is 'a socially constructed domain of cultural effects' that makes the text matter in a specific historical situation and place, and makes it come alive, giving it a resonant tone. In that sense, affect *guides* the whole possibility of emotion and is meta-emotional. By structuring collective 'maps of mattering,' affect organizes *why things matter* (see Hills 2002a, 91). Yet it is a somewhat hazy idea. Despite Grossberg's carefully constructed definitions of the differences between the two concepts, other researchers have argued that he frequently equates affect and emotion. Many writers have also tended to use 'affect' as a form of academic shorthand for 'emotion' or 'emotional resonance' when in fact it highlights the way that *shifts* in context can change *how much* a cultural form matters and the strength of emotion that the public feels about it. As Grossberg explained:

> The very form of affective difference . . . [means] the subject [here the fan] is constituted nomadically, by its movement across different fields of affective difference. The affective subject is always transitory, defined by its qualitative and quantitative trajectories. . . . Affect defines, then, a condition of possibility for any political intervention; it is however,

ideologically, economically and libidinally neutral except as it is articulated into these systems under specific historical conditions. (1997, 160–1)

Here Grossberg emphasizes that when societies move through contrasting eras (say, the 1960s to the 1980s), patterns of collective feeling seem to shift so that some things matter and others feel irrelevant as time goes by. Attention to affect means examining the redrawing of the playing field within which we experience a weight of feeling about what matters. Grossberg's idea of affect is interesting because it locates emotional resonance as a kind of fluid essence that can be attached to and detached from specific social and cultural forms (here from socialism and counterculture). It advances upon crude notions of social control by asking us to see collective emotion as part of a process of political engineering.

In recent years 'affect' has been widely adopted as a term within academic studies of culture. Introducing their edited collection on the subject, Seigworth and Gregg (2010) clarify and explore the nation a little further. For them, affect is an open-ended concept that refers to both potentials, spaces and forces of encounter. It is both impersonal *and* intimate, a force of encounter that impinges on us from the outside. In this formulation affect is always in situ and always *in process*. It is also unconscious, at some times seductive, and at others impelling:

Affect arises in the midst of *in-between-ness*: in the capacity to be acted upon. Affect is an impingement of extrusion of a momentary or sometimes more sustained state of relation *as well as* the passage (and the duration of passage) of forces and intensities. That is, affect is found in those intensities that pass body to body (human, nonhuman, part-body and otherwise), in those resonances that circulate about, between and sometimes stick to bodies and worlds, *and* in the very passages or variations between these intensities and resonances themselves. (1; emphasis in original)

Quite apart from the seemingly ever-expanding nature of both the concept and its definition, what is interesting here is that notions of affect rather wrestle with the idea of human agency. Even used as a loose template that simply draws attention to the way that human emotions are not individual but emerge from a context of wider shifts, the idea is still freighted with certain assumptions. At worst, it is in danger of reproducing the questionable notion of contagion ('intensities that pass body to body') without explaining *how* it happens. Nevertheless, affect is still an interesting and flexible idea.

Why might it be useful to discuss the weight and direction of emotion? If we take affect more loosely to mean emotional intensity, it gives us another dimension beyond semiotic meaning through which to examine the role of popular culture in people's lives. 'Meaning' is a head-led term, not a term for bodily sensations or passions, yet its operation is intrinsically related to affect (Jenkins 2006, 24). That is important because a 3D version of meaning is greatly needed to grasp signs which have an emotional weight as well as interpretational dimension (25). We might therefore think of semiotics and affect as two opposite potentials by which we can place or measure a text, for instance, as 'simple and emotionally arresting,' or 'complicated and boring'. Although the text's meaning and emotional pull can be envisaged along two dimensions, in reality they work together. For example, a symbol – perhaps a deep, primal, archetypal one, like a mother figure – has a meaning and at the same time, for that reason, it strikes us as having an emotional weight for us. The term 'affective semiotics' captures this inevitable union combining semiotic interpretation and emotional charge. For Hills, however, good academic work should be able to speak about fandom in a way that everyone can immediately grasp; even the term 'affective semiotics' is itself therefore alienating (see Hills in Jenkins 2006, 27).

Personal fandom originates in a process of emotional investment. It starts with a frisson of excitement, even if that then motivates some less immediately exciting practices like critiquing or discussing texts. Fan loyalties and disputes frequently and perhaps inevitably raise strong feelings. Furthermore, fans tend to report feeling empowered by their interests. They often describe their connection in terms of a pleasant sense of shock, captivation or reinvigoration. Performance generates feelings of connection and exhilaration, a 'high' felt by *both* the performer *and* their fans (Cavicchi 1998, 90). In some discussions, this boost becomes a source of sustenance that helps people to get through difficulties in their lives. The emotional dimension of most forms of fandom is, nevertheless, hard to describe. Sue Turnbull (2005) has talked about 'ekphrasis': the attempt to recover in words the emotional effect that a performance has on its viewers. When Springsteen stopped lingering over past glories and played more recent songs, Cavicchi noted, 'As a result, I felt less relaxed nostalgia and more strong feelings of empowerment and energy; the rapid transitions between songs filled me up with electricity and sound and a strange sensation that I could do or be anything I wanted' (1998, 31). Researching fans of David Bowie, Nick Stevenson found that 'Apparently during periods of stress and emotional turmoil, many of the male fans suggested that Bowie's music had helped them . . . Bowie is rediscovered at times of intense insecurity or emotional vulnerability' (2009, 84 and 94). There are many stories about personal fandom helping people through episodes of illness, divorce or bereavement. These stories suggest that rather than compensating for an essential 'lack,' fandom is a source of personal power that people turn to at different points on their life journey. As Stevenson explained, 'During many of my interviews, it was striking how a connection to Bowie acted as a relatively permanent anchor through many men's lives' (85). Although the emotional impact of fan attachments is hard to describe, what can be said is that it has a powerful effect.

Another aspect of fan attachment is that it can restructure notions of what is public and what is private. The sense of connection that each fan feels for a famous actor, singer, writer or musician can alter and restructure their spatial experience. As the last chapter showed, traditional narratives of celebrity describe fans as something akin to human swarms physically intruding upon their icons. Stars are portrayed as in danger of having to abandon their privacy – and sometimes even their sense of self – in exchange for the social and material benefits of being publicly celebrated by their fan base. In reality, the private and the public are psychological domains not so clearly bounded as by any physical spaces that people inhabit. For example, writing on the nature of public rituals Jack Santino has explained:

> Many apparently public events are in fact private, and some are personal, conducted in the company of only one other, or even alone. Still, many of these kinds of solitary actions might be understood to be performed for or in the company of a 'virtual' or an assumed imaginary audience . . . whenever I see a penny on the street I pick it up, because my deceased mother used to do this. When I do it, there is a very real way in which she is present, despite whatever else I may or may not believe regarding death and the afterlife . . . there is an imagined audience that not only witnesses but shares in the ritualized activities. (2009, 11)

Santino's discussion demonstrates that the received distinction between public and private space is radically challenged by ordinary experience. In that sense, fans who connect with their heroes in different contexts can find themselves inhabiting public and private spaces in a dualistic or contradictory way. Introducing a piece on horror fanzines by David Sanjek, his editors explain, 'all fanzines are, in essence, public expressions of private pleasures' (see Sanjek 2008, 419). They also talk about 'private fandoms for Erotic thrillers' (see Mathijs & Mendik 2008, 5). Television viewing has further weakened the distinctions between the public and private sphere (Harrington & Bielby 1995, 117). A surprising number of rock fans find their passions by watching recordings of live concert events. Their private viewing experience is informed by indications of their band's popularity as they view its public performance in their living room. Music fans actually present at the events talk about 'being in the same room' as their heroes, even if that room is a large capacity arena. Locating moments of connection between the star and fan as private can also make them feel more personal and intimate. For Cavicchi a successful Bruce Springsteen concert can change the valence of its location: 'It felt less like a concert and more like a private party' (1998, 34). If music fans acknowledge that they are in a very public space where the collective mass of the crowd very much matters, then *they can also act out a more personal, private, emotional connection to the figure on stage* as part of that experience. Academics like Henry Jenkins have strategically described fandom as a public, communal activity, but many fans operate much more in private: Sue Wise explained 'mostly my interest in Elvis took the form of a solitary hobby, a private thing between "him" and "me"' (1990, 393). Sometimes this can reflect a sense of social ostracism. Laura Vroomen, for instance, described how individuals can pursue 'private fandom' in order not to upset family members or house mates who do not share their taste (2004, 246). The point here is that fandom facilitates conceptions that *combine* the private and public in ways that ultimately serve the individual.

Whether experienced in public or private, the emotional 'buzz' that people get as fans is worthy of attention. In instances where fandom is about celebrity-following, it can be extended to say people get a buzz from the idea of meeting a celebrity on an individual footing. Everybody to some extent tends to follow a humanist epistemology of celebrity: we know that behind the texts and images are 'real' people – individuals with bodies, minds and hearts just like us – but individuals who are both more popular and less private than us. In a media culture everyone is surrounded by electronic traces of these celebrities. Modern media forms – television shows, Websites, films, recorded music – constantly offer us a wealth of sounds and images as promissory notes, evoking the idea of intimacy with them. One thing that attracted some American fans to *Doctor Who*, for instance, was that the actors who made it visited fan conventions and were more accessible than Hollywood glitterati (Nye 2010, 109). The question for scholars researching affect and fandom is, therefore, why does the idea of immersing oneself in a particular narrative or getting closer to a favoured celebrity give rise to such strong feelings? A first step in answering that question is to realize that while feelings originate in the body (Ahmed 2004, 5), and many therefore claim they are natural, their meaning comes from the ways that we inadvertently *generate, understand* and *frame* our experiences. A good analogy for this is to consider the idea that two people go on a rollercoaster ride, one knowing that he/she will love it and the other dreading it. Although each one's body has the same *physiological* experience, they interpret it differently in relation to what their minds anticipate, feeling excitement and anxiety respectively. In that sense, unspoken and shared assumptions can determine individual beliefs which then prompt the emergence of emotions. Fandom is not *entirely* a personal emotional activity. It is, in fact, a common experience based on the fulfilment of *shared unspoken* assumptions, translated by the individual into their own sensations, then *later* manifest in communal experiences.

Religiosity

This sculpture is a disgrace. Instead of honoring Michael Jackson for his many contributions to the music industry, you chose to ridicule him in this manner. For your information, MJ was not dangling his baby, but showing the baby to his fans who asked to see the baby. I urge you to remove this sculpture and replace it with one that honors Michael Jackson's amazing talents and humanitarian accomplishments.

DANIELA HAIRABEDIAN, a Michael Jackson fan[4]

In November 2002, Michael Jackson visited Berlin to pick up Germany's most coveted entertainment award, the Millennium Bambi. A large crowd of fans gathered to welcome the superstar at the Adlon hotel. Appearing on a fifth-floor balcony, Michael greeted the appreciative throng by showing off his young children. He partially covered Prince and Paris with blankets to protect their privacy. In the excitement, Jackson accidentally dangled nine-month-old Prince Michael II over the railing and cradled him with one arm only. Some of the onlookers were shocked and the incident prompted a media frenzy. The story was reported by *The Sun* in Britain with the headline 'You Lunatic' while *The Daily Mirror* settled for 'Mad Bad Dad' and its editor urged for Jackson's arrest. Berlin authorities launched a preliminary probe to determine if his actions constituted the endangering or neglect of his children, but then decided not to open an investigation. Critical of the lack of prosecution, German welfare advocates of the Child Protection Association said that Jackson was shielded from the law because of his fame. Soon he issued a statement via his lawyer in which he called the incident a 'terrible mistake . . . I got caught up in the excitement of the moment. I would never intentionally endanger the lives of my children'. There is no evidence to contradict Jackson's interpretation and in retrospect it is easy to see how his actions were framed by antagonistic media perceptions that dismissed him as an eccentric, perhaps insane, unfit parent.

Especially when stars have long running careers, their reputations are fluctuating concerns. Michael Jackson's death in the summer of 2009 catalysed a widespread resurgence in appreciation for his musical contribution and in part eclipsed his 'Wacko Jacko' image. In April 2011, his fans were dismayed, then, to see that the Los Angeles-based artist Maria von Kohler recreate the baby dangling incident as a clay sculpture on the first storey of Premises Studios in Hackney Road, East London. The statue, which von Kohler called *Madonna and Child*, predictably raised the ire of Jackon's following. A barrage of angry messages were posted on the company's Website, with one fan even threatening to set the studio on fire. Its chief executive, Viv Broughton, replied in *The Daily Mail*:

> How can a work of art that's faithful to a real event be construed as an attack on anyone? Madonna and Child is as much about extreme fan worship as it is about Michael Jackson. Lots of people have come here to view it. Most people think it's brilliant.

What was the artist trying to do? A gallery description of themes in her work explained:

> A consistent interest in the portrayal of heroic or propagandist figures, acts and symbols in their countless forms often provides a starting point for von Köhler's work. It references historical, religious and political propaganda and iconography in art, toys, junk shop trinkets, the media and public spaces . . . The underlying feeling permeating the work is a sense of living up to a seedy, desperately coveted yet sinisterly unattainable, non-existent ideology.[5]

As an example of fan-baiting, Kohler's *Madonna and Child* did its job in creating controversy by manipulating the fans and the media. The sculpture's aim, evidently, was to equate fandom to fundamentalism and it did so by exposing fandom as a moralistic structure of feeling. The implicit claim that it made was that fans are characterized by their bias: their loyalty to the star, their selective perception of his or her public image, and arguably their blindness in relation to Jackson's less appealing moments. A much-followed performer is, to many fans, like a friend or family member: someone that they feel they know, love and try to protect. The Michael Jackson fans and Kohler became locked into a predictable contest over how Jackson *should* be seen, which was itself a moral question. Henry Jenkins has described how fans share values and collectively lever what he calls a 'moral economy' (2006, 55). If communal fandom so frequently involves voicing a shared morality, would it be fair to say, as Kohler implied, that it is a religion?

Many academics have directly compared fandom to religion. David Giles (2000), for instance, likened fan texts to religious scriptures of the Middle Ages. Similarly, reporting on John Frow's work, Nick Stevenson showed how

Frow inferred a metaphysical basis for celebrity culture: 'Basically, Frow argues that by identifying with a star we attempt to defeat death. By connecting with a more-than-human being, we seek to move beyond ordinary human temporality into the mythic and sacred' (2009, 89). Notions of fandom as a search for the sacred are common currency (see, for example, Neumman 2006). Yet even if the fans use a spiritual vocabulary, there are also strong reasons for questioning the idea that fandom is simply a surrogate for religion. One of the most obvious is that the idea is, at worst, somewhat derogatory to both fans and religious worshippers. In popular culture, the notion that fandom resembles religion is an ongoing joke that acts to normalize mainstream audiences by locating fans as misguided, irrational and servile zealots, people who believe in their heroes against all the evidence and at any cost. Matt Hills (in Jenkins 2006, 17) suggests that religious analogies contain a kernel conception of 'false worship' that limits them. The central problem of applying notions of religious conviction to fandom – even sympathetically – is therefore that the comparison maintains a derogatory perception of the phenomenon.

One of the reasons not to entirely dismiss the idea that fandom is like religion is that the Judaeo-Christian roots of Western society have subtly saturated it with a legacy of archetypes and ideas. As Chris Rojek has put it: 'Celebrity culture is secular. Because the roots of secular society lie in Christianity, many of the symbols of success and failure in celebrity draw on myths and rites of religious ascent and decent' (2007, 175). Another reason is that enthusiastic fan-academics, even self-declared 'insiders' like Rupert Till and Daniel Cavicchi, maintain the comparison. Matt Hills, for example, has claimed:

> Fandom both is and is not like religion, existing between 'cult' and 'culture'. 'Cult' discourses are thus not entirely hollow and empty . . . Undoubtedly one of the major problems with linking fan cultures to either religion or religiosity – and this is a problem for both fans and academics – lies in identifying what is actually meant by 'religion' in the first place. (2002a, 118)

According to the *Oxford English Dictionary*, a 'religion' is a system of faith and worship; a human recognition of superhuman power, and, especially of a God figure who is entitled to obedience. Rupert Till has reduced the prominence of worship in this definition by saying that a religion is a genuinely-held belief, not an opinion or view based on provisional knowledge (2010, xi). The predictable, spectacular, public displays of collective exuberance around stars mean that casual comparisons between fan phenomena and religion are widely circulated. Many media performers exploit the analogy, particularly in popular music, where – as the famous 'Clapton is God' graffiti found in a London station in 1967 demonstrated – the 'rock god' epithet is longstanding. Some *acts* have directly evoked the comparison in their stage shows. Michael Jackson did so in 1996, when he performed 'Earth Song' at the Brit Awards in England and pulled a crucifixion pose on stage. Cliff Richard has made allusions to the promise of redemption in his lyrics and videos, not just through lighting, elevation, gesture and posture, but also by adopting themes such as asexuality and benevolence to the poor (see Löbert 2008, 77). Springsteen has sometimes played the role of an evangelical preacher in his shows (Cavicchi 1998, 30). Artists from Jim Morrison to Jon Bon Jovi have struck crucifiction poses on stage, arms outstretched as if encompassing or saying they belonged to their audience. Still other performers have knowingly parodied the idea that the public worships them. Beyond these popular comparisons, fans themselves sometimes use spiritual figures of speech and a religious vocabulary. Though sensitive to its sensationalist connotations, *both performers and their audiences* borrow the language of religious conversion to talk about their experiences. *Star Trek* fans sing about being 'born again' and their duty to see that everyone is 'saved' (Jenkins 1992, 250). As Cavicchi explains, 'fans often talk about introducing someone to Springsteen's music as "converting" them . . . Often fans use the idea of conversion in a specifically religious sense, logically seeing the act of introducing someone to Springsteen's music as a kind of proselytizing' (1998, 42). In other words, religious figures of speech are a way to talk about the personal experience of having so rapidly transferred allegiances.

Discussing fans' use of spiritual language, Matt Hills said in one interview that fans used religious metaphors in their becoming-a-fan stories, but Jenkins noted that political conversion narratives also use the 'conversion' metaphor. Hills countered that fans do not use party political language (see Jenkins 2006, 22). It seems that spiritual metaphors are more useful as they capture the emotional transcendence of fan experience. Fans often refer to a live rock show as a religious or spiritual experience. They report being filled with the spirit, or feeling a sense of closeness to their star. According to Daniel Cavicchi, 'Fans even talk about the importance of the larger audience in terms of their own fandom, and the power of being part of the audience is a common theme in accounts of concerts' (1998, 88).[6] **Communitas** is an idea proposed by anthropologist Victor Turner which suggests that individuals at live mass public events can feel blissfully united and are thrilled to realize that they at one with the assembled community. For Cavicchi, however, fandom is not primarily about communitas: 'While social, celebratory abandon with others is important in fans' encounters with the music, it is always secondary, whereas individual, critical appreciation is primary' (1998, 122).

Why do fans, then, use religious terminology? Religious discourses highlight instances of shared faith that do not require external real world 'proof' or 'evidence' to come into play. Fans use religious language in quotes or to describe specific moments, but commentators forget that such fans are speaking the same language in a very different way to others outside their community. Hills suggests that religion provides a shared vocabulary that *sanitizes* (makes sane) fans' common experiences (see Jenkins 2006, 20–1). The vocabulary can then allow them to avoid the question, 'Why are you a fan of this particular object?' Instead they can celebrate their conviction without having to justify their attachment or explain why rational comprehension seems irrelevant (Hills 2002a, 122). This raises the issue that religious language could be no more than a convenience: a way to speak about experiences that are hard to directly express in words.

Some researchers have sincerely pursued the comparison between fandom and religiosity. Music fan specialist Daniel Cavicchi has produced one of the most sympathetic and discriminating insider discussions of fandom and religion so far. According to Cavicchi, 'while religion and fandom are arguably different realms of meaning, they are both centred around acts of devotion, which create many similarities of experience' (1998, 51). Fandom is more than *metaphorically* connected to religion because, for Cavicchi, it contains several *structural* parallels: the development of a close attachment to an unobtainable other, a kind of moral orientation, a daily life devoted to interpretation and a community based on a shared if vague assumption of devotion (186). However such parallels 'do not mean that fandom is religion; rather they point to the fact that fandom and religion are addressing similar concerns and engaging people in similar ways' (187). According to Cavicchi, then, fandom and religion are similar experiences that have different meanings (51). He makes the closest connection when discussing narratives of fan initiation:

> On the whole, fans use the idea of conversion only as a metaphor to signify the degree of dedication and commitment Springsteen usually inspires. However, a closer look at fans' accounts of their experiences shows that the concept of conversion serves as more than simply a metaphorical description of fans' degree of feeling; it actually describes in detail the process of becoming a fan. In particular, the descriptions of transformations found in narratives of becoming a fan are remarkably similar to those found in the conversion narratives of evangelical Christians in the modern United States. (43)

While Cavicchi's comparison is carefully considered and sympathetic, part of the issue here is that a comparative metaphor can never be factual. Indeed, there is only a limited empirical fit between fandom and religion as there are probably *more* differences than similarities (Jenkins 2006, 20). As Cornel Sandvoss has stated, there is a significant difference between references to religion *in* fandom and the idea that fandom *is* a religion (2005a, 62).

Any solid analysis must face three crucial problems that directly challenge the idea that fandom is a substitute for religion. These are, first, that it has no central theology, second that fans can 'worship' more than one 'deity' at a time, and third, that the idea rests on a questionable conception of human need. Taking each in turn, the first thing to notice is that fandom 'lacks an absolute, other-worldly framework' that would make it resemble religion (Sandvoss 2005a, 63). While any fan may report mysterious emotions and experiences, he/she is not connected to sacred texts that explicitly offer promises of salvation in an after-life. Also, unlike monotheistic believers, fans can pursue several dominant and lesser interests *at the same time*. Erika Doss' 1999 study *Elvis Culture: Fans, Faith & Image* illustrated how fan researchers can encounter problems if they do not aim to inductively understand fandom. Doss started her analysis in rational comparative mode by asking:

> Why Elvis? Why has Elvis Presley been sanctified as the central figure in what some are calling a quasi-religion? Why not some other popular culture matryr who died young like John Lennon, Buddy Holly, Janis Joplin, Jimi Hendrix, or, more recently, Kurt Cobain or Selena? Why is Elvis – more so than Malcolm X, Martin Luther King, Jr., and JFK – consistently held up as 'icon of the twentieth century'? (1999, 2)

Beyond the difficulty of calling fandom a 'quasi-religion' what Doss misses here is that fans are not arriving at their attachments by making comparisons between *either* Elvis *or* Buddy (they can like both); or Elvis *rather than* Jesus or Martin Luther King. My own PhD research with 150 Elvis fans suggested that only a fraction of them listened exclusively to Elvis (Duffett 1998, 222). If they have a picture of him, it suggests that they have developed an interest, but it does not necessarily imply a decision to ignore Buddy Holly, Malcolm X or anyone else. A fan's passion for Elvis may actually inspire him/her to learn about such people. In another example from the world of a sci-fi, we can see that individuals can embrace multiple fandoms. It is the relationship between different personal fandoms that is intriguing here:

> Many fans accepted *Doctor Who* as their secondary fandom, coming to it from *Battlestar Galactica* (the original series with Lorne Greene, that is),

Star Wars or *Star Trek*, but a few of us had *Doctor Who* as our primary or sole favourite . . . I liked *Star Wars* and *Star Trek* and many of the others, but I loved *Doctor Who*. (Nye 2010, 108)

Much like this non-exclusive fandom, furthermore, people often follow their fannish interest *and* practice their chosen religion at the same time, without any necessary conflict. Fundamentally, the notion that human beings have, at root, a *universal need* that can be served by either religion or fandom is very much open to question. Insofar that they imply fans need God but find Michael Jackson or *Star Trek* instead, the frequent comparisons between fandom and religion resemble a widely-challenged 1970s media research paradigm: *uses and gratifications*. In other words, the religion or religiosity idea *essentializes* religion as a universal and ahistorical human need when it might be more insightful to reverse the equation and see it as a *product* of social discourses. What we never see from advocates of the argument – and this is indicative of their stance – is the logical counterpart to their theories: the application of ideas *from* fan research *to* religious worship. Fans are (mis)taken as worshippers, but devoted Christians and others are never analysed as 'fans of God'. Even the phrase sounds sacrilegious.

Grappling towards a compromise, some writers have attempted to square the circle and explain how fandom is like *but is also not like* religious activity. For Aden (1999), fandom is not a substitute religion, but it does contain a place-bound conception of a better society in the shape of a 'promised land' (also see Sandvoss 2005a, 63). While there may be some credence in the idea that the media can offer interested viewers certain kinds of utopian fantasy moments based on constantly deferred intimations of equality and intimacy with stars, the question here is whether God should form part of an explanation. Some more recent writers have updated their terms of reference, by moving beyond religion. In the 1990s, the idea of religiosity emerged in academic circles to describe the place of religious practice in a changing society. Writers increasingly contested the notion that modern life was experienced as a purely secular and rational activity which squeezed out any personal need to explore faith. Instead they argued that ordinary people remained enchanted by spirituality in daily life and practiced their faith in less formal but more diverse ways. Bowie researcher Nick Stevenson noted that recent consumers have rather a casual 'pick and mix' relationship to religion (2009, 89). Matt Hills (2002a, 117–19) and others have therefore begun to explore the idea that fan researchers should think in terms of *neo-religiosity* rather than religion. This may be an attempt, however, to stretch an idea that does not quite hold up.

For better or worse, metaphors allow us to talk about things that we can only just see. In the rest of this section, using a case study approach, I will explore why researchers have pursued the religious comparison and how we might salvage one element of the sociology of religion without creating an explanation that lends itself to lambasting dedicated fans. What is interesting about the religiosity explanation is that it so frequently gets applied to fandoms that are considered *lower* on the cultural hierarchy: populist, low brow, lower-middle-class or working-class. It is rarely suggested that fans of Bob Dylan, for example, have substituted fandom for religion, even though they may be every bit as dedicated as Elvis fans. In an examination of the widespread application of the religiosity idea specifically to Elvis, in 2003 I demonstrated that what began as a joke about the perceived tastelessness of certain forms of fandom soon became an academic concept describing the perceived religious zeal of real fans who never, as such, claimed the label for themselves (see Duffett 2003). The religiosity comparison therefore shows the subtle but significant power that academics can wield, especially when they create theories based on metaphors that purport to explain the intentionality of other people. Comparisons are always interpretive devices rather that empirical facts. A strategic approach in this context would be to sidestep issues of the accuracy or actuality of each comparison and instead examine theorists' motivations. 'Religious' representations of stars like Michael Jackson and Elvis by middle-class cultural commentators – and their academic equivalents – imply a shared concern about the emotional overload of star performances and the public's ecstatic response. Moreover, they tend to coincide with moments where the reputations of such icons are becoming more legitimate and established, posthumously welcomed by mainstream society. For example, around the time Graceland first opened to the public, Albert Goldman's infamous 'hatchet job' biography (perhaps that should read hatchet job 'biography') *Elvis* subjected its charge to a full character assassination and unleashed a grotesque parody of Presley into the mainstream media. By the mid-1990s, Elvis was in the news again because members of the babyboom generation were pushing to make one of their most-loved performers part of America's cultural furniture.[7] As Greil Marcus said, 'He had put his stamp on the nation, just as the nation was now putting his stamp on its mail' (2000, 175). For a man who had been dead for well over a decade, Elvis's prospects were looking good. In the wake of this process of rehabilitation, however, scholars increasingly began to create religious interpretations of Elvis fandom.

In 1994, Simon Frith reported that 'the academy never had much interest in Elvis Presley' (275). He went on to explain that Elvis had been dismissed by critics of popular culture and virtually ignored by musicologists, sociologists and writers from cultural studies. However, within five years Gilbert Rodman's *Elvis After Elvis: The Posthumous Career of a Living Legend* (1996) was joined by Vernon Chadwick's conference reader *In Search of Elvis: Music, Art, Race,*

Religion (1997), and Erika Doss's 1999 volume. Theologians, sociologists and folklore scholars were now among those who increasingly pondered whether Elvis fandom was religious practice. In other words a sea change took place as the decade moved forward. In the years after Simon Frith's declaration, folk anthropology, cultural studies, popular music studies and the fine arts joined forces in a sustained effort to explore and explain Elvis as a religious icon. When labelled by academics and not by fans themselves, theoretical fan 'religions' are *cultural constructions* that reflect the anxieties of social groupings that constitute themselves through academia. Instead of making an objective, neutral comparison, Doss used the notion of religion because it supported her concern as a representative of bourgeois culture: 'I am a middle-class, highly educated and highly opinionated college professor. Perhaps more important, I'm not an Elvis fan – which I explained in conversations with fans when they asked me who I was and what I was doing' (1999, 26). Having access to the means of representation placed such researchers in a position of authority and enabled them, by continually making the comparison, to sustain the idea of religiosity. They could then interpret Elvis fandom as a 'cult' to fill their own sociocultural agenda.

The religiosity notion became so pervasive that it operated as an assumption and a structuring device, presiding over academic interpretations of what fans actually had to say. Once the metaphor was accepted, others were effectively forced to speak through it, either in a confessional or resistant mode. When it became more entrenched, the comparison then operated as a guiding assumption in research. Fans who denied the religious quality of their experiences were interpreted, in the eyes of their own disbelievers, as either lacking or lying. Writers like Ted Harrison discounted what they said. Harrison looked for reasons why they seemed to cover up. After asking whether fans *prayed* to Elvis, Harrison said, 'some will admit it, others not' (1992, 67). Later he added:

> So it is that many Elvis fans will hotly deny any religious suggestion that they have turned their hero into a cult religious figure. In addition to the possible Protestant reservations, they sense that for it to be perceived that they have 'deified' a pop star will attract unwelcome ridicule. Fans are very sensitive about the way people laugh about the very idea of devotion to a rock and roll singer. Yet from time to time a fan will 'come out'. (75)

Though Harrison is a popular writer, academics reached similar conclusions by similar logic. Erika Doss asked, 'What does it mean when adherents deny the religiosity of something that looks so much like a religion?' (1999, 73) It meant they could be presented as inflexible and blind to their own predicament, or hypocritical and shamefaced. The idea that fans' interview statements provided an honest and straightforward record could not be entertained because they were supposed to be too obsessed or ashamed to give a realistic picture of their own experience. In effect the religious metaphor could then be used to challenge the social practices of fans (Jenkins 2006, 19). It encouraged them to reign in their displays of emotional conviction for fear that middle-class circles would reject them as lacking in taste. It also silenced their views in the face of estranged 'experts' who contended otherwise.

If the religious analogy has been used to attack fandom, is there anything from the sociological theory of religion that sympathetically and selectively might be worth salvaging? Suprisingly, perhaps, I am going to suggest an affirmative answer. In his classic 1912 book *Elementary Forms of Religious Life*, the French sociologist Emile Durkheim studied the social ecology of Australian clans engaged in totemic religion. These societies were based, according to Durkheim, on a fundamental division between the secular and the sacred. Totems are material objects (sometimes people) that embody the contagious essence of the sacred. Each totem functions to mediate the emotional force of the social collective. As part of this, Durkheim explains that the totem feels energized as a focus of the spectacle who recognizes his or her connection to the whole of the congregation:

> This unusual surplus of forces is quite real: it comes to him from the very group he is addressing. The feelings provoked by his speech return to him inflated and amplified, reinforcing his own. The passionate energies he arouses echo back to him and increase his vitality. He is no longer a simple individual speaking, he is a group incarnate and personified. (2008, 158)

Clan members who gather to worship a totem therefore unknowingly help to channel collective energy gained from the group through the totem, who then gives back to the individual worshipper. In a key moment that Durkheim calls 'effervescence', each emotionally heightened crowd member experiences a life-changing jolt of electricity as they subconsciously recognize a personal connection to the totem. The energy in turn boosts the individual's strength and confidence. In this way he/she is connected to the social body on a primal and mysterious level.

Academics such as Chris Rojek (2001, 56) have applied Durkheim's ideas to celebrity. However, elsewhere I have cautioned against both the casual comparison of fandom and religion and any *wholesale* application of Durkheim's ideas in popular music studies (see Duffett 2011a). The French sociologist's work rests on a distinction between the sacred and the profane that seems inappropriate when applied to commercial music or other forms of popular culture. It also defines religion through a metaphysical conception of afterlife that seems irrelevant. Nevertheless, more attention to *one* mechanism from Durkheim's framework may be useful: in effect, celebrities *are* like totems. As Pramod Nayar (2009, 4) explains, 'A celebrity is an individual or event that the public watches'. We also know that people get a thrill from meeting their idols. For Durkheim, 'religion is above all a system of notions by which individuals imagine the society to which they belong and their obscure yet intimate relations with that society' (2008, 170). To elaborate, the crucial aspects of this are twofold. First, social electricity only exists insofar that individuals *feel* it. The process of rousing such excitement is based on shared *assumptions*, *perceptions* and *experiences*. Although nothing literally leaps between people, those involved feel an intense and undeniable human chemistry. Second, the mechanism of effervescence is essentially *productive*. By shaping believers' commitment to the group, loyalty and morality, it helps to generate a part of their identity. The energizing loop of human interaction, in which *engaged participants* feel thrilled by gestures of attention from a more socially valued person (the focus of attention), is therefore highly productive. I mention 'engaged participants' here precisely because not all audience members feel a strong positive link to the performer.

To adopt Durkheim's ideas is not to reduce people to proverbial cultural dupes, but instead to account for the intensity of feeling experienced by a convinced fraction of the audience.[8] As Kerry Ferris puts it, 'One person's exciting encounter may be another person's routine "celebrity sighting", which may be yet another person's uneventful trip to the supermarket' (2001, 46). By routinely aligning performers and audiences, the media – and most obviously the live music industry – brings the individual and collective together in a way that I have previously described as a 'symbolic economy' (see Duffett 2009). To further focus on the affective dimension of performance using Durkheim, we can follow the process across three stages (though in practice they happen together): in the first, the crowd has power in its collectivity; in the second, the performer has a foundational sense of well-being from the support of their audience; in the third, each individual fan feels a thrill from the performer's attention.

To deal with the first two phases, I wish to build on the work of Steve Waksman (2007), who analysed the emergence of arena rock in the United States during the early 1970s. According to Waksman, the mass popularity of recorded music had long given artists their relative status. However, events such as the Beatles 1965 show at the Shea Stadium and the countercultural festivals of the 1960s *directly equated* the size of the *live* crowd with a sense of collective power and freedom. Waksman looked at how the hard rock band Grand Funk Railroad pioneered the practice of arena rock touring by co-opting a certain language that celebrated the sheer size of their fan base. The group's manager Terry Knight said, 'Anybody that can draw 55,000 people together at one time has got some kind of power' (Waksman 2007, 161). Whatever the historic development of the arena rock idea, the assumptions that undergird Knight's statement are more than hollow rhetoric. Contemporary music audiences tend to share them. Music is widely seen as creating a sense of community. As Simon Frith suggests, 'Live music performance . . . is a public celebration of musical commitment, a deeply pleasurable event at which our understanding of ourselves through music is socially recognized' (2007, 14). In our society, popular music therefore tends to come freighted with a pleasurable inequality of popularity between the performer and individual listener.

We are taught to understand that musical performance always implies an audience: either a set of spectators for a mediated product or a face to face crowd.[9] We are also taught to understand that a musician's success depends on the audience's approval. Successful musical performance is a means of mutual social empowerment. Charismatic performers are credited with actively bringing the audience together. Describing punk rock veteran Iggy Pop, one journalist in the NME recently explained, 'In transforming rock'n'roll concerts from mere spectacle into a profound manacle-smashing collective experience, he truly is the ultimate frontman' (McKay et al. 2011, 13). Indeed, because popular music is understood through romantic tenets that invest it with an air of intimacy *in public* (as that is where singers express personal emotions), it may be an especially good vehicle to consolidate and augment what Robert Cialdini (2001) has called 'social proof'. Confident performers know that they have been chosen to embody the focus of the event and enjoy the power of that position. Tom Jones expressed his experience of singing on stage by saying, 'It's a high that you just don't get from anything else. When you're on there, and the band and the people, and it's like – wow! – you've gone into another place'.[10] Here the important point is not just that Jones is describing a thrill; it is that his fans are feeling it too. Similarly, reporting on David Bowie fans, Nick Stevenson noted that 'during periods of stress and emotional turmoil, many of the male fans suggested that Bowie's music had helped them' (2009, 84). If such responses were previously understood as results of *sonic* enchantment or psychological lack, attention to Durkheim's schema suggests that music – or film acting for that matter – can operate as a vehicle for stars to touch fans by demonstrating both personal charm and mass popularity.

In response to the thrills they get, fans sometimes write back, opening up the communication from their end. As one, reproduced in Fred Vermorel's book *Starlust*, wrote, 'Here I am, a little speck on Earth, sitting alone imagining that I could actually be communicating with David Bowie' (1985/2011, 157).

This strangely familiar correspondence verifies Durkheim's theory by locating a fannish thrill in momentarily surmounting the power relationship between an ordinary person and a performer of Bowie's social value. Professor Daniel Hertitz added to the discussion here by saying that 'no star aura is found within the aesthetics of the medium itself' (2008, 65). It comes, instead, from our collective embrace of the performer. Through the repetition of that process of embrace the imagined world of deserved celebrity acquires a kind of distant glamour. As Nick Couldry has explained:

> It is 'common sense' that the 'media world' is somehow better, more intense, than 'ordinary life', and that 'media people' are somehow special. This is not based either on fact or on a cultural universal, but rather is a form of unconsciousness ultimately derived from a particular concentration of symbolic power. The media sphere itself is not different in kind from the world in which viewers live; it is a part of the same world dedicated to mediating it. Yet, through the naturalized hierarchy between constructed terms 'media world' and 'ordinary world', this division of the social world is generally reproduced as legitimate. (2007a, 353)

There is a danger here in thinking that stars simply emerge from a privileged 'media world' when instead that realm simply represents an accumulation of stellar personalities; it is the sum total of the performers deemed worthy of creating and fronting popular media products. Although electronic mediation can guarantee an audience that is both 'real' (a statistical collective) and imagined by us (an 'imagined community' that is the sum of the other private viewers or listeners), it is the *approval* of this audience which allows each performer to become successful in a Durkheimian sense. Finally, if such a performer convinces each of us (as individuals), we only need to be reminded of his or her popularity to feel thrilled by (the idea of) a personal connection.

Becoming a fan: A mysterious process

Very few studies address the origins of an individual's fandom; for many scholars 'fan' is a kind of consumer category into which someone simply falls or does not fall . . . In such studies, there is no 'becoming a fan'; rather 'being a fan' simply appears as a mode of audience participation, part of a larger historical context of industrialization or the rise of mass entertainment.

DANIEL CAVICCHI (1998, 41)

For someone to *be* a fan, at some point they have had to *become* one. Very few academics have studied this particular phenomenon, but not due to a lack of material. Fans tend to periodize their lives around autobiographic turning points when 'everything changed' and they became interested. Their initiation frequently becomes an important personal memory, recalled and discussed with others. Autobiographical first-person 'becoming a fan' stories are usually the first things that fans talk about when they get to know others, whether in person or online. Such stories allow each individual to locate his or her fandom as a shift in personal history. They enable people to mutually position their identities by comparing and contrasting their particular histories. Becoming a fan is marked by changes in both an individual's subjective, inner self *and* social role. Personal narratives seamlessly join those two aspects together.

Any attempt to understand the reasons for each individual's emergence as a fan, and the exact way in which it happened, present a minefield of research problems for interested scholars. Nobody first consciously plans to become a fan. It is not something achieved by rational design. Individuals are rarely conscious of the process until after it has happened. In other words, becoming a fan is rather like driving past a roadside spectacle on your biographic highway: your perspective changes radically during and after seeing it, and you might report the experience differently at various points along the journey. This means that we have to treat 'becoming a fan' narratives very carefully as documents of experience. Furthermore, while certain performances or events have prompted large numbers of individuals to become fans, the process cannot be predicted, pre-arranged or stage-managed on an individual basis. In different cultures, for different objects, emergent fandom also happens in very different ways. Traditional ideas claim that mass culture is immediately accessible to all comers and therefore different to high culture since no need for a process of cultivation or apprenticeship is required. Depending on the object of interest, though, a degree of immediate social mentoring sometimes happens before or after the key moment. Media genres such as soap operas actually require sustained attention to understand nuances of character and plot. Existing fans can act as mentors and initiators, providing an education that reduces the time needed to realize why episodes matter. As Harrington and Bielby explain, becoming-a-fan stories that involve a gradual journey of personal shifts are sometimes tied to relationships with others:

Most [soap] watchers depend on more experienced viewers to help them make sense of the unfolding narratives, and people must be patient enough to overcome their initial confusion before they can become regular soap watchers . . . Most people can clearly remember who introduced them to soap operas and how old they were when they first started watching them . . . Most of our respondents first began watching soaps in a supportive environment, surrounded by others with similar interests. (1995, 87–8 and 89)

Individuals who become fans do not exactly *transform* their identities, because they never actually *leave* any aspect of their previous identity *behind*. Instead, they find that a new vista opens up of self-identified possibilities. The individual changes *how they see* their identity. Before any social proclamations, this form of affective change and self-recognition must first take place *inside* the individual. After a frisson of emotional connection and – perhaps more importantly a recognition that it has happened – the crucial moment in the emergence of a person's fandom really comes when *they* recognize their own fandom ('I realized that I was a fan'). Its particular process of emergence, however, can sometimes be a gradual or drawn-out experience. Indeed, Cavicchi compares 'becoming a fan' narratives to the two kinds of religious conversion outlined by William James: moments of *self-surrender* (in which a troubled person gives up their struggle and is converted) and *volitional* (a gradual move into new habits) (1998, 43). Some fans *do not* have a clear moment of discovery and understand their shift more in retrospect: 'I have no real memory of 'discovering' *Doctor Who*; it's just something that's always been part of my life, for as long back as my memory goes' (McGuire 2010, 118). After the internal shift, further moments of outward initiation and discovery then take place and individuals usually start to track down performances and speak to like-minded fans.

Bacon-Smith (1992) examined how fans become self-identified and go through various levels of initiation such as watching broadcasts, recording shows and learning about fanzines and fanfic. Media playback technology is vital here in allowing convenient access to material. Sometimes people find it easier to maintain their fandom either because of an interest in an ongoing (serialized) product, or because this interest is boosted by an ongoing community:

Doctor Who wasn't the only fandom I followed: *Star Trek* in its various forms, *Star Wars*, *Scarecrow and Mrs King*, *MacGuyver*, *Blakes 7*, *Remnington Steele*, *The Avengers*, *Sapphire & Steel*, *Adderly*, *Robin of Sherwood*, *Beauty and the Beast*, *Babylon 5*, *Stargate SG-1* – as well as others. Many of those fandoms vanished as soon as the shows went of the air. Others lingered awhile before their fans moved on. I stayed with a *Doctor Who* fan because the fandom continued to exist even after the show didn't. Thanks to the Internet, I could find like-minded fans to discuss stories and themes . . . In time, I didn't attend *Doctor Who* conventions because a particular star or stars would be there (since I had already heard most of their stories before), but because it was a chance to visit with friends I only saw once a year. (Sullivan 2010, 130)

In an internet age, intrigued potential fans can increasingly exploit media convergence to create their own points of contact with a phenomenon (Jenkins 2008, 57). However, access to distributional technologies and exposure to cultural materials does not *determine* the emergence of individual fandom. They are, in effect, facilitators: necessary, but not sufficient conditions.

Individual fandom can be conceptualized, partly as a squaring of identities where the potential fan discovers things they like about the text. This squaring can mean a recognition of pleasures, an understanding of creativity, or an appreciation of attitude. Traditionally, referencing the metaphor of addiction, such elements have been called 'hooks'. Harrington and Bielby found that various points of access attracted fans to soap viewing:

While viewers are usually introduced to soaps by another person, different access points (Whetmore and Kielwasser 1983, 111) within the genre hook the viewer: actor, character, writing, storyline, costumes, or some other identifiable feature. Some respondents follow favourite actors, writers, and directors from show to show; others are loyal to a specific show and its familiar community of characters. The idea of different access points is important because it is central to differentiating viewers from one another. Fans who scrutinize acting skills, for example, can become frustrated with viewers who are 'hung up on the story', and those who are loyal to the entire fictional community of Genoa City, Corinth, Llanview, or Bay City are aghast at others who can pick up or drop a program seemingly at will. (1995, 89)

Individuals in the audience can at first be resistant to a performance, but, as Cavicchi explains, 'This indifference or negativity is then radically altered. An individual hears a song on the radio, reads a line in a book, or is dragged to a Springsteen concert and simply becomes "hooked". Such a transformation is an epiphany, often described as mystical and inexplicable' (1998, 43). Hooks are important as they allow people of different identities to follow the same phenomenon. For example, stars can have both deaf fans and blind fans who find different ways to enjoy the performance. *Actions* can also be hooks as they encourage fan commitment; following a live show one fan explained to Cavicchi (1998) 'I can't believe someone has that kind of power over me [laughs]. He made me stand on a chair and yell, "Goobah, goobah, goobah!" [laughter] But I did!' (90). The idea that hooks can include audience actions suggests both that they are diverse and not directly causative; not everyone 'gets' them. New fans can initially be engaged as much by *performances* as by performers as individuals: 'Having a personal relationship with Springsteen means that one feels deeply about Springsteen the performer; in "becoming a fan" stories, fans are not so much touched by Springsteen himself as by his performance' (55). This is particularly interesting as it demonstrates that fans are less in love with stars, or, for that matter, authors, than with *the pleasures and possibilities that those individuals can offer to them*. Because they are inevitably *more* emotionally engaged than the rest of the audience, dedicated devotees can be both highly supportive of the performer and highly vocal about below par moments – paradoxically wishing for further glory in difficult times. Unending attention is never guaranteed: if a hero reneges on the relationship in some way, criticism and desertion can follow. Singer Ricky Martin, for instance, disappointed many of his Hispanic fans when a photo circulated online of him headlining at George Bush's 2001 inauguration ball.

An associated issue with hooks in the context of people becoming fans is that fans can be familiar with a performance for years *before* they perceive the hooks that finally attract them. When Daniel Cavicchi married a Springsteen fan, he had known the Boss's music for a long time, but he explained that, 'After we got married, I truly became transformed'. He noticed a sign that his fandom for Bruce Springsteen had started when he repeatedly played a b-side to the 'Brilliant Disguise' single called 'Lucky Man' (1998, 51).

Given the methodological difficulties of engaging with the process, it is not surprising that researchers have generally kept away from the topic of how people become fans. When they have done, their discussions have tended to focus on questions of the role of *individual agency* in the process. One way to explore that is to begin separating collective and individual elements *in theory*, while admitting that they always happen together *in reality*. Following Bourdieu's work on taste, the first *social* element to notice is that certain objects *are licensed* and available to be chosen within shared structures of taste. Fan identity necessarily begins as a personal interest, but it can grow or wither due to the local social context:

> Fandom does not seem to flourish in a resolutely hostile environment; its passions and attachments have to be linked to a localized sense of cultural value and legitimacy, even if this only occurs within the household or a small circle of friends rather than the 'imagined community' of the fan subculture. (Hills 2002a, 78)

In other words, while there are many cultural passions that we *could* have in theory – focused on anything from boybands to soaps, horror films to ballet – traditionally there have been some things that are socially encouraged, and for Bourdieu they depend on our local social environment and identity: nationality, ethnicity, age, gender, (dis)ability, class and subculture. This does not mean that licensed, tasteful objects are chosen every time. It means instead that individuals are *more likely to encounter and feel comfortable choosing* those objects. Furthermore, an individual's personal fandom does not always last:

> I drifted away from *Who* fandom because of a teenage estimation that if I continued with this all-consuming passion I would never, in a million years, have any chance of getting a girlfriend. Now, whether or not this was true, the fact that this decision made cultural sense to me indicates the operation of one aspect of a cultural system of value whereby media fandom is/was linked to a sense of 'failed' or inadequate masculinity. Living with this dimension I was not able to simply pursue my fandom. Like [Sue] Wise, I felt under pressure to reject it, even if I cannot recall any direct challenge to my sense of masculinity. (85)

Matt Hills links the end – or perhaps more accurately the temporary cessation – of his *Doctor Who* fandom with social pressures that framed the world of *Doctor Who* fandom as not fully masculine. In this case fan attachment is also connected to the life cycle: on the same page Hills explains that he took up horror fandom because it would allow him to express a more mature adolescent masculinity. His reasoning is critical, analytical and necessarily in retrospect. What is also interesting is that although the experience of fandom begins as a kind of innate impulse or moment of self-discovery, it sometimes seems to *end* through pressures such as gender ideals or notions of appropriate taste. The existence of undeclared, 'closet fandom' implies that this is not always that case and, in the face of potential social ostracism, some fans carry on their passions simply by hiding them.

One of the issues with the idea that there are social forces guiding us to choose particular objects is that individuals can make odd or awkward choices in relation to their social identities. Moreover, particular configurations of events seem to have a relatively predictable effect on increasing or decreasing specific fan bases. Imagined friendship, which can be an important element of fan attachments, is greatly affected by the star's death: 'I was suprised at how much his [Elvis'] death touched me . . . As I listened to records and delved into clippings . . . the memories that were evoked had nothing to do with sex, nothing to do with romance. The overwhelming feelings and memories were warmth and affection for a dear friend' (Wise 1990, 337). Yiman Wang (2007) has investigated fans of the pop and film star Leslie Cheung, who died in 2003. As one fan posted on the social networking site LiveJournal, 'I may sound like I'm a freak for being sad over a dead celebrity, but . . . almost everyone who grew up in Hong Kong in the '80s was, at one time or another [aware of Cheung]'. Wang compares Cheung's popularity to Princess Diana and explains, 'The term "posthumous fandom" is meant to highlight Cheung's *increased* charisma after his death. As a dead celebrity, the iconic Cheung acquires a spiritual dimension' (2007, 327; emphasis in original). Perhaps due to a combination of loss assessment, increased publicity and reason to feel pity, star deaths are often moments when fan bases extend considerably. Since most of the public *already know* the star to some extent, repeated exposure to their performance cannot account for the whole phenomenon. Instead the star's passing as a human being changes what we know about them and makes a qualitative difference to what we can feel (i.e. a shift of affect). The question then becomes why a star death does not make *everyone* a fan. Cavicchi notes, 'Throughout my fieldwork, I did not come across any stories about groups of people becoming fans *en masse* while, say, at a concert or listening together. In fact, I would surmise that many fans might frown upon such an occurrence as too connected with the uniformity of a mass audience' (1998, 53). In other words, although certain events may sometimes prompt large numbers of people to become fans, we have to conclude that individual fandom still has a crucial, personal dimension. Some fan conversions happen alone, others in the presence of fellow initiates, but each must be *experienced* as a kind of individual, personal event.

While fans have as great a capacity for conscious and rational self-examination as anyone else, their own stories of becoming a fan are usually characterized by an inability to explain exactly how and why the process happened. We may find the hooks, but it feels as *if they* have found *us*. One male Bowie fan said to Nick Stevenson, for example, 'It was like I was meant to find him' (2009, 91). As Matt Hills said, 'Fans do not claim agency in their "becoming-a-fan" stories, but they do claim agency through their later "performances" of fan identity' (2002, 159). To cite a parallel example, Judith Butler (1990/1999) has examined gender. Contesting essentialism, she has claimed that even if gender *feels like* an innate identity, it can be seen as a *social performance*. Butler does not mean this in a voluntarist sense (i.e. masculinity or femininity as something we elect), but argues instead that each growing child responds to language and expectation, growing up as if he/she matures by copying other people. Gender can therefore be seen as something gestural: *a performance without an origin*. Fandom is often championed as an act of consumerist free will primarily pursued by each individual – but, like Butler's idea of gender, it also *seems* like an iteration-without-origin (Hills 2002a, 158–9). This idea implies that fandom is not just the result of an individual process of connecting with popular culture. It presupposes that fandom itself is primarily a role, an unconsciously learned predisposition to the media – an idea that effectively returns us to issues of contagion. Before completely dismissing it, however, one might ask: *Is it possible to be a fan without fandom?* This question seems strange, but if it is then fandom is more like a deep state of consciousness. I am holding back from saying an 'existential' state here because – even if fans sometimes feel and speak of it in these ways – I do not think there is an innate human need to be a fan (or fans would have existed in all times and eras) and I do not think that fandom is something inherently spiritual or metaphysical (attained like a state of nirvana). Instead, various phenomena like the emergence of fandom (seemingly, often in private), social ostracism and closeted behaviour, suggest that fandom is a passion that has deep personal meaning, not something acted out for the sake of its performance or solely deployed to gain 'face'. In a sense, then, on any scale of conviction of identity, fandom is pitched on a level that is deeper than a casual role (one held and expressed to socially manipulate others) but less than an innate aspect of a person's natural, existential or instinctual being. To offer a parallel example, if someone has a baby, they are a mother. Once they are a parent, they cannot adopt or disregard the role as they chose, but may, for social reasons, decide to express or conceal it at different times. Unlike motherhood, however, fandom is neither the marker of a one-way existential shift (you cannot be an ex-mother, but you can an ex-fan) and fandom has to involve a positive attachment at some level (whereas, once you are a mother then you always are one, even if you do not *feel* like it).

Given that fandom is something that initially happens as an experiential shift inside each individual fan's head, a central point to realize is that the fan object can be real or imagined, alive or dead. On one level it does not matter. For Daniel Cavicchi the fannish self is in a constant process of self-discovery and reshaped by its own sense of reflexivity (1998, 136). A characteristically celebrated, self-absent quality both locates the individual's fandom as something overwhelming – bigger than and beyond themselves – and has led to its false and highly problematic social stereotyping as something that is inevitably addictive (as if nobody ever *stopped* being a fan), and, more important, the *opposite to* rational subjectivity. However, formulations that retain the mystery of the process of becoming a fan tend to assume that we must be conscious of that process in order to understand anything about it. If our fandom begins in ways that we do not consciously understand as individuals, does that mean such processes are inexplicable? Might it instead mean we have unconsciously adopted *assumptions* – about the social function of media in general, and about specific authors, texts or performers in particular – that *when activated or fulfilled* allow us to create, access or unlock our fannish identities? The symbolic economy associated with Durkheim's theory of religion discussed in the previous section may offer some hope here by giving us at least a working hypothesis of affective mechanisms by which each individual becomes a fan, particularly in a cultural field like rock music. It suggests that the moment of enlightenment comes from *a double realization*, as each fan both (a) recognizes the semiotic resonance of the text *for him/her as an individual* and (b) fully understands its social popularity. Because these *two* realizations may occur at different times (or indeed both at once), the process may remain hard to fathom from first appearances.

In the knowing field

In the early 1990s a series of books were published featuring random dot autostereograms, optical illusions more commonly known as 'magic eye' puzzles that relied on viewers diverging their focus in order to see 3D shapes that emerged from flat pieces of paper. The magic eye craze had many readers squinting at strange puzzle pages, trying to see ordinarily hidden shapes and patterns. In a sense, whether fast or gradual, fandom begins like those magic eye puzzles. Fans start to 'see' some things that others cannot. Their experience may be informed by a range of factors. In television fandom, for example, it is often a slow process because the narrative gradually exposes an appealing play of creativity. Rather than divergent pupils, the shift comes about through *a combination of two assumptions*: an emotional attachment to someone or something and a recognition that he, she or it has social power (usually denoted by popularity). Since neither of these assumptions is fulfilled by conscious intent, fandom *feels* both overwhelming and empowering.

Sceptical of the idea that empirical studies such as interviews could help researchers find new ways to understand the music audience, Theodor Adorno claimed that 'every answer one receives *conforms in advance* to the surface of that music business which is being attached by the theory' (1938/2001, 45; emphasis mine). In other words, for Adorno, music audience members are like *fish in water*, unable to lead researchers to new discoveries because they can only repeat terms from the hype that contextualizes their cultural interest. If fandom actualizes unspoken assumptions, then, a bit like the Adorno's famous fish in water, even highly critical or reflexive fans may have limited discursive resources at their disposal to comment on the origins of their interest. After all, most ideas about fan initiation draw on *limited discursive resources*: 'passive' manipulation by the culture industry, pathological 'vulnerability' to contagion, 'blinding' religious insights or the 'active' construction of resistant identities. In this section I wish to introduce a new term to the literature on fandom: that of fandom as entry into a 'knowing field'. This term orginates from Hellinger's work in family constellations therapy. What follows will describe the nature of a 'knowing field' and explore its usefulness as a heuristic device in fan research. My argument is that attention to the experience of individual fans can deepen our understanding of fandom as a phenomenon.

Family constellations therapy emerged from the unique career trajectory of the German therapist Hellinger whose biography included a long spell as a Catholic preist and missionary to Zulu tribes in Africa. During his work with tribal rituals, Hellinger began to devise a workshop-based form of therapy that allowed individuals or couples to see their family-of-origin traumas embodied by fellow participants:

> Representatives are chosen for essential family members and are placed in physical relationships to one another . . . The representatives are not asked to 'play a role' or to participate in a psychodrama. They are only required to note carefully and precisely what they feel during movements in the constellation. One of the phenomena that occurs is that the representatives begin to feel movements, feelings and reactions that seem foreign to their own personal lives. These reactions may not be an objective truth about real family members, but they allow hidden dynamics to come out into the open and provide enough information to help the therapist find movements that facilitate healing. (Hellinger 2001, 8)

While Hellinger himself does not use the term 'knowing field,' it has been widely used to describe the representative's emotional experience of participating in a constellation. Entry into the field primarily occurs when the participant is asked to become a representative for the duration of the constellation. Once they agree to being placed somewhere in the room, it seems to them that they come to partially *embody and incarnate* the feelings of the family member for which they stand. This embodiment is a mysterious and mystical process, an experiential leap which realigns part of their identity. While fans are not in need of healing and fandom has no obvious relationship to family dynamics, I think that a loose borrowing of the 'knowing field' idea does capture some important elements: that fandom is not (just) a performed role, but rather a means of entry in to a realm of emotional conviction where one's feelings can seem highly personal and yet not quite one's own, since the experience of feeling something strong and positive is shared by many others. At least as a youth phenomenon, if fandom still seemed foreign in the 1950s, its strangeness has now become something to which society has grown accustomed. It is also – arguably – the product of individual reactions to hidden, and not so hidden, ontological assumptions, social dynamics and cultural resonances. The 'knowing field' is therefore a terrain of affect, bounded by a threshold beyond which one can say, 'Yes, I know that I am a fan'. Different forms of fandom have affective differences. Nevertheless, if adapting Durkheim's mechanism of effervescence can help explain the affective rewards of celebrity-following, then in several ways the 'knowing field' idea can also help us understand personal fandom. First, the notion reminds us that fannish emotions are *both produced and productive*. In other words fannish emotions emerge from assumptions and their fulfilment, but they can go on to shape other things such as the collective, moral economy of fandom. Second, the idea helps us to recognize that that personal fandom for a particular object unites a *process of emotional change* with *a residency on a territory of affect*. By 'a process of emotional change', I mean feeling an affective shift by traversing a threshold that separates fandom from disinterest. This can be thought of as the would-be fan surpassing a base line, but it can also be understood by recalling that if and when his/her interest wanes, he/she will effectively cross back down in the other direction.[11] The *territory of affect*, meanwhile, is a positively charged space: the 'knowing field' denotes a place that is *both* inside each of us, and something notionally shared by everyone in the fan base.

6

Fan practices

Starting points

- Why do fans repeat particular actions?
- Why do fans who participate in different phenomena behave in similar ways?
- What are the relationships between fan activity and social identity?

We need only say her first name. The name 'Marilyn' conjures up magical and diverse images of her phenomenal presence. Immortal Marilyn *is built by contributions from a group of Marilyn fans who have been working together already for years running the largest Marilyn Monroe fan club in the world (of the same name). Now our efforts are focused on this Website . . . Planning to go to Los Angeles for the 50th Anniversary (5 August 2012) of Marilyn Monroe's passing? Marilyn fans will gather to pay their respects, attend events that honor and celebrate her life. Immortal Marilyn members always stay at the Hollywood Orchid Suites, situated in the heart of Hollywood, mere steps from Hollywood Blvd, The Kodak Theater, Grauman's Chinese Theater and so much more!*

IMMORTAL MARILYN WEBSITE[1]

Fans are active in pursuit of their pleasures. The network of individuals who run the Immortal Marilyn club do not just put their energies into creating a Website. They hold pilgrimages to Hollywood, make and upload their own videos, write articles, create wallpapers, hold memorial services, raise charity donations, review books, sketch pictures and much more. Fan practices give the lie to the idea that fandom is passive. Indeed we might say that not all activity is consciously and critically examined, but our minds and bodies are always active in some way unless we are forced to do things against our will. Our activities show the ways that we collude with what holds our attention. Most people who talk about fandom tend to connect it to a particular set of practices that either signify fascination (wearing a t-shirt, collecting media products), engagement with celebrity (writing fan mail, attending film premiers, impersonating) or collective sociability (going to fan conventions, contributing to forums). Writers in cultural studies, on the other hand, have primarily discussed fandom in terms of practices of resistance ('spoiling' narrative plots, lobbying corporations, rewriting script scenarios). Fan studies has placed particular emphasis on the way that female fans have rewritten the sexual relations of male fictional characters in 'slash' fiction. At this point it has to be said that the *primary* practice of media fandom is simply consuming the text or engaging with the performance – listening, watching, thinking and feeling, finding yourself through its gestural embrace. Such seemingly 'passive' and less prominent practices are, however, more complex than might be assumed at face value. Fan practices blur the distinction between reading and writing (Jenkins 1992, 155). Without claiming to be comprehensive, this chapter will recategorize fan practices in terms of three types of pleasures associated with fandom: connection to connection (to a hero or story), appropriation (of its meaning) and fresh kinds of performance (enacted by the fans themselves).

Pleasures of connection

Beyond engaging with the text, for many people some of the primary pleasures of fandom stem from their aim of encountering the performer and perhaps talking to them or receiving their autograph. Stars vary in their attitudes about serving fans as an audience. Richard Witts has described how prominent musicians have kept their live audiences waiting for up to two and a half hours (2005, 152). Rather than seeing Bruce Springsteen as a marketed star (he is evidently uncomfortable and generally refuses interviews), a commercial producer or even the next Dylan, his fans celebrate his values and argue that those make him genuine and approachable (Cavicchi 1998, 67). Although not all celebrities are interested, those who generously greet their fans often become celebrated for it.

Autograph hunting is a common fan practice. It has roots in much earlier times, where aristocrats made collections of manuscripts to mark out different periods in history. By the nineteeth century, contemporary heroes from politics, business, theatre and music were all targets for autograph collectors. Autographs inscribe a cipher of the person. They indicate individuality, both in terms of *exchange value* (rather like signing a work of art or cheque) and *use value* (reminding us that we once met the individual, that he/she acknowledged us). The pleasures of connecting with stars, even through autograph collections, are, however, limited. Autographs and media products are understood as *alienated* traces of personality and performance. Intellectuals have sometimes spelled this out. Discussing the mediating value of snap shots, Daniel Hertitz reported:

> Roland Barthes says photography is a memorial to the dead, a way of making the dead present again among us while also confirming their absence, since the photo reminds us it was *then* that we knew them (and no longer). (2008, 72)

Some of the most recent research on celebrity encounters has come from the symbolic-interaction work of sociologists Kerry Ferris and Scott Harris (2011). According to the two researchers, while fans often form relationships outside of actual physical meetings with their heroes, they seek out moments of actual physical co-presence and long for mutual, face to face encounters. Star-fan meetings are necessarily based on asymmetries of knowledge (favouring the fan) and of power (favouring the star). Hence 'the ways in which fans seek out and notice celebrities certainly differ from the ways that celebrities orient to and take note of fans' (Ferris & Harris 2011, 18). Because fans see performers as 'intimate strangers' they may feel a particular sense of entitlement: 'Fans may feel they are entitled to knowledge of and contact with celebrities (strangers) just like they do with friends, family and colleagues (intimates)' (31). Face-to-face meetings are seen as better than moments of media consumption, because they enable fans to expand their knowledge of the performer into new areas and also to redress some of the asymmetries typical to the fan-celebrity relationship. Such meetings also provide opportunities for fans to acquire souvenirs. They use their agency here to advance their structural position. 'Staged encounters' – set up for fans or by them – put the audience is in control. Determined followers can even use the celebrity's workplace as a gateway to enter locations that define his or her private life. One fan of a celebrity actor, for example, used a public golf tournament to pursue her quarry. She videotaped the actor's mother at a golf tournament and offered to post her a copy. When the woman quickly offered her home address, the fan had automatically acquired a coveted piece of 'access information'. She could then reach the actor through his mother at any time. The two sociologists sharply contrast such staged events to chance meetings: 'The celebrity encountered in an ordinary setting is seen by observers as being "in his personal life", and this status somehow creates a social shield for him that is to be breached only under particular circumstances' (46). They explain:

> [There are] two types of interpretive, interactional work are revealed in seers' narratives of celebrity sightings: recognition work, in which seers struggle to define and comprehend the presence of a celebrity in their ordinary world, and response work, in which seers present themselves to the celebrity, engineering an encounter to create a particular definition of the situation. (39)

In the 'recognition work' category, fans do 'double takes' and search for proof identity; in the 'response work' category, enthusiasts stay cool, work out a reason to say hello, protect themselves from embarrassment and make sure the celebrity stays in relative 'public privacy'. They judge the celebrity's response to the interaction, to make sure he/she stays comfortable. When talking to celebrities, fans' verbal strategies can sometimes 'redefine the encounter as mutual rather than unilateral, and, therefore, more like an ordinary, consensual friendship' (27). Hence Ferris and Harris argue that there is a 'moral order' to celebrity sightings (xii). In other words, fans often use shared norms and standards to help define precisely where their personal, ethical lines might be drawn.

Pleasures of appropriation

Spoiling

Spoiling is the act of publicizing information that will give away a show's central plot mystery or other crucial information before its release or broadcast has occurred. Critics who review television shows and movies sometimes issue *spoiler warnings* to tell readers that their commentaries will 'give away' important plot details. Meanwhile, the fans who have an urge to practice spoiling understand it as the purposeful discovery of crucial developments in the plot of a fictional story of a film or TV series before the relevant material has been broadcast or released. Many of the arguments about fans consuming and appropriating texts over-simplify the situation. Cultural power does not operate systematically in this context and no one group holds *all* of it (Hills 2002a, 43). Amateur games of guesswork and attempts to spoil represent an *ordinary* pastime pursued by the dedicated audience. A degree of textual speculation is *invited* in that sense and represents an activity that fans characteristically pursue. Will Brooker found, for instance, that *Star Wars* fans engage in educated prediction work that is akin to 'spoiling' in some ways (2002, 116). Spoiling allows fans a kind of intellectual and literary pleasure; they must devise strategies to go beyond the forefront of their community's collective knowledge. For Jenkins, fans who go to extremes to find answers are in fact *the most dedicated sort*, a kind of unwelcome elite (2008, 25). Some have suggested that those who spoil are looking for recognition. Online communities have debated whether to see spoiling as a process of engagement with the text, or as a boastful contest 'won' by the most skilled investigators (51).

In the game of spoiling, neither the fans' nor producers' role is a passive one. *Doctor Who* series producer Phil Collinson criticized a fan for sneaking into a costume workshop and leaking pictures online. Matt Hills consequently explained:

> It may seem strange for a media professional to attack a fan verbally in this way. Symptomatic of the producer-versus-fan info-war – sometimes won by fandom, sometimes by *Doctor Who* production team – this nevertheless indicates the intense emotional value ascribed by fandom to experiencing *Who*, whether ahead of broadcast (for 'spolied' fans) or during transmission (for the 'unspoiled'). (2010b, 11)

The passage reflexively categorizes fans into those whose pleasures come from pursuing the practice and those whose pleasures come from denying it, suggesting that different perspectives on the value of spoiling can become a way to differentiate the identities of particular types. The practice of spoiling is also a clear example that a balance of power exists between fans and media producers, beyond any co-operative alliances. Indeed, the evolution of their mutual game of one-upmanship allows each side to speculate on the other's activities. *Survivor* fans who received spoilers tended to carefully examine the credibility of the source (Jenkins 2008, 55). Trust became very important to them. Sometimes fans have believed that a producer has misinformed them in order to divert attention away from the truth (46). In that sense, the game of spoiling allows them to enter into intellectually adversarial – but more intimate – contact with television show producers, film studios or record companies.

Of course, perceptions vary about whether it is better or worse to know the plot of your favourite show in advance. In line with the views of many media producers, non-spoiling fans may see the behaviours of those who actively pursue spoiling as inappropriate. Aggressive forms of spoiling have sometimes even been seen as antithetical to normal fandom. Indeed, some

purists hate spoiling as too intrusive (41). When the *Survivor* fan community
found out about one fan who rented a hotel room to get photos of the cast and
crew, it debated where the lines should be drawn (37). Those who gleefully
spoil a plot, for themselves or others, are, in a sense, 'cheating' everyone
and are seen as disloyal by many. Interestingly, though, academics rarely, if
ever, offer spoiler warnings. They are interested in unpacking the meanings
of texts, not in preserving their pleasurable mystery for viewers: 'Although
scholars are aware of the issue of spoilers, again often because they are
fans themselves, academic work is typically produced without any regard
for whether or not it will "spoil" fans' enjoyment of the TV episodes under
discussion' (Hills 2010b, 9). In other words, *researchers act as casual spoilers
after a show is broadcast*. Spoiling may be ethically controversial, but it allows
those interested to engage with the product on a more intensive level: they
conceptualize it as a puzzle that they can solve through active investigation.
The activity therefore offers the thrill of code-cracking.

Fanfic

Narratives are accounts that present a series of connected events. Everyone
understands life through story structures since they offer an accessible way
to perceive the world. Even media forms that might seem immune to the
creeping ubiquity of storytelling cannot escape it. For example, newspaper
reports about the private lives of famous actors present recognizable plots
and characters to the audience. Most media products – whether feature films,
games or soaps – offer up a world of narratives and characters that can be
enjoyed in a conventional sense, but can also be enjoyed in a new way if they
are appropriated in imaginative writing. As the basis for their own creative
ventures, fans adopt, organize and fictionalize these narrative worlds. **Fanfic**
is fictional writing created by the fans inspired by the objects of their interest.
Its content can be divided into different categories such as 'AU' (alternative
universe). Many are labeled by specific terms. Genfic, RPF and slash offer
three examples of different fanfic genres.[2] **Genfic** is simply 'general interest
fiction' which refrains from sexual or romantic plotlines. It can include 'darkfic',
a category that contains graphic violence (Brooker 2002, 145). Fans also
write 'cross-universe' stories in which, for example, *Doctor Who* appears in
Star Trek or *Star Wars* (Sullivan in Thomas & O'Shea 2010, 125). **RPF** means
'real person' fiction. It fictionalizes the lives of celebrities. **Slash**, which is
about same-sex trust, intimacy and eroticism, will be discussed more in the
next section. These styles are not just limited to television or science fiction
fandom. Reams of 'popslash' and 'rockfic' are now generated online by music

fans who reinvent their heroes. 'Bandom' has become a recent music fanfic subgenre associated with emo (goth music gone pop for younger audiences). The material in such subgenres is emergent, however: television and film fanfic remains dominant.

The academic interest in fanfic relates, perhaps, to the fact that it is obvious evidence of fans leaving their creative mark. It shows the capacity of ordinary people to use the media as a resource which can be actively reshaped in order to meet their own specific needs or interests. Fanfic can act as a public display of a writer's creativity. RPF writer Mario Lanza has written stories about the cast of *Survivor* that have been enjoyed by the contestants themselves. He has even received fan letters from the show's actors (Jenkins 2008, 38–40). By starting a conversation based on the shared fandom of its writers and readers, fanfic also functions communally to create social and cultural bonds. Any character portrayal in genfic or slash is part of this potential dialogue (Busse & Hellekson 2006, 28). Fanfic can vary from copying and extending the narrative universe of a media product to parodying and subverting it – although, of course, the idea of subversion depends on *who is interpreting* the original text (Jenkins 2008, 199). Fanfic is not universally accepted or practiced within fan communities. Indeed, many fans see it as 'character rape' for its distortion of stories that have already attracted support (Jenkins 2006, 57). Fanfic writers can also use *genfic to critique the original text,* for example by creating a parody if they think a show is getting a little too camp (Brooker 2002, 156). While it is often seen by producers as a marginal or unlicensed activity, fanfic's informal creation and distribution fosters an abundant sense of creative freedom within fan networks, allowing writers to play God, have things their way, evolve universes and challenge taboos (Jenkins 2006, 86–7). Fan writers can change their texts by expanding the series timeline, recontextualizing key scenes, shifting attention to minor characters ('refocalization'), making moral realignments, genre-shifting, dislocating characters emphasizing particular personalities, intensifying emotional encounters, eroticizing texts or hybridizing series (see Jenkins 1992, 162–77). Fan fiction therefore allows fans to feel more invested in characters and to explore them in richer, deeper narrative worlds. It allows people to speculate on missing episodes or to extend their pleasures by creating variations on a theme (Dickins 2010, 178).

One reason for the emergence of fanfic is that fans' expectations become set by stories that have either been discontinued, lost or mooted to soon appear. The 1968 *Doctor Who* story 'Fury from the Deep', for example, is no longer retained by the BBC. Fans of the series have used their imaginations to invent what they might have missed (Hills 2010b, 55). Fanfic can thus be understood as a kind of laboratory space: a device that allows writers to rethink different aspects of *their own* worlds and even *their perception of their object*. Brooker (2002, 93) found that one fan used secondary material to help reconceptualize *The Phantom Menace* (Lucas, 1999), for instance, as a subtle and more complex text.

Slash: A fanfic subgenre

What is slash?

'Shut up . . . we're by no means setting a precedent.' He was quiet . . . and not merely because he was used to obeying that voice implicitly. He was being peeled, slowly, like a delicate fruit, in time to some far off pagan rhythm and he found his logical mind was swathed in a white mist of sensual well-being. Gentle hands spread warm oil slowly, in ever-widening circles over his chest.

DIANE MARCHANT, A Fragment Out of Time[3]

For many decades, a lively minority of fans have been writing romantic or erotic fiction about the male objects of their affection. Kirk/Spock (K/S) or **slash fiction** is a prominent fanfic genre that usually puts the two main male characters from the series into a homoerotic relationship.[4] It illustrates how fanfic differs from the primary text. Since Kirk and Spock come from different planets, their relationship can help fans work through questions of otherness (Jenkins 1992, 203). A fluid sense of identity – expressed in the Vulcan mind-meld – allows the male characters in slash to share a certain intimacy, consciousness and set of sensations. Elizabeth Woledge (quoted in Busse & Hellekson 2006, 26) suggests that rather than pornography, slash is about explicit intimacy. The subgenre often uses sex as a *pretext for affection* – a place where characters' personalities and relationships can be carefully assessed. Stories in the genre tend to shift from homosocial friendship to homosexual desire through predictable plot steps re-inhabited in different ways in each story: an initial co-working relationship or friendship, the stress of emergent unspoken desires (indicating the painful taboo of masculinity), a moment of confession and the plateau of a utopian relationship. Slash can be about the sacrifices one must sometimes make in order to live with integrity, or the pain of pursuing a secret identity (see Jenkins 1992, 206–16).

Depending on the original show, the content of slash stories can range from soft core to S&M: *Blakes 7* (1978–81) slash emphasized the *dystopian* element of male-male desire, whereas *Star Trek* slash stories have been about *utopian* male-male love (206). The genre also has multiple subgenres: alternative universe, porn without plot, hurt/comfort, first time, angst, BDSM, point of view and comic parody (see Brooker 2002, 144). Hurt/comfort stories feature characters that face a threat or emergency and are then able to say that they care about each other.[5]

Why write or read slash?

Slash has a controversial reputation. While the authors of this fanfic genre are usually female, the stories marginalize female *characters* and bring 'female' *pleasures* into focus instead through the *portrayal* of male characters. Slash tends to explore sexual fantasies (Jenkins 1992, 200). Constance Penley talked about the 'pornographic force' of much of the genre (see Sandvoss 2005a, 74). While this seems like a valid perception, it is essentially based on the difference between slash and other genres, but does not encompass all of its pleasures. Sex can, in its intimacy, subtly express the personality of a character; it is an up-close form of character revelation (Dickins 2010, 178–9). Slash has also been perceived as an experimental extension of female sensuality to men: for example, in its emphasis on extended foreplay and exploration of extra-genital erogenous zones (Jenkins 2006, 80). In that sense, the important thing about slash is that it represents a way for fans to reshape the text to suit their interests. Slash helps women deal with their feelings within a society that has made men superior (74). Writers accept that media producers can never fully satisfy their female desire for a perfect episode (as they see it). Consequently, slash authors exploit gaps in character motivation and other opportunities (Jenkins 1992, 104). Some argue that the genre allows female fans to increase their pleasure in the text. After all, viewers are traditionally encouraged in most shows to identify with the key *male* characters because those are the main protagonists. Female viewers can sometimes feel like 'tourists' (Jenkins 2006, 67–8); slash allows them at least a kind of *voyeuristic pleasure* in the worlds of these characters. Some of its writers see slash as a branch of female erotica that can express women's sexual interests in the men by seeing them as sensual creatures who enjoy each other (Brooker 2002, 135). In that way, slash is not just any kind of fan erotica. 'Lieutenant Mary Sue' fanfic stories are ones criticized as presenting idealized versions of their female authors. Fanfic enthusiasts often dismiss these unimaginative stories as mere 'groupie fantasies' and instead write fiction to see what happens when a romance confronts mundane realities and professional duties (Jenkins 2006, 51). Within the bounds of an intimate relationship, slash narratives represent a utopian attempt to find mutual equality and autonomy and therefore offer an *indirect critique of the rigidity of masculinity* as it is currently practiced by most men (Jenkins 1992, 219). According to Sarah Katherine, *slash rewrites manhood*, presenting it as emotional responsible, nurturing and sustaining (see Jenkins 2006, 71).

Slash is often about exploring trust. The two main characters usually retain their perceived masculine strengths, but acquire some new ones as well. Both can be strong and vulnerable, dominant and submissive. Slash therefore removes the masculine masks that can hide personal feelings and it teaches people how to recognize signs of emotional caring (72–3). Will Brooker's respondents explained that 'the appeal of slash lies not so much in its erotic qualities as in its playing with gender roles and liberated treatment of male relationships' (Brooker 2002, 136). Slash writers often use pseudonyms as they play with multiple identifications and break taboos (Jenkins 1992, 200). Like other fanfic, the genre can be used in a similar way to *gossip* insofar that it can build social ties between writers and their fan-readers (222). As fans write texts that are closer to the realm of their lived experiences, their re-readings play a role in creating a shared, ongoing communal experience (53). Brooker found that the *Star Wars* genfic was generally written by women while male fans tended to make their own digital films or computer animations. He added 'it does seem to be indisputably the case that women do one thing with the films, and men do something entirely different' (139). Perceptions of slash are therefore often highly gendered.

Is slash oppositional?

Not everyone is comfortable with slash. Many fans feel that the idea of a sexualized *Doctor Who*, for example, is embarrassing, cheapening and selling-out his story (Dickins 2010, 177). Explicit slash even makes some insiders uncomfortable, partly because it can depart from female sensibilities about what 'good porn' might mean (Jenkins 2006, 82–3). In some ways slash can reflect closeted forms of fandom in that writers lead normal lives and use pen names. Other fans who object to slash have sometimes tried to 'out' its authors (Jenkins 1992, 201). Even those researching slash are, Jenkins has argued, in danger of getting swayed by its 'scandalous' reputation, forgetting to see it simply as 'a mode of textual commentary' (202). Indeed, slash is an archetypal example of ordinary people deciding that they can take the text to its next level and see it as a social project rather than a commercial property. For Jenkins, when slash writers filter, emphasize and reinterpret aspects of the primary text, they provide a theoretical model of textual poaching: 'What K/S does openly, all fans do covertly' (Jenkins 2006, 58). Some fans even see themselves as having greater expertise than professional writers, due to the extreme dedication and rigour with which they pursue their writing projects (Jenkins 1992, 70). Slash also asserts the inventiveness of fans in the face of less exciting versions of the story. The 1996 television movie of *Doctor Who*, which featured Paul McGann in the title role, contained the show's first kiss which and meant 'it was [then] impossible *not* to think of the Doctor as an erotic object' (Rose 2010, 46; emphasis mine). Similarly, at *Star Trek*'s fan conventions when the show's spokespeople denied that the android Data had emotions or that Captain Picard and Beverly Crusher had a history of romance, fans pointed to series events and their own perceptions (Jenkins 1992, 38). Cornel Sandvoss made an interesting point here:

> While the reasons for the reluctance to deal with sexually explicit fan fantasies are thus easily understandable, we must nevertheless avoid pasteurized representations of fandom and its underlying mechanisms – not least because the sexual desires and fantasies that underlie fandom and audienceship are of course utilized by the media industries. (2005a, 76)

For Sandvoss, *it is the media industries that sexualize stars and narrative products*; yet fans' sexual perceptions are in danger of being suppressed if they take those narratives in other directions. While this raises issues of agency, it begins to suggest that sexuality is one terrain on which fans can explore their interests in terms of expressing adventurous impulses, making social alliances and fighting battles. In fact, slash varies greatly in its fidelity to the canon (Brooker 2002, 160). Speaking about Harry Potter slash, Green and Guinery are therefore careful to distinguish canon and **fanon**:

> Canon is used to describe the HP oeuvre as approved by Rowling, her publishers, and her copyright assignees (for example, Warner Bros). In contrast, 'fanon' is the name used by the fans to refer to a body of work that results from their creative / subversive interactions with the core texts, such as 'slash' (homo-erotic / romance) fiction. Differentiation between the two terms acknowledges the likelihood that JK Rowling or her assignees might not approve of [the] fanon. (2004, online)

Insofar that they can be collectivized, the media industries do not quite know how to react to fan creativity (Jenkins 2008, 154). This is because fanfic and other fan-created texts (things like artworks) are simultaneously an *advertisement* for the social popularity of the commercial media, a *training ground* for emergent professionals, a *creative contribution* to popular culture and a *cultural form* – one that has the potential to damage public perceptions, directly reduce profits and set precedents which could then be exploited by unlicensed competitors. Media organizations encompass a diverse set of interests and voices too. At worst, they can take an authoritarian stance and attempt to use legal means to police and prevent fan creativity. Stars like William Shatner – who played Captain Kirk, the original lead from

Star Trek – have deemed fan readings as illegitimate based on their own judgements about what program-makers intended (often claiming 'pure entertainment', as if there was only one kind, as a series' main goal). Sharing such views, media corporations have sometimes sent 'cease and desist' letters to fans. However, since popular culture is a *shared* set of social myths based on resonant stories, legal wrangling can stifle its inevitable extension (Jenkins 2008, 158). As one *Star Wars* fan explained to Henry Jenkins, producers have no right to legislate over whether fans can experience the feelings other than those intended by author (1992, 30–2). It is interesting to note that the *Star Wars* franchise team have also officially sponsored fan film competitions (Jenkins 2008, 153). This is not an unusual pattern: Elvis Presley Enterprises offers another example of a media organization that has *incorporated and licensed* fan creativity on one hand – adding fan art to displays at Graceland and turning fan artist Betty Harper's sketches into postcards – *and simultaneously attempted to scotch or rein in fan expressions* when they ran counter to its financial interest (see Wall 2003). While elimination and incorporation represent extremes, some organizations negotiate with the fan community to balance those interests, building *new participatory associations and technologies* which allow fans and companies to interact in other ways. **Game modding** is the user-generated reworking of role-playing or real-time strategy computer games.[6] It represents a case where modification of the root product is *invited, expected and encouraged* as part of the regular process of consuming the product. Here the commercial producer continues to exert constraints even as the work is incorporated into a grass roots community: to the producers, fans' enthusiastic activities represent both free labour and free creativity (Jenkins 2008, 167–9). As online role-playing platforms proliferate, perhaps practices like slash writing, too, will be absorbed by this collaborative approach to cultural evolution. The problem is that slash tends to be consumed by only a fraction of the fan audience. Some fans dismiss it as character rape (Jenkins 1992, 187). Yet the idea of 'character rape' is also used by other fans to dismiss aired material (Jenkins 2006, 58). It implies that a past version of a particular character should be *frozen in an arrested form* that dictates the grounds for his/her ongoing participation in the story. Good fiction, however, is about the *transformation* of characters.

Is slash gay fiction?

While series like *Glee* (2009–) mark a sea change in the gradual acceptance and representation of gay characters on mainstream television, historically it was relatively rare to see homosexual characters represented on-screen outside of marginal, comical or occasional tragic roles. *Star Trek*, which claimed to be socially utopian, refrained from presenting gay characters (109). Furthermore, gay male celebrities have often kept their sexualities out of the limelight for fear of loosing sections of their fan bases. Gay pressure groups have often aimed to 'out' prominent but closeted gay men as a first step towards ending homophobia (Jenkins 1992, 189). Slash seems to be a place where the characters explore an emotional terrain somewhere beyond the heteronormative horizon of the straight world. The fanfic genre covers a wide range of same sex relationships from friendships, through erotic encounters to hardcore sex. Creating charged moments between male characters, it could easily be (mis)identified simply as homosexual fiction. One writer told Will Brooker that no straight men write slash because they do not imagine homosexual acts between males (2002, 134). Yet slash has a complex relationship to gay identity and discussions about the topic prompt a wide range of responses. The rest of this section will draw largely on Henry Jenkins' excellent analyses of slash.[7]

The issue of interpretation arises partly because heterosexual female fans usually create slash, but there are also gay slash writers. Some slash authors deny that their characters are gay at all. Others use the form squarely to explore homophobia and gay identity. Many female writers see the form as the quintessential *female genre*: an expression of desire in all senses, and an unpoliticized, uncensored forum for female networking. Constance Penley noted that female writers assert the straightness of their slash characters in order to continue their own imagined relationships with these characters, even while the characters have sex with each other (Jenkins 1992, 198). Lezlie Shell of the *Women of Houston in Pornography Group*, for example, said, 'Two heterosexual males becoming involved in a sexual relationship is my standard definition of slash . . . 'Slash' characters excite by being extensions of female sexuality.'[8]

Because of slash's subject matter, some of its writers have found a productive alignment with gay activism. Fans who view slash as a forum for queer identity have been distressed by what they see as homophobia within the slash community. Some writers see the denial of gay identity to slash characters as a form of homophobia. They suggest that slash writers *are in a process of coming out to themselves*, and that they portray their characters in parallel denial of *their own* gay identity. Critics of slash argue that it is highly polysemic, refuses to explicitly acknowledge characters' sexual identities (as opposed to their practices), rarely explores sustained relationships, sometimes treats female characters in misogynistic ways, isolates characters from the real issues of the gay lifestyle, rarely contains lesbians and has occasionally 'romanticized' rape.[9] The counterargument is that as a dramatic genre, slash has no duty to accurately reflect gay male experience. It is, after all, *fantasy* fiction which makes no claims to represent the truth.

Perhaps the benefit of slash actually springs from its ambiguity. It can help to blur the lines between different types of sexual identity. Character bodies provide a shared space where queer and straight fans can discuss their desires outside the polarizing realm of identity politics. In a patriarchal society, both women and gay men have been excluded from legitimate structures of power. Both groups can also identify through sexuality and form underground social networks. Slash is exciting partly *because* it reflects similarities between their parallel, historically marginalized positions.

What, then, can be said about slash as a genre of fanfic? According to Will Brooker, 'Slash fiction . . . has received a considerable amount of academic attention, yet many *Star Wars* fans seem never to have heard of it, and those that have tend to keep their distance' (2002, 129). In other words, for their own reasons researchers may have overplayed the importance of slash as living culture of fanfic. Slash is a relatively marginal, subcultural practice but it has often come under the academic and journalistic microscope; it has been confused with the entirety of textual poaching. Ironically, too, academic ideas about slash have mainly been adaptions or refinements of fans' ideas. Scholars and fans often talk about slash differently: scholars tend to focus on K/S fiction whereas fans can sometimes be *purely slash followers*, joining together different shows in their writing (rather than focusing on just one); fans understand slash in relation to various genres of writing (such as romance); women of all sexual identities write slash; fans focus on slash's links to other fictional genres, not its uniqueness; slash fans see a genre in flux while academic accounts look for a unifying theory that explains why people write slash. What we might say, then, is that slash is a small corner of fan activity that has become important to researchers because our *academic traditions* seek out creative and resistant activity. This does not mean we should dismiss the genre's transgressive quality however. Veteran fan researcher Cheryl Harris (1998, 6) has argued, 'Fan writings seem to be central to the practice of fandom: newsletters, fanzines, "slash" fiction, and songs are some of the communications produced'. Slash and other forms of fanfic are, then, what some fans *do* with their interests in media culture.

Pleasures of performance

Participating

Perhaps the primary pleasure that unites fans with performances is simply *enjoyment through engagement*. This enjoyment is more than a passive process of consumption or reception. It involves the fan being active in suspending disbelief, making meaning and participating. There is a sense here in which *performance sets the tone* and fans, making meanings as they go, *engage in various adaptive forms of counter-performance*. At live music events, for example, these counter-performances are visibly and audibly expressed in ways that can include delightedly screaming, heckling, calling for attention, singing along and applauding. Such events are usually a summation of each fan's ongoing engagement with media products that reflect previous performances. As we make sense of what we see, however, the process of paying attention to these media texts also involves less obvious kinds of participation. In our everyday lives we shout TV catchphrases, sing karaoke, hum along to the radio, or recite dramatic monologues from the movies. In that sense, we are *always participating* in popular culture's realm of meaning in mundane ways while we use it as a personal and social resource. As Tia DeNora explained, 'Music is a device or resource to which people turn in order to regulate themselves as aesthetic agents, as feeling, thinking and acting beings in their day-to-day lives' (2000, 62). The same goes, I would argue, for their use of other media forms. Beyond this seemingly mundane but important field of participation, there are more obvious practices expressing the performative engagement of dedicated enthusiasts.

Collecting

Collecting is the bringing together of a number of items that are connected to a particular theme. In media representations such as documentaries and press stories, this highly structured process of material or digital accumulation is especially linked to fandom. The public display of a large personal collection both marks its owner out as visibly different *and* references his or her supposed obsession. A clear example of this is Jeanie Finlay's 2011 film documentary *Sound It Out*, which features the last surviving vinyl record shop in Teeside and shows one fan at home, surrounded by his collection, explaining that he is considering being buried with it. A relatively recent trend for the accessible archiving of media products in the 'cloud' of online storage and the streaming of those products raises crucial questions: Is collecting an inherent pleasure of fandom? To what extent is collecting premised on the *ownership* of the collected items or their rarity value? Is fandom itself necessarily premised on collecting?

Although many fans do collect, fandom is not *all* about collecting, and collecting is a hobby activity that exists well beyond the world of fandom. In effect, then, fandom and collecting have historically overlapped; collecting gives people a way to extend the pleasure that defines their fascination and dedication; many people collect items like posters or lobby cards which are only symbolically related to orginal performances. We can distinguish at least three objects of collecting. The first is the accumulation of *mimetic traces of the performance itself*. For example, a music fan might buy all the albums made by their favourite artist to listen to the songs. The second object of collecting is *merchandise*: mass-produced material associated with the original text, series, author or performer.[10] A third object of collection is *memorabilia*: unique and personal material that is intimately linked to the original object of interest. Memorabilia collectors combine an interest in getting closer with a concern for the rarity of the items in their collections. *When researchers think about collecting, sometimes they forget the first type of object*: fans may simply be accumulating examples of performance that they can assess to enjoy. Collecting can also be a pleasure in its own right, appealing to those with a completist type of personality or economic investment motivation.

While some would argue that collecting represents a process that should be examined in its own right *as an obsession* – the evocation and temporary satisfaction of a desire to possess – there may be other ways to understand it, ways which do not emphasize identities built around collecting as a general process. In sociology and anthropology there is a small tradition of study know as material culture research. All cultural studies researchers are, in a sense, political storytellers working in different traditions. Material culture researchers use physical objects as entry points in to the particular stories they tell. These objects are socially *practiced* (used) in particular ways in relation to time and space. The organization and display of objects can also demonstrate a lot about the identity of the collector. Attention to his or her archiving practice, the way that things enter, stay in or leave the collection, can uncover interesting and often quite personal aspects of identity. For example, just as an individual can have multiple personal fandoms at the same time, so they can have multiple collections. With each collection, they must make regular decisions about what to include and exclude, what to reject and what to keep. Most collectors have precise, specific and highly organized rules for the 'systematic' acquisition of their collections. Their vast accumulations can therefore be seen as open-ended historical documents which leave clues to the collector's identity in recognizable traces of the way he/she selects, organizes and arranges relevant items. Because of this some collectors have become more self aware through their hobby.

Different authors suggest different reasons why fans collect. The traditional answer – connected to a pathological view of fandom – is that collectors are, in effect, *object fetishists*. Walter Benjamin famously once said that for a real collector, 'ownership is the most intimate relationship that one can have to things' (1931/2005, 492). Fetishizing means making a *symbolic* investment in a particular material object; the use of the term in this context implies a link between fandom and pathologies. Yet fetishism is not a simple term to understand as it emerges from multiple fields of meaning. *Sexual fetishism* is about maintaining attachment while warding off the anxieties associated with loss; it is therefore a kind of displacement activity, the busy work of an anxious mind. *Religious fetishism* indicates the maintenance of a relationship with a more powerful metaphysical force by means of a prized symbolic object. Finally, in Marxist terms, human labour is separated from the goods that it creates by the systems of exchange; *commodity fetishism* is the attribution of magical qualities to these alienated objects. In each of these formulations, the fetish becomes a kind of mask: *a substitute physical* item that surreptitiously orchestrates or compensates for a more awkward social reality or set of relationships; perhaps it is a kind of a refuge. In that sense, the choice to fetishize is a displacement activity: a process of disavowel of the self and act of projection that *displaces* issues of self-identity on to a particular physical object. Fetishism therefore raises questions of rarity, authenticity, pilgrimage and loss.

Rather than defining identity around the collecting process – at worst by describing collectors as 'fetishists' – however, it may be useful to consider how they directly and indirectly *use* their pastime to narrate their self-identities. In a classic study, Susan Pearce (1992) distinguished between the collecting of *fetishes* (which have a metaphoric relation to the world) and the collecting of *souvenirs* (which stand, metonymically, for events in the collector's past). Souvenirs are things that represent their original contexts: artefacts of memorabila, such as concert set-lists, review clippings or celebrity encounter photographs. They enable the fan to narrate a retrospective notion of his/her biographic self moving through an ongoing process of growth and development. Collectors therefore use book shelves, web pages, photo albums, scrapbooks, diaries and other spaces as containers to help them accumulate a stock of aids to memory. In short, artefacts used as souvenirs express identity as *a retrospective construction of a fan's life lived.*

A further dimension of collecting as a means to form and express identity comes when fans *socially use* their accumulated collections as treasure troves for *public* display or resources for the dissemination of esoteric knowledge. Domestic collections are often housed in particular rooms or parts of rooms. Researchers such as Erika Doss (1999) who located fandom as a pseudo-religious activity saw these rooms as 'shrines'. However, while they allow fans to contemplate their interests, it is unlikely that anyone actually *prays* to their heroes in a worshipful sense. As any viewer who has watched a haunted house film implicitly knows, houses can symbolize the individual self in a metaphorical sense. In domestic spaces, collections therefore represent the way that personal fandom is *bounded* within a particular part of a person's identity. Collectors who share their houses with other members of the family place their items in rooms specifically associated with them as individuals (bedrooms), or at least dissociated with the non-collecting members of the household (garages, attics). Fan collections can therefore become contested as *spatial markers* that represent personal identity and territorial ownership. Even a domestically displayed collection can manifest the individual self in a way that is a potential focus for either shared pleasures or anxieties and conflicts; many fans have to re-organize their displays, for example, when they get married (see Cavicchi 1998, 139). Collections can also be used for semi-public or public display. In that respect one interesting example is a private home in Holly Springs, Mississippi, owned by two Elvis fans, Paul MacLeod and his son. Graceland Too as been open to the public for well over a decade as a monument to their fandom. It is, in a sense, also *a semi-commercial space of public exhibition* which relies on its domestic setting and owners' folksy enthusiasm to mark it out as a craft business that says something interesting – though perhaps ultimately stereotypical – about the power of fan fascination.

Identities are also expressed around collecting, then, in the way that fan *knowledge* (associated with the quest to collect) is displayed in social settings. Alan Zweig's documentary *Vinyl* (2000) opens with its protagonist, a monologue-prone bachelor, explaining:

> I used to keep a diary up until recently, on my computer, and of course in that diary all I talked about was women, and here all I'm only going to talk about records. But maybe the point, somehow, will be the same. Making this film is all about record collecting and vinyl and I could probably do the whole film just here in my house.

The equation being made here is between a lack of success with women and the habit of collecting records. Insofar that collecting stereotypically – and unfairly – represents an absorbing distraction from the life cycle and an outlet for autistic tendencies, the public often associate it with inadequate masculinity. Will Straw (1997) has published some interesting research in this area. Straw classified four different kinds of male record collectors depending on *how they used their knowledge*: *nerds* (who have knowledge but do not tend to display it), *brutes* (who have no knowledge to display), *dandies* (who are more interested in displaying than acquiring knowledge) and *cool* males (who modestly display their knowledge). In the year 2000, Stephen Frears' film production of Nick Hornsby's novel *High Fidelity* explored the gendering of collecting in a funny way. Barry, a record shop assistant played by Jack Black, tutors one unsuspecting customer:

Barry: We've got Echo and the Bunnymen albums.
Customer: Yeah, I've got all their other albums.
Barry: Oh, you do? Well, how about the Jesus and Mary Chain.
Customer: They always seemed –
Barry: They always seemed *what?* They always seemed *really
               great*, is what they always seemed! They picked up where
               your precious Echo left off and you're sitting around
               complaining about no more Echo albums. I can't believe you
               don't own this fucking record – it's insane!

A minute later Barry is seen again holding a Bob Dylan album and yelling at a customer, 'You don't have it? That is perverse. Don't tell anybody that you don't own fucking *Blonde on Blonde*!' In his role as an independent record store clerk, Barry therefore uses cultural capital that he has acquired as a record collector to 'help' his customers.[11] In that sense, *High Fidelity* clearly makes the argument that collecting is a way to accumulate and assert cultural capital. There is at least *some* truth in this. After all, many collectors reject easily-available, mainstream media products and develop a kind of committed, 'hunting' mentality. However, collecting is more complex than this stereotype suggests. As Roy Shuker's study of record collectors explains:

> The *High Fidelity* stereotype is just that; there is no 'typical' record collector. Contemporary record collectors have a shared interest in sound recordings as significant cultural artefacts, with associated notions of discrimination, musical canons and rarity. They also share the dominant characteristics of collectors more generally, albeit with particular inflections of these: the thrill of the chase; obsession, linked to accumulation and completism; at times a preoccupation with rarity and economic value; and a concern for cultural preservation. The last often involves self-education and public/vernacular scholarship, drawing on the collection as a resource. These traits are subsumed into collecting as a significant aspect of social identity, involving the acquisition of cultural capital, overlaid with a patina of nostalgia. (2010, 33)

Such research draws attention to the fact that collecting is *both* a personal and a social process; items and information that fans accumulate *almost always* get used in a social sense. Indeed, fans have often contributed to public exhibitions, left legacies to archives or provided material that was previously assumed to be lost. Websites such as YouTube have been populated by their efforts to preserve performances as a shared heritage. What is interesting here is that fans – whether individually or collectively – act as archivists and curators, moving material between the public and private domain in interesting ways. The *White Feather* exhibition presented in 2010 at *The Beatles Story* centre in Liverpool was a case in point. Organized by John Lennon's first wife Cynthia and their son Julian, the exhibition featured items connected to the famous Beatle's first marriage. Many of the private letters and other possessions had fallen into the hands of collectors and circulated as memorabilia. Before Cynthia and Julian could show these remnants of their own family history to the public, they therefore had to buy back 'their' items from private collectors. In pursuing that quest – as Julian explained on the exhibition's Website – the family *became collectors themselves*: 'I started collecting these personal pieces because I felt they belonged back in our family.'[12]

Blogging and writing fanzines

In the pre-internet days, one of the main ways that fans could communicate with each other was through independent and ephemeral publications called fanzines (sometimes just called 'zines'). These niche publications were often little more than photocopied pages, stapled together. They featured drawings, pictures and typed sections, and focused on topics such as film, music, hobbies and politics. Produced on a small scale by individuals or small networks of fans, fanzines were not usually designed for profit. While independent record and video shops sometimes stocked self-published items, fans would often tip each other off about them and obtain copies by mail order. Some zines were so hard to find, in fact, that dealers made 'bootleg' copies of them for resale without their maker's permission (Jenkins 1992, 160). For those who made and read fanzines, they mattered as opportunities for creativity and free expression operating outside of the professional, metropolitan media.

   While not all fans read or wrote fanzines, those who did felt bonded to particular networks within their fan communities.[13] The kinds of pleasures discussed were often similar to those found by Harrington and Bielby for soap viewing: the illusion of eavesdropping, gossiping without guilt, hoping for classic moments, exploring twists in the private lives of the actors off screen, feeling the reassuring familiarity of a long-running series and even tracking the use of props for continuity errors (1995, 119). Music fanzines contained record company news, letters, articles and analyses, fan fantasies, concert announcements, personal and merchandise ads, contests and announcements for fan conventions. Fans would monitor the press for news about their heroes. They would also share bootlegging and ticketing strategies, swap memorabilia and circulate reviews about events and recordings. Some fanzines carried advertisements for pen pals or were an outlet, primarily, for fanfic stories. Science fiction zines were often 'multi-universe', featuring a range of associated fan objects. Fanzines came in all styles and orientations. Before the internet, some *Doctor Who* fans even made video 'zines featuring interviews, lost material, extras and fan films.

What was the function of fanzines? They offered a place in which fans could socialize and express their own creativity. Fanzine narratives would often fill in the gap when broadcast series went off the air (Jenkins 1992, 151). They kept the conversation going and continued the dialogue if an artist or product was temporarily away from the spotlight. According to Cavicchi, 'Like record company hype about a star, fanzines are hype about being a fan' (1998, 162). In other words, fanzines provided a space in which fandom could be glamorized, made to seem quirky and interesting. Fanzine editors often remained more responsive to their readers because they saw themselves as closer to them that any professional publisher (Jenkins 1992, 159). Fanzines were also a less censored space. Their content could also vary in terms of public acceptability from family-friendly newsletters to twisted commentaries bordering on obscenity. David Sanjek distinguished various kinds of horror fanzines: 'In addition to these sarcastic or archivist fanzines, others, including *Subhuman*, *Trash Compactor*, *Cold Sweat*, and *Sheer Filth*, nihilistically identify with repulsive imagery' (2008, 426–7). Such zines were significant in helping to politicize particular fan cultures. Chris Atton, a prominent alternative media researcher, has claimed:

> The rise of the fanzine as an integral part of punk subculture of the late 1970s was instrumental in generating a second wave of underground-like publications that dealt as much with the politics of liberation, direct action and anarchism as they did with popular music. (2001, 1)

While their political edge was significant, it is important to remember that not all zines were, however, political. Some were semi-official and carried fan club news items. Many had cash flow problems and never broke even. Their writers were often paid in copies, not money. In sum, zines ranged widely in quality and mattered because they explore issues that media producers either would not have dared to examine or would just never have considered.

The internet provides a free or low-cost public forum in which ordinary people can conveniently express their views and creativity. It has consequently reduced interest in fanzine culture. *Blogging has become the new zine culture*, but blogging is a subtly different cultural form. In theory, blogs are more instantly accessible, though in practice surfers need to know where to find them. Despite the networks of the 'blogosphere' and mutual comment posts, blogs have generally been used more as *individual* spaces for the expression of opinion. They are also more public, more globally accessible, more subject to potential surveillance, more able to carry different forms of information and more easily archived. For example, some music blogs are little more than 'link farms' that allow fans to download obscure albums as shared media files. Blogs are also supremely convenient. In that sense, the users are more like consumers; circulating a zine was perhaps a more committed activity. However amateur the product, the actions involved in creating a zine made it more like a guerrilla activity: taking a stand through the use and abuse of office photocopy technology. Zines were therefore a historically important form of fan culture. When fan publishing entered the digital era, it was as if *the underground went overground.*

Fanvids

The video uploading site YouTube is – less than a decade after it first started – currently the third most popular destination for surfers on the internet. Yet long before non-broadcast video became a central mode of public communication, fans were making videos to circulate to each other. Indeed, a verb – 'vidding' – developed to describe the process and some argue that the practice of vidding dates right back to the 1970s. Henry Jenkins' discussion about vidding in *Textual Poachers* remains important because it shows fans at work before watching uploaded internet videos became a communal spectator sport. According to Jenkins, fan videos both comment on the original text and help to bond the fan community. They are a testament to the dedication of the people who made them and they also articulate the fan community's mutual interests, shared understandings and collective fantasies (Jenkins 1992, 248–9). Rather than simply being postmodern mash-ups, fan videos emerged as a new *narrative* art form. They could be used to situate shows in new genres by editing them in different ways. While official music videos for the series *Miami Vice* (1984–9), for instance, emphasized the consumerist fantasy of driving through the city, fan videos made by editing footage from the series focused on the bond between the two male leads (see 234). In effect the show was re-imagined as a soap opera. Fan videos have also helped shift attention towards subplots or minor characters. For Jenkins, 'fan videos centre on male bonding, romantic awakening, and group commitment. These themes reflect not only central concerns of fan gossip, criticism and fiction, but also speak to the desires for affiliation that draw people into the fan community' (237). Video reworking gives fans an opportunity to relive iconic media moments and recall the memories associated with them.

In an age where the tools to manipulate images, recorded sound and video are widely available, the work started by fringe vidders has been taken up by a much wider community. Three aspects of this are worth mentioning here. First, the use of new media has allowed fans to extend and globalize media consumption. For example, **fansubbing** is a practice of unofficially subtitling foreign film footage. It allows fans of manga and other foreign genres online access to a much wider variety of material than they might get through the commercial marketplace. Second, as public life becomes more mediated, participatory culture is a way for ordinary people to express their creativity and political opposition. Parody videos bring larger issues down to a human scale (Jenkins 2008, 289). However, rather than getting political for the sake of it, fans are usually more interested in modifying the text in ways that extends their pleasures. Indeed, they may not take kindly to others who disrespectfully mash up their favourite shows. Third, many fans use video to provide commentary and make product reviews. In that sense, perhaps vidding can best be seen as a way to express the same creativity that used to animate fanzines.

Filking

Filking is the singing of popular tunes by fans with lyrics adapted to reflect a shared interest in a favourite media product. It represents an open space for fan creativity. The practice allows fans to comment on their texts, bring minor characters and subplots to the surface and pull together interesting new combinations of popular music and television storytelling. Filking also allows fans to 'answer back' by reworking – resisting, grotesquing or parodying – the negative media stereotypes thrown at them. Filk singers are dualistic poachers, taking *contents* from TV and *forms* from pop. Like folk artists they sing in a community-led oral tradition, gaining a sense of identity by linking to the past (Jenkins 1992, 268–9). Both men and women play prominent roles in the filk singing community. In that sense, filk singing is like folk singing: there is no formal separation between performers and spectators, and it operates in a casual atmosphere where amateur performers can, without disapproval, sing off key or forget words (see 256–7). For early writers in fan studies, filking was important because it could be taken as a relatively non-commercial and potentially subversive form of folk culture. Researchers could perceive fans who sang filk songs not simply as dreamers but as people who took action.

Impersonation and cosplay

For much of the 1980s, one entrenched stereotype of media fandom was that the most dedicated fans were likely to be nuts dressed in Elvis jumpsuits or Star Trek vests. Impersonators made an impact in the press and on television because, again, they were visibly different. As more and more popular music groups attracted their own tribute acts, 'secondary performance' became seen as a more common activity and professional opportunity. It became apparent that tribute artists were often specialists doing it for money, rather than fans doing it for love (see Homan 2006). Because impersonators appear to be neither 'independent' individuals, nor has their identity fully disappeared into that of their hero, their passion might *notionally* be seen as *troubling the self*. Hypothetically, the practice might appear to threaten the performer with a loss of self as they melt into the role of the star. Occasionally, tribute acts like Kay Kent as Marilyn Monroe have *acted out* the tragedies of their icons (Hills 2002a, 162). By doing so it seems that they are tragically authenticating themselves, prooving an *inner world* just like that of their hero. Indeed, *authentication* is a crucial issue for any impersonator as they can so easily be dismissed as a fake. Yet the impersonator's seeming loss of self is, according to Matt Hills, actually a period of *passing through self-absence* that leads to an *expansion of self*. Hills has suggested that impersonation has become *othered* as something 'bad' and *mediated* in ways that emphasize fans' lack of agency: a feminized and feared loss of self that returns us to issues of possession (see Hills 2002a, 167–8). Rather than a lapse of personal autonomy, however, impersonation is more often a *marketing opportunity* or *performative pleasure*.

The notion of *fans* as impersonators is a both a stereotype and something of an overestimation. A small minority of media enthusiasts seriously claim impersonation as their cultural practice, acting out an interest that allows them to articulate their identity through that of their favourite star. In most fan cultures they remain a tiny – if visible – fraction of the fan base. For Nightingale, amateur impersonation is a *narcissistic* pleasure: as impersonators, fans 'strive to be instantly identifiable as the "loved object"' (1994, 9). Yet cosplay and impersonation more clearly reflect *playful immersion* in the mythos of particular shows, stars or genres (see Lancaster 2001). Because dedicated fans often see their favourite artist as unique, however, they can *more easily* recognize the smallest of differences between their star and his or her imitators. Many prefer tribute artists who maintain a kind of *dualistic identity* that loosely links the image of the original star to the individual identity of the performers.[14] William McCranor Henderson has argued that 'the top impersonators use Elvis as a platform for *their own* personality' (1997, 252; emphasis mine). Sometimes, if an impersonator can perform material that the original artist did not, they are supported as a kind of extension of the icon's performative style. Impersonators can also have *their own* fan followings and fan clubs.

Fandom can *visibly resemble* impersonation in one area. In the practice of 'cosplay', fans dress up as their favourite anime characters (Jenkins 2006, 152). As Matt Hills has noted, Western cosplayers have to negotiate the issue of nationality when they do this (2002b, 13). He argues that their different national identities are 'tactically deactivated or backgrounded' when they participate in the pleasures of cosplay. In effect that makes the practice similar – on some levels – to fancy dress. Fans adopt the garb of fiction characters as a way of extending their participation, exploring their identities and interacting with others. Cosplayers also use their own *costume-making* talents to express their fandom. They can explore issues of performativity in the way that they use their bodies. As Nicolle Lamerichs (2011, online) explains, 'Cosplay makes the ambiguous relation between the fictional and actual explicit'. In another piece on cosplay, Jen Gunnels reported the experiences of one *Star Wars* cosplayer:

> As he remarks, aspects of the character are specifically tied to donning the costume. He may not believe that he carries specific aspects of character identity over into everyday life, yet they are available to his identity when in costume. (2009, online)

While wearing a costume gives some people license to explore new horizons, it facilitates others to express their own identities *as fans*. If they know that their performative identities are accepted by those around them then they may feel safer expressing them. If a female wears a costume in a more male-orientated sci-fi convention, for example, she may also be showing that she is not being dragged along against her will. A few fans who dress up are really involved in 'crossplay': they appear as characters from the other gender (Mead in Thomas & O'Shea 2010, 58). Hence cosplay is a diverse practice that ranges from playful fancy dress to a more profound realization of social identity than might be accepted in wider culture.

As fans take up avatars and roam multi-player virtual reality environments like *Second Life*, internet technology increasingly facilitates our longstanding urge to play with alternative identities. Makers of the crime fiction show *CSI: NY* (2004–present), for instance, collaborated with *Second Life* creators Linden Lab to construct a virtual environment for the series (Jenkins 2008, 124). Cosplay and impersonation at fan gatherings might even now be seen as *enacting virtual community in physical space.* Presenting empirical research on cosplayers at the New York Comic Con event, Jen Gunnels suggested that cosplay should be understood as a kind of *social coping strategy*:

> The *Star Wars* cosplayers are clearly tapping into their childhoods: today's social context eerily mirrors the context that members of Generation X grew up in, and the children born to Generation X are growing up in parallel circumstances characterized by economic instability. For some cosplayers, dipping into the *Star Wars* universe may be a way to cope, as well as a way to share coping strategies with their own children – to pass on the same myth that enabled them to negotiate their own growth within our culture. Will we point them in the direction of Luke Skywalker and Obi-Wan Kenobi to learn how to best negotiate the times? In all honesty, I would like to think so. Perhaps they will forge a New Jedi Order to balance the mistakes of the Knights of the Old Republic. (2009, online)

7

Fandom, gender and sexual orientation

Starting points

- Do male and female fans always behave in the same way?
- How is fandom used to express different sexual identities?
- To what extent can fandom create 'gender trouble'?

Gender is the cultural – as opposed to biological – differentiation of the sexes. In order to think about its relationship to media fandom, the phenomenon must be discussed in more detail. Gender is associated with particular social conventions, rules, roles and expectations. They emerge from *socially-projected distinctions* that designate and distinguish 'masculine' and 'feminine' identities or practices. Gender is therefore a *cultural construct* only *notionally* claiming legitimacy in the biological difference between male and female bodies. Feminists argue that Western society has historically been organized as a *patriarchy* (led by men), so women have at worst been oppressed and at best relatively excluded from public life. There have, however, been exceptional moments and gradual shifts. In the 1940s (during the Second World War) and 1960s (after the mass adoption of the contraceptive pill) more women entered the workplace and gained access to prominent roles, catalysing the changes to come and helping to accelerate a collective re-evaluation of gender.

Masculinity traditionally conferred male self-esteem by reproducing male privilege. It naturalized gender as difference and difference as hierarchy, creating shared notions of ideal and acceptable behaviour. In a society where many authority figures were male, women were defined through their place as domestic assistants who internalized a certain passivity, vulnerability and reticence. They were, paradoxically, also celebrated as objects of desire. Because femininity was perceived as weakness, feminine behaviour itself became othered as an object of scornful disdain and hidden fear. This fear of femininity also permitted contempt for 'effeminate' behaviour in men. Masculinity was therefore not just a way to separate the sexes: it challenged homoerotic male bonding and homosexuality as weak and inadmissible forms of male behaviour. Since it also encouraged individuals to compete for status and placed emphasis on defiant achievement, masculinity promoted particular traits such as independence, rivalry, rationality and self-mastery (see Easthope 1990). Since traditional masculinity understood women as decorative trophies, they were reduced to objects of conquest and tokens of exchange. It therefore turned sex into an arena for the competitive assertion of manhood. These masculine norms have historically led and defined public life, but in many cultures and countries traditional gender expectations have changed quite significantly in recent decades and a wider variety of behaviours has become acceptable. Demands and changes gained in the name of equality have, researchers suggest, challenged the absolute notions of gender that held up patriarchy. As new roles and behaviours become available to both men and women, researchers have suggested that masculinity is 'in crisis' and should be understood as pluralized (i.e. *masculinities*). Understandings of the nature of femininity have also shifted. David Gauntlett explains:

> Femininity is not typically a core value for women today. Instead, being 'feminine' is just one of the performances that women can choose to employ in everyday life – perhaps for pleasure, or to achieve a particular goal. There's plenty of evidence that traditional femininity is no longer popular. (2008, 11)

In other words, women have begun to recognize traditional, heteronormative femininity as a role organized in relation to *male* needs and desires like sexual objectification and domestic service. After rejecting traditional femininity as strategy to make them feel insecure, women have begun to recognize that it *can* also offer pleasures. Sometimes they have therefore perceived it – in a collective and unspoken way – as free space of autonomy, hedonism and camaraderie: a garment that can be worn at will. This shift has impacted different age groups, cultures and classes to different degrees. Changing modes of femininity and masculinity indicate that all gender is malleable and even 'queer' to some extent: arbitrarily constructed on unstable boundaries. This recognition of the relational quality of identity has been celebrated by those who build their gender identities on relatively marginalized sexualities: gay men and lesbian women. It was only in 2003 that homosexuality was nationally decriminalized in the US Supreme Court, bringing the last 13 states in line with laws that had been passed in the 1970s elsewhere in the union. The struggle for homosexual rights in terms of the legal recognition of same sex partnerships, not just as civil unions but as marriages, is ongoing. Gender and sexuality therefore remain a complex and contested cultural terrain, a place where the personal and political intersect. What, then, is their relation to fandom?

When talking about gender and fandom we need to avoid two significant pitfalls. The first major trap relates to what could be called 'textual essentialism' and is connected with believing that we can make any reading that easily connects the portrayal of gender *in* the text with, first, a gendered interpretation of what it means and, second, a perception that it would therefore automatically suit particular social groups in the audience. For instance, it would be wrong to say just from hearing a soppy romantic ballad that its fan audience was entirely female. The idea forgets that gendered portrayals can be perceived in different ways, that individual viewers or listeners can read portrayals quite differently (sometimes identifying across gender), and that each person can accept or reject gendered interpretations as *discursive resources*. A second trap goes beyond the text to *essentialize the audience*. If the cultural world is seen entirely through the prism of gender, there is a danger that we will think that the ways in which male and female – or for that matter gay and straight – fans pursue their fandom are *inherently different*. Henry Jenkins (1992, 112) argued that reading strategies which can differ between the sexes are grounded in social experience, not essential difference. His idea takes us a step away from biological determinism to focus on gender as a set of contingent roles and norms. However, there may still be some senses in which personal fandom *is actually the same* for individuals of different genders. A focus on gender *as difference* is in danger of hiding this similarity. With those two warnings in mind, there may still be things that can be said about fandom, gender and sexuality.

Identifications

Textual identifications are made by fans in social context where whole fields of media culture are associated with particular genders. In the broadest sense, this applies to notions of a feminized mainstream and more 'masculine' cult margin. The notion of a feminized mainstream is not true, however, since specific genres – consider rock music, soap or horror, for example – are marketed either differently to each gender, more to one gender than the other or, sometimes, to both male *and* female viewers equally (consider products appearing under the banner of 'youth programming' or 'family viewing'). It is, rather, that the mainstream has so frequently been *linked* to the mass audience that it has become associated with *passive viewing and listening*. Because women have generally been socially categorized as less rational than men, and more vulnerable to 'seduction' by the text, they have inevitably – and wrongly – become associated with passive spectatorship. Society has therefore viewed 'sitting close to the text' as feminine activity (61). In commentary and criticism this gendered coding of the mainstream has rolled outward to a perception of the fan community in general. Of course, some genre-based fan cultures *do* primarily consist of one gender or the other. Back in 1992 Henry Jenkins said:

> [The telefantasy fan community is] largely female, largely white, largely middle class, though it welcomes into its ranks many who would not fit this description . . . Perhaps my most difficult claim will be that such a widespread and diverse group may still constitute a recognizable subculture. (1)

He added that 'Male fans are less common than female fans, though certainly not unremarkable within this culture; we have learned to play according to the interpretive conventions of that community' (6). Conversely, the *margin* of the mainstream – cult media, exploitation cinema, esoteric music – and its followers have often been coded as masculine. Studying cult film, Joanne Hollows explains, 'the processes of classification and categorization through which "cult" gains its sense of masculinised identity are produced in opposition to a feminized mainstream' (2003, 41). Yet the central distinction hides a variety of fans of both genders. Those who both identity across type, such as male soap followers, for example, are rendered abnormal or invisible *by the process of categorization*. The gendering – as opposed to just 'gender' – of texts and genres therefore operates primarily *as a discourse*.

Within this picture of the mainstream and margins, certain cultural fields – in part because of the generic appeals of their texts – tend to be more associated with audiences dominated by one gender or another. Fandoms for different products are therefore *perceived as* gendered in different ways (see Jenkins 1992, 108). Local discourses used by fans here can offer indications of which gender norms control the discussion. A good example is provided by the displacement of female fans in the horror genre. Where female audiences *are* more public – as in the case of the vampire film – female fans are also more prominent. They appear less visible as fans of other subgenres. Brigid Cherry's (2002) research on female horror fans in the United Kingdom suggests that they are relatively marginalized by male-orientated genre conventions, but also that they discursively exclude themselves by internalizing and expressing perceptions of what they do as 'strange'. The judgement then translates into them avoiding organized fan gatherings, for example, or strategically describing their primary interest as 'sci-fi' fandom. Illuminating the macho side of horror fandom in the audience research journal *Participations*, David Church has discussed Passolini's famous 'sick' film *Salò* (1975):

> Based upon empirical research on gendered tastes in horror films – specifically, female horror fans' distaste for what Brigid Cherry calls 'excessive or gratuitous displays of violence, gore, or other effects used to evoke revulsion in the audience' – we can infer that most 'sick film' fans are probably male or at least have stereotypically 'masculine' tastes. For example, a study of viewer responses to sexual violence, which used several 'sick films' as objects of inquiry, found that viewers embracing these films were indeed predominantly male or aligned themselves with 'masculine' tastes. Fan discourses about 'sick films' are indeed suffused with masculinist notions of challenging oneself to withstand them, treating the completed viewing of each one as, like the label 'sick' applied to fans and films alike, a badge of honor: as one fan says, Salò 'is challenging on a whole lot of levels but getting through it is a trudge', while another claims, 'I always try to challenge myself because so far nothing's really made me sick, but I've never seen Salò and I heard that's pretty messed up'. (Church 2009, 349)

Horror is an interesting case, since its modern set piece – the shocking and repulsive gore scene – does not necessarily dissuade the *entire* female audience. According to Carol Clover:

> Although girls too went to slasher movies, usually in the company of boyfriends but sometimes in same-sex groups (my impression is that the *Nightmare on Elm Street* series in particular attracted girls in groups), the majority audience, perhaps even more than the audience for horror in general, was largely young and largely male – conspicuously groups of youth who cheer the killer on as he assaults his victims, then reverse their sympathies to cheer the survivor as she assaults the killer. (1992, 23)

While Clover goes quite far here in generalizing a gendered pattern of audience response, it is probably the case that any female fan going to see a slasher movie *alone* in the cinema would be widely perceived as exceptional. In that sense some spaces of fandom are *uncomfortable* for male or female fans that feel in a minority and *out of place* in relation to the majority audience. This is particularly the case for women, who can feel physically threatened or socially excluded from certain spaces. Studying transgendered heavy metal tribute bands – female performers who emulate male artists – Georgina Gregory recently explained:

> The audience for Lez Zep and The Iron Maidens concerts contains a far higher number of female fans than would normally be expected, and some of those I have spoken to have said that they feel safer and enjoy the atmosphere more when the audience is more evenly gendered. (2012, 13)

Gender differences can carry over to *fan activities* too. Many fan practices are more common in one gender or the other: fan fiction writers, for instance, are usually female (see Pugh 2005, 7; Jenkins 2006, 43). Female fans are sometimes discriminated against because of their practices, for example, erotic fiction writing is sometimes critically dismissed compared to the more commonly male-coded pursuit of film making (Jenkins 2008, 158). The traditional association of femininity with passivity and servitude has consequences here. Australian researcher Catherine Lumby has made interesting points about female pop fandom in this respect. As Lumby sees it, the sexual side of this kind of fandom is as much about constructing a space where the fans can discover their own identities as it is about meeting the band. Describing one of her research subjects, Lumby explains:

> For her part, Sue was planning to get laid again. She wanted to learn more about what she liked and didn't like about men, but most importantly she wanted to escape from the scrutiny of parents and teachers long enough to explore her own sense of self. She told me in detail about sexual feelings and practices – she was the first person who ever talked like that to me. And the excuse for sharing this information was always a discussion of a pop star we liked. I was a lot less adventurous than Sue as a teenage girl. But I do clearly remember that the genuinely erotic dimension of fandom related to a fantasy of escape. It was a virtual space for reinventing the self, for exploring sexuality, for playing with and laughing about that state of being female. And my memories of those intense times with Sue, when [we] were just 14, are as powerful as the memory of standing endlessly in line, waiting and weathering the cold. (2007, 351)

Fandom can therefore offer a space where individuals can investigate the possibilities of their gender identities. Sometimes this can happen when people discover particular fictional characters. Exploring the persona of Catwoman from the original *Batman* television series (1966–8), for example, was a way for female fans to resist male constraints to be a 'good little girl' (Jenkins 1992, 35).

To suggest that certain social spaces of fandom are *socially coded* 'male' while others are 'female', however, is to forget that these spaces are historically contingent. As media texts change, the patterns of gender making up fan communities can change significantly too. The *Doctor Who* fan community provides an example worth discussing in more detail. Russell T. Davies' version of the series included a strong female lead and romantic subtext, allowing more women to enter its traditionally more male-orientated fan culture. While *Doctor Who* was always presented as family viewing, before the series was reinvented there was a perception that the members of its fan community were male. When the new series arrived in 2005, the traditional notion of an asexual Doctor was cast aside. The new incarnation of the central character suddenly seemed capable of both sex and romance. To examine the accompanying shift in the 'Whovian' community, I will draw on Thomas and O'Shea's edited collection *Chicks Who Dig Time Lords* (2010), a book which voices the experiences of a number of female *Doctor Who* fans. One contributor recalled:

> Being a relatively new fan, I've only heard second-hand stories from the days of the classic series, but it seemed that *Doctor Who* fandom always carried a whiff of the Old Boys Club and in the hierarchy of *Who*, the girl fans hovered near the bottom. Is this perception correct? It depends on who you talk to and where they fall in the hierarchy. I've met girls who swam through the waters brilliantly and girls who ended up creating their own niches and formed their own hierarchies within larger fandom. Perception is a tricky thing, but in terms of fandom power, influence and control, it's a man's world . . . There were no fireworks or beating down the glass ceiling. It's been more an experience of existing in intersecting circles rather than forming a great fandom melting pot. There is often a sense of talking at entrenched fandom rather than engaging in any real dialogue. I wondered if the boys in already established hierarchies had continued on as if nothing had changed. (Stanish 2010, 35)

As new fans entered into what was previously a fan culture *led by male fans* and their interests, a fascinating series of shifts took place. Female fans of various ages and marital statuses became increasingly visible. At first, this new cohort was chided by some existing male fans for the general nature of its attraction to the series, expressed as **squee** and fan fiction. One of the female fans recounted:

> Now, 'fangirl' is a word with a slippery meaning. I polled people in my LiveJournal for their definitions, which ranged from 'silly screeching teenager' through 'a self-depreciating term used by female fans to refer to themselves' through simply 'a fan who is a girl'. In this essay, I use the word with the lattermost meaning in mind. But many female fans are keen to dissociate themselves from 'fangirl' behavior, and not just because they see it as adolescent. In 'Cyberspace of Their Own: Female Fandoms Online', Rhiannon Bury writes that members of the David Duchovny Estrogen Brigade would play down their association with the group to avoid ridicule and to be 'taken seriously' – by male fans . . . The same was true of Australian *Doctor Who* fandom: I was a rare fangirl in a sea of fanboys. (Orman 2010, 144)

As the female 'Whovians' began to contact each other and discover their collective identity, they reconsidered the show's past and celebrated that Verity Lambert was the show's first producer back in 1963. She was, at the time, the BBC's youngest and only female producer. **Shippers** are fans who are much more interested in the triumphs and tribulations of romantic relationships than in other aspects of the dramatic text. Male fans *assumed* that the female *Doctor Who* followers were shippers demanding greater chemistry between the Doctor and his assistant Rose Tyler so that they could enjoy a soap set in a sci-fi context. Their assumption was at least partially correct. Some female fans were intrigued by the possibility of romance between the characters:

> The shipwar, or 'relationship war', is a squabble over true love: Harry Potter, or the Doctor, or whomever should find true love with the right female character (i.e. the one they personally happen to identify with). Plus – often in tandem with the shipwar – there's harsh criticism of female characters (Rose, Gwen) who seem to get too much approval from the showmakers or from the male characters. (Orman 2010, 152)

This seems to suggest that fans of different genders can *sometimes* identify in different ways. For instance, fanfic writers like Jacqueline Land have said that men generally like characters to face physical problems whereas female readers are fascinated by psychological ordeals (Jenkins 2006, 50).

As the transformation of *Doctor Who* demonstrated, certain media products can *articulate* (and re-articulate) particular versions of gender. For example, Jason Eastman (2012) has shown how Southern rock performers and audiences share an expression of rebellious masculinity that has emerged from the poorest parts of the world's richest country. Even if they may not operate all the time, differences in identification are to be expected since male and female fans operate from different, socially constructed positions. Cavicchi noted the gendering of his own sample: 'Whether men actually outnumber women among Springsteen fans I cannot say conclusively. During my fieldwork, however, I did encounter almost twice as many men as women' (1998, 143). He added that 'female fans have reported that men often see them as second-class fans because of an inability to really relate to the music and have protested such stereotypes' (144). Bruce Springsteen's 1995 tune 'Secret Garden' sparked discussion in his fan community as men and women had different interpretations of what the song meant when it described how a woman could possess a hidden, inaccessible. Male fans read it as a lament about the nature of femininity. In contrast, one female fan suggested it had more of an empathetic resonance: 'Quite frankly I think you have to be a woman to fully understand it – or at least in close touch with one. The fact that Bruce writes a song that comes that close to our souls is . . . well, it's downright scary and that strikes hard' (Cavicchi 1998, 145). This suggests not only that people of different identities interpret the same music differently, but that they each seek affinity on the basis of their own pre-existing identifications.

Fandom and sexual identities

The capacity for misrecognizing and marginalizing identifications and practices is exacerbated when sexual identities are considered. Homosexual practices were illegal for most of the twentieth century and direct references were largely absent from media culture. Even after events such as the June 1969 Stonewall riots helped to prompt the decriminalization of homosexuality across the majority of American States, for years mainstream media culture was neither open nor welcoming. This lead to the idea that gay readings had to be speculative, investing in polysemic characters and 'hijacking' mainstream texts. D. A. Miller's study of Alfred Hitchcock's 1948 film *Rope* suggested that closeted gay audiences read the sexual identity of the main character via 'the shadow kingdom of connotation, where insinuations could at once de developed and denied' (1991, 125). Before the 1970s, appeals to gay spectators had to be indirect because programmers feared that openly gay characters would alienate mainstream audiences. Gay identity was initially portrayed through subtle drama or comedy stereotype: for instance, in the

British film *Victim* (Dearden 1961), Dirk Bogarde played a judge who was blackmailed for his closeted identity. Casual gay characters did not appear in the mainstream for decades. Gay audiences tended to confer iconic status upon individuals – often women – who *did* appear in the mainstream and offered even the smallest relevant signs with which they could associate. According to Richard Dyer (2004), such audiences liked Judy Garland, especially after MGM suspended her contract in 1950 and she tried to commit suicide. She failed in her marriage and struggled with alcohol, but just soldiered on. Dyer argued that gay audiences saw Garland as a survivor who had trouble fitting traditional marriage and family structures. Heterosexual fans, however, have not always taken kindly to seeing characters who appear to express gay identities. As Rob Lendrum (2004) explained:

> The *Batman* TV-show of the 1960s used the ambiguously gay relationship to their advantage. By acting out the comic book, the show drew attention to the absurd and homoerotic qualities of superhero masculinity. Some bat-fans felt that the silly TV-show had ridiculed their beloved character, so in an effort to 'dignify' Batman, the writers set out to re-heterosexualize him. (70)

Fearing that mainstream audiences would reject their media products, television networks and other businesses often acted to silence gay readings. For example, although *Star Trek* represented a utopian future for Earth, the show never had a gay character until 2007. Fans speculated that one female character called Tasha Yar was a lesbian, but a bedroom scene between her and the android Data was soon written into the show. In this respect, Michael DeAngelis' work on *social distancing* is relevant. DeAngelis (2001) offers case studies contrasting the images of three male stars and their fluctuating separation from gay audiences. James Dean died at the age of 24 in 1955. DeAngelis argues that around 15 years later, during the start of a significant era of gay rights struggle, Dean's ambiguous sexuality was levered to reshape his public profile so that the gay community could celebrate him as a 'working class hunk'. In his second analysis, DeAngelis notes that while Mel Gibson's early roles have contained an element of homoerotic camaraderie, once Gibson arrived in Hollywood in the 1980s, his image was shifted towards that of a heterosexual, family-orientated, and even homophobic man. DeAngelis claims that this was, in part, an attempt to close down readings that might allow a gay following to claim Gibson. Finally and in contrast, during the more tolerant era of the early 1990s, according to DeAngelis, Keanu Reeves' ambiguous sexual identity made him 'pan-accessible' to audiences of different sexual orientations. Despite the title of Michael DeAngelis's book – *Gay Fandom and*

Crossover Stardom – the voices of gay cinema fans are not always directly audible in the account. Nevertheless his work increases our understanding of how celebrity images may be used strategically to allow particular audience members to square their sexual and gender identities when image-makers attempt to shape fan bases.

Some fan communities have become spaces where gay men can feel accepted and make connections. With visions of a future utopia, certain areas of science fiction fandom have offered gay readers a special kind of acceptance. Jim Kepner's 1950s homophile fanzine, *Towards Tomorrow* was seminal in that respect. Homosexual science-fiction lobby group, the Gaylaxians, are another interesting example discussed in Henry Jenkins' much-reprinted 1995 essay 'Out of the Closet and into the Universe'. The Gaylaxians were a group of gay *Star Trek* fans who staged a letter-writing campaign which asked Paramount to have gay men represented on board the Starship Enterprise. Though the Gaylaxians were simply genuine *Star Trek* fans who were also gay, the studio saw them as a pressure group bent on 'outing' particular actors and characters. Among excuses given to the fans were that the producers had no decent script, that sexual orientation had to be in the drama and not just in passing characters, that no character's preferences should be obvious (unless they were straight), that representing homosexual characters would go beyond the action genre's remit (by being too character driven) or that a revamped show would reveal offensive sexual practices or stereotype gay people. None of those claims sounds convincing in retrospect.

Finally here, when communities or practices are predominantly shaped by the concerns of one social group, those in a minority have to inhabit a world in which the cultural conventions may be different to what they desire. Jenkins (1992, 116) argues that men have learned to read media texts using the codes created by female-dominated fan cultures, just as women have learned to read within the norms of patriarchal culture. For example, the same subtext of homoeroticism that might previously have been of interest to gay fans is useful to female fanfic writers who wish to put those characters in slash situations. Some producers – of *Xena: Warrior Princess*, for example – knew fans wanted a gay subtext (Jenkins 2006, 145). Joss Whedon is interesting in this respect as the scriptwriter who created the series *Buffy the Vampire Slayer* and *Angel*. Talking about the rivalry between his two characters Spike and Angel (sometimes called 'Spangel' by fans), Virginia Keft-Kennedy (2008) commented that their mutual rivalry over Buffy has created an intimate kind of connection between them that has consequently inspired slash stories:

> The source of their rivalry is usually Buffy, the teenaged Vampire Slayer, who, despite her calling to fight vampires, becomes romantically and sexually

involved with both Angel and Spike at various points throughout both series. Eve Kosofsky Sedgwick's reworking of René Girard's notion of the 'erotic triangle' is useful in looking at the ways in which fans conceptualise the relationship between Angel and Spike in slash fiction, and the tangential relationship the two vampires share with Buffy. In her book *Between Men*, Sedgwick writes that the 'bond that links the two rivals is as intense and potent as the bond that links either of the rivals to the beloved' (1985, 21). This notion of the erotic triangle – with Buffy at the apex – is both played out on-screen in *Buffy* and *Angel*, and explicitly enacted in many slash fictions . . . Angel and Spike, however, were never really friends. Even during their reign of terror their relationship was a tenuous one, marked by competition, jealousy, and violence. This emphasis on violence and on the homoerotic bonds of shared hostility, are themes that are constantly highlighted in Angel/Spike fanfic. These tensions form the foundation of many of the stories. With Angel and Spike pitted against one another, sex and violence become the sites at which masculinity, homosociality, and the vampiric are negotiated. (Keft-Kennedy 2010, 69)[1]

Alterations

As Rhiannon Bury's (2003) study of the *X Files* fandom suggests, female fans use texts designed by men to discover shared pleasures. Yet to fully enjoy such texts, such readers have to perform a kind of 'intellectual transvestitism', identifying against their own cultural experiences and constructing countertexts to express their own desires (Jenkins 2006, 44). In other words, women who participate in some forms of media culture habitually find themselves identifying with characters of the opposite sex – something that men did not traditionally need to do and therefore found harder to contemplate. A good example of this comes from the recent and phenomenally popular film series *Twilight*. Edward Cullen is a vampire character who must fight his own lust for Bella Swan because he fears that he might kill her. Jennifer Stevens Aubrey et al. (2010) report that female fans saw romance in a certain way and often identified with Edward in his struggle to wait:

Research documents that girls, not boys, typically act as the sexual gatekeepers in romantic relationships . . . For some of the fans we interviewed and surveyed, *Twilight* can be viewed as a shelter in a hypersexualized media environment. Our data suggest that at least some of the fans want media messages of romance rather than explicit sex. Further, we are sensitive to girls viewing Edward as the ideal romantic partner because he epitomizes the conflicting needs of adolescent girls who have sexual feelings but are nervous about acting on them. It also appears that *Twilight* connects with this particular generation of girls because many of them have grown up in a time when abstinence-only sex education was commonplace in their schools and communities. (online)

When they have the chance, it is not surprising, therefore, that female viewers have sometimes altered and rewritten male dominated texts to suit their own needs. Female fan writers can be critical of the primary text for misrepresenting women. In their sci-fi fiction, they have repurposed the genre by turning it into romance, rereading it as a type of women's fiction (Jenkins 2006, 50). For example, there were around 400 *Star Trek* fanzines by 1980, many of which were written and edited by women. Despite the show's originator Gene Roddenberry proclaiming the possibility of social equality in space, women on the Starship Enterprise in the orginal series had menial, supportive jobs, wore mini-skirts, were called 'girls' and received attention only as the volatile love objects of male lead characters. Often they were portrayed as repressed workers or emotional wrecks. Consequently, female fanzine writers began to play with Lieutenant Uhura's character to reveal the 'glass ceiling' of patriarchal assumptions held by men of the Federation, for instance the idea that a woman could not lead the fleet in a war. In order to show softer, more novel aspects of masculinity, they began to rewrite the interplay between the assertive Captain Kirk and emotionally cold rationalist Mr Spock. From 1974 onwards, some imagined that Kirk and Spock had a same sex relationship – hence the development of K/S or slash fiction (Pugh 2005, 91). Female writers also extended the world of *Star Trek* by imagining the relationship between Spock's parents or marriages between other crew members. Rejecting a genre convention of romance that said a man should be perfected before marriage, these fan stories saw partnerships as adventures 'boldly going' into new fields of conflict and making fresh discoveries. Female fans thus used the utopian mandate of their favourite series to directly challenge patriarchal frames of reference. As Henry Jenkins claimed, 'The fans' particular viewing stance – at once ironically distant, playfully close – sparks recognition that the program is open to intervention and active appropriation' (1992, 155).

Social uses of the text

Given that fans often participate in public communities that share celebrated texts, it is important to consider how those texts are *socially practiced*: how they are used in everyday life to shape and create the ordinary relationships between people. Because their connection to particular series and performers suggests something in common, fans can form communities of mutual care. Female *Star Trek* fans created a social network which allowed them to meet and support each other.[2] When shared with those around them, their diaries and letters became vehicles for bonding. Henry Jenkins noted that male readers often assessed the authority of the author, while female readers tended to locate themselves as part of a conversation (108). Communal fan practices may therefore represent the institutionalization of an approach to texts usually coded as 'feminine' (89). Before the legalization of homosexuality, informal spaces of socialization and public media consumption were particularly important as places where like-minded men could meet. Judy Garland concerts, for example, allowed gay fans a space to 'come out' and encounter other gay men in a public place (see Dyer 2004). Equally, the pen pal sections of fan magazines such as *Films and Filming* were places where men looking for pen pals could ask, 'Are you a friend of Dorothy?' The line deployed the name of Garland's character in Victor Fleming's famous 1939 film, *The Wizard of Oz*, as a shared reference point. Once gay identity was more accepted, fan groups like the Gaylaxians formed closer-knit social niches within gay culture. They contrasted *their* particular community with the wider gay world, seeing their own society as more welcoming and supportive of their cultural interests.

Gender trouble

Unlike audience research, film studies has traditionally concentrated on psychoanalysis, spectatorship and the notion that media products offer their audiences relatively narrow, gender-defined subject positions in relation to the text. While this approach has led to ideas that politicize the pleasures of cinema, it does not account for the variety of identifications and interpretations that audience members can make. Equally, work on fandom and gender is in danger of, at worst, essentializing gender, pinning it down as a static form of identity and assuming that each gender inevitably interprets the text from an entirely different perspective. It is easy to forget *similarities* in the ways that people of different sexual orientations can identify with and interpet the same text or perform. There is another danger in perceiving that gender identity can never transform or adapt to different situations. According to Judith Butler (1990) in her book *Gender Trouble*, *all* gender is a performance without an origin. She meant that the actions by which we pursue gender are not indications of biological human identity, but instead they can be seen as socially conveyed and performing a *constitutive* function. Rather than *expressing* gender, they actually *enact* and *(re)make* it in one and the same process. Gender performance can therefore include everything from the way we talk as individuals to the way we walk and style our hair. As we enact these signs of gender, we also *internalize gender.* Our gender is therefore an imitation, approximation and replication: something that we automatically borrow from others around us and yet *feel* as our own since it allows us to identify ourselves. From this perspective, what is interesting about the parallel subject identity of 'the fan' is that – while we feel it as an emotional conviction and strong form of identity ('I realized that I was a fan') – it is also enacted and performed in actions that separate us from non-fans. Those actions, moreover, can sometimes reinforce our gender identities and sometimes contest them. In the latter sense, certain aspects and kinds of fandom can themselves cause 'gender trouble'. By this I mean that we must not preclude the possibility that our gender and fannish identities can be in conflict with each other.

For women, the gender trouble of fandom has sometimes taken the shape of the collective expression of 'unladylike' desire in public. In a famous essay on the forces behind American horror films, Robin Wood (1979) argued that society enacted a 'severe repression of female sexuality/creativity' which went along with 'the attribution to the female of passivity, her preparation for her subordinate and dependent role in our culture'. He added that this entailed, 'the denial to women of drives culturally associated with masculinity: activeness, aggression, self-assertion, organized power, creativity itself'. (9) **Liminality** is, broadly speaking, the idea that certain threshold spaces operate under social rules in opposition to the norm. One perspective on rock'n'roll is that it allowed young and adolescent females a kind of liminal space in which to express sexual desires and characteristics that had been marginalized and stifled elsewhere in public life (see Ehrenreich et al. 1992). While it would be tempting to follow this line and say that repressed female sexuality has been *unlocked* since the 1950s by the seductive male sexuality of such musical performances, it might be more useful to think of things in a slightly different way. Female desire for stars from Elvis to Justin Bieber has been publically *produced* as one symptom of what is going on. The *claim* propounded in the 1950s, that the activities of female audiences represented a kind of mass hysteria – the return of sexual energy that had been repressed elsewhere – was itself an indication that Americans felt intense social anxiety about the collective *expression* of female desire in public places. If we have, as a society, gradually got used to the phenomenon, the lingering critical attacks on boybands – apparent, for example, on Facebook hate pages – arguably indicate that outbursts of female desire are still seen as problematic in public life, particularly if they are *supposedly misdirected* at wholesome, young musicians.

For male media enthusiasts, fandom can cause gender trouble in other ways. As Henry Jenkins suggested in *Textual Poachers*, fans are perceived as 'feminized and/or desexualized through their intimate engagements with mass culture' (1992, 10). This means that the social stereotype of media fandom *itself* has traditionally led to perceptions of male fans, in some fields, as socially inadequate and somehow defective in their masculinities. If a mature male fan loves a genre generally aimed at a female audience – like soaps or romances – he is perceived as especially suspect. The practice of being a fan *itself* also involves *devoting* your days to exploring the creativity of another person, often a man, suggesting a bond of affinity and admiration that *can trouble staid forms of masculinity*. After reading a sample of 2,500 pre-internet fan letters sent to six different artists, Elaine Elder reported that 'many heterosexual male fans seemed unable to admit they were indeed fans of male stars' (1992, 77). Interestingly, though, a reluctance to express admiration – lest it be considered subservience – has also been articulated by female fans writing to celebrities in cultural fields that promote more masculine norms of behaviour. A good example of this is punk. In my own work I discussed a fan letter sent by two girls who wrote to Johnny Rotten, the lead singer of the Sex Pistols:

> John, don't get the impression that we only like you for your fame (and fortune!); it's not like that . . . You are you, you don't give a fuck about what people expect you to do, you just want to be yourself . . . We are two 16-year-old Dublin girls who are individualists. We don't give a fuck about anyone's views. We have our own views on life and that's all that matters. (in Duffett 2010c, 103)

It could be argued that these two girls, operating in a domain which celebrated values that were traditionally associated with male identity (independence, rebellion), decided to enact a kind of 'female masculinity' as their way of approaching their hero (see Halberstam 1998). Such examples highlight that rejecting or adopting norms associated with gender can be a kind of strategic activity, designed to create an advantageous result.

Discussing fandom for David Bowie, Nick Stevenson described what he saw as a masculine denial of vulnerability:

> It is finally the emphasis that our culture places upon self-reliance and the rejection of dependence that continues to inscribe masculine dominance. Here I would suggest that by identifying with 'an alternative text', many

of the men were actually learning to banish more difficult feelings of helplessness and dependency. (2009, 95)

To the extent Stevenson's Bowie fans went as far, however, as they could go – within a culture dominated by heterosexual norms – in discussing their hero's seductive allure, even they were seduced by his aura. A male Bowie fan explained, 'I am heterosexual, but I found him very attractive. You know, like you see lots of actors on film. Like James Dean. I just could not take my eyes off him' (Stevenson 2009, 91). In the 1993 film *True Romance*, directed by Tony Scott but scripted by Quentin Tarantino and Roger Avary, the lead character, Clarence (played by Christian Slater), went further and exclaimed, 'I always said, if I had to fuck a guy . . . I mean had to, if my life depended on it . . . I'd fuck Elvis'. The claim, which I have occasionally heard repeated by male Elvis fans, implies the production of a current of same-sex desire evoked by socially valued, handsome and pretty male performers. In that sense, some fan connections may be so intense that they begin to 'queer' gender identities. Nick Stevenson noted, though, there is a great taboo against discussing such desires:

> These features were quickly closed down and were mostly avoided by the other men interviewed. Again, the reasons for this are complex, although admitting sexual feelings for another man is still a difficult achievement in a culture where men are encouraged to be ashamed or embarrassed about such feelings. (2009, 95)

Nevertheless, it seems that the bonds of fandom can go beyond a kind of imagined camaraderie into a place of seduction. When I asked one male fan about Elvis for my research he explained, 'I'm ODed on the guy. I have to have some Elvis music. I have to listen to him'. He continued, 'I suddenly hear an Elvis track on the radio and I think, God, it's *my bloke* on the radio!' (see Duffett 2001, 402). Such exclamations and statements of ownership ('my bloke') indicate both a kind of power relation and energy of seductiveness that can begin to reshape the most alienated elements of masculinity in the context of a fan attachment.

8

Myths, cults and places

Starting points

- In what ways do fans pursue their interests beyond discrete textual boundaries?
- How might 'cult' phenomena be defined?
- What do fans' geographic pilgrimages actually mean to them?

We believe that life can be as circular, as karmic, as rich and as deep as art. That is life, too, theme repeat poetically, and sorrow ends. That is, in the end, what fan activity is: seeking ourselves, seeking meaning in stories. We choose our idols out of dozens, hundreds, and clothe ourselves in the appropriate vestments and icons. We buy, say, an absurdly long scarf, or Converse shoes, to identify ourselves as these acolytes. In a very real way, television is the new mythos. It defines the world, reinterprets it.

CATHERYNNE VALENTE 2010, 181

Myths, cults and places make up the stuff of dedicated fandom. These three elements respectively highlight magical dimensions of meaning, audience dedication and geography. Attention to them reminds us that particular fan objects can appeal by having an unusual, striking quality and are therefore able to sustain continued fan interest. Popular cultural phenomena define the territory within which fans find themselves. Some stars, like Bruce Springsteen, have maintained steady careers and never disappeared into obscurity (Cavicchi 1998, 13). As fans, we sometimes immerse ourselves in the minutiae of our objects to a point where they provide an affective context *through which we circulate* in real and imagined ways. One question is whether this comes from a fannish tendency to obsess, or the richness of our fan objects. Henry Jenkins has argued that fandom is about resonant myths, not false faiths (2006, 17). Discussions about 'cultishness' get us away from the text and idea that fandom is simply an aesthetic practice. Speaking about *Doctor Who,* Matt Hills has said, 'Whereas fans generally display a tendency to read the series intratextually – in relation to itself and its own histories – academics frequently read it intertextually via specific theoretical frameworks' (2010b, 4). To make intertextual and intratextual readings there has to be complexity in the text. Even performances that seem simple can contain subtle nuances and deep resonances for those who get drawn into them. What is the best way to talk about texts that seem to attract sustained fan phenomena? Discussions of myth, cult and place highlight the specialness of particular objects, leading to the question of whether a general discussion can be fruitful at all. Ideas about place, for example, suggest that certain locations are not just spaces but are meaningfully unique. These concepts, then, allow us to narrate uniqueness and grasp the special appeal of particular phenomena that can sustain strong fan bases.

Myths

Rather than, as is commonly thought, being a confabulation (something *entirely* false), in dictionary definitions a **myth** is a popular and satisfying way of telling a story. This suggests that as well as the affective dimension of legend, myth also has an ideological dimension; its social meaning appears to make it a 'natural' focus of attention. Russell T. Davies, talking about *Doctor Who*, distinguished mythology and continuity by saying that mythology is more about emotion (Hills 2010b, 212). Are myths, then, the cause of stardom or its result? They are both. If an intriguing celebrity image can help to make good copy, only a highly popular performance can cause mythic narratives to multiply and compete with each other in a bid to unlock the thrill of their subject matter.

Because fandom happens inside fans' heads, its objects can be real or fictional, alive or dead, fantasy people or fantastic drama. Contrary to the extremely relativistic idea that popular phenomena form total 'blank slates' (i.e. are place holders for projection upon which different audience members can see whatever they like), myths are neither entirely blank nor entirely restricted to one meaning. Instead they have contours that can encompass what matters by tapping into the anxieties and desires at the heart of present-day society. Think, for example, of the story of Cinderella: a resonant cultural myth not because it is meaningless, but precisely because it connects desire, romance and social mobility. Cinderella relies on the acceptance of certain ideas about gender, monogamy and class to sustain its symbolic resonance; if those things changed radically, the Cinderella story would lose its appeal. It is precisely such shared elements that then allow young girls to identify with the Cinderella role and to project themselves as desiring subjects into the story. Other narratives and performer's images have mythic power for exactly the same reasons. They sustain a longevity of appeal because their contours follow specific concerns. Unlike press discussions often assume, as fans we may *not* want *to be* the central characters, but we might want to be *like* them or be *with* them instead. The social relevance of each myth therefore offers a thrilling space into which we project our identities to envisage a kind of fit. In other words, the 'blank slate' has a position and borders that make it matter. From the point where many implicitly understand a myth's relevance, it can become more like the kernel of something larger: a nexus or point of intersection around which further narratives can form and adhere.

When they become larger, the most resonant myths – the ones that appeal most – are characteristically unfinalized (open in content) and ongoing (open in authorship). As Matt Hills has noted, cult texts facilitate endless unfinalized, speculative narratives. Attention to *Doctor Who* as a fan favourite suggests one possible source of its textual richness:

> *Doctor Who's* time travelling is linked to a range of hybridized genres including SF, comedy, soap drama, and adventure. The show's format involves articulating these different genre discourses via a 'generic function' that sets discursive parameters (and consistencies) in Who's identity. (Hills 2010b, 105)

In other words, texts that combine an array of different genre conventions and other elements can offer a wealth of opportunities for different readings and extensions. Official and unofficial developers of the text can steer it in different directions. The new *Doctor Who*, for instance, was, branded in some ways to avoid the connotations of the sci-fi genre by using an action-adventure score, for example (203). A rich, resonant, multiplying, regenerating text can offer opportunities for fans to find their own entry points into the myth. Each follower of *Doctor Who* has their own favourite Doctor: 'This was the fourth incarnation of the Doctor, who quickly became *my* Doctor' (Nye 2010, 104; emphasis mine). Texts that have a foundation of appealing core qualities can then go on being updated and reinvented, extending across a palate of possibilities and bringing the franchise to new generations of followers. Busse and Hellekson (2006, 7) explain that 'fan academics have begun to think of the entirety of fan fictions in a given fannish universe as a work in progress.' Open textuality can also be associated with open authorship, particularly if the auteur at the centre of cultural production for the phenomenon has died. A good example of this was the development of new James Bond novels when endorsed writers, such as the television comedy presenter Charlie Higson, attempted to take Ian Fleming's place. In the case of the new *Doctor Who* (from 2005 onwards), multi-authorship of the series represents 'an industrial consecration of fan approaches to multiple authorship' and also aligns it with the tradition of *quality television drama*, a form often created by teams of skilled writers who work together (Hills 2010b, 30). Rather than seeing a multi-authored text as liberated from the stamp of auteurship, fans instead look for how the range of creative individuals involved in a project have jointly put it together. They tend to read multi-authored texts through the collision of various agents who collaborate and leave their 'signatures' on the work (31).

Further fuelled either by studio production, star publicity or fan discussion, as popular myths expand they become part of larger and more complex bodies of knowledge sometimes known as **mythologies**. A mythology is not an *extension* of one media product itself so much as a constellation of myths and ideas that surround at least one text or its maker. When central tropes or explanations emerge as guiding forces in a mythology, they are called the **mythos**. The mythos of Alfred Hitchcock, for example, would include his Oedipal anxieties, his fascination with icy blondes his fear of birds (of the feathered variety). These elements do not directly explain the creation of his films, but they may help audiences unlock the meaning of subtexts within them. In other words, mythology marks an extension of fan fascination beyond the boundaries of the primary text – in this case Hitchcock's film *The Birds* (1963) – into a much wider realm. As Daniel Hertitz has explained, discussing cinema, 'Film stars like Marilyn carry the aura of their on-screen presence into their off-screen lives, and nothing is more mysterious than this transition' (2008, 63). **Literary biography** reads the maker's life through the themes of their text. A literary biographer's aim is to show how the life of the person was expressed in the text that they created. At their most poetic, literary biographers are therefore also explorers – and perhaps *performers* – of mythology, plotting the shape of a mythos that frames both the auteur and their text. Rather than just examining stars as workers in the culture industry, popular approaches tend to follow literary biography in promoting an equivalence between – or downright confusion of – the text and its maker. Thus, for example, Hitchcock is portrayed through *The Birds as* Hitchcock. Indeed, if a fan's quest to get closer to their hero is about seeking intimacy and bonding, then one motive for this – beyond any temptation to bask in reflected glory – is to know the 'real' person: the individual beneath the mask of myth. As sociologist Kerry Ferris (2001, 34) has noted, fans often have an 'interest in distinguishing the actor from the character she plays and in gathering information about the actor's personal life as well'.

Sometimes, under guidance of the mythos, the text itself can also be re-established, re-imagined or extended.[1] According to Matt Hills (2002a, 137), the term 'hyperdiegesis' denotes the creation of a vast or expanded narrative space only partially covered by any one text. In recent years this phenomenon of textual sprawl has sometimes begun to eclipse central narratives. As audiences get used to moving across different media platforms in their everyday lives, storytelling has turned into a complex art of world-building that is as much about creating an immersive cultural and artistic universe as it is about pursuing one central narrative: '*Who* has become more than just an "unfolding" text, instead aspiring to the status of a multi-platform, multi-layered mega-text from which fans and academics can only ever consume a cross section' (Hills 2010b, 4). There are limits, though, to how far a mythos can expand. Feelings of closeness to the text only continue when fans believe in its credibility and coherence. Members of the fan community reject leaps in the plot or gaps in the motivation of particular characters (Jenkins 1992, 106). *Doctor Who's* narrative universe, for instance, is a fantasy world stitched together by a sense of truth that actually comes from 'emotional realism' (Hills 2010b, 100). By bringing *Doctor Who* together with the England of Dickens, Queen Victoria and Shakespeare, its producers could be accused of desperately drawing on high culture to avoid the charge that *Doctor Who* is a lowbrow phenomenon. For Hills, this is one of the ways that the production team have defined the new *Who* franchise as a brand. In the context of significant shifts or emergent gaps in the text, fans can find their own perspectives on its characters. For example, *Harry Potter* is yet to have a romantic relationship, so his fans have filled the gap with a range of speculations (see Green & Guinery 2004).

Another way to talk about the mythos is that it reflects the interests or value systems of the fan base. In phenomena as diverse as hip-hop, telefantasy and comic books, genre fans do not just stick to the output of one cultural producer; they explore many others of a similar nature. Henry Jenkins (2006, 20) has argued that such fans are not so much being 'religious' – finding spiritual sustenance by sticking loyally to one text – as *sharing common values* that allow them to create and enjoy multiple texts. In this way, it could be said that each *genre* has a guiding mythos.

Icons are stars who have acquired their own myths and mythologies. Such figures are *always already* a focus of fan attachments (Hills 2002a, 138). They become *cult* figures when their image is wrested from the industry and adopted by the audience (141). Given a kernel worthy of fascination, a myth can grow into a mythos: something that is much larger and shared precisely because it circulates within the same channels as the society itself. The images of figures like Elvis and Marilyn are not only part of the cultural furniture (always there to be used) but they also represent points of intervention in the broadest moral discourses that define society, such as the American dream (the idea that talented representatives of the poorest classes can make good) or the vacuity of glamour (the idea that fame is not worth the price because it cannot make its recipient happy on the inside). At such points, the star transcends myth and becomes the focus of a mythos: a kind of black hole reconstituting popular culture in their own image, stamping their mark on everything because they seem to set the boundaries within which it appears. As Daniel Hertitz (2008, 133) explains, 'This is the transcendent aspect of the icon: that the media seems to levitate around her.'

Iconic performers are not just recognizable. They are recognizable *by the merest signs and ciphers* of their identity: silhouettes, items of clothing, first names, catch phrases. They have specific styles of performance. Bruce Springsteen, for instance, is known for telling his famous 'growing up' stories on stage. His image therefore works in conjunction with his musical performance (Cavicchi 1998, 28, 65). Icons are not limited to film or popular music. Telefantasy viewing can foster a kind of personality cult, in so far that fans prefer episodes which either confirm an existing character's personality or reveal new sides to it (Jenkins 1992, 98). In *Doctor Who*, 'The Doctor is a flawed, damaged, brilliant, dangerous alien. He's also the hero' (Jones 2010, 173). He is constant and yet mercurial as he reincarnates across time. He can also examine what it means to be human by being an outsider.[2] Rather like James Bond, Doctor Who is an icon that has been played by more than one person. Such icons are also like genres in that they represent a personification of specific conventions and audience segments. They reduce the uncertainty of profitable media production, carve up and format the consumer market place, and they can also act as sales people, endorsing their own or others' wares (see Hesmondhalgh 2005, 116). In more humanist terms, icons represent constituencies; they *speak for the people*, and it is actually a mark of their iconicity to say that they have transcended their origins, moved beyond their first audience, intrigued everybody and become a stake in wider discussion. For Matt Hills, the emergence of iconicity is based on mystery: Elvis is perhaps a cult icon because the meaning of his demise was mysterious (2002a, 142). Mystery certainly *fuels* fascination, but it does not necessarily act to guarantee that what is behind it is worthy. There has to *already* be something interesting about a performer for their mystery to matter.

A different way to talk about mythic worlds of meaning in popular culture is to consider them in relation to the idea of textuality. Whether the primary text is a cult film or key album, a constellation of other, secondary texts necessarily circulates in relation to it. They can include advertisements, interviews, community speculations and 'bibles' (Jenkins 1992, 99). A **meta-text** is a combination of *both* the primary text (or texts) and an entire collection of secondary texts that refer to it. Attention to meta-textuality suggests that the primary text does not contain its own inherent, transparent meaning, but is accompanied by a range of by-products that can in turn shape or reshape what it seems to say. Some commentators have drawn on the literary studies of Gérard Genette (1997) to dub more ephemeral, secondary texts as 'paratexts' and highlight their unlikely importance.[3] Without the primary text, in theory they would cease to matter. Johnathan Gray, however, argues:

> Paratexts are not simply add-ons, spin-offs, and also-rans: they create texts, they manage them, and they fill them with the meanings we associate with them . . . a film or program is but one part of a text, the text always being a contingent entity, either in the process of forming or transforming or vulnerable to further formation or transformation. (2010, 6–7)

For Gray, these paratexts – which can include trailers, advertisements, opening credits, merchandise, t-shirts, secondary texts like documentaries and biographies, spin-offs, commentary, online postings, reviews and even adaptions or edits of the text itself (the director's cut for example) – continually change what any show means to its audience (11). Hence 'Paratexts are the greeters, gatekeepers, and cheerleaders for and of the media, filters through which we must pass on our way to "the text itself", but some will only greet certain audiences.' (17) It is also important to realize that distinctions between the primary (main) text and secondary (para) texts start to break down once producers expand across a range of media to tell the story. Directors like Andy and Larry Wachowski have created central texts that necessarily require their viewers to have engaged with texts created other media. This process is not simply one of adaption, but rather a tale of two media in which some of the same story is told in one medium and the rest in another. Hollywood is now targeting a young audience that is familiar with video games, music and films, and can see the connections being made when narratives expressed in one form refer to those in another. The Hollywood writer's strike in 2007 showed that 'promotional' material was now considered a *central* part of transmedia storytelling (Jenkins 2008, 125). This shift can be understood, in a sense, as the demanding of a fannish practice from *all* modern audiences as they meander across the surface of different media in their quest for meaning.

Two more textual formations are worth discussing in relation to their role in preserving and sustaining myths: canon and fanon. A **canon** is a selection of texts that represent the supposed essence or highest quality examples of their form or phenomenon. Texts take up their meaning because they are read in relation to the canon (Busse & Hellekson 2006, 27). By representing the supposed cream of the crop, canons are tools for cultivating audiences. While the idea of canonicity comes from the era in which critics and other appointed guardians of elite culture could operate unchallenged in their educational role, in recent years the right to specify the canon has been wrested by fans into their own hands. As Will Brooker (2002, 106) suggested, the 'canon is a slippery thing'. Talking, for example, about a moment where some fans had drawn upon the canonical authority of Stephen Sansweet's *Star Wars Encyclopedia* (1998), he explained:

> While the Encyclopedia is accepted as canonical in this specific instance, this is not always the case; the group still makes a distinction between 'official' texts on one hand, and on the other, novels, computer games or comics that, despite their Lucasfilm branding, have less credibility. The line between the two is hazy. (Brooker 2002, 52)

The professional bodies that construct key texts and licence them as franchises frequently attempt to canonize only specific versions of the text or assert only particular versions of the canon. This policing extends to merchanize too: when BBC Wales produced *Doctor Who* they made a *Style Guide* to ensure that merchandise for the new series had a consistent look and feel (Hills 2010b, 67). That process created a coherent taste-image for the franchise. Yet sometimes such ideas can backfire, because fans are consumers who can also make their own choices about what should be included in the canon. For instance, greatest hits packages have a mixed reputation in popular music. Fan communities can dismiss them as commercial fluff or embraced them as tools to extend the fan base. The role of Bruce Springsteen's 1995 *Greatest Hits* album was debated in terms of marketing and (mis)canonization, but many fans still bought the album (Cavicchi 1998, 85). A more recent example with a different outcome occurred in the summer of 2011 when Kiss was included in the roster of a proposed Michael Jackson tribute concert. Because the band's notoriously outspoken bass player Gene Simmons had said publicly, 'There's no question in my mind he [Michael] molested those kids,' Jackson fans did not want him at the concert and put pressure on promoters, Global Live, to drop Kiss from the October 2011 event. Kiss might have been central in most people's hard rock canon, but – whether Michael Jackson fans saw the rockers as talented or not – Simmons' comments effectively meant that his band was expelled from *their* music canon. Tense mismatches like this one can reveal the operation of the fan base as a 'moral community' and highlight a deep divide between the commercial canon and the one agreed by fans.

The fan bases' own canon – usually discussed in relation to fan fiction – is sometimes called the **fanon:** a selection that can also include fan-created texts and meanings (Pugh 2005, 41). According to Busse and Hellekson:

> Most important to treatments of fan texts are understandings of canon, the events presented in the media source that provide the universe, setting, an characters, and fanon, the events created by the fan community in particular fandom and repeated pervasively throughout the fantext. Fanon often creates particular details or character readings even though canon does not fully support it – or, at times, even contradicts it. (2006, 9)

The fanon can include slash fiction and other material, and, in a sense, is a way for fans to mark a difference between their own and the 'official' versions of the meta-text. While many find the fanon's products dubious (in so far that they can alienate mainstream fans), those same custodians of the canon can become attracted to the most popular creators of the fanon because they represent whole swathes of the fan community (see Green & Guinery 2004). The fanon is not just important because it shows that fans can canonize their objects in a different way to the text's official creators or guardians. It can also change the meaning of the primary text for the fans by altering their perspective:

> By looking at the combined fantext, it becomes obvious how fans' understanding of the sources is always already filtered through the interpretations and characterizations existing in the fantext. In other words, the community of fans creates a communal (albeit contentious and contradictory) interpretation in which a large number of potential meanings, directions, and outcomes co-reside. (Busse & Hellekson 2006, 7)

Will Brooker (2002, 72) has also noted that fans' consumption of secondary texts and the quasi-canon of *Star Wars* might mean that they misinterpret or even hallucinate different or additional elements of the main texts. Henry Jenkins describes the process in more detail:

> The ongoing process of fan rereading results in progressive elaboration of the series 'universe' through inferences and speculations that push well beyond its explicit information; the fans' meta-text, whether perpetuated through gossip or embodied within written criticism, already constitutes a

form of rewriting . . . These fan stories build upon the assumptions of the fan meta-text, respond to the oft-voiced desires of the fan community, yet move beyond the status of criticism and interpretation; they are satisfying narratives, eagerly received by a fan readership already primed to accept and appreciate their particular versions of the program. (Jenkins 1992, 155)

Crucially, because fans are *primarily* orientated around identifications and meanings and only *secondarily* to assenting loyalty to the encouraged process of consumption (and then, mainly as a way to sustain the production of the text), the fanon is *not necessarily* a fake, amateur or secondary phenomenon. There is a possibility that fan fiction can *sometimes* have *more* fidelity to the original text than new professional product (Brooker 2002, 134). In that sense, while dedicated fans often buy into the fanon, anyone can express a sense of concern about the text. Fan communities are therefore courted by the text's industrial custodians, but primarily concerned to protect their own pleasures.

Cults

The word **cult** has become commonly used for fan objects that have evoked a special intensity of interest, type of audience, strength of popular commitment or longevity of appeal. 'Cult' is a term that is complex and hard to define not only because different people use it differently, but also because it can be applied either to a primary text (as a 'cult text') or a fan base (as a 'cult phenomenon'). It also has existing connotations from fields outside of fan studies, implying the veneration of esoteric religious material or the fashionability of a niche product. While only a tiny fraction of cultural products become designated as cults, media cults are not rare. There are now many 'cult' films and TV series. As one of the longest-running cult figures and someone whose contribution dates back to well before the electronic media, William Shakespeare has long been at the centre of a thriving stage and literary phenomenon. In the age of digital media, he is, according to Matt Hills (2002a, 134) perhaps the perfect example of a media cult. For Hills (xi), such cults have three elements: affective (evoking intense fan attachments), linguistic (the adoption of cult discourses) and temporal (suggesting longevity). Sherlock Holmes is excluded from cult status: Holmes is one of the most famous fictional characters, but he 'cannot be firmly classified as a media cult despite the existence of otherwise compelling similarities' (xiv).[4] Perhaps the two main reasons for denying the famous detective's cult status are that he has consistently inhabited the *mainstream* of popular detective fiction and has not been *labelled* as cultish by his own readers or viewers. The example offers a window on the variety of elements at play in the use of the term 'cult' as a tool to label particular fan objects. What follows will disentangle some connotations of the cult appellation.

One proposed answer to the puzzle of cult status is to think about popular cultural phenomena as religions. To describe a social movement as a 'cult' is to attribute an external label that evokes particular connotations and frames it in a certain way. Enthusiatically describing his own fan interests, Rupert Till has explained: 'Popular music cultures are a common form of popular or implicit religion. Rather than describing them as NRMs (new religious movements), I have described them as cults . . .' (2010, 7). Till notes a series of similarities between popular music culture and religion, including a focus on creative icons, the evocation of strong commitment in followers, and 'brainwashing' (8). By playing with notions of the sacred, for Till, popular music has ventured towards a 'sacred popular' form (5). Till's stance on pop fandom could be debated by asking what it is really saying about fandom: would most fans *like* to be described as cult-followers? If they would not, are they *deceptively misrepresenting* their own beliefs and practices?

As a discursive resource, labelling something a 'cult' can be understood as a term of abuse. Analysing fans use of social media after Michael Jackson died, for instance, in their otherwise sympathetic article Sanderson and Cheong (2010, 331) talk about 'Michael Jackson's global influence and cult-like following.' The use of the term 'cult-like' here (rather than 'exclusive' or 'dedicated') evokes conceptions of abnormality, otherness, suggestibility and perhaps even insanity. It fails to explain why a mainstream superstar can have a global fan base that is also supposed to be a 'cult'. The term 'cult' generally has a negative stigma because it implies group members who are weak-minded, isolated from (social) reality and emotionally manipulated or brainwashed (immersed in false beliefs) (Hills 2002a, 123). It implies that fans might have to be 'rescued' from a star's grip. The 'cult' label has been approached by some writers like Jensen (1992) as a 'cultural symptom' of wider society, offsetting the anxiety that comes from attaching the label to the unsettling practices of fan cultures. In other words, rather than assume that fan communities are inherently cult-like, we need to explore *why* the term is being used. While Sanderson and Cheong and Till are not intentionally maligning the fans of whom they speak, they are indirectly reinforcing the notions of religiosity that were discussed in Chapter 5. 'Cult' fandom does not indicate the social relocation of religion to a place outside of the church, or even the collapse of religion into purely private moments. Rupert Till, however, remains unconvinced and suggests, 'There is evidence of brainwashing type activities. Fans repeatedly sing along to, or listen to, music that is in itself repetitive' (2010, 8). One argument in favour of this view, perhaps, is that fans themselves sometimes use the term 'cult' to describe what they do. Given its stigma, fans must be using 'cult' in a different way than those referring to religious groups. For Hills (2002a, 124) they adopt such terms to safeguard their 'self-absence', but I think there is a more simple explanation: cultdom implies *cultivation*, and cultivation is a badge of honour. It implies the dutiful pursuit of a dedicated apprenticeship to a particular object. Consequently, analytic attention should not just be placed on the term 'cult' itself, but *on the connotations and power relations involved in attributing the term*. We also need to be careful to investigate each 'cult' on a case-by-case basis, looking at *who* is attributing cult status to *whom* and *why* they are doing it.

There is a tradition of study that locates cult appeal in the structure of the text itself. In this writing the cult text is a world already equipped for fans to explore it. Umberto Eco's (1995, 198) description of films like *Casablanca* (Curtiz 1942) as texts that involve 'the furnishing of an entire narrative world' is crucial in that respect. For Eco, a cult film displays a completely furnished world that is encyclopaedic, yet it need not be especially well made or coherent; in fact its *incoherent elements* invite a degree of fan participation (see Jenkins 2008, 101). On the other hand, Matt Hills has proposed that one of the motivating forces behind such worlds is that cult texts are characterized by generative central mysteries. *Doctor Who*, for example, has been 'regenerated' through mystifying the identity of its central hero (Hills 2002a, 135). For Hills, three features that help to structure cult textuality. Cult texts tend to contain certain defining resemblances that include *auteurism, endlessly deferred narrative* and *hyperdiegesis* (131). An **auteur** is a leading individual – usually a film director – who stamps his/her creative 'signature' on the fabric of the text. Auteurism is connected to the idea of *quality drama*: mass culture given an artistic stamp that can be assessed by using high cultural (literary) reading strategies (133). 'Endlessly deferred narratives' involve plots that continue to run because their stories are constantly re-opened or never quite come to an end. **Hyperdiegesis** is the process of continually constructing an extended imaginary world that forms a backdrop to the text, but cannot be contained within any one of its instances. Attention to mystery can draw fans through each of those elements. Can 'cult', then, be thought of as a genre? Cults cannot be seen as genres, but some genres give rise to more cults than others. This is because they facilitate the recognition of auteurs, hyperdiegetic narrative worlds and endlessly deferred narratives (143).

Taking a slightly different perspective, film studies scholars Ernest Mathijs and Xavier Mendik (2008) have attempted to define cult cinema in several ways that we explore in what follows. The two researchers describe several definitive features: *innovation*; *blurring of genre boundaries* (or grotesquing of genre elements); *intertextuality*; *openness* (leaving stylistic or narrative loose ends); pure gore, aesthetic or moral *'badness'*; ability to *obliterate the barriers* between 'good' and 'bad' film; and *ability to trigger nostalgia* (2–3). Of course, some of these 'features' are actually judgements attributed to the films *by* cult spectators and discourses. What is interesting about their list, however, is not just that it provides a more specific elaboration of Hill's three-part schema (for example innovation can be seen as a reflection of auteurism and openness creates endlessly deferred narratives), but it also includes features such as innovation and intertextuality that are not inherently part of the text itself. These reflect ways that people *talk about* the text as, for example, 'good' or 'bad'. Furthermore, Mathijs and Mendik actually suggest 'that the term fandom is too generalist and tame to actually capture particular kinds of persistence and dedication involved in cult' (5).

An associated school of thought on cultdom suggests that cult products have to be in some sense genuinely organic or rescued by fans. Cult fans can be seen as repeat viewers or heavy niche media consumers (see Abercrombie & Longhurst 1997; Robson 2010, 212). Moreover, *fan-made artefacts*, like the digital cinema parodies of *Star Wars*, can also have their own 'cult' followings (Hills 2002a, x). The 'fan-rescued' reading suggests that cult texts have to be found by fans rather than planned for them. For example the series *Nowhere Man* (1995–6) was planned cult television that failed (136). Hence 'neither can cult texts or icons be too obviously 'manufactured' by producers (143). This approach challenges any notion that the industry can determine what is truly popular and it puts agency back into the hands of the fans themselves. Scholars want to talk about 'cult' fans as being particularly dedicated (x). Yet what the fan-rescued definition of cultdom cannot quite grasp why certain texts attain cult status and others do not. In other words it is a way of describing cult objects, not explaining them. For Hills, the notion of 'cult' therefore forces us to think about how – despite fans protestations otherwise – 'fan objects are perhaps ultimately arbitrary' (nobody was born a *Doctor Who* fan, for example) and yet fandom is not just an interpretive practice; it can be a deeply felt conviction.

If the idea that fans 'rescue' cult text seems like a truism, it helps us to focus on another dimension of the cult label, that they attribute it to anything they like. As Matt Hills asks, 'If they use the term 'cult', why would fans make use of a term which may well be culturally devalued outside fan cultures? What cultural work can the discourse of 'cult' be made to perform for fan cultures?' (121) While Rupert Till's description of pop fandom as a cult activity seems out of touch with how other fans understand it, he does attempt to rehabilitate the term:

> This book will describe popular music scenes and movements as cults, not in order to suggest that they are wrong or bad, but rather as a joyous affirmation of their glorious transgression of all those things that those who would use the word cult negatively hold dear. (Till 2010, 1)

In this instance, Till is attempting to lever the term against its own reputation. This time discussing cult films as a *consumption* phenomenon, Mathijs and Mendik (2008, 4–6) suggest that such films elicit continuous intense participation which involves a discrete set of elements: *active celebration*; *communion and community*; *liveness* (the films are often watched in social events); *audience commitment*; *renegade audiences* (who like the oppositionality of their texts, and who canonize an alternative set of the products). In some forms of 'cool' fandom, there is no need to see the label as disparaging; 'cult' has connotations of exclusivity. For someone to self-identify as a fan of 'cult' 1950s and 1960s rockabilly, for example, implies that they are 'in the know' about *that* relatively exclusive form of music. For *non-fans* to, in turn, label *Star Trek* or Michael Jackson fandom as a 'cult' activity, however, has exactly the *opposite* meaning. This makes it hard to talk about cultdom as a universal phenomenon. To complicate the discussion, according to some sources all cult audiences are actually fans. Mathijs and Mendik (5–6) suggest that beyond any casual viewers, *cult film audiences* watching movies like the double feature *Kill Bill* (Tarantino 2003 and 2004) are made up of: *fans* (who enthusiastically follow particular films); *'avid' audience members* (analytical readers who explore the many subtexts of one rich text); and *cinefiles* (viewers who prefer intellectually challenging texts and make detached aesthetic judgements). Highlighting different viewers' sources of pleasure, senses of attachment and perspectives on the text, Mathijs and Mendik create a set of distinctions that break down, somewhat, under sustained scrutiny. For example, fans can be avid viewers, and cinefiles are often, in effect, genre fans. Nevertheless, Mathijs and Mendik's categories can help us differentiate different kinds of cult fan.

Following the notion that cult texts are 'rescued' by fans, one attempt to describe cult status locates cult textuality as outside the mainstream. In this formulation, cult texts are alternative, underground and off the radar of the ordinary media. Ernest Mathijs and Xavier Mendik (2008, 8–10), again, note that cult films get their *status* from four elements: *curiosity-attracting strangeness*; *allegorical meaning* (cult films are often adaptations of other cult objects and set in imaginary times and spaces); *an ambiguous approach to controversial material* (exploring or exploiting topics such as insanity, rape or animal cruelty); and *political resistance* (for example, portraying punk or countercultural subversion). Cults have been similarly designated by scholars as something separate from, and different to, the mainstream (Hills 2010b, 203). Mark Jancovich and Nathan Hunt (2004) suggest that there is no single quality that characterizes a cult text; instead they argue instead that an *arbitrary* system of classification separates cult from mainstream and defines something as a cult. Indeed, *subcultural* celebrity can help us understand cult audiences, and 'cult' can simply mean *outside of the canon* (Hills 2002a, 84 and 2010a, 238). The cult/mainstream distinction is therefore useful to fans who wish to mark out their separation from ordinary viewers. It also allows producers to negotiate the fan community as one among a number of constituencies that it aims to please (Hills 2010b, 203).

The argument that cults are non-mainstream certainly has problems. One is that cult status is not simply a distinction in relation to the mainstream, but is also 'a multiple set of differential reading strategies' which can *bring about* cult status as a residual or emergent property when audiences begin to invest in a text (218). A second problem is that there are cults *within* the mainstream. For example, *Star Wars* remains an extremely popular film franchise at the heart of the mainstream Hollywood film industry, yet it sometimes gets described as a 'cult fan phenomenon' due to the visible dedication of its followers. This leaves us with the question of whether it is possible to have a cult *within* the mainstream, or whether mainstream promotion excludes a text from the attribution of cult status. One answer to that is to challenge the notion that says dedicated fandom only happens when a franchise is out of the mainstream. For example, Green and Guinery explain:

> The temporal gaps between the books and the films – coupled with the expanding possibilities of Internet communication – mean that fans can feel both creative and connected while circulating the cultural materials derived from their engagement with the *Harry Potter* 'canon'. (2004, online)

Cult fandom may therefore not be so much about the intensity of collective interest in a media product or the social organization of fan base around it, but rather has a temporal quality: cults often form in the absence of official new material (Hills 2002a, x). There are the *forms of fandom* that support the text while it is out of the public eye and unpromoted. *Doctor Who* is especially interesting in that respect. The series has regenerated itself across the four decades by shifting from mainstream BBC television to the margins of broadcasting (off air, video, American public access cable television), then back to the heart of British terrestrial television. Writing about the show Matt Hills explained:

> Rather than being a 'cult' TV show threatened with 'mainstream' status, *Doctor Who* has had a more complex textual history in which 'mainstream' status, according to fan lore, declines into 'cultdom' before being restored by BBC Wales . . . This 'mainstream' status is embraced by Who fandom, almost as if it represents the restoration of a prelapsarian condition – reversing the programme's 1980s fall into 'niche cultdom.' (Hills 2010b, 209).

Doctor Who's return to the mainstream had to be negotiated in relation to its middle phase as cult object, with many of the show's fans and makers (many of whom also claimed status as fans) wishing to keep its cult cache without having that damaging its mainstream popularity. Indeed, when *Doctor Who* was being regenerated, its fans did not necessarily want to claim cult status as they wanted to show to re-enter the mainstream. The new production team aimed to assimilate and incorporate 'cult' status *as part of the show's mainstream appeal*: 'New *Who* may deny strenuously its 'cult' credentials . . . but by fusing 'genre' and 'authorship' it falls squarely into the domain of 'authored' cult telefantasy' (27). As Hills added:

> Whereas the fan community has, by and large, embraced 'mainstream' status, bridging 'cult' and 'mainstream' textual classifications, the BBC Wales production team has insistently othered cult fandom in extra-textual publicity discourses contributing to the show's 'text-function'. . . . 'Cult' was not just a dirty word for *Doctor Who* fandom, it was also a badge of failure for the early noughties BBC1 Saturday night line-up. And it was within this industry context that BBC Wales was tasked with remaking *Doctor Who* . . . As film critic Danny Peary has suggested, 'the work cult implies a minority'. (210–11)

Hill's study suggests that cultdom can be claimed and discarded when it suits the fans and makers of a show. This is important because, contrary to traditional formulations, a version of 'cult' status is frequently fabricated within the media industry as a way to locate the fruits of a specific regime of production. In that respect producers of various kinds can take very different stances. By using word of mouth promotion they can attempt to co-opt fan communities and use them as a spearhead to push flagship productions *into* the mainstream. Alternately, they can distance new media products from such communities in order to position such products *as* mainstream. Distributors and production companies can also court specific niche communities to *create* cult status (Jenkins 2008, 142). Finally, less popular material may specifically be released *for* fan audiences who are targeted as niche markets (Hills 2002a, 36).[5]

Is the cult label just about branding? Examining the *political economy* of cult fandom, Mathijs and Mendik (2008, 7–8) noticed several regularities: *unplanned elements in production* (personal setbacks, studio accidents, unusual interventions); *unusual promotion*; and *continuous presence of reception*. They note that cult texts spawn endless additions: serializations, franchises, remakes, retrospectives restorations, revivals, re-releases, directors' cuts, spin-offs, rip-offs and spoofs. These things are, however, more about the *verification* of cult status than its creation. To sustain the success of such commodities, producers rely on existing audience interest in stories, for example, about how the texts were made.

Places

Fans are not just textual readers, they are people. They do the same things as everyone else, including going on vacation. Sometimes they enjoy social events and visits to places themed in relation to their specific pleasures. Traditions accounts of place and the media – a good example being Joshua Meyrowitz's 1985 book *No Sense of Place* – either tend to leave place out of mediation or assume that every place has been redefined in the public imagination by the world of the media. Yet *space is cultural* and *culture is spatial* (Hills 2002a, 151). Electronic mass media may have created non-territorial, virtual spaces of media consumption, but fandom itself is an in situ activity. In other words, we literally live on and move across the meaningful terrain of an actual finite planet. Whether we define any particular portion of that territory in terms of abstract space or unique concrete place depends on the conceptual overlay we chose to attribute.

Cornel Sandvoss has developed some interesting ideas in that respect. Sandvoss argues that landscapes of fan consumption are often 'placeless' – ordinary parts of everyday life (like living rooms and arenas) – and this is what allows them to be appropriated as part of fan's readings (2005a, 58). (It could also be argued that their relative *timelessness* also plays a role.) Additionally, he suggests that fandom is itself connected to a feeling of 'Heimat': a zone of physical, emotional and ideological safety that fans can call home, which offers them a sense of security, stability and emotional warmth. In this formulation, as a home, fandom itself becomes a kind of portable haven, a place in which people can belong (64). So there is a mismatch: we can be 'at home' in the text, but not necessarily in the physical place where we consume it.

For Sandvoss there are actually several spaces of fandom: physical spaces of consumption (living rooms, concert arenas, cinemas), spaces of representation of those physical spaces, the virtual realm of fan narratives and public spaces of fan 'pilgrimage' (54). Sandvoss' schema therefore carefully distinguishes the *emotional space* of fandom itself (Heimat) from both the *actual place* of consumption and the *imagined space* of each text: the 'promised land' or mythic world that somehow relates to it. The latter category can include celebrity mansions, film sets, famous landmarks and on-location spots. The inhabitation of these extra-textual spaces can express fans' relationships to their texts (Hills 2002a, 144). Rather than simply being destinations for after-the-fact trips, particular places may be visited by fans while filming is still happening. Visitors to those places must sometimes need to use their initiative to find out where they are located (148). In a sense, the whole process is rather akin to fans 'spoiling' the text or literally putting themselves in the picture. What media-induced tourism shows is that fan activity cannot be purely reduced to the consumption and reading of texts (156). Fans are not just textual poachers, but *textual roamers* who go on symbolic pilgrimages that create new social interactions (Sandvoss 2005a, 54). As they do this, however, it could be argued that their fandom sometimes forms a kind of affective and semiotic territory from which they see the outside world.

Some places of fan engagement are simply spaces *themed as places* that represent particular stars or narratives. If conventions, music weekends and holidays seem ephemeral sites for fan engagement, the communities that sustain them are not ephemeral. Sandvoss notes that 'the virtual spaces of media consumption are re-manifested in place through the creation of new landscapes of fandom that find their point of reference in a particular fan narrative' (54). Whole amusement parks, like the *Star Trek Experience* in Las Vegas, have also been created with media franchises or icons as their theme. Dolly Parton is unusual in being a living icon with a whole amusement park, Dollywood, licensed and organized with her consent. Museums and exhibitions offer other spaces that become devoted to particular moments, stars or genres. These spaces are *designated* as relevant places by business or public activity: they have no direct link to the fan phenomenon except as a form of branding. Indeed, fans are only likely to be a fraction of their visiting (usually paying) public. While devotees can be curious about the artefacts kept inside, such spaces seem opposite to the private, non-commercial places more organically linked to the star. Celebrity graves, for example, appear a more natural place to visit. Of course, distinctions between commercial space and organic place do not always completely line up: public spaces can become places of commemoration, celebrities endorse specific locations and their homes are occasionally opened to the public after they die. Nevertheless, it is important to say that not all places of celebrity *feel* important or become a focus of fan desire. There has to be something significant, perhaps historical, about a place in order to make it a 'mecca' for touring fans.

Much of the discussion of fan tourism is framed by the metaphor of 'pilgrimage', a term that relates fandom to both religiosity but also attempts to capture the emotional value of visiting places of magical interest. Springsteen fans make 'pilgrimages' to the New Jersey Shore looking for his hometown and locations mentioned in his songs; many admire that he has not severed his ties to the area. Cavicchi noted that fans' pilgrimage stories often involve tales about commitment in the face of adversity or the magic of the experience upon arrival at the destination, about whether they found it as expected, and how the experience reinforced their realization that Springsteen was an authentic, regular person (1998, 170). Rather than 'rituals', however, fans' visits to important locations can be seen as affective-interpretive practices that define material space for them. As Matt Hills explains, 'Sacred spaces do not simply reproduce sacred/profane oppositions, neither are they merely 'containers' for the purity of the sacred, as these forms of behavioural legislation emerge after the fact' (2002a, 154). Unlike some ordinary tourism, where mediation comes between the material place and its travelling audience, in fan tourism the media text is always the *first* point that guides fan-tourists interpretations and valorizes those places for them. Indeed, researchers such as Brooker (2007) and Aden (1999) have therefore interpreted media consumption itself as metaphorical travel. Fans latch onto spaces of narrative significance in the text and then desire to visit those places (see Hills 2002a, 156–7). This means that researchers need to consider how fans' a priori *perceptions* of the relationship between the text and the place help to actualize it for them.

Discussing the symbolic power imbued in places by the media, Nick Couldry (2000) has shown how fans' distinctions between ordinary locations and the enchanted set of *Coronation Street* resemble the sacred/profane dichotomy (also see Sandvoss 2005a, 62). While the term preferred by many writers is 'sacred', perhaps a less religious term for these unique locations is 'magical'. We can never get inside the text, but we can enter into the physical space to which it refers (Hills 2002a, 146). For Gilbert Rodman, Elvis Presley's home Graceland is not a passive and neutral space where Elvis' already-constructed stardom just happened to make itself visible over the years (155). Instead, fans imbue it with a particular power as the place where their dreams might have come true. **Hyper-reality** was a term that emerged out of the French thinker Jean Baudrillard's writing to describe a world in which mediated image and reputation precede and govern what we expect to find, aiding a perceived eclipsing and restructuring of reality. Living so much of our lives in a bubble of knowledge engineered by the media means, for Baudrillard, that we fail to see what is in front of us in the real world. The idea of fan tourism raises the issue of hyper-reality (151). Visiting fans are tourists whose frames of interpretation are shaped by their favourite media products (145). This suggests that fandom can at worst become a bubble or at best, an inspiration for learning about the world. Hyperreality is also not an either/or term: some places can be *more* (re) constructed for our pleasure (like Disneyland), or *less* so (like the Manchester) (152). Seeing the residential homes of icons helps fans understand that their stars are just like the rest of us: real people embodied and located in particular times and concrete places (Sandvoss 2005a, 61).

Accounts that involve notions of hyper-reality or sacredness seem rather simplistic. They tend to oppose textuality to 'real' place and prioritize textuality, but fan's imaginations are also shaped by what is extra-textual: performative and pertaining to real life. An encounter with place is therefore an encounter with 'the real' location even if our interest in it is *displaced in time*. There are some interesting discussions of nostalgia in that respect. Describing the viewing habits of one family of 'anti-fans' called the Walkers, Diane Alters (2007) found that they affirmed a specific notion of family values by only watching rerun 1950s television shows. To talk about the Walkers' viewing preferences, Alters drew on the Russian scholar Mikhail Bakhtin's notion of the 'chronotope' which she translated as a 'time-space' of media output (2007, 344). Alters reasoned, 'The Walkers' chronotope, then, brought the 1950s into the present so that they could control the present in their home' (349). This idea suggests that viewers – here anti-fans, but in theory this could just as easily apply to fans – can imaginatively inhabit specific time-spaces that reflect the original eras and locations of their favourite texts or heroes. For example, fans currently visiting Graceland do not think about it in the present, but prefer to imagine it when Elvis lived there between April 1957 and August 1977. As one fan guide book explains, 'We cannot go back in time [though we might wish to], but we can go back in place' (Urquart 1994, 1). Shifts in media archiving and other social practices have made the chronotopic imagination not marginal but central to the ways that popular music and other media forms are consumed and enjoyed. Simon Reynolds has recently discussed this in his 2001 book *Retromania*:

> Eventually, after pop built up enough history, it became possible to fixate on an earlier period you preferred to your own time. Ariel Pink: 'When people like sixties music, they live there forever. They live in a moment when the person that they are listening to was growing their hair long for the first time. They look at the pictures and they feel like they can actually live there. For my generation, we weren't there' – he means biologically

alive in the sixties; he was born in 1978 – 'so we really live "there". We have no concept of time'. (Reynolds 2011, xxxvi)

It is not just that archival media more easily facilitate fans in their quest to imaginatively inhabit the past; cultural histories can also prioritize particular events from specific periods and places over others. Investigating this, I borrowed the term 'imagined memories' from Beatles biographer Ray Coleman (see Duffett 2002 and 2003). An **imagined memory** is the product of a fan's desire to have experienced one of the early performances of their favourite star. Alison Landsberg's (2004) notion of socially implanted, 'prosthetic memories' is quite a similar concept.[6] Seeing the first concert by the Sex Pistols in Manchester's Lesser Free Trade Hall on 4 June 1976 is a classic example of an imagined memory. The first thing to notice is that such an incident *did actually happen*: it can be located in time and place. For any individual audience member who experienced that moment, it was supposedly magical and transformative. There were many more who never had the actual experience and wished they did. An imagined memory is not exactly a fantasy, because it *really happened* to someone else. Precisely because *it happened to someone else,* however, it is not *your* memory, either. It is therefore a kind of fantasy which authenticates itself as a (desired) 'memory' by a process of valorization in the narrative of history and the media. The term points to the inadequacy of phrases like 'cultural memory' when used to describe popular music's past: for a few people these memories are real enough (although, even for them, the meanings of the memories have been inflected by the subsequent success stories of the performers). Imagined memories are spaces of emotional investment that are necessarily contradictory: they only matter because of what came after them. In a sense, then, they are *commodity templates* – valorized (made to matter) by stories and characterized by their own rarity value. Not everyone has the 'real' memory; we did not all share the original experience, but we all partake of its 'memory'. This is precisely why those who were originally there become privileged witnesses, starting points for further commodities (such as documentaries, heritage tourist sites, exhibitions, re-enactments and anniversaries).

If they recall prized moments in the early careers of iconic artists, how do imagined memories come about? Through what sociocultural processes are they fabricated? They tend to emerge from a four-stage process of collective appreciation. The first part of this is *mass performance*, when a classic performance (live or on record) marks a new peak of an artist's mass adulation. The second stage is *historic narration*. Biographies and other ways to tell the story are created to contextualize, romanticize and therefore extend the pleasures that fans have invested in the artist or piece of music. These narratives say things like 'it all came about by accident' or 'it almost never happened' or 'there was a unique confluence of circumstances'. They are designed to show that the emotions motivating the original performance were 'real' rather than fabricated by technicians or commentators in the culture industry. The third part of the process of activitating imagined memories is *recognition*. Cultural entrepreneurs *recognize* an early moment in the star's career narrative that appeals to fans because it shows the artist at their rawest and seemingly most powerful (not yet diluted by the industry). The imagined moment then becomes a touchstone in retellings of the narrative. With the template now complete, fascinated fans begin to discuss and imagine those unique historic moments. New cultural products are formed around the reminscences of those who experienced the moments. Privileged interpreters are given a mediated chance to speak about what happened. A final stage in the process of creating imagined memories is *extension:* the imagined memory finally becomes a generative resource for other narratives and commodities. In time, of course, even those later, popular performances can themselves become imagined memories as more people start talking about their previous viewing experiences and fewer fans have access to any 'real' memories of the event.[7]

I want to briefly mark out some subtle differences between imagined memory and myth. The key thing here is that imagined memories and myths are not quite the same. Myths are ways to tell an artist's story that satisfy the public. They need never actually have happened. *In theory*, imagined memories may be *based on* myths, but usually they are not. Also, myths do not have to be imagined memories: a myth can be about almost anything, whereas an imagined memory pertains to a specific moment of performance: a time and place that many fans wish they attended. There is much work to be done on the intersection of imagined memories and other fan practices. One example here is the question of cultural capital. Given that imagined memories are recognized retrospectively, in what ways does their construction as invitational containers for affect then facilitate the display of cultural capital? Fans do not need much capital to locate these moments, since they are usually prominent in discussions about cultural phenomena. Nevertheless, such moments may become foci for the collection of further facts and stories that allow those interested to play elaborate games of distinction. What I hope to have shown here is that we are steered as fans by affective attachments that come from our engagement with crucial performances. This process valorizes an earlier time, the significance of which only becomes fully recognized in retrospect. Consequently, although *narratives of cultural history tell the story by moving forwards, we create such narratives, as fans, by looking backwards.*

'Authentic' places do not just matter not because they form the real locations that accommodate fans' chrontopic imaginations. We can also surmise that the most magical heritage sites are also, in a sense, *performative*. Not only do such places let fans feel intimate with the actuality of a famous person with whom they identify, but they can also *re-perform* the image of the celebrity in situ. According to Matt Hills (2002a, 153), Graceland, for instance, is not jarring, precisely because its reflects the hyper-commodified value system of its late owner. When you walk through the front door, you are greeted by the contradiction between a giant chandelier in the front room and a headset that explains, 'It all began with the dreams of a poor boy from Tupelo, Mississippi'. The prescribed route through the mansion strategically confronts guests with alternating visions of the splendour and humility of Elvis writ large in the house that he made his own. The mansion's upstairs is also off limits to fans and retains an aura of mystery. In a sense, then, Graceland does not just *represent* Elvis' legacy: it is organized in a way that tells his story and *performs* his image.

To discuss the 'performativity' of a place is to raise issues of agency: how much can a place guide us to have an emotional response? Does that response occur because of what it is, what it represents to us, how it has been arranged, or a combination? Can places *do things* to those who visit them? Or is the experience entirely down to what mental expectations visitors bring along? Is a place like a text? And if it is, are visitors like readers? If they are like readers, then, following the argument that readers are *active*, what are visitors doing when they connect with the place and make the experience come alive for them? Some visitors to Graceland scrawl their names across the stone wall at the front of the estate compound, near the music gates. Derek Alderman (2002) has argued that such visitors are not just consumers shuttled round the mansion, but they are also, in effect, participating by 'authoring' their own involvement. It could be argued that the idea of 'authoring' one's own memory of Elvis takes things too far. On one hand, the idea of fans as individual authors of their experiences implies that they are inscribing their projections onto a void, which brings us back to the 'blank slate' idea. On the other, hypothesizing an authorial approach either leads us back into the text (negating its collective authorship as myth) or beyond it to issues of shared social context (to discourses, identities and other concerns that fan-authors share). If we adopt an 'open source' model of networked authorship – which seems an interesting idea in relation to myth – it may be possible to talk about 'place participation' in that way, but what remains is the issue of why so many people desire to experience something so similar and whether they all leave with the same experiences.

UNDERSTANDING FANDOM

Authorship is not the only form of agency. Fans tend to use their agency to fulfil their structural position – their role as fans – and to connect, individualize and enhance their experience, in effect *unlocking the thrill of being* in situ *as fans*. I will conclude by examining Sharon Colette Urquhart's 1994 tour guide *Placing Elvis: A Tour Guide to the Kingdom,* which was written by an Elvis devotee for her fellow fans. Urquart makes a number of points that are common sense to Elvis followers, yet marginalized by some fan theory. She begins discussing Graceland by saying, 'Here you will find Elvis, the man, rather than Elvis, the media sensation . . . Though thousands of people have stood at Elvis' grave, it is only the moment when you are present that an abstract place suddenly takes on personal meaning' (1994, i). In other words, *beyond* enjoying any classic performances on film or audio recording, visiting Memphis is a way for fans to get closer to Elvis, to experience his world in an embodied way, in a way that *uses experiential geographic knowledge as a gateway to intimacy.* Urquhart continues, 'Graceland is a powerful place because it meant so much to Elvis . . . By being where Elvis was, we draw closer to him . . . until we stand where the King stood, walk where he walked and saw what he saw, we will remain distant from him' (11). Having made the case for visiting the mansion, she then suggests two other practices that might enhance the experience. The first asks fans to locate their biographic trajectory in relation to Elvis' own:

> Think about *where you were when he was there*, reflect on how your life experiences have been similar to or different than his. Empower yourself by realizing that regardless of when and how he touched your life it happened *in a way entirely unique to you*, and the relationship should be celebrated as such. (11; emphasis mine)

Here Urquhart encourages each fan to differentiate himself or herself from the mass of the fan base, and establish a connection by way of comparison between the dual pathways of two different lives. In physics, the term for this process might be 'entanglement' (see Kassabian 2004). By thinking about biographic differences in a focused way, the fan can increase the strength of their connection. The second practice that Urquhart suggests is less private. It uses communication to define a fannish identity:

> Remember the details of your history with Elvis. Discuss these with details with your family, friends and other fans, compare similarities and differences, and recognize the unique value and qualities inherent in the way you came to know the King . . . Encourage your kids' imaginations, fill them in on a little of your own past. (1994, 12, 14)

In this second practice, Urquhart encourages each reader to dialogically explore the social and subjective place of his or her Elvis fandom. Personal stories allow Elvis fans to identify common reference points, decide what is shared and what is idiosyncratic, and feel more together. Shared fandom can also bond families.[8] Urquhart suggests that fans can use the momentary experience of *being in place* as an opportunity take stock of their personal memories, then weave stories that can both narrate their fannish identities and nurture their family memories. Fandom becomes *owned* here as a signifier of the personal: children get to understand their parents by hearing nostalgic tales about the role of fandom in their remembered lives. Such discussions also bring a unique geographic place *back to life* – not only as part of the star's chronotope, but also as an already-imagined realm for the fan: an indication that going to Graceland is, in a way, like coming home.

9

The fan community: Online and offline

Starting points

- How do fans organize themselves into social groupings?
- To what extent has the internet transformed fan cultures?
- Why do fans find their communities beneficial?

As in Nancy Baym's observation that fans interacting with a computerized environment, fan discourse works to create a specific kind of community that becomes more important than the object of fandom itself. Fans are also motivated by self-invention, in which fandom provides an opportunity to live in and through a set of symbols that are expressive of one's aspirations rather than 'reality'.

CHERYL HARRIS 1998, 6

In the last three decades, Western society has seen a shift so significant that it parallels and perhaps surpasses the introduction of television in the 1950s. The rise of the home computer as a focus of attention and its subsequent networking via the internet have wrought major changes in society. Although the hardware network emerged over a long period, the worldwide web is much younger. It began when physicist Tim Berners Lee created a language that would allow researchers to exchange electronic pages of data. By the early 1990s, university campuses regularly sent and received student email, but it was the emergence of Google and dawn of affordable broadband services in the late 1990s that supercharged internet computing as a domestic activity. For many people, fandom was already an important part of everyday life. Various objects often invited fans to consume across more than one medium to extend their pleasures (see Nikunen 2007). The internet transformed and further facilitated the whole phenomenon of fandom. Constance Penley reported in 1998 that fan communities were 'enthusiastic yet thoughtfully cautious about the new Internet culture'. (116) Her claim applied most readily to more official fan organizations that were concerned about losing control of their empires. As the internet made fan activity more public and put the distribution of media content into the hands of ordinary computer users, the changes threatened the organizations and individuals who depended on intellectual property for their revenue streams (Jenkins 2008, 141). Fans were, in fact, early adopters of both the internet and the world wide web, participating in multi-user dungeons and bulletin boards, then constructing home pages and 'shrines' full of pictures of celebrities, creating web rings, forums, news groups, blogs, wikis and fan club pages, and quickly embracing the era of social networking. The National Association of Fan Clubs shut down in September 2002. With older clubs moving online and new ones springing up rapidly, the burden was overwhelming. Although the organization provided a service for a quarter of a century, it eventually struggled to up keep up with its task of confirming the legitimacy of fan clubs and responding to e-mail requests asking for information on clubs dealing with obscure fan bases.

How has the internet shaped fan cultures?

Since both the internet and fandom are vast cultural phenomena, any question about how each has transformed the other has many answers and inevitably leads to limited generalizations. Fans have supported the new medium and it has made them more visible. They have the luxury now of increased access to information, a greater speed of social interaction, and a new means of public performance.

Digital archiving has greatly increased fan access to information. Beyond some members-only fan sites, the main model for information distribution online is that it is supplied free to users: rather than membership subscriptions, most sites make a profit though link, banner and video advertising. That means fans can download and stream text, pictures and video to extend their knowledge of particular texts and performances. For instance, Youtube.com has become a repository of footage uploaded by fans from their videotape collections, subtitled clips, camera phones, camcorder footage, reviews and commentaries created by fans sharing their *cultural capital*. Film studios, record labels and star individuals also have their own Youtube channels. Repositories like Youtube function as resources for those interested in pursuing new trails of discovery, increasing their exposure to performances and adding to their personal knowledge. Before the net caught on, fans could have tracked down desired material through other means – such as trading pirated products – but it made life much easier. Fanzine editors also moved their creations from print to web, because the costs of publicizing self-created electronic material online are marginal. Various forms of content – stories, pictures, video – can be integrated in valuable ways. The web allows people to conveniently archive all their stories and pictures for public enjoyment (Jenkins 2006, 143).

Beyond the streaming of data, we might add how fans legally and illegally download vast quantities of audio and video material for their enjoyment. The story of Napster, a peer-to-peer file-sharing application, provides a case in point. In 2000, the heavy metal band Metallica protested to the United Senate that over 300,000 users were illegally sharing files of their *Mission Impossible II* (Woo, 2000) soundtrack song 'I Disappear'. When the band's founder Lars Ulrich spoke to the Senate, he explained:

What about the users of Napster, the music consumers? It's like each of them won one of those contests where you get turned loose in a store for five minutes and get to keep everything you can load into your shopping cart. With Napster, though, there's no time limit and everyone's a winner – except the artist. Every song by every artist is available for download at no cost and, of course, with no payment to the artist, the songwriter or the copyright holder.

Ulrich did not refer to the users as 'fans' here, and indeed, illegal downloading sparked discussions within fan communities since many fans wanted to remunerate artists to preserve their careers. However, other sources, such as Janelle Brown writing in *The Salon* (2000), did refer to the Napster users as Metallica fans. Suddenly, as file sharers 'looted' – or liberated – digital music, the possibilities unleashed by the net caused commentators to confuse fandom, consumption and the abuse of intellectual property.

The net has created new opportunities for fans to feel closer to their stars. Fandom can often be realized as an attachment to heroes who are 'unobtainable yet accessible' (Urquhart 1994, 12). Since so many communicate with their loved ones long distance, the internet has made the idea of intimacy at a distance more normal and acceptable. Writing about global media events in 2010, Alberto Ribes argued that 'distinguishing between face-to-face and mediated interaction is no longer useful in this discussion' (2010, 2). David

Beer's work on the British singer Jarvis Cocker is interesting in this respect. Beer explains that Cocker is an 'active wikizen' who frequents the online world. He then argues:

> [N]ot only do people 'make [online] friends' with Jarvis the pop star, with the potential to alter the relations and organization of music culture, but also that Jarvis acts to introduce people as they orbit around his online profile and meet to discuss shared interests, tastes, and so on. (Beer 2008, 224)

As well as providing a wealth of information that helps fans find out more about the singer, Jarvis hosts his own online social networking area – Jarvspace – where he has approved over 60,000 friends who communicate with him and each other. Beer continues:

> The analysis offered here begins to illustrate that Web 2.0 is facilitating a shift in the relations of music culture as people 'hang with the stars' in the flattened environments of the social networking site . . . [where] the audience are communicating 'directly' or at least they are led to believe they are, with the performer . . . The visitor, as we can see from the posts directed at Jarvis, has the perception that Jarvis is intermittently present and his is communicating with them . . . It is possible here that the user may even be participating in a kind of Orwellian 'double think'; they know it is highly likely they are being misled but they continue to participate in the charade . . . there is a perception of (pop star) accessibility, or a *perception of proximity*, that is being cultivated here that fits with the broader rhetoric of democratiziation and participation that has ushered in Web 2.0. (232; emphasis in original)

This is an interesting quote because it shows that Beer is careful to negotiate the ambiguities of the online world. On one hand, for some the net has made geography seem like a less important parameter when it comes to establishing human intimacy. On the other hand, virtual intimacy presents problems of veracity and authenticity: Is Jarvis really there communicating? Even if he is, isn't he doing it more at his own convenience, with the social networking platform as both a means and a barrier at the same time? If famous tweeters or networkers like Jarvis and Lady Gaga now seem to connect individually with their fans in a virtual environment that allows a *full exchange* of communication, they only have *limited time* available to offer personal attention. There are 60,000 plus visible 'friends' but only *one* Jarvis available to greet those in his fan base. He *can* only have limited time for each person, so the pleasurable inequalities of celebrity are still there, not least because Jarvis has a reputation and aura from his professional and public life *offline* as a broadcast musician. Nevertheless, online media have changed fans perceptions of the remoteness of stars. Twitter, for example, can be used to pursue one-on-one conversations in public with others online, thus creating networks of personal interaction. As more people adopt mobile internet viewing practices and virtual co-presence becomes more accepted, the distinction between the virtual and real is becoming more blurred. *Digital media have exposed the parasocial relation as a theoretical artifact freighted with assumptions from the mass culture era.* In the digital realm, fans do not see stars as quite so distant and they have developed increased expectations of interaction. The lucky handful who manage to have extended exchanges with their heroes online arguably compare, though, to those who, for example, waited outside John Lennon's home at the Dakota Building. They form a visibly elite fraction of the fan base.

Whether stars make themselves available in fan forums or not, alongside the increasing access to information and material, what social networking sites demonstrate is that fan cultures themselves have become more public in the last 20 years. The community for each object has (re)emerged itself as an online entity. As more and more people adopted the net, some of their activity was devoted to publicizing existing fan clubs, communities and events to an increasingly wide audience. Since people from different countries participate in shared conversations more easily, the net *globalized public fandom*. Will Brooker (2002, xiv) reported, 'most of my correspondents have never met the other fans they communicate with regularly and know them only through the text'. There was some academic debate about whether these were 'real' communities:

> While the debate as to whether online networks can be accurately described as communities is ongoing (Rheingold 2000; Turkle 1997), there can be little doubt that many fans themselves imagine these networks as a community and equal to other friendship ties. (Sandvoss 2005a, 56)

Previously, fans had communicated at conventions, through face-to-face circles, fanzines and pen pal activity. Now online interaction turned the fan community from a network of local cultures or periodic rituals into a non-stop process of social effervescence (Hills 2002a, 181). When people used online discussion boards alongside their television viewing, technologies of convergence enabled communal rather than individualistic modes of reception. The fan community had to shift its normal ways of processing and evaluating information (Jenkins 2008, 26). Furthermore, our practice of the net is never entirely virtual; its use is *mediated by everyday life*. Paul

Hodkinson (2002) has discussed how subcultural participants have formed 'translocal communities' online which *both* network in the virtual world *and* arrange periodic public meetings in concrete locations like North Yorkshire, United Kingdom, where the annual *Whitby Goth Weekend* takes place. Deterritorialized online networks can therefore manifest themselves in specific times and places (also see Sandvoss 2005a, 57).

Another point here is that the net has changed the pace with which *new* narratives, performances, media personalities and producers emerge and are celebrated as fan objects. Fan phenomena can now explode at a very fast rate. The concerted efforts of the mass media and internet fan community have made fame and franchises grow more efficiently than ever. J. K. Rowling, for instance, published her first *Harry Potter* novel in 1997. By 2004 she led a book and film franchise that reportedly made her richer than the Queen of England. On one internet site alone (fanfiction.net), there were almost 150,000 *Harry Potter* fanfic stories compared to about 33,000 for nearest rival, the *Lord of the Rings* (see Green & Guinery 2004). Fan phenomena since then have moved even faster with social networking. In my own research, I compared the speed with which Elvis Presley and Susan Boyle found global fame (see Duffett 2011b). Two years after Elvis released his first single on a regional independent record label, he emerged in the global spotlight as an RCA recording artist. The first flush of global interest in Susan came after she appeared on one UK television show. Within a matter of hours a video clip of her 11 April 2009 performance on *Britain's Got Talent* had been uploaded to Youtube and went viral as millions of people watched. Boyle's instant fans immediately set up their own club sites and discussion boards. Her story even appeared in *The Wall Street Journal*. All that happened *before she had ever released a commercial recording of her own*.[1] It was not that Susan was a better singer than Elvis, but rather that she emerged in a very different era of media technology. Any significant celebrity story, notably the news of an icon's death, is a test case for how fast media technology allows information to travel. Other recent warp speed online phenomena have included responses to Michael Jackson's death on 25 June 2009. Anthony Elliot (1998) discussed the social registration of John Lennon's demise in 1980 as an 'experience of despatialized simultaneity' that featured 'the decoupling of time and space, such that information and communication originating from distant sources filters into everyday consciousness instantaneously, or virtually so' (841). Playing with this idea, we might say that contemporary media technologies – televisions in public places, the internet, mobile devices, social media – have removed the need to say, as Elliot did, 'or virtually so'. As news broke of Michael Jackson's passing, Twitter and other social media saw a rapid surge in postings and providers like America Online were unable to handle up to 90 per cent of their new traffic (see Sanderson & Cheong 2010). News does not just travel fast now. It arrives instantaneously. Fans mobilize their responses just as quickly.

As well as giving fans the opportunity to find out about their objects, to get closer and commune with each other, the net has provided a forum for them to productively express themselves in different ways, for example through commentaries, blogs and exchanges. Online newsgroups are not a transparent form of mediation, however, since they serialize the fan audience *as a text in itself*, creating a second order of commodification where audiencehood is *performed* by the participants. What the people call fan culture, the media industries call 'user generated content'. One way to see it as that the users make the content and the corporations make the profit (Jenkins 2008, 177–8). Nancy Baym (2007) has noted that 'online [music fan] communities are also taking a new form somewhere between the site-based online [discussion] group and the egocentric network [like Myspace or Facebook], distributing themselves throughout a variety of sites in a quasi-coherent networked fashion'. According to Hills (2002a, 181) the fan audience online 'constructs itself extensively as a mediated and textual performance of audiencehood'. This means that publically performed online fandom has *become a commodity-text in its own right*.[2] The disillusioned words of a 1990s online poster called humdog are instructive in this respect, especially in an age of social media. Complicating notions of the active audience, the critique paraphrased here reminds us that online communities inadvertently make profits for site owners and sponsors:

> It is fashionable to suggest that cyberspace is some island of the blessed where people are free to indulge their individuality. This is not true. I have seen many people spill out their emotions – their guts – online, and I did so myself until I began to see that I had commodified myself. Commodification means that you turn something into a product that has a money value. In the nineteenth century, commodities were made in factories by workers, who were mostly exploited, but I created my interior thoughts as commodities for the corporations that owned the board that I was posting to, like Compuserve or AOL. That commodity was then sold on to other consumer entities as entertainment. Cyberspace is a black hole. It absorbs energy and personality and then re-presents it as an emotional spectacle. It is done by businesses that commodify human interaction and emotion, and we are getting lost in the spectacle.[3]

Such words draw attention to the nature of the net as a very public space. Yet humdog's claims are not entirely true in an age of blogging and tweeting:

depending on the platform and given sufficient traffic, users can increasingly decide whether or not to retain advertising profits *for themselves*. Because blogs make no claim to objectivity and often tend to be read by those with similar views, they allow a particular kind of fan self-expression (Jenkins 2008, 227). Technology columnist Andrew Leonard has questioned whether the blogosphere might be becoming an 'echo chamber' (248). This means that the net *enables* some fans to speak but stay bounded in their own 'moral communities' even while they have a discussion in public. Indeed, some quarters of the media industry have tended to see fans in *isolation*. A number of businesses have perceived the net as an opportunity to organize and manipulate whole groups of fans. FanLib, for instance, was a business that tried to get them to create user-generated content, but forgot that it was addressing an established community (180).

Now that the fan community can organize itself online in a particular way, people can distribute their own understandings and interpretations to each other without a need to be mediated through commercial channels. The social role of professional critics has also shifted. Far from being autonomous voices, they now function as consumer guides and offer suggestions about what to see, hear or avoid. Their assessments have become aggregated on sites like RottenTomatoes.com and placed *alongside* those from ordinary audience members. The net has therefore contributed to a reduction in the autonomy and power of professional reviewers. Now there are multiple authors and multiple critics (133). However, this does not mean that contemporary culture has become an entirely liberal space where everyone is celebrated for liking whatever they chose. Instead, online discussions enable the dissemination and assertion of shared positions that act to articulate shared values, police areas of controversy and close down debate. Older fans can be critical of newer fans for encroaching on to their interests without appropriate displays of cultural capital. Facebook hate pages have also been opened by people who gleefully question and abuse 'uncool' forms of fandom for pop bands and other outfits. Youtube and Amazon comment sections are peppered by fans defending their objects from the savage barbs of outsiders.

Media technologies do not liberate, but social interactions sometimes can (Jenkins 2006, 135). The combination of open, communal, public discussion and instantaneous responses to cultural events has created an environment where, perhaps more than before, fans can be involved in collective action. **Convergence** is the flow of content across different media platforms, the migration of audiences and co-operation between different media industries. It means that the onus is on consumers to make connections and seek out new information in a rapidly changing environment where the hierarchical relationships between different kinds of media are changing. According to Jenkins (2008, 185), convergence culture requires certain skills: ability to connect information, pool resources, express interpretations, circulate creative expressions and compare value systems. Fans are increasingly acting in a concerted way to forward their concerns – that can include anything from 'spoiling' plots to lobbying networks, or 'outing' singers – in a context made possible by the opportunities that the internet has presented. They can, for instance, act with antipathy towards a competing media franchise because they fear it will eat into their community (Jenkins 1992, 91). Some fans police irrelevant kinds of discussion out of their community unless they directly reference the text (84). Beyond external or internal threats to their community, fans organize themselves communally for other reasons, such as re-imagining fictional scenarios or fighting censorship. In order to consider how they do those things, it is appropriate to examine the nature of fan communities in terms of their organization and functions.

The social organization of fan communities

How do fans organize themselves collectively? Is there something intrinsic to fandom that means it has to be a public and collective activity? Is there any meaningful difference between a fan base and a fan community? Academic studies always seem to assume that the fan community is 'pre-constituted'; a set of norms against which individual fans measure up. Consequently they have nothing to say about how *new* fan cultures – and new fans – emerge (Hills 2002a, xiv). Traditional sociological discussions, meanwhile, have tended to propose that modern society is characterized by an increasing tendency towards alienation: pre-modern communities have long since largely disappeared and extended families broken down into smaller units. This interpretation locates alliances of internet users and fan clubs as replacement communities that offer their members a sense of belonging in an otherwise lonely world. Like most interpretations, the fandom-as-community idea is an oversimplification. **Anomie** is the feeling of rootlessness and alienation that sociologists have described in modern society. Members of Western nations are not quite as anomic as the theory suggests. Instead they often belong to *several* communities and diffused networks at once – workplaces, religious communities, schools and universities, political parties, circles of friendship – albeit with different kinds of obligation and degrees of dedication. Harrington and Bielby (1995, 102) noted that previous research on soap operas had suggested that they allowed isolated people to participate in an imagined community (the audience), yet this picture was limited because soap fans usually participated in *real* communities, including their fan networks.

Fandom can begin in private, though 'private' is not quite the requisite term: friends and family make recommendations, and potential fans always engage with media products and performances that they know are *collectively valued*. Texts come freighted with multiple indications of their popularity, from the knowledge that they were socially important enough to finance and produce to the ensuing reviews, endorsements, chart placings and audience ratings. **Closet fans** are a minority of people who live their lives as fans without making it a talking point with others. Those fans do exist. According to Harrington and Bielby (91):

> Some viewers downplay their own viewing habits; others report they have 'tried to stop watching' but could not; still others know people who watch daytime television but 'pretend not to' . . . we were told of loyal soap viewers among fundamentalist Christian organizations who keep their viewing secret because they think that watching defies the teachings of their ministry. Awareness of public derision is also evident in the case of a longtime *General Hospital* viewer, an attorney who during one job-hunting phase refused to watch GH because she didn't want people to know she was at home without anything 'productive' to do. Once she found a job, she resumed watching.

Even if contagious contact is *not* always necessary to engender fandom, unless a fan finds that he/she dislikes fan club members, entry into the fan community can (and usually does) help to *maintain* his/her fannish interests. The community is a way to perpetuate and support personal fandom. Although its members can mentor new recruits, they are often already attached to texts *before* they enter clubs and other forms of social organization (Hills 2002a, 63). While an artist's *fan base* is the collective made of people who feel a connection to him/her, the *fan community* is a physical manifestation of the fan base, a mutually supportive social network of people that can – and do – regularly communicate with each other as individuals. The fan community can enhance an artist's appeal in various ways: sharing information, lobbying to get their artist greater media exposure, demonstrating mass support, offering a friendly welcome to new members. Public social groupings act to foster, facilitate and maintain fandom. Many fans characterize their entry into fandom as a move from social and cultural *isolation* – whether as rogue readers, women in partriarchy or gay men in heteronormative culture – into more active communality with kindred spirits (Jenkins 2006, 41).

Since fan networks are communities of common interest, they offer people a sense of belonging (Jenkins 1992, 23). Speaking about her first visit to a *Doctor Who* fan convention, Tara O'Shea (2010, 99) explained, 'The thing that struck me immediately on walking through the lobby doors of the hotel was the intense sense of community'. Lynne Thomas had a similar experience:

> I had found my tribe. These were my people. For the first time in my adult life, I felt as though I belonged. In a fandom for that show that, in 2000, wasn't currently on the air. Upon reflection, this seems to fit; I'm a professional rare books librarian, after all . . . (Thomas 2010, 83)

Fans describe conventions as *utopian spaces*: welcoming, tolerant, accepting, multicultural and enlightened (see Nye 2010, 105). This sense of belonging is not limited to *Doctor Who* or sci-fi fandom and is extremely widespread across different fan cultures. Daniel Cavicchi's work with Bruce Springsteen's fan community offers some relevant insights. According to Cavicchi, fans use Springsteen's concerts as common talking point (1998, 37). They develop community ties online, through printed media, at concerts and other social events (161–6). This is not just a matter of sharing the same musical text:

> Springsteen's music is certainly a unifying force among Springsteen fans . . . However, simply sharing the experience of the same music does not completely explain the strong relationships between Springsteen fans. Many people hear the same radio programming, for instance, but not all radio listeners feel a strong bond with each other. And, as we have seen, not all Springsteen fans interpret and understand Springsteen's music in the same way. (166)

For Cavicchi, fans' face-to-face interactions *come after* and *are premised on* a pre-existing sense of shared community: 'Fans create community or a 'sense of belonging together' not with actual shared experience but with the *expectation* of shared experience' (161; emphasis mine). In other words, before the fan community actually materializes, shared fandom forms a necessary premise. This may be because fans assume that they share certain values, like those held by Bruce. It is also because *his fan base is already one collective entity* in fan's imaginations. Springsteen devotees refer to themselves as 'tramps' and sing the line in 'Born to Run' to enact it (34). They are not unusual in this respect. Many, perhaps most, pop cultural phenomena include nicknames for members of the fan base, as if they were members of a specific grouping. For instance, *Doctor Who* fans are called Whovarians; Sherlock Holmes buffs, Sherlockians; Star Trek fans, Trekkers and so on. Equally, made up words, like 'Beatlemania' and later 'Leomania' – a term once used to reference the response of

Leonardo DiCaprio's young fans – name collective phenomenon through their supposed hysteria. In a very informal way, these nicknames and labels portray the fan community as a singular mass of dedicated individuals, a veritable army.

A common term used to describe the sense of welcome and strength of common bonds within the fan community is to refer to it as 'family'. Cast member India Fisher (2010), who played the companion to Paul McGann's eight incarnation of *Doctor Who* explained, 'Cheesy as this may sound, the fans have always felt like a *Doctor Who* family – I was taken into the fold and made to feel part of that instantly, and it's still the same ten years on . . .' (51). The notion of 'family' here goes beyond cast and crew members of famous shows and is frequently used by fans themselves. Erika Doss (1999, 150), for example, noted that a dedicated female Elvis fan described her network of over 200 pen pals as her 'family'.[4] Fans of other texts have found themselves in 'family' support networks as part of the fan base (Aldred 2010, 72). The notion of family signifies the role of the fan community as a close-knit network of people who look after each other on the basis of shared interest and values, taking each other's fandom as a vouchsafe. As a community, fans operate a 'moral economy' in which *consensus* can be levered to legitimate, protect or promote particular positions (Jenkins 2006, 55). Indeed, the way that these 'families' share certain rituals and moral values has its own important range of functions. One is simply to bond people. On Kate Bush's birthday, for instance, her fans have held 'Katemas' gatherings in Glastonbury every year from 1988 onwards (see Vroomen 2004, 248). Recent research by Sanderson and Cheong (2010, 328) analysed fans' collective responses to Michael Jackson's death in 2009. They suggest that 'social media served as grieving spaces for people to accept Jackson's death rather than denying it or expressing anger over his passing'. The two researchers described how grieving fans held 'Michael Mondays', saving up all their Michael discussions for a particular weekday and only talking about him on that day. Such collective fandom operates by affiliating its members with joint rituals and mutual evaluations (see Jenkins 2008, 81). Cavicchi has explained how fans are also bonded by *shared discourses and practices of storytelling*:

> What is created in Bruce stories is not simply a conception of self but rather a conception of self as a member of a specific group . . . Bruce stories also shape expectations of group behavior. They identify general values important to being a fan and . . . serve as models for thinking and acting in specific situations in which fans might find themselves. (Cavicchi 1998, 169)

The values of fan communities connect and stabilize the fan base around a set of shared interests. Henry Jenkins (2006, 54) argued that fan communities have their own norms that police and ensure some uniformity of reading the text. In *Textual Poachers* he explained: 'Fan texts, be they fan writing, art, song, or video, are shaped by social norms, aesthetic conventions, interpretive protocols, technological resources, and technical competence of the larger fan community.' (Jenkins 1992, 49) In that sense, the community exists as more than a common context within which fan activity takes place; it is also a shared resource that facilitates specific actions. These may include representing or levering the fan base in shows of support for the text or performer. For Matt Hills (2002a, 80), fan communities allow fans to ward off the criticism that the intense emotionality of fandom is somehow strange and alien. In other words, collective unity can help to mount a challenge against the stereotypes of abnormality that have dogged fandom in the past. Indeed, fan communities can become *self-referential microcosms of support that create their own minor forms of media fame*. In May 1981, MediaWest*Con was an example of a convention held by and for fanzine writers – not conventional celebrities (Sullivan 2010, 123). In sci-fi fandom the notion of enhancing one's reputation with other fans has a name: 'egoboo' (ego boosting) (see Green & Guinery 2004, online). This opens up the possibility that fan communities are not the unprecedentedly egalitarian organizations that some portrayals of fandom claim.

So far in this chapter the fan community has generally been discussed as if it was a uniform and monolithic social entity. Beyond the competition between official and unofficial varieties of fan club (see Cavicchi 1998, 3), there remains, nevertheless, a degree of hierarchical structuring and competition *within* fan communities for specific objects. Fan clubs often have hierarchies, usually consisting of a president, an elite panel and perhaps chapters in different geographic territories. John Tulloch has described those high up in the hierarchy of fan clubs as 'executive' fans (see Tulloch 1995, 149). Internal hierarchies are a common feature when any social system grows large and starts to organize, but their emergence in fandom does not impress those who believe that it should be about the creation of utopian communities of equal people. Some try to escape the power structures of clubs:

> On that fateful day, a new organization was founded – not a club with a strict power hierarchy, but a fan co-operative, banded together because of common interests and the desire to prove we could be a different kind of organization . . . one that served all the group members and television shows we were interested in, not individual egos. We called ourselves . . . The Federation. . . . (Adams Kelley 2010, 76; ellipsis in original)

As individuals compete with each other for status and position, the hierarchical development of fan clubs, forums and other manifestations of the fan community can make organized fandom very political.[5] Furthermore, there may be differences of opinion between whole sections of the community. For example, in the wake of rumours that said that Bruce Springsteen would be reuniting with the E-Street band at a 1993 charity concert in Madison Square Garden, his fans felt disappointed when he introduced the soul pop singer Terence Trent D'Arby instead. Some of Springsteen's loyal followers *booed their own hero* to express their consternation. In the next issue of the fan magazine *Backstreets* they justified their actions amidst debates about whether criticism of Springsteen's artistry was 'proper' fan behaviour (see Cavicchi 1998, 105). The Springsteen example is typical, in so far that some fan communities can be in a perpetual state of discussion or disagreement within the context of a shared set of interests. Collective intelligence does not always mean a unified 'hive mind' in which individual voices are suppressed (Jenkins 2006, 140). Describing one online community, Deborah Stanish commented:

> It was business-as-usual – which within any fandom means ideological debates, canon battles, ship wars and n00bs v. establishment. There were debates on what classified a 'real fan' as opposed to a poseur opportunist. Hierarchies were summarily judged and found lacking. (Stanish in Thomas & O'Shea 2010, 35)

'Ship wars' are discussions, usually between female fans, about who the best partner would be for their favourite character or artist, a classic example being the debates over whether Yoko Ono was good for John Lennon. Meanwhile, 'n00bs,' of course, are newbies (novices) who – in the eyes of their more experienced peers – have yet to fully grasp the concerns and protocols of the fan community. Seasoned community members who may have notched up decades of involvement can be critical of new updates to the franchise and new ways of interpreting what they see as *their* text (see Brooker 2002, 99; Cavicchi 1998, 103). Such concerns often reflect a division between casual or new fans, typical fans and an ultra-dedicated elite. The first contingent may well represent the next generation coming into the community. They often break taboos and do things to challenge the claims that their experience is invalid.[6]

New waves of interest mark new times, but they can also help to create them. Whether the old guard or new vanguard win out depends, in part, on the relative size of the total of new fans, and whether they have access to the hierarchy and media outlets controlled by the old guard. In the case of Russell

T. Davis' signature post-2004 era of *Doctor Who*, the influx of new fans was large enough to create changes:

> Established fans found themselves in the position of being casually dismissed by the new order. There was an element that declared classic *Who* was dull and plodding, while simultaneously vowing loyalty to RTD and all that he espoused. They ignored cries that they were 'doing it wrong' and embraced the new sensibility. Sola scriptura mixed with a healthy dose of authorial intent became the new canon. Was this only a girl thing? Depends on where you decided to hang your fannish hat. On LiveJournal, a new hierarchy of girl fandom was evolving . . . In traditional male fandom, allegiances were often based on which Doctor or era you preferred. In the fandom culture of Livejournal, lines were quickly drawn based on which companion you preferred. (Stanish 2010, 35–6)

Sometimes theorists can be guilty of over-emphasizing fans as a community. According to *Star Wars* analyst Will Brooker (2002, 113) in some cases 'to talk of the fan reaction or the fan viewpoint . . . is to impose an imagined consensus on a community that thrives on debate'. Fan audiences are therefore 'communities of imagination' that – unlike some other imagined communities – cannot be taken for granted as organic groupings and are always seen as in danger or fragmentation (Hills 2002a, 180). Television fans often drift between series as part of an extended engagement with fandom itself (Jenkins 1992, 40). Furthermore, there is no *automatic* connection between membership of an imagined community of fandom online and actual social ties (Sandvoss 2005a, 57). Although fan communities are not, therefore always stable or harmonious, their primary function is to act as a support network and manifest the unity of the fan base:

> One of the beautiful things about *Doctor Who* and its fandom is that there's room for everyone. We don't have to agree on our favourite Doctor, our favourite companion and our favourite episode. Instead we all agree that we love this show (and bicker good-naturedly about the details). . . . (Thomas 2010, 85)

The cultural functions of fan communities

Fan communities have both internal and external kinds of function. Internally, they welcome, support and socialize individuals. Externally, they organize to act as a collective bodies that represent both the fans and their heroes.

We shall focus on each of these categories in turn. While mutual support is not the only reason that people enter fan clubs, it can become a strong reason for staying. Clubs offer a space where individuals can find friends – and sometimes partners – among those who share common interests. Lynne Thomas has discussed the role of the fan community in supporting her while she raised a disabled daughter:

> In the nearly seven years since Caitlin was born, *Doctor Who* has become a talisman, a touchstone for our family as we continue to build a community of friends and acquaintances that share our love for the series. This fandom community has become our solace, our support, and our occasional escape from the difficulties inherent in raising Caitlin. They know us not just as Caitlin's parents, but as fans and as people, and they let us be all of those things at once. Our fandom community has acted as the Doctor does, accepting change and committing acts of kindness for which we are deeply grateful, which help us keep going. . . . (86)

This sense of mutual support through community ties also fosters processes of reception of the text. Fans often view texts in groups in order to multiply their pleasures. According to Henry Jenkins, 'For most fans, meaning-production is not a solitary and private process but rather a social and public one' (1992, 75). Group reception allows people to discuss their shared object, to explore it together, to turn its reception into a celebratory social event and in that sense to experientially affirm that it matters. Music fans can find direction and meaning by discussing particular songs (Cavicchi 1998, 108). Furthermore, although interpretative communities can promote particular ways of seeing a text or performance, they do not prevent individual idiosyncratic interpretations (Jenkins 1992, 88).

By shifting reception from a private to a public practice, fans can also develop other pleasures. Watching television allows them to talk, which in turn facilitates more watching (58). The process of mulling over the text opens up new interpretations and opportunities for consensus. It enables people to understand what they see or hear through novel frames of reference and sets in train a productive multiplication of perspectives. They may start to understand their favourite character, author or performer in new and more intimate ways, or to recognize of the depth of their text on new levels. As fans do this, their ongoing debates create new interpretations. Sometimes this process can take the form of gossip. Fan gossip gives people things to talk about that do not directly affect their lives (83): by exploring and critiquing the actions of others, gossip allows people to discuss their own experiences, self-disclose, create social ties, build common ground, reinforce norms and share expertise (84).

In various ways, pop culture enthusiasts do not just bond and explore their texts. *They also actively help to determine the ongoing shape and prominence of those texts.* Fans are collective actors in the realm of media culture. Henry Jenkins describes this changed terrain in a particular way. **Participatory culture** is, for Jenkins, the idea that the distinction between active producers and passive consumers has been reduced or erased because both are now actively engaged as players in the flow of media culture. Fan creativity is not simply derivative here, but part of a two-way traffic with the media industries instead (153). This shift of perspective does not entirely negate the power relations between and within the two groups, however, but actually helps us to reformulate them. As Jenkins explains:

> Just as studying fan culture helped us to understand the innovations that occur on the fringes of the media industry, we may also want to look at the structures of fan communities as showing us new ways of thinking about citizenship and collaboration. The political effects of these fan communities come not simply through the production and circulation of new ideas (the critical reading of favourite texts) but also through access to new social structures (collective intelligence) and new models of cultural production (participatory culture). (257)

For Jenkins, no one group can now control media access and participation. Collective intelligence can be seen as an alternative source of media power. As a practice, the formation of participatory culture is therefore like singing folk songs chosen from the public domain: anyone can participate and modify content (162). Fan culture is similar to a folk culture in so far that it constructs a group identity, articulates its ideals and defines its relationship to the outside world. Its artists are *supposedly* equal to audiences and commune with them. The culture is transmitted informally. It also exists beyond commercial institutions and depends on voluntary participation to populate its ranks. It draws on a tradition of appropriation and a vocabulary of community: 'Using these images facilitates communication within an increasingly alienated and atomized culture' (Jenkins 1992, 273). In other words, fans now act communally and creatively as media producers. As moral economies, their networks tend to set their own rules about where to draw the line between acceptable and unacceptable appropriation of media content (Jenkins 2006, 38).

Drawing on the work of Pierre Levy, Jenkins has suggested that fans online can now express their intelligence collectively in ways that are beyond the capability of any one individual. They can find information, protest, create happenings and persuade with greater speed and impact than ever before. At its most extreme, participatory culture is a form of contestation that resists and challenges externally imposed limits. Some oppositional groups now create their own new media spectacles to manufacture dissent (Jenkins 2008, 284). However, to focus on this is to misunderstand the new media regime: 'The depiction of media change as a zero-sum battle between old powerbrokers and insurgents distracts us from the real changes occurring in our media ecology' (274). Instead of the push–pull of dominance and resistance, the collective agency of fans can be envisaged more as part of a process of bargaining and negotiation in which different groups aim to accommodate or manoeuvre round each other. Media corporations are never utopian, but they can be bargained with (260). According to Jenkins, the fan community 'must negotiate from a position of relative powerlessness and must reply solely on its collective moral authority, while the corporations, for the moment, act as if they had the force of law on their side' (173). Pondering his own ideas, Jenkins asks:

> Have I gone too far? Am I granting too much power here to these consumption communities? Perhaps . . . I am trying to point toward the democratic potentials found in some contemporary cultural trends. There is nothing inevitable about the outcome. Everything is up for grabs. Pierre Levy described his ideal of collective intelligence as a 'realizable utopia,' and so it is. I think of myself as a critical utopian. As a utopian, I want to identify possibilities within our culture that might lead toward a better, more just society. My experiences as a fan have changed how I think about media politics, helping me to look for and promote unrealized potentials rather than reject out of hand anything that doesn't rise to my standards. (258–9)

His perspective sometimes forgets that fan concerns are *essentially tangential* to other actors on the playing field of the contemporary media. Each party is a necessary part of the game, but none is respected any further than its abilities to facilitate the aims of the other. Consequently, to place a constant focus on the role of fan communities in relation to professional media producers is to intentionally misread the aims and meanings of fandom. In the industrial process of creating culture, fans have, at various times, seen other agents as useful facilitators or annoying barriers to their pleasure, for example representing their star at his or her best, or abusing him/her as a shoddy mass commodity. Beyond engaging with this, fans are, essentially, both collectively and personally *relatively indifferent* to the issue: their primary emotional relationship is with the performer, the author, the story, the character – not with the industry. Because of *their own* academic traditions and history, scholars are much more concerned with fans' relationships to the sociology of media culture than are the majority of fans. This is not to say that such scholarship does not matter; it disrupts false ideas about consumer satisfaction and social harmony that are often assumed in public discussion.

To move beyond the participatory paradigm, it may be useful to return the focus to within the fan community, or at least explore how the community interacts with other institutions in more mundane ways. In the unstable, sociological regime of participatory culture, fans can individually and collectively adopt any number of different roles, some of which are operated tangentially or in unusual alignments with cultural producers. For example, fans are increasingly becoming recognized in their role as historians, curators of material and spokespeople for generational memory:

> With no primary texts forthcoming between *Jedi* and *Phantom Menace*, it was arguably up to the faithful longtime fans to become curators of the mythos, to keep it alive, to cherish it, and to sustain it both through their financial investment in all the secondary texts – following the characters through the Expanded Universe – in some cases, by participating in folk activity like fan fiction or amateur cinema. (Brooker 2002, 88)

Will Brooker's notion of *curating the mythos* is important here, as fans are often concerned that their icons are losing prominence and popularity. Another tangential relationship that fan communities can have is that some media producers aim to *deputize* them. Official approval or licensing schemes can be used as ways to both support, control and profit from fan activity. Sci-fi fandom is linked to the professional sci-fi writing community and fans have their own awards. They also gather at conventions as marketplaces for semi-professional product (Jenkins 1992, 47). A few of these fans can 'go pro', specifically because of the niche targeting of their marketplace in the first place (Hills 2010b, 57). They often identify with those of their own kind who participate as creatives in the franchise:

> [*Doctor Who* actor David] Tennant is also my Doctor because he is one of us, a lifelong fan of the show . . . I love knowing that deep down, there's an eight-year-old boy inside him that jumps up and down with glee every time he steps though those blue [TARDIS] doors.. . . (Thomas 2010, 85)

The internet has mediated fandom as a collective public practice, and fandom has, in turn, helped to reshape the nature of the internet as the newest popular electronic medium. Contemporary fan cultures are now so open that they have become complex cultural negotiations 'in which personalized, individual and subjective moments of fan attachment interact with communal constructions and justifications without either moment over-writing or surmounting the other' (Hills 2002a, xiii). Jenkins' notion of participatory culture shifts attention from 'poaching' the text towards exploring the fan community itself as a social actor in the realm of new media. The idea recognizes fans as political citizens and sets out a charter for critically exploring how they use their collective agency as power players in the realm of contemporary media culture. It brackets off personal fandom and tells us much less about processes intrinsic to it, both on an individual and collective level. The real question now, though, is how we get between the individual and the collective, between fandom as subjective quest, moral economy and participatory culture.

10

Researching fandom

Starting points

- What are the central methodological debates in fandom research?
- What key issues does researching fan culture raise and how might they be addressed?
- Given that academia and fandom are overlapping cultural fields, how can they be brought together in ways that will benefit everybody?

In media studies and other disciplines, the focus on texts and textuality has meant that researchers have often tended to neglect both audiences and wider contexts. Discussing Britain's most prominent science fiction television series, Matt Hills (2010b, 11) has said: 'Treated academically as something finished, completed and fixed under analysis, *Doctor Who* is instead decontextualized, cut adrift from the temporal cut-and-thrust of the informational economy circulating around it, as well as from viewers' emotions.' Unfortunately the limited approach that Hills describes there remains common, but the academic field is gradually shifting to include more about reception. Fandom research moves the focus from the text to a dedicated fraction of its audience. Even here, however, there is a danger of *speaking for* the fans. 'In the discussion about fandom', claimed Cheryl Harris, 'the authentic voices of fans themselves are rarely heard' (1998, 5). This begs questions of *how* those fan voices might be heard, understood and represented, and *what role the researcher's own fandom (or lack of it) may have* in that process. All research comes from a particular perspective. **Methodology** refers to the process by which the researcher critically justifies their own choices. These choices will include a particular *research philosophy* (i.e. perspective on knowledge); *research design* (the best way to shape the study and gather data); the usefulness of chosen *methods*; and an awareness of associated *ethical* issues. After evaluating existing studies, experienced researchers will reflect carefully upon the issues that necessarily emerge in light of their particular methodological choices. They will consider the politics and power dynamics of their own identities and roles in the research process. The truth is that fandom is quite a difficult area to study. Asking fans to be self-reflexive can change their stance. The outlook of each fan and their experience of fandom can be different depending on who they are, where, when and how they became interested, and how much time has elapsed since. Casual fans will offer different comments compared to committed devotees. New fans will say something different compared to seasoned ones. Lapsed fans may say something different again. In other words, *the situatedness of the research subjects* must be taken into account.

In different ways and to different extents we are all fans. Yet scholars have been involved in a 'writing-out of the self' when discussing fan cultures (Hills 2002a, 63). Fandom can only appear within academic space if it is channelled through appropriate conventions. The established demands of cultural theory mean that fans have often been othered within that space. Before the emergence of fan studies, their marginalization happened through perceptions of their supposedly atypical status as obsessives. In fan studies, their supposedly atypical status as creative readers and political agents has become a key focus of attention. The trajectory of fandom research has, in many ways, been towards a kind of self-listening and self-acceptance: academics have embraced the ordinary miracle of fandom and radically questioned the distinction between 'them' and 'us'. Yet *fandom and academia are not exactly the same cultural realm.* The two fields have distinct histories, values and ways of understanding. The way that individuals envisage their social responsibilities can determine whether they see the distinction between the two cultural fields as mutually problematic or mutually beneficial. A central fan studies question has been: *How can we rehabilitate the popular image of fans?* It may, though, be just as appropriate to ask: *How can we get further in creating an understanding of fandom in a way that does not alienate fans?* The two concerns lead towards convergent understandings. One examines fans as creative people. The other asks how and why they enter that place of creativity.

Initial issues

There is one seemingly obvious question that is overlooked by a surprising number of researchers: *Am I gathering data from actual fans?* Beyond the difficulties in defining fandom discussed in the first chapter, the issue of respondent self-labelling arises. Sometimes people may self-identify, as 'cult fans' even, without displaying any enduring commitment (Hills 2002a, xiv). The poorest approach to research is to interview students *under the assumption* that they are dedicated fans. Any researcher who uses snowball sampling – getting the initial research contacts to recruit others – can also find this a problem. Before he or she knows it, the researcher can be swamped with data from casual fans who are not at all dedicated. Since fan club membership is an indication of both self-identification and dedication, one way round the problem is only to interview fans from clubs. However, by ignoring new comers, closet fans and others currently outside of organized communities, this strategy creates its own biases.

Any issue of respondent selection is compounded if the research is pursued online. Research conducted by the solicitation of data over the Internet is convenient, but respondents can easily disappear, it allows for various kinds of deception, and it can hide the variable contexts of everyday fandom. Self-identification as a fan online might reveal precious little of the poster's social identity in terms of race, age or gender. Forum membership and comment-posting does not *necessarily* signify fannish dedication, although it can act as a sign of it. Unless the net is used to arrange face-to-face research encounters, online profiles usually have to be taken on trust. Beyond this, results can change considerably depending on what sort of methods are used to obtain the data. The benefits of emailing never-met respondents include removing some potential forms of researcher-bias – such as ageism – and allowing respondents to mull over their answers. However, as Cavicchi (1998, 17) noted, email is based on distance and contains fewer cues to help the researcher calibrate and understand what is being said.

As is the general protocol in qualitative research, the names of the fans should be changed or otherwise not given if any such material is published. This itself helps to collectivize and anonymize both the sample and wider fan community (in effect representing it as a fan base), but some research respondents may wish their own names to be used. Because many fans feel that their fandom expresses the core of their identity, they are often willing to contribute and can be enthusiastic if they like the researcher. Some may be pleasantly surprised that an academic cares about their experiences, memories and emotions. Depending on whether they trust the research, fans either tend to say an awful lot or very little in research encounters. Since dedicated fans have often been misrepresented by journalists, academics or others in control of the public record, it is not surprising that they can sometimes be unwilling to talk, especially if they participate in marginalized or stereotyped communities. Cultural research can, however, offer fan communities a voice and provide additional legitimacy or justification for

their passion. For example, scholarship saying that *Star Trek* was one of
the first series to promote progressive multiculturalism helped the show's
fans to positively represent their interests in wider circles (Hills 2002a, 67).
For better or worse, academic attention has often been viewed as a form
of public endorsement for particular texts or their fans. Perceptions of such
endorsement vary in both the mainstream media and in fan communities.

At interesting example of comes from the research of Michael Goddard and
Ben Halligan (2010). They held an academic symposium at the University of
Salford on 9 May 2008, to discuss a particularly creative post-punk musician:

> This symposium, *Messing up the Paintwork*, set out to engage with the
> art and politics of Mark E. Smith and the Fall and from the beginning
> encountered antagonism and questions of territory, even before the day of
> the conference itself. From the time it was first proposed, there was a lively
> discussion thread about the conference on the unofficial Fall Website, *The
> Fall Online*, most of it sceptical. The contributors questioned everything
> from the price of admission to the value of highbrow academic discussion
> led by 'chin stroking grey haired professors' on the Fall or indeed on
> rock music in general. This antagonism far from being a discouragement
> was taken as a positive sign, in that the event was engaging directly
> and conflictually with a unique fan culture who in some cases exhibited
> highly sophisticated responses to the event even while disparaging it. An
> example of this interaction was one contributor to the discussion, 'Granny
> on Bongos', who offered up a series of 'pre-cog' conclusions to the
> conference topics such as the following:
>
>> * *Mark E. Smith and (northern) working class culture: Likes a pint, doesn't
>> keep pigeons, may or may not like leek soup. Can't keep whippets due
>> to touring.* (the Fall online, 2007)
>
> Ranging from the flippantly sarcastic to the incisive, these ideas about The
> Fall would have been perfectly at home at the conference itself, even if
> their intention was to save Fall fans £30 and the waste of a day with a
> bunch of academics.
>
> (GODDARD & HALLIGAN 2010, 1)

There may have been all sorts of reasons for the 'flippantly sarcastic' fan
talk online assessing the idea of an academic symposium in Salford about
Mark E. Smith and his band the Fall. The rather incisive comments reflected
the value system of punk and post-punk, where dry, quick-witted heckling is
an enjoyable part of the process. They also perhaps indicated a discomfort
at Smith being recognized as legitimate cultural icon and losing some of

his caché as an outsider. Fan responses clearly registered a concern that comparatively privileged, middle-class professionals ('chin stroking grey haired professors') could pay so much attention to a working-class hero who discounted intellectual interpretations of his music.[1] In a sense, Mark E. Smith's fans *did not need* the object of their passion endorsed by an 'outside' research group, yet even to say that assumes that the 'chin stroking grey haired professors' were not fans themselves – an assumption that seems at least a little questionable given the efforts necessary to organize the symposium. The controversy over the Salford event definitely showed that fandom and academia were not perceived as the same thing *by fans*, at least in this case, and that fans could use their creativity to express discomfort that 'their' text – and perhaps, therefore, *the source of their oppositional identity* – was being perceived as a research object.

By reproducing an online comment from the fans, Goddard and Halligan (2010) were using a particular kind of data. **Unsolicited data** is material that pre-exists the process of investigation and unlike, say, interview transcripts, is not bought into existence by the research project. Many studies of fandom use unsolicited data sources, quoting things like letters to fan magazines or online comment posts. Using these data sources can allow researchers to save time and sidestep several issues that might otherwise prove awkward to them. Already written fan talk raises issues of interpretation, but because it is already available in public, the researcher can avoid some issues of *confidentiality* (deciding whether to disclose information) and *veracity* (being able to show the reader that research evidence exists). That said, one must be still careful about quoting from closed or commercial online forums. Unsolicited data also allows the researcher, potentially, to work greater critical distance and less immediate concern for their subjects – though that choice is ultimately one of ethics, rather than method. Further problems can occur if comments said in public are radically misinterpreted or used without regard for the original context. Several books, such as Fred Vermorel's influential compilation *Starlust* (1985/2011), have shown the dreams and fantasies of fans. Items like fan mail, however, need treating with special care. On one level, any analysis of fan correspondence has much to say about the meaning of famous performers for their audiences and the way that their image is used as a public resource. On another, even though it is always addressed to a public figure, fan mail arguably represents a private form of communication and to publish such material is therefore a potential intrusion of privacy. This becomes especially problematic when the material has never been published before or when it has been stored in a semi-public archive. Beyond such concerns, it is easy to forget that the fan mail is a communication that emerges from a power relationship with a celebrity. Rather than being taken as an indication of helpless fantasizing or total submission, fan mail needs to be understood as a form of beseeching in a context of unequal power: a fan-initiated attempt to momentarily eclipse a perceived lack of attention. *Decontextualized* renderings of unsolicited material do not always help us to fully understand fan behaviour.

The issue of respect for privacy can also occur with solicited data. Kay Turner's fascinating compendium of Madonna fantasies, *I Dream of Madonna* (1993) revealed a lot about the way that the public used an iconic star as a symbolic resource. However, any gathering of data for a similar investigation would either mean mounting an exhausting hunt for unsolicited material or staging a *perhaps unwelcome* inquisition into the dreams by strangers. Some people perceive their dreams as very private events reflecting their deepest selves. They might feel offended if asked to share. Others readily discuss their dreams, but attempt to self-censor any coverage. Either way, any researcher pursuing a psychoanalytic study of fan dreams that uses solicited data could encounter a form of bias in the material that they gather. To help fans to open up about the nature of their worlds and experiences, one thing that can help is to spend more time with them and understand their experiences *on their own terms.*

Ethnography and othering

Cultural anthropology is the study of human culture. **Ethnography** has frequently been its central approach: the study of human behaviour *in the situation of its occurrence.* Henry Jenkins (1992, 8) has claimed that researchers can learn a lot about, and more crucially *from* fan communities. Traditionally, to create an ethnographic study, researchers stay with the social group that they are studying and 'immerse' themselves in an experience of its cultural world. In theory, observations from the field should lead the investigator towards a process of recognizing patterns and drawing conclusions. The ethnographer's horror is perhaps that after immersion in the community he/she may end up with a pile of data about which little can be said because no interpretation is evident that can decide on its significance. However, as an encounter with the 'real' world, ethnography is *always already mediated* by the theoretically informed role adopted by the researcher. In that sense, no study can ever be entirely inductive (see Hills in Jenkins 2006, 30). While the emphasis on initial description suggests that ethnography does not begin by immediately making theories, it can still be used to challenge and refine them (Jenkins 1992, 286). Critics might argue that ethnography leaves too much room for subjective interpretation and researcher bias. The ethnographic approach is based, however, on both an assumption of social distance and of power relations. The researcher acts as a kind of *cultural translator* who is privileged to explain the alien ways of a different cultural world because he or she has entered it as a surrogate for 'normal' readers. At worst, there is a danger that ethnographers can use their informants as an alibi, reducing fandom to a figment of theory and not an expression of emotional conviction. Certainly, a crucial factor in determining the shape that the study will finally take is how the researcher is labeled and considered by both themselves and their subjects.

Them and us: The outsider approach

Being an 'outsider' who arrives to interrogate the fan community has its own benefits and limitations. Academic distance allows scholars autonomy and critical purchase. The ability to look at fandom from a separate place allows the researcher to step back and judge or instruct. Erika Doss' book *Elvis Culture* (1999) offers one example of a work in which the investigator maintained critical distance from her research subjects. The Elvis bibliographer Mary Hancock Hinds (2000, 265) called it 'an example of the narrowmindedness and stereotyping that Elvis fans endure'. Hancock Hinds' claim is open to debate, but what we can say following the discussion in Chapter 5 is that *Elvis Culture* – like any other academic study – pursued a very specific interpretation of its object. If complete objectivity is neither possible nor desirable, then the question becomes one of exactly what a particular study is trying to achieve. After the long era in which Marxism broadly informed the social sciences, it is no longer possible to claim simply that researchers should aim to *understand* things, their mission – either directly (through the process of the action research) or indirectly (by making work that persuades readers) – is to try to *change* the world. One might ask, then, what relatively unsympathetic outsiders are trying to achieve, except for affirming their own prejudice and freedom to criticize. Is there something valuable to know about fandom that only someone working from an outside perspective can express?

Several decades ago, when academics were widely esteemed as authoritative critics, there was a perceived danger that by studying popular culture – an object that was widely taken as trivial but fun – universities would be succumbing to commercial pressures and dropping their mandate to preserve the very best of human culture. Unless it was roundly critical, academic attention to mass culture and its audience was seen in that environment as *trivial by association*: mistakenly equating mass popularity for cultural worth, devaluing academic authority, wasting time, dumbing down and celebrating the wrong things. In drawing attention to the politics of popular culture *as a social practice*, cultural studies challenged all those assumptions (see, for example, Seiter et al. 1989). Fan studies emerged once that critique had been sufficiently accepted. However, ethnography has a much longer heritage as a methodological approach. It emerged from anthropology, a discipline that originally – if we look back far enough – served the colonialist project by exploring human behaviour in 'primitive' societies.[2] Analyzing more local cultures, late twentieth-century ethnographers often worried about 'going native' and maintained scholarly distance to allay their fears. Their research has been defined by its *academic impartiality*: the researcher's ability to demonstrate a critical, independent stance. The problem with this is that it can facilitate arguments that are unsympathetic and/or inaccurate. Rather than use fandom to *challenge* their own theoretical frameworks, some of the more distanced scholars *explained it away* (Hills 2002a, 5). The distanced approach meant that researchers even 'transformed fandom into a projection of their personal fears, anxieties and fantasies about the dangers of mass culture' (Jenkins 1992, 6). By starting to project ideas into the social grouping that they were studying, such scholars were, in other words, *seeing only things that they wanted to see*.[3] 'Outside' research, then, even of a sympathetic variety, is always held back because its investigators cannot leap into the mindset of their committed and enthusiastic research subjects. It therefore runs the risk of misunderstanding key identities, experiences, concerns and desires. One way out of this dilemma is to ask fans about their practices directly, rather than making judgements from outside their world. Daniel Cavicchi has suggested that academics have all too often projected their own agenda onto the fans and made the immediate understanding of fandom tangential to their interests:

> Fans value their fandom for the ways that it addresses the existential reality of their daily lives . . . [and] are not necessarily thinking about where they stand in an abstract, larger social order or how their fandom can change that order; rather they are concerned to get through each day and how their participation in performance helps them to understand the fluctuating and contradictory experience of daily life and to make connections with other people around them. (1998, 185–6)

For Cavicchi, then, fandom is shared, but is also an intensely personal thing. His experience of similarity to those he studied helped him ask intelligent questions and understand their points of view.

Only us: Are insiders actually double agents?

When conducting his research, Daniel Cavicchi (12) claimed, 'I tried simply to "be myself", to interact with the fans with sensitivity and respect and, though a reflexive consideration of my presence in the different contexts of fieldwork, carefully interpret what fans were (and were not) telling me.' The quotation marks that he leaves around the phrase 'be myself' indicate that it is contradictory: after all, if you are yourself, you do not have to *try*. It suggests that the roles of fan *and* fan researcher are therefore like different hats to wear. One common argument is that *an ethnographer should ideally be an 'insider' who knows the culture that they are studying well enough to really allow it to speak for itself*. Henry Jenkins' work is interesting here. Prior to the release of *Textual Poachers* (1992), the most prominent discussion of fans was *Enterprizing Women* by Camille Bacon-Smith (1991). Like Bacon-Smith, Jenkins presented an audience ethnography. Unlike her book, his one did not follow a traditional 'going into the field' narrative; its author claimed that he was *already* an insider in the telefantasy fan community. For Jenkins, being 'inside' translated as adopting a highly reflexive, ethical position when representing fellow fans: 'Writing as a fan means as well that I feel a high degree of responsibility and accountability to the groups being discussed here' (Jenkins 1992, 7). Insiders like Henry Jenkins have a passion that can motivate them through their studies. Like Jenkins, many fans now go into the research process with the aim of *legitimating* and *representing* their own communities. Furthermore, fellow fans may welcome their sensitivity and experience. Insiders can be useful *map makers* who already know the territory (Hills 2002a, 18).[4] Claims to insider status carry the implicit assumption that no fan will represent their own kind in an uncharitable way. Ordinary fans can speak more freely to their fellows precisely because those individuals are trusted not to misrepresent the community without facing immediate consequences (Brooker 2002, xiii).

The advocacy of 'insider' research throws up a question for the direction of academic work as a whole: *If fan research is only conducted by passionate insiders, where will fandom for 'regressive objects' (say, racist skinhead bands or homophobic reggae artists) be represented? Will it only be studied by using unsolicited data and secondary accounts?* Academic work tends to be welcomed most readily when its audience follows the same cultural tastes (Jenkins 2006, 32). Some might say that scholars have *their own* cultural realm, just like fans, so, 'perhaps . . . they are, in part, describing a cloaked version of themselves' (Hills 2002a, 54). All too often, the result is that privileged middle-class commentators talk about *their* film, record and comic book collections or fan communities – and they therefore *remake fandom in their own image*. Interest in relatively 'uncool' or regressive kinds of texts goes underrepresented.[5]

Fan studies has been marked by the rise of a whole generation of scholars who proudly proclaim that they love pop culture. If scholarly and fan identities have, to an extent collided, does it mean that anyone with fannish experience has the right to speak as an academic *purely* by dint of their real world knowledge? In his book *Fan Cultures* (2002a), Matt Hills discusses this knot of associated issues. What follows in this section will draw heavily on insights from his work.

Elite, scholarly, expert fans-turned-critics are sometimes celebrated by academics, but they are, in effect, inevitably dismissed too for having no proof of their academic credentials. In other words, academics sometimes view fans as having encyclopaedic popular expertise, but do not promote them at the expense of their own authority. A significant difference remains: academics are trained and recognizably qualified within a specific discipline (say, media studies), and they possess a certain set of skills accordingly: subject knowledge, critical thinking, public speaking, experience in conducting qualitative research and adopting an appropriate academic subjectivity. Fans, meanwhile, pursue a different cultural field and set of experiences. They have a separate *way of knowing* about their specific object, a parallel set of collective values, and a different understanding of the fan base as a community of common interests. Of course, it is not impossible for academics to realize or discover that they hold fannish attachments, or for fans to undergo additional education in order to speak as academics. The roles are, furthermore, not quite as inflexible or opposed as might be imagined: 'Academics are not resolutely rational, nor are fans resolutely immersed' (Hills 2002a, 21). Both groups aim to articulate their experiences in different ways. Unmediated fan discussion cannot pass for academic work. However, in the process of academic discussion, fandom can be 'curiously emptied' of the very things that define it: passion, attachment, affect.

Matt Hills distinguishes two intermediate breeds of commentator: *scholar-fans* (academics who wear their fandom in public) and *fan-scholars* (amateur experts from the fan community). Both are subjected to criticism:

> Academics and fans both value their own institutionally-supported ways of reading and writing above those practices which characterize the other group. This creates a type of mutual marginalization . . . Imagined subjectivities and their simplistic moral dualisms possess cultural power. This means that scholar-fans are typically looked down on as not being 'proper' academics, while fan-scholars are typically viewed within fandom as 'pretentious' or not 'real' fans. (20–1)

Nobody is suggesting here that a person cannot be a fan and scholar at the same time. Rather, they are distinct *roles* that the same person can simultaneously occupy. Given that a certain degree of separation between those roles is necessarily the case, the real question then becomes one of how academics – whether or not fans themselves – can *use* their position to *fairly represent* their research subjects. This issue of fairness comes in several forms at different stages of the research. The first is research practice. A crucial concern here is that the researcher should recognize it when they may be projecting. After talking to 17 David Bowie fans as part of his research, for example, Nick Stevenson (2009, 96) recognized his own role in the process: 'None of the men interviewed actually told me that they were lonely, isolated and depressed although this is evidently what I felt.' A second key issue connected with fairness is theorizing fandom. Nick Couldry has talked about developing 'accountable theory' in which the language and explanation we use to describe others is *always consistent with any we would use to describe ourselves* (see Hills 2002a, 73). The third key area is the presentation of the study. The politics of language is crucial here: one of the interesting things about Sue Wises' thoughtful account of her Elvis fandom, for instance, is that she writes accessibly and plainly, avoiding academic jargon. There is another question connected with inclusivity and control over the process of academic representation: *To what extent do the fans speak with their own voice in the research?* Ethnography can be a way to introduce accountability into academic work. Henry Jenkins encourged fans to comment on manuscripts of his work and wove their response back into the finished piece. He used a dialogue with the fan community in his early research to integrate his experience of fandom and his academic writing (see Jenkins 2006, 31 and 61). *Beauty and The Beast* fans accused Jenkins of incorporating too much dissent from a small minority of the fan base into his work; in a process of dialogic editing he included their feedback as part of the discussion (Jenkins 1992, 130). What we see, then, is that there are a variety of ways for scholars to respectfully collaborate with fans.

Beyond the interaction of 'researcher' and 'fan' as separate identities, the last two decades have seen academics claim positions that more closely associate the two roles. Specific frameworks govern how cultural capital is attributed. In the old climate where fandom was relatively marginalized from academia, the academics studying it were seen as double-agents: either playing a useful role as cultural translators or doubly dismissed. At worst, they were viewed as improper scholars (who had a scandalous object) and improper fans (who had too much rational distance) (Hills 2002a, 12). Despite evidently possessing a high level of cultural capital, fan-scholars could thus become marginalized within academia and their own fan communities. To escape any perceived taint of pathological abnormality, when negotiating confessional styles of self-presentation, scholar-fans had to hide their enthusiasms and display rational, expert public personae. Since fan studies has become recognized as a body of knowledge, all this has undoubtedly changed. On the other hand, leading fans have expertise that is increasingly being recognized by academic authorities. Simon Frith has argued that 'many fans of pop who are not academics are certainly intellectuals' (1992, 183). Ordinary fans can be conflicted: sometimes in favour of intellectual support and sometimes – like the Mark E. Smith fans – wary of it. Reproducing the division of 'them' and 'us', they can both draw on academic authority to support their points and dismiss scholars for being out of touch with their experiences (see Jenkins 2006, 15). Hills (2002a, 19) suggests that although 'fandom and academia are not mutually antagonistic' academic writers agree that 'fans are wary of academics, and that academics cannot simply assume the mantle of "fan" '. Fans can therefore help academics examine their own interpretive practices (Jenkins 2006, 33). Another emergent, recognized hybrid meanwhile is the *fan-academic*:

> [The fan-academic is] the fan who uses academic theorizing within their fan writing and within the construction of a scholarly fan identity, as opposed to the professional academic who draws on their fandom as a badge of distinction within the academy. For, curiously enough, while the academic-fan or 'scholar-fan' has become a highly contested and often highly visible topic for theorists the fan-academic or 'fan-scholar' has been passed over in silence. (Hills 2002a, 2)

If the separate roles of fan and scholar have become increasingly entwined in mutually productive ways, can we therefore say that they are approaching a kind of mutual equality? As part of the project of appropriately presenting fandom, several recent academic writers have strived to place academia and fandom on an *equal footing*. For Hills, 'Academic practice – regardless of its favoured theorists and theoretical frameworks – typically transforms fandom into an absolute other' (5). His own work has therefore asked how university research might be reconstituted to avoid that happening. Hills has radically interrogated conventions of academic research for places where it maintains authority in subtle and often hidden ways: 'Cultural studies may be keen to critique and remake the world, but it has become amazingly adept at ignoring its own power relations, own exclusions (of which fandom is, finally, only one) and its own moral dualisms' (184). One example is that researchers who endorse *vernacular theory* – ideas and ingenuity stemming from fans *not* universities (as if the two were inevitably separate and opposed) – often want to maintain their academic authority too. Hills asks, 'how can the mutual marginalization of fandom and academia's imagined subjectivities be challenged?' (9) To what extent does this mean, at an extreme, dissolving academic privilege and identity? According to the work of Jürgen Habermas (1962/2005), the **public sphere** is an unfettered space beyond government control, where ordinary people can participate in public discussion. Given that academic research can still have a persuasive, talismanic effect in the public sphere, and that the public, to an extent, still trust researchers as knowledgeable, ethically aware authorities, it may be better to ask how the – admittedly changing – place of the contemporary academic can be used to present fandom in a respectful, insightful and dignified way. Academics *can* use their privileged voice *dialogically*, without erring towards the egocentricity, arrogance and blinkeredness that can all too easily come with the pursuit of their role. Busse and Hellekson (2006, 8) argue that:

> Fan and academic discourses can contain mutually exclusive readings and are not primarily focused on synthesis . . . But in connecting fannish and academic practices here, it is important to emphasize that we are not trying to colonize fan spaces with an academic value system. In fact, if anything, it's the reverse: we use our fannish knowledge and values and apply them to academic practices. Rather than privileging a particular interpretation as accurate, we have learned from fandom that alternative and competing readings can and must coexist.

Academic traditions based on electronic media (such as cinema or recorded music) often emerged when their industrial agents were recognized as creative figures. Andrew Sarris' 1962 essay on Alfred Hitchcock for the French journal *Cahiers du Cinema* is a prime example. As popular culture and fandom have increasingly become seen as legitimate objects of study, different forms of fan phenomena have been examined and scholars have claimed that their fannish identities are foundational. Researchers who self-consciously serve and speak for fan communities by using their own identities as fans are, in effect, academic fans or 'aca-fen' as they are known (the second part of this hybrid term denoting a plural of fans). Jenkins summarized this position when he stated: 'I come to both *Star Trek* and fan fiction as a fan first and a scholar second. My participation as a fan long precedes my academic interest in it' (2006, 251). Similarly Will Brooker (2002, xv) was quick to declare his own fandom and its role in his study: 'I am writing about *Star Wars* partly because it constitutes one of the most potent cultural myths of my life, and I am writing about fans because I am one myself.' He later adds, 'This entire book is an example of a childhood passion channeled into an academic career' (19). Scholars like Jenkins and Brooker represent, in effect, a new elite. They are ethical and articulate popular culture enthusiasts who are schooled and equipped, ready to use the space of academia to their advantage *as fans*. These aca-fen tend to focus on and promote the creative ingenuity of ordinary members of the fan base (see Jenkins 2006, 13). Such scholars have not only dropped the old concern to maintain a critical distance from their object of study. They have also reduced the distance between fandom and the academy by proclaiming their dual identities. Aca-fandom has therefore questioned the norms of academic subjectivity. *Textual Poachers*, for example, challenged academics' self-conceptions (35). Perhaps because aca-fen often teach in fields based on the interrogation of media cultures, their status as fans has not, moreover, led to their pedigree as academics being questioned. They have managed to make the dual identities work together. In this case academic authority has also been used by skilled fans to dignify the wider presentation of their communities and adjudicate in their immediate debates (14).

From the perspective of the old guard, aca-fen seemed to have divided loyalties. Are they not reducing academic objectivity and autonomy by simply *being 'native'*? The **affective fallacy** says that those emotionally swayed by a text will lose insight and objectivity. In this view aca-fen appear to be in danger of being too subjective and creating biased research (27). The idea, though, that any researcher can escape from his or her situatedness and enter a space of total objectivity is itself a questionable fantasy. Objectivity is, in fact, an adopted *strategy or stance* constructed *from within* concrete, situated identities and perspectives. Impartial rationality is a *rhetorical claim* rather than absolute tenet. It can also be a dangerous claim, however neutral it appears, because knowledge has political consequences. Questions about the narrow nature of fans' perspectives forget that having a fannish identity is like having a sexual identity. Being of a particular persuasion does not mean that a person drops all rationality. From their own perspectives, fans can be as articulate and objective as anyone else. Indeed, when they hold up their heroes in public, aca-fen challenge the flawed notion that 'good' rationality is always neutral and impartial (Hills 2002a, 4). *All academic work is autobiographical* in some – usually indirect – sense, but we must remember that aca-fen who proclaim a life-long love for their object of study, also speak as both academics and fans from a *very particular perspective*. Some critics have also argued that such scholars can never *unreservedly* embrace their fandom in the space of academic writing, because they reserve the right to determine its political significance. In theory, their situatedness means that aca-fen also face the 'experiential leap' problem *from the inside*: not being able to talk about *how* fandom happens, because there is no automatic shared intersubjective space of experience between themselves and any non-fan readers. In reality, this underestimates aca-fen as skilled communicators who can create the intersubjective space by being articulate in their writing. Indeed, they could stand accused of exploiting their autobiographies to make claims about the truth and value of their research.

Milly Williamson has cautioned against simply championing fans. She questions the way that aca-fen have occasionally compared their own position as organic intellectuals speaking for a particular social constituency to that of prominent African-American authors like Henry Louis Gates and Cornel West:

> To liken the way that a fan scholar speaks from within 'a skin' of experience to the way that an African American scholar does, is untenable. Fan scholars who position themselves as intellectual activists and fans as subordinate rebels achieve these claims by ignoring the hierarchies that exist in fandom, and by inadequately characterizing 'dominant' culture. (Williamson 2005, 104)

There is a therefore danger that aca-fen may have distorted, or at least selectively presented fandom itself as a way to fight the academy from within (Jenkins 2006, 32). By self-consciously maintaining that the aca-fan is in some way an academically unconventional 'scandalous' category, researchers have retained an increasingly obsolete frame of interpretation that accuses academia of disregarding fandom and assuming a superior position (Hills 2002a, 15). From this perspective, fandom represents the 'real' (authentic passion): a state romanticized by academics as something they can never quite achieve. In actuality, however, fandom no longer represents a return of the repressed in academia but instead forms a parallel identity that scholars can choose to embrace, exploit, explore or ignore.

Beyond bounded fandom

Both 'outsiders' and 'insiders' tend to see their cultures as clearly delimited and bounded wholes. James Clifford's work offers a critique of the assumptions of cultural uniformity and absolute difference that underpin the ethnographic approach. Clifford suggests that ethnography can border on a form of projection. By representing other cultures as different, ethnographers are *constructing* what they purport only to *sample*. As part of their own academic enterprise, they actively give wholeness and otherness to tribes and similar cultural phenomena. In other words, they help to create what they simply claim to reveal. This can be translated to interpret fandom research. Daniel Cavicchi (1998) notes that 'insider' status may be problematic because the notion of an 'inside' depends on a mutually shared definitions that ignore other differences between participants, and that 'fandom tends to enhance problems of being a native, since most people are not wholly defined by being a fan, and their identities are always shaped by various other social connections and relationships' (11). Cavicchi is correct here: fandom is a vocation for some, but simply one aspect of identity for many. He adds that 'being able to think about fandom as part of my profession has separated me from other fans' and that his age and gender 'complicated my insider status' (12). Jenkins has also grappled with this issue:

> Historically, academics have abused power, constructing exotic and self-serving representations of fans. Even many of the most sympathetic audience ethnographies signaled their distance from the communities they described. I did not have the option of distancing myself from the fan community. What I knew about fandom I knew from the inside out. (2006, 61)

Because it gives *the illusion*, at least, of an encounter with 'the real', the task of constructing an ethnography comes with a mantle of responsibility (29). Like other academics, ethnographers are, in a sense, then, storytellers working within certain conventions and assigning their respondents particular functions and places within the academic stories they tell (Hills 2002a, 70). One way beyond the ethical issues that inevitably arise from the social relations of ethnography is for the ethnographer to speak *only* about *their own* interests.

Autoethnography

> Too often our scholarly efforts exempt us from the daily problems we document with such passion. We escape by taking flights into the heights of theory, explaining, yet again, how structural inequality works or why racism persists. Theory is not a free pass allowing us to travel though these territories unscathed; neither is theory a protective shield against our own culpability. Understanding capitalism, structural inequality, racism, sexism or any other of the myriad social ills does not inoculate anyone from perpetuating the very structures we seek to destabilize.
>
> ELIZABETH CHIN (2007, 352)

If most academics working on fandom are also fans, then, rather than talking in our research about *us* (academics) and *them* (the fans), we can offer 'inside' pictures of our fan experience: conveying an 'us' to a potential 'outside' readership. The problem here is both scientific and political: *Whose experience and which culture (within the fan base) should be shown?* An extreme answer to this question is that the researchers should self-consciously discuss their own fandom, either to *position themselves* and expose the privileges and biases that come with their role, or perhaps because they are making the even more radical – and less often made – claim that they cannot actually speak for other fans *of the same object*. The process in which the researcher critically assesses and reflexively reports on their own fandom in depth is called an **autoethnography**. Autoethnography is a process of voluntary self-estrangement that operates through the practice of persistent self-questioning. Rather like a public form of therapy, the process can at best expose the adoption of tropes and conventions about fandom, showing how a personal 'cord of our cultural identity as we perform it – is always borrowed and alien' (Hills 2002a, 72). Autoethnography should therefore aim to reveal how the self of the aca-fan is structured by processes of 'common sense', self-rationalization and commodification. Any thorough autoethnography should reveal the role of the social world – the family, peer group or fan community – to which the fan belongs (76–8). Accounts of such heroic reflexivity might also help to reveal the narcissistic limits to common sense and academic writing, but there is also a danger that they might also ignore the social and cultural context, make the writer's self seem artificially isolated, and forget the role of discourse (76). In autoethnography, there is a possibility that narcissism can arise at precisely the point where self-interrogation reaches its limit. John Fisk (1990) analysed his own responses to *The Newly Wed Game* and declared, somewhat bombastically, that he held 'vulgar tastes' antithetical to his own bourgeois position; his work showed how ethnographic theory could reflect the self, but Fiske did not register this as an imposition, unlike his claim against psychoanalytic approaches. Oppositely, Scott Bukatman's (1994) autoethnographic account reflected on his time as a young reader of superhero comics and suggested that he was compensating for not fulfilling a masculine ideal (see Hills 2002a, 73–5). At its most intense, autoethnography can therefore help to expose theory as a situated project, a disguise for the theorist's own personal attachments.

There are multiple dangers with the autoethnographic approach. Does it produce good research? From an *objectivist* viewpoint – where the real world exists as facts and researchers just have to sufficiently *sample* it – the subjective view of one aca-fan is too small, too skewed and too self-conscious to be of much value when explaining a whole fan base. However, almost by definition ethnographers are *not* objectivists: they tend to squarely recognize the role of perspective and importance of interpretation in the construction of meaning. Daniel Cavicchi mixed both ethnographic and autoethnographic elements in his own work. He made no claims to represent *all* of popular music fandom in his study of the Springsteen phenomenon (see Cavicchi 1998, 14).

Neverthless, autoethnographers still face a legacy of objective thinking that permeates most academic work – including qualitative research – and are not immune from charges of undue bias from other ethnographers who deal with entire cultures or communities. Sometimes their approach is dismissed altogether. For example Matt Hill's 2002 book *Fan Cultures* was criticized *not* for being too empirical, but for never quite getting to actual fan cultures. Ironically, his critics ignored the carefully constructed autoethnography that he included in his account (see Jenkins 2006, 29).

European cultural studies research has tended to exclude or at least relegate individuality: taking its theoretical inspiration from Marxism and identity politics, the tradition has at best perceived 'the individual' as a placeholder to be interrogated by cultural theory and at worst as an entrenched but ultimately distracting bourgeois notion. While we can agree with Hills (2002a, 92) that there is a danger of excluding ordinary lived experience – and therefore ignoring our own lives – when pursuing impersonal theoretical approaches, the opposite may also be true at the other extreme: if autoethnography is not pursued and conveyed in appropriate ways, it can make such an individual statement that it reveals little of interest to other people. At worst, it might become a licensed exercise in egotism: indeed, authoethnography tends to be the province of particular kinds of scholars and subjects.[6] Rather than simply using autobiography, it is interesting here that Henry Jenkins chose to speak both from *within* and *about* the wider fan community (Jenkins 1992, 5). Nevertheless, autoethnography's focus on individuality *can* be used in productive ways, for example by talking about how the same individual's various passions are really linked together and make sense in relation to their personal journey. While Matt Hills critiqued John Fiske and Scott Bukatman for avoiding a discussion of their families in their autoethnographic accounts, he also avoided the topic in his own account of fandom until he corrected himself, noting how his life as both a fan and academic had been encouraged by his family. One use of autoethnography is, then, to ask why specific fandoms become relevant and irrelevant for an individual at specific times and to chart how multiple fandoms are linked as an individual realizes his/her self-identity (Hills 2002a, 81–2). Jeanette Monaco's (2010) recent autoethnographic study of viewing television series *The Sopranos* (1999– 2007) provides a good working model of this. Monaco combines an awareness of fandom research and the twin subjectivities of the fan and academic. She also places an emphasis on pursuing self-reflective 'memory work': using her viewing experiences to make meaningful connections between the personal and cultural field, recalling earlier moments of her situatedness within the constraints of social identity, and in turn drawing on this to make sense of her predicament in the present. The following quotation shows some of this process in action:

> The birth of my second child Eva, not long after my son turned three and I completed my part-time MA in Visual Culture, is a useful starting point . . . Exhaustion was one reason for watching lots of TV during the day accompanied by my increasing academic interest in the series, which was fuelled during a time when pre-and post-broadcast British press reviews hailed the show as a masterpiece example of 'quality' television . . . Eva is sleeping in the Moses basket another friend from Bristol (UK) lent us which is placed in front of the Ikea bookcase that is tightly packed with a selection of my partner's old vinyl LPs, a mixture of novels, and oversized art books, some of which I shipped over from the States. This bookcase sits in one alcove next to the fireplace while the TV and its cupboard occupies the other. I remember nothing much of anything else now except that I recall feeling a heaviness in my body of the same type that weighed me down many of those mornings and I now imagine myself slowly sitting up to turn off the TV after *The Sopranos'* credits roll down the screen. I see my hair in a mess and imagine there are dark circles under my puffy eyes. I then see myself sobbing, and searching through my pockets for tissue to wipe my eyes and runny nose. I am now looking at this newborn baby and I think about my father's mother, the woman after whom I named my daughter. I then say her name 'Eva' and I tell my deceased grandmother how much I miss her.

> My memory tells me this sadness had something to do with viewing a *Sopranos'* scene involving Livia Soprano (Nancy Marchand), the monstrous mother figure with whom the central character Tony (James Gandolfini) struggles to come to terms throughout his long-term psychotherapy sessions. This flash of recognition that takes me to the memory of my grandmother, whom I have since then claimed bears a striking resemblance to Livia, however, is still difficult to discern. As a way of attempting to revisit the emotional event I decide to rewatch the pilot episode which first introduces Livia. I am soon reminded, after only watching the opening credits, that I feel an immediate sense of familiarity with the New Jersey industrial and suburban landscape, the 'real' locations chosen by the show's creator David Chase, which contribute to the series' claims to authenticity. My proximity to the text is enhanced, however, by the series' representation of an Italian-American working-class community's habitus. This experience, I feel, in spite of the series' obvious play with the tropes of the American gangster genre, eerily reflects remnants of my own past, which is articulated in the characters' distinctive eastern

sea-board working-class accents and dialect, their choice of food, clothing and hairstyles.

Monaco's highly reflexive and self-aware style creates an interplay between her everyday life, her multiple identities (as a mother, fan and academic), her situated viewing experiences, her family memories and *The Sopranos* itself. As she weaves her discussion, each resonates to inform the narrative and build something more emotionally moving and intellectually informative that a simple chain of descriptions. While it may *look* superficially like a stream of consciousness, this type of work actually offers an advanced way to explore how personal experience and cultural theory are relevant to each other.

Like other academics, autoethnographers work with specific audiences, briefs and sets of conventions. Each must work to approach his/her own experience with the right strategies, to unearth blind spots and develop the discussion in an appropriate way. To be a good autoethnographer takes training in academic protocols and strategies of conscious self-interrogation. Simply being a fan does not qualify the writer: 'The fan cannot' Hills explains, 'act, then, as the unproblematic source of the meaning of their own media consumption' (2002, 67). Fans may have trouble explaining *why* they like their texts. Research is generally a process of intelligent modelling in which the researcher analyses and learns from other studies that have gone before. Consequently, researchers have often tended to subordinate fan discourses to academic ones. Any budding autoethnographer should study examples of good and bad practice and look carefully for their strengths and weaknesses. We all have blind spots. Matt Hills (2002a, 71) has argued that ethnography needs to be reconceptualized so that it can speak about any potential gaps when reflecting upon academics' and fans' identities. For example, celebrity and fandom are now themselves to an extent modes of conducting scholarly transaction. Public intellectuals like Slavoj Žižek are celebrity figures who have their own fan bases (readerships), and can evoke fannish connections as they contribute their ideas to the public sphere. Yet few researchers talk about the implications.

Ultimately, what cultural theory should be doing, I think, is bringing about a mutually satisfying unity between self and other under the guise of 'understanding and changing the world'. Ethnography aims to artificially negate the self in a process of discovering the other. It is an important way to socialize early career researchers and make them aware of the cultures and perspectives of the fan community. However, ethnographic and autoethnographic approaches rely on *a frisson of cultural difference*, either between researchers and their objects, and/or between researchers and their readerships. One way to end this chapter might have been to pursue an autoethnography of my own. However, I shall only go *part* of the way in that direction. When I embarked on my own research, I was interested in fandom and I therefore chose a figure with a prominent fan culture. I did not know very much about Elvis – either good or bad – so I studied his phenomenon in an open-minded way. Through the process, I became much more of a fan. I went to Elvis events for years and met my partner through the community. Since I also publish academic pieces on Elvis, I now feel like a professional fan in some of my research time, which is a great privilege. However, I do not think that I need to wear my fandom as a badge in my writing because – beyond any social duty to position myself – I think that by *not* proclaiming my own fandom may actually be more useful. It is not shameful to be a reflexive fan within academia any more, but I would prefer scholars to reach a place where the issue is dropped and we just take it for granted that anyone – fan or not – can potentially write with insight about fandom *if they do so with respect*. In that sense, rather than a fan-first-and-foremost, proudly fighting his corner again potential academic disapproval (which does not exist in the same way that it once did), I want to be seen as a respectful, fan-positive researcher. I don't hold anything against prominent fans who are also cultural scholars. There are now many great ones. Neither do I think, however, that we should always have to promote the personal when discussing socially important culture. There is now a crucial role for researchers who *do not* proclaim their own fandom. By devoting their careers to the study of fan phenomena, such scholars suggest, through their actions and ethics, that a wider foundation of support exists for the importance of their object; much more so than if fans only studied their own communities. Positioning oneself is an inevitable process, but sometimes it can remain all the more effective by being an unspoken one.

11

Conclusion: The frontiers of fan research

Starting points

- What do perceptions of fandom suggest about power and agency in a media culture?
- To what extent has the project to socially habilitate fandom been successful?
- How is research on fan culture developing now?

Interested in audience studies, media studies and consumption studies in ways that advance all these areas of inquiry (as well as others), recent studies of fans and fandom force us to rethink key questions of identity, performance practice, genre, gender, sexuality, self, affect, race, ethnicity and nationalism.

C. LEE HARRISON AND DENISE BIELBY 2005, 799

As a cultural phemomenon, media fandom is now into its second century. Compared to its long empirical history, fandom has attracted sustained attention as an object of study for a much shorter period. It is only in the past few years that fans have really become a widespread object of enquiry. Harrington and Bielby (2005) have recognized the diversity of this flourishing interdisciplinary academic field. To really conceptualize the focus of a growing scholarly tradition, we have to understand how fandom simultaneously encompasses *both* individual engagement and social participation. To fully understand its mechanics, individual and social elements must be positioned as elements in a causal chain that moves forward from widely circulated assumptions to individual connections, communal pleasures and collective actions. This book has aimed to situate fandom by examining how individuals become fans, as well as how fandom becomes social. However, historic divisions between different academic disciplines have placed a greater emphasis on *either* the personal (psychoanalysis, phenomenology, autoethnography) *or* the collective (taste cultures, fan communities). Furthermore, to understand fandom, we must recognize that it is actually two things: a social experience and topic of debate. On one hand, then, it is an inspirational experience and common social pursuit. On the other, it is a *discursive construct*: something *represented* by journalists, scriptwriters, academics and fans. This chapter has a section on each of those aspects. By way of introduction, what follows will first examine three overlapping academic perspectives: the sociocultural, the historical and the political. In a sense, all of these locate fandom as both personal *and* social, although they often focus more on the latter side of that equation. None of these traditions is necessarily 'better' than any other. Indeed, they are *all* useful in developing a greater understanding of a complex object of study.

The sociocultural approach primarily sees fandom as a sociological phenomenon *in* and *of* itself. This phenomenon is something that evidently comes with a range of *elements and features*, mechanisms that might eventually be fully understood by interested researchers. *Understanding Fandom* has largely taken that approach. It has shown that although fandom has sometimes been discussed as a form of deviance become social (a disease), it is actually the result of *shared assumptions that circulate in wider culture*. Fannish interests are neither the same as religion nor religiosity. Ideas about piety or sacredness are of little use in explaining why fans get fascinated, although a selective application of Durkheim's notion of totemism may go some way to explaining the affective *buzz* that they feel. Furthermore, to be a fan does not mean living your whole life wishing you were actually someone famous. Shared goals and dreams suggest that rather than a *predicament* (something to be escaped), fandom is actually an important social role *in itself* for many people. Ideas about agency (authorship, poaching, resistance) tend to forget the way that fans often use their ingenuity is *to fulfil their structural position*. Rather than economic production or consumption, this position, however, primarily relates to an object (a text or star), an individual identity (being a fan) and a community (the fan base). Economic consumption is often a means by which fandom is facilitated and practiced, yet neither the process of buying nor its associated ideology (consumerism) fully captures the phenomenon. Since fans are necessarily more than consumers, neither the process of buying nor its associated ideology (consumerism) fully captures the phenomenon. Fandom begins with shared values and unspoken assumptions. It then becomes actualized (it 'clicks') inside *individuals'* heads and that leads to common experiences. Since fans can be critical, they are in love with the pleasures that they discover, not necessarily with objects in themselves. Pursuing a deeper connection with one's favourite text or performer becomes a motivation that shapes the lives and characteristic practices of many who become interested. Fans explore myths and imagined memories as part of a continuation of their own interests, and they use their fannish passions as inspiration to create a further culture that matters in its own right.

Sociocultural insights such as these see fandom as a kind of functional subjectivity that becomes collective and communal in various ways. They treat it as something relatively unchanging that *exists* 'out there' in the society. The sociocultural approach is fruitful because it analyses common mechanisms and shared connections. A recent example of the approach comes from studies that have examined the role of fandom in relation to ageing and the human life cycle. As part of a will to understand fandom as a personal resource, in the last few years more researchers have begun to think about how it is connected to the life cycle. Prominent phenomena from Beatlemania to descriptions of teenaged 'Twihards' have associated media fandom with adolescence in the public sphere.[1] Widespread perceptions therefore see it as an immature or adolescent escape: a compensatory activity. Laura Vroomen (2004, 243) has noted that commentators often frame fandom as a way to *resist* social ageing: 'there is an assumption that intense popular music investments cannot be carried over into adult life, and that contradictory practices and identifications cannot be sustained.' Yet fan cultures are not always quickly abandoned or cast off by their participants. As accepted norms shift, fandom has become a cultural process in which people can engage at any age; perhaps it is *easier* to pursue in later years when those interested have greater free time or disposable income. The centrality of popular culture as a social currency in recent years has been associated with whole cohorts of people clearly continuing with their fannish interests even as they move through the life cycle. Some discover their fan interests for the first time in later life, drawing on memories of earlier experiences. Finding fandom at a later age can put a person behind on the learning curve, but their stronger sense of their own identity can mean that they have escaped earlier needs for social approval and will happily affiliate with 'uncool' fan objects.

For many of those who experience it, fandom is a continual process. Some move nomadically from one phenomenon to the next and therefore experience their fandom as a kind of lifestyle (Jenkins 2008, 57). Others are dedicated to singular objects. Although audience members often lose interest or get disappointed by fresh updates to the text, dedicated devotees claim that their fandom remains relatively constant even as *they* change.

Aided by the opportunities for social interaction offered by fan communities, seasoned fans can sustain their interests over long periods of time, never seeming to waver far from their paths. Time becomes marked for such individuals by each new phase of experience *as a fan*. New passions, media technologies, releases, broadcasts, tours, practices and communities can all act as way stages marking different eras that come and go. Following the renewed success of the *Doctor Who* series in 2005, for instance, there was 'literaturisation' of *Who* fandom, as a coterie of public figures began talking about their generational memories (Hills 2010b, 55).

For those who stay interested, reflecting on the past helps to narrate a version of individual identity across the changing passage of time. This process is especially evident in activities like collecting. In fans' lives, first runs of television series, music charts, box office schedules or anniversaries can act as markers of time. For the continually dedicated, a box set can become a condensed form of personal biography. Fans are able to mull over their collections as if they were looking at a home scrapbook or photography album, discussing where they were and what they did at the time that the product appeared.[2] Indeed, many people now see their interests as a kind of resource that they periodically dip into when they require renewed support. In Chapter 5, using Hellinger's notion of the family constellation, we considered the idea that fandom as a territory of affect (the 'knowing field') within which individuals can settle or across which they can traverse. Some people enter the field, some depart and many come back.[3] Others linger on the border and remain casual fans. One of the limitations of fandom research has been the tendency to assume that fans are 'one hundred percenters' dedicated to singular objects. As Matt Hills has argued, 'media fandom has been restrictively defined in cultural studies to date as a matter of faithfulness to singular fan objects' (2005, 18). It is common for fans to move nomadically between different interests – a process sometimes called 'serial fandom' – or to engage with multiple objects at the same time.

Hills has examined a process that he calls 'cyclic' fandom: '[It] combines a self-reported level of affective "intensity" and activity with cyclic shifts away from discarded fan objects and towards newly compelling objects' (2005, 803). Drawing on the psychoanalytic theories of Christopher Bollas, Hills describes the cyclic fans' endless chain of fancies as 'aleatory objects': 'The emotional jolt of the aleatory object is seemingly gradually digested and transformed into fan knowledge, as a scene is gradually "sussed out".' (814) The cyclic fan accounts for his serial interest in terms of recapturing a first thrill:

There's always that just 'Wow!' feeling of 'Wow!' at the start. I think that's what I'm addicted to, as you keep going along, that feeling gradually fades away, and then its probably like an addiction, you wanna get that buzz again, so you start heading off in another way. (815)

This interviewee does not seem to be following the emotional process that could fully define him as a fan in the traditional sense. Although his 'buzz' appears fannish, his rapid lack of loyalty indicates that perhaps he does not feel the performer, text or scene quite resonates with his own identity. Indeed, he seems to shy away from commitment to a fan identity, saying, 'I'll, I sort of channel myself into something . . . it's like drilling for oil or something, and stopping before you hit the big . . . if you keep going and going you risk losing yourself within something, basically.' Here the interviewee seems to be afraid of identifying as a *dedicated* fan, perhaps because fans have been so highly (and so wrongly) associated with mass manipulation. Instead, he is always ready to jettison his old interests in favour of new ones and is defined by a process of learning. He identifies continued engagement with a 'problematic' form of identity.

Media technologies and platforms provide a changing context within which many fan engagements are organized. Significant shifts in production, distribution and marketing have favoured particular genres and types of media output at different times. For example, reruns represent a cheap and lucrative form of programming that can significantly change the viewers' relationships with the text in terms of genre expectations, recognition of seriality, emotional responses, and perceptions of its role in their life story (Jenkins 1992, 68–9). Periodic returns can be associated with a kind of nostalgia for earlier eras in the individual's life and/or their society. Discussing *The Empire Strikes Back* (Kershner 1980), Will Brooker said:

There is a sense of nostalgia to this group's enjoyment of *Empire*, based partly on shared memories of what it meant to be a *Star Wars* fan in 1980: the first wave of toys compared to more recent models, the limited scope of home computer games, the discussions in the playground when everyone else had seen the film and you only had the figures. (2002, 56)

Fandom therefore becomes about more than just pursuing an object. Friendships made through the process can become an important in their own right. It can be the pretext for participation in a more general realm of sociocultural activity that characterizes an ageing population.[4] The pleasures associated with later-life fandom are more accessible precisely because ageing fans are unencumbered by the responsibilities of the life cycle. Media fandom does not have to be a youthful infatuation. It can be a life-long love affair. As a form of individual subjectivity, then, fandom can be used to mark time, stay young, look back or carry on.

The discussion above shows that each person pursues his/her hobby during different phases of his/her life cycle. As an example of a sociocultural approach, it explored links between two categories (the fan and the life cycle). In reality, such static theoretic categories do not exist. There are only *real fans* living everyday lives in actual times and places. As a theoretical aggregate of the actions and experiences of those people, fandom has had a long history and varied geography. Different eras and localities have inspired different forms of fan community. Rather than create a typology, it may be better to recognize that the phenomenon is rich in empirical detail. After all, making ahistorical generalizations can sometimes be limiting rather than productive. Different fandoms are necessarily different. Compare, to name but a few, the highly subcultural following of the Grateful Dead, the cineliterate intellectual elite who became fascinated by French New Wave cinema, the adoring crowds who loved Harry Potter, and the avid television enthusiasts who supported *Buffy the Vampire Slayer*, pondered *Lost* or enjoyed *Glee*. In terms of demographics, public profiles, values, practices and other variables, fan bases are all different. Thinking about their actual histories allows us to make connections and discover nuances that previously went unrecognized in fan scholarship. Though there have been some *ethnographies* of particular fan cultures and communities, there are far fewer *historical studies*.[5]

More broadly, fandom itself has a specific history as a social phenomenon. From the movie fanatics of early Hollywood to flash mobs on Youtube, specific cases and examples have captured the zeitgeist at particular times.[6] Fandom itself has also functioned within the wider *context of modernity*, not just as a surface phenomenon, but rather a dynamic constituent. In each specific place and historic moment it has marked out what it means to be a visible social subject and engaged member of the media audience. Of course, individuals identify across multiple fields of social identity (like age, gender, nationality or race) that are equally situated. There is still much work to be done in exploring the ways in which personal fandom has functioned in relation to nationality, family ties, ethnic affiliations and other components of social identity.[7] Because these forms have never been static, their empirical relationship to fandom necessarily places it in a changing historic context. Changing times also make us consider that as modern subjects, fans have – as well as being othered by their own society – *themselves sometimes participated in social othering*. For example, they have taken part in global cultural transformations as tourists or cultural curators attracted to orientalist media spectacles. There is still a great deal of research to be done in inductively understanding this historic dimension of fan culture. The predicament of the phenomenon in an era of globalization offers an example of its changing context. Just as Western popular culture has globally proliferated, a new generation of Anglo-Americans have enjoyed global culture. The current generation is inhabiting a globalized, cosmopolitan popular culture. In Japan the term 'otaku' denotes obsessive consumers who have lost touch with their surroundings; by claiming 'otaku' status, American fans are signalling their allegiance to popular culture in the widest geographical sense.[8] Equally, more studies of fans in cultural contexts other than the English-speaking world may greatly enhance our understanding of fandom (see Gray et al. 2007, 14).

Finally, there are more political approaches to fan phenomena. The joys of being a fan can lead individuals to feel emotionally empowered and ready to contribute to a wider world. Part of the emphasis of fan studies have been to explore exactly what such people – usually as part of a collective – *do* with their personal fandom. Assembled in communities, fans have often aimed to maintain a visible presence and contribute to society. Since they have been misrepresented by the media so frequently, they know that their collective representation can help determine how others both see them and see their heroes. Not only have fans have often spoken out against their own restriction or exploitation; they have also lobbied TV networks, record labels and others to reverse decisions to drop their favourite shows and performers. In his book *Convergence Culture*, Henry Jenkins (2008) highlighted this type of fan activity. He showed that because fans in specific communities often hold the same values, they have been able to fight for their own specific causes. Various organizations, celebrities and alliances have, for example, mobilized younger people to vote.

Jenkins views the fan base as a collective agent *in its own right* that has the autonomy, creativity and power to achieve goals. In an era of social media and reality television, researchers have shown that fans are not only *active* but have also been political subjects who could *operate as activists*.[9] Fans at play can develop skills useful to political campaigning and activism. Blogging, for example, is 'spoiling' the American government (Jenkins 2008, 226). Lines between popular culture and politics seem more blurred than ever because the same skills which consumers develop by participating online as fans can be used to pursue political change. Communities can mobilize to create box office hits or to vote for particular politicians (234). In this environment, pop culture matters precisely because it does not *seem* to be about politics.

To support his ideas, Jenkins has focused on two particular kinds of activism. **Narrative activism** is the notion that fans can disrupt unfolding shows like *American Idol* and other broadcasts by influencing events that are happening on-screen (53). Another type of fan activism refers to the visible deployment of iconic figures for political uses. **Avatar activism**, then, for Jenkins, represents the way that 'citizens from around the world are mobilizing icons and myths from popular culture as resources for political speech' (Jenkins 2010, online). This form of protest captures the way that iconic figures have been used to make political statements. It is named after an incident in February 2010, during which Palestinian, Israeli and international activists painted themselves blue – to resemble the Nav'l beings from film 'Avatar' (Cameron 2009) – then marched through the occupied village of Bil'n. The protesters were filmed with camcorders and the footage circulated on YouTube, sparking global controversy. Not all avatar activism is, however, initiated, organized or executed by fans. For example, the Fathers 4 Justice campaigner who dressed as Batman and scaled Buckingham Palace in 2004 may not have been one. Some campaigns, however, clearly *do* connect with fan communities. One example is the Harry Potter Alliance, an organization that used the ethos of Harry Potter's character from famous franchise to mobilize over 100,000 young people to raise money to campaign for workers rights, protest against genocide in Africa, support gay marriage and combat the disaster in Haiti (see Jenkins 2008, 206 and Jenkins 2010). The most visible aspect of such protest is, in effect, *a spectacularly politicized form of cosplay* that re-articulates the affective charge of stars or famous fictional characters to spark media interest, engage audiences and prompt political action. However, according to Jenkins, cultural activism is not a universal answer. The problem now is that new media have increased the opportunity to pursue diverse tastes *at the same time as dividing* social groups within public sphere.

We can see from the latest phase of Jenkins' work that the active audience tradition is about fitting fandom for a role to which it *notionally* connects: once the textual poacher, now the political activist. In the absence of there being one definitive truth about fandom, the benefit of this approach is it goes some way to habilitating the public image of phenomenon. It is, in some ways, rather like an academic version of the charity drives that fan clubs hold: as much as any general good consequences it may cause, it is also a very public way of encouraging outsiders to think again about fans as progressive social beings. Framing fandom as a counter-culture may also encourage existing fans to see their role as socially worthwhile, to *envisage themselves as political subjects* and to align with radical causes.

As a deductive practice, the dominant strand in fan studies also raises key issues and dangers. Fandom research has always held in tension the parallel questions of how to *understand* and *best represent* its object of study. Those two concerns are inevitably linked, especially since total objectivity is impossible and obsolete (the imperative is to *change* the world not just understand it). However, it is also true that the history of discussion about fandom, whether negative (as pathology) or positive (as celebration), has been characterized by *selective and partial representation* both inside and outside the academy. What has been missing has been a will to *momentarily* depoliticize the object and simply to understand it *for what it is,* as a first base for political support work. Without belittling fans, perhaps we should accept that fandom is a positive and adaptive form of human identification that has survived and transformed in each new regime of media production. The danger of the fan activist agendum is that it will offer an idealistic perspective that romanticizes its object as a utopian cultural form, and forgets that fans often *collude* with other agencies to pursue their ends. A focus, instead, on fan complicity could help to demonstrate that fans often participate in power relations, even where they do not set the agenda or have the upper hand. Collusion is not always an act of subservience; it can be viewed as an expedient practice of mutual development.

Fan studies has come a long way. It is important to realize that each of the methodological perspectives discussed in this concluding chapter has its own strengths and weaknesses. Sociocultural approaches bracket off the situatedness of fandom in order to consider recurrent elements of the phenomenon and how they connect with common dimensions of identity. Historical accounts carefully refrain from generalization, but may be swayed by available sources or fail to grasp wider connections. Political work, exemplified by the research of Henry Jenkins, recognizes that its object is caught up in an ongoing social debate and therefore habilitates fandom's image, enabling individual fans to recognize their own agency and speak from new position. However, the active audience tradition has sometimes tended to *reduce* fandom to a progressive social position. At worst it has perceived fandom in a utopian, idealistic fashion, confusing contingent associations with intrinsic functions. The way that fandom has been academically discussed has sometimes had less to do with analytical explanation and more with policing stereotypes. If psychologists have misguidedly framed fandom as a form of borderline insanity associated with intensified consumer behaviour, fan studies has treated its object as form of social identity that is increasingly socially accepted.

Evidently, as fans, we are not stooges. We are human beings with the full range of human capabilities. This does not mean, however, that our primary aim is *always* political in the traditional sense: to poach, subvert or negate corporate culture or intellectual property. In reality, fandom is inspired by media output but not restricted to it. Its concerns escape the matrix of corporate production by raising more humanist issues: seeking pleasure, exploring creativity and making social connections. Challenging widespread misunderstandings about fandom remains an important project; doing so by paying exclusive attention to a narrow spectrum of practices *deemed* creative or political by our research paradigms, though, appears to lose sight of fans' core motivations.

Fandom as a discursive construct

I took up an invitation in February 2012 to present a keynote speech on music fandom at the annual MARS conference in Seinäjoki, Finland. MARS is a mixed event that brings together academics, students and members of the Finnish music industry. My hosts explained that immediately after my speech a Finnish music journalist would interview me on stage and they would stream the interview live online. The keynote went well on the day. My interviewer's questions then proceeded along certain lines. He wondered if I had been a fan, asked me to explain the links between fandom and religion, explored fandom as a gendered issue, and raised the spectre of John Lennon's killer: 'Is there something wrong with our brains when we are fans? Because there's lots of obsession – mania – kind of disturbance?' It was, sadly, all rather typical fodder for non-academic discussion. I managed to ask my interviewer which musicians *he* liked as a fan, if *he* saw fandom as religion, and who *he* worshipped. At the end of the Q and A, with the cameras still rolling, he whipped out a signed photograph of Tom Jones and pressed it to my forehead, saying, 'Tom will bless you! Tom will make you happy! Tom will save your life! Now go on with your life and be a happier person!' All I could do by that point was be a good sport, so I said, 'I've had the benediction now.'

My interviewer's not-so-subtle antics were a reminder that maybe we should not take fandom too seriously. After all, if you cannot laugh at yourself, what have you got left? Beyond that, though, they implied that there was something rather questionable about a professional scholar spending over a decade of his time analysing something that seemed so trivial. The episode reflected a continuing divergence between popular and academic perceptions of fandom. Where do all the negative ideas about fandom come from? Even as we shift further and further into a digital culture, the legacies of television, radio, cinema and sound recording significantly define the ways in which fandom has been understood and lived. The critiques of modern mass culture that were associated with various academics and commentators – notably Theodor Adorno – secured a socially autonomous space for critical theory, but did so in a way that made damaging assumptions about the place of the audience. Those critiques located fans in various ways: as prime representatives of the masses; as consumers alienated by broadcast media and separated from cultural production; as sexually repressed, clinically obsessed or spiritually misguided; as crowds of unruly sychophants or isolated, infantilized, fetishists. More than that, though, the critics implied, first, that fans' lives were characterized by daydreams, delusions and fantasies, and, second, that they focused on an imagined relationship to compensate for social inadequacy or personal loss. It was suggested that as supposedly vulnerable and unfortunate human subjects, fans could be broken out of their predicament by showing it to them for what it was: contesting the merit of mass spectacles, celebrating elite cultural forms, shaming bad taste, educating the untutored or deliberately pursuing obscurity. This discursive framework contested the production of mass commodities by denigrating their audiences. If it offered more powerful roles to some speakers than others, it nevertheless provided a place from which everyone could speak. Fans could talk about their interests in terms of obsession, addiction and manipulation. More than the vitriol of a few lofty academics, the framework therefore *shaped a shared way of seeing everyday culture that spread well beyond lecture theatres into the rest of society.* Adopting the stance allowed people to hierarchically align themselves with the elite minority that had always contested common taste (see Marshall 1997). Posited as both mysterious and familiar, in this scenario fandom was not so much 'alien' as an attributed form of inferiority or sickness striking at the vulnerable sections of modern society: the women, the working class, the masses, the marginalized, the new generation.

In the recent decades, some things have changed. Scholars working inside the academy have created a social space beyond fan clubs and forums where fandom can be explored and expressed without falling back on the disrespectful discourses that have dominated public life. Yet we are still, nevertheless, in the shadow of mass culture thinking. Society has not yet fully jettisoned it. Many ordinary fans still speak through it, whether belittling others or questioning themselves. By championing fans as creative, productive and political subjects, the active audience tradition has *contested the mass culture critique by inverting it*. However, to borrow from a recent piece by Gunkel and Gournelos (2012, 5), 'any attempt at transgression is always and inescapably contextualized and regulated by the very system or structures from which it endeavours to break away'. Fully breaking away would mean sorting through our concepts and language to avoid both mass culture perspectives and their aftermath, but to that we need new concepts. Language is a starting point. Throughout this book, I aimed to use the words 'dedicated' and 'fascinated' rather than 'obsessed' or 'fixated'. However, the trouble with 'clean' language is that fans do not always use it. They often retain value-loaded terms like 'pilgrimage' or 'obsession' to register fandom's emotional impact.[10]

Although fandom has historically been seen as a scandalous, emotionally exuberant form of attachment to media culture, one of the interesting things about it is that *it has never been a recognized term for seriously scandalous objects*. Fandom was categorically separated from fanaticism, which was the result of ideological immersion. In the stricter usage, a person can be a fan of transgressive or taboo entertainment, say, the film 'Cannibal Holocaust' (Deodato, 1980), but they could only be 'fanatical' about Adolph Hitler.[11] This made fandom itself seem 'safe', a funny and tame category. In discussing fandom we are perhaps grappling indirectly with multiculturalism and the 'end' of traditional politics. The anxieties of a multicultural world continue to focus on fandom as a way to broach the issues of social difference. It can function as a proxy for those who want a wider discussion about forms of personal attachment that cause social anxiety: fundamentalism, fanaticism, fascism, fixation and blind loyalty. Even though various social commentators still use the term 'fan' to talk about those things, as I have shown in this book it is really about none of them. Fandom is about consumption *and* production, resistance *and* collusion. It reflects circulating assumptions, subjective feelings, shared experiences, common practices, imagined communities, collective values, social formations and group actions. *Sympathetic research will continue to separate fandom from all the things that uninformed commentators misrecognize it as being.*

In various ways, fandom means *making social connections and exploring pleasures in the context of a shared media culture*. Texts and performances provide a common territory, a way to recognize ourselves through the prism of our passions, but experiencing them is only part of a process that is immensely personal and yet wonderfully social at the same time.

Is a master theory of fandom, then, either possible or desirable? Over a decade ago, Cheryl Harris (1998, 4) argued that fan research has tended to closely examine practices but failed to successfully integrate them with the theoretical models that explain fan behaviour. There remains a sense in which fan studies seems to have given up on or perhaps lost sight of that goal. 'After a period when various rival models of fan practices have emerged in competition with each other', argues Nick Couldry, 'we may now be on the threshold of a different phase where the interpretive challenge is different: how to find the right [theoretical] mix . . . for interpreting *this particular* fan practice?' (2007b, 140) A master theory of fandom may never be found, but it remains a worthy goal to understand the phenomenon as a special bundle of processes that interact in contingent ways. As we naturally bring them together, those processes inspire delightful experiences and meaningful pleasures.

Glossary

Aca-fan ('Aca-fen', plural): an academic who usually teaches in cultural studies, studies fandom, supports the cultural legitimacy of fandom as a social identity and proudly attests to being a fan in his/her own life and work. In that sense, although academically initiated, aca-fen are *fans first* (by experience, choice and proclamation) and use their academic role to support the wider acceptance of fandom.

Active audience John Fiske's term for an audience that does much to *appropriate* popular culture. The term primarily makes sense through its opposite (the supposed 'passive' audience of the mass culture critique). It makes less sense as an oppositional term in the internet era where audience members have become users and their 'activity' is facilitated by commercial platforms.

Affect the idea popularized by Lawrence Grossberg that behind the emotional resonance of ideas and media products is a transferable substrate that makes things matter. Affect is often used by some as a shorthand for 'emotion' in academic discussion, but the term also has connotations that connect it to hegemony. It describes a form of the socially-organized energy that compels individuals to express feelings and/or act *in particular directions*.

Affective economics Henry Jenkins' idea that the makers of media franchises such as *American Idol* systematically capitalize on and exploit central mechanisms by which fans emotionally identify with their heroes. For Jenkins, affective economics represents a new configuration of marketing.

Affective fallacy: the contested idea that those who are emotionally persuaded by a text will lose all insight and objectivity. In the era before fan studies emerged, the affective fallacy kept some scholars from declaring their fandom.

Agency: the ability of real and specific individuals or groups to make a difference in society. Agency is often described in relation to what seems to be its opposite: structure (rules, constraints, obligations). In reality, agency and structure are related: structures have sometimes shifted to accommodate fans, but fans have also used their agency to fulfil their structural roles.

Amateur theory: the propensity of ordinary people to come up with ideas outside of formal educational frameworks. Amateur theory has different aims than formal, for example, scientific, theory.

Anomie: the feeling of rootlessness and alienation that sociologists have described in modern society.

Anti-fans: a complex term developed by Jonathan Gray to describe audience members who express a strong disapproval of a particular text. The term is problematic as 'anti-fandom' indirectly links disgruntled viewers to fandom. By definition, fans of any kind love pleasures they get from their texts. There are two further issues. First, fans can be highly critical of their own texts if those texts fail to continue supporting their pleasures. Second, despite the appearance of the term's literal meaning, 'anti-fans' are not necessarily *against the fans* of the text they hate – although in various ways they may often be that too.

Apa: an acronym for 'amateur press association', a term that emerged within sci-fi fandom to describe a kind of group letter circulated between members in which each member writes a contribution and copies it to every other member. Apazines were a form of fanzine (see Jenkins 2006, 64).

Auteur: a leading individual who leaves a consistent creative stamp or signature on the media products that he/she helps to design.

Auto-didactic: pertaining to self-teaching.

Auto-ethnography: the self-reflexive academic study of *one's own* behaviour by subjecting one's tastes, values, attachments and investments to a rigorous and systematic analysis. It attempts to answer the question of what can be learned about fandom by critically examining how one performs the identity oneself.

Avatar activism: Henry Jenkins' term for how the public uses figures from popular culture as a spectacular resource in political protest. It can range from dressing up as a fictional character to attract media attention to using the name

and ethos of a franchise in order to mobilize its fans.

Black box fallacy: the idea that convergence will eventually mean we have only one piece of media hardware with a screen to deliver the entire array of media content. In reality, although *content* has converged, the desire for immediate consumption means that individuals use *various* hardware devices to engage depending on where they are: laptops, iPods, TVs, BlackBerrys or PCs, for instance (Jenkins 2008, 15).

Blank slate: the idea that star images are essentially empty vessels (blank slates) devoid of meaning that function as canvases upon which audience members can *project* different meanings and desires on the basis of their own needs.

BNF: a 'big namefan' who has a large following of his/her own. Usually this is a label applied by other fans, sometimes as an insult. BNFs can include fan club leaders or 'superfans' who participate in media stories about fandom (see Zubernis & Larsen 2012, 30). Also see **egoboo**.

Boosting: a process in which fans collectively lobby media producers to float the careers and raise the profiles of their favourite performers. Boosting relates to **totemism**.

Brands: intellectual properties that symbolize the key qualities and values of particular media franchises.

Brand community: an industry term for a group of loyal consumers. Fans represent a rather unruly brand community.

Camp: an aesthetic or performative sensibility that means taking delight in artificiality and frivolity.

Canon: the media universe created by the makers of a text; a set of texts chosen by critics or prominent fans as the best or most indicative of a particular cultural field. To understand any genre or area of media output requires you to be familiar with its canon.

Casual: industry terminology for a drifting, unengaged broadcast viewer.

Casual fan: a person who may self-describe as a fan and repeatedly return to a particular cultural interest, but does not sustain any further kind of dedication.

Celebrity: used to describe a form of social status conferred on a celebrated individual ('he coped . . .'), or, more recently, to categorize famous people ('celebrities'). *Stars* are purportedly famous for their charisma and talent (skills such as singing or movie acting); celebrities are, classically, however, famous for being famous. Mimetic media have always encouraged a fascination with celebrity, but this interest has changed in form and value as the role of the media in society has shifted.

Character rape: an idea circulating within fan communities that the first series of a show produced the only proper interpretation of the personalities of particular TV characters, and that experienced fans should police later re-workings created by either media professionals or other fans (see Jenkins 2006, 56).

Chronotope: a term suggested by Mikhail Bakhtin to denote a specific segment of time and geographic place found in literature. Fans who are nostalgic for particular eras can select media products that come from or reference those periods.

Closet fans: fans who keep their particular fandom private because it appears to contradict public norms or their individual public image. Closet fandom can relate to issues of genre, taste, social identity and cultural capital.

Collective intelligence: an idea Henry Jenkins ascribes to Pierre Lévy, suggesting that fans are, as a group, harnessing new media technologies to rapidly discover, collate and circulate information that individuals, by themselves, find impossible to piece together.

Communitas: an idea proposed by anthropologist Victor Turner which suggests that individuals can feel blissfully united at large, festive public events.

Convergence: a complex process of change in the landscape of contemporary media that entails a paradigm shift towards the flow of the same content across different media platforms, the migration of audiences and new co-operation between the different media industries. Convergence is happening in a relatively unplanned environment where the hierarchical relationship between the different kinds of media is changing. It makes the consumer responsible in seeking out new information and connections, and it involves the interplay of corporate-driven elements – like franchising and synergy – and consumer-driven elements (see Jenkins 2008). Also see **black box fallacy.**

Cosplay ('costume play'): dressing up as characters from popular culture. This is not unique to fandom and is perhaps not as common in fandom as supposed. The pleasures of cosplay are complementary to those of fandom. Impersonators and cosplay enthusiasts cannot simply be understood as extreme fans. Furthermore, cosplay is encouraged by photographers and cameramen because it visually distinguishes fans from other audience members. Fans in unusual dress, however, also maintain fan stereotyping. For these reasons cosplay forms a controversial corner of fandom.

Contagion: the idea that individuals begin their personal fandom through contact with existing fans.

Crowd funding: the online practice of drawing on fans and others to collectively fund projects.

Crowd sourcing: the online practice of collective planning that draws on fan communities.

Cult: a term with many connotations that references unusual cultural interests and/or social formations.

Cultural capital: a term developed by the late French sociologist Pierre Bourdieu to describe how people use learned affiliations of taste to place themselves just above anyone who is close to them on a social hierarchy. Cultural capital operates between fan cultures (some, such as Elvis fandom, are seen as relatively uncool), but also within fan cultures (as 'hip' fans show they are more 'in the know').

Cult fandom: fandom for a cult media product.

Cult media product: a media product that continually inspires a particularly dedicated and socially organized set of fans. *Doctor Who* is one example.

Deduction: an approach to research that first uses theory to create expectations and then contrasts those expectations to data from the real world. Also see **induction**.

Digital natives: the generation born roughly after 1990, who have grown up within the environment of digital media.

Discourses: loosely, shared ways of talking about particular things. The French theorist Michel Foucault developed a more strict approach to the term and suggested that discourses produce accepted versions of the truth in order to govern specific objects in society. Foucault was interested in the rules defining who could contribute to specific discourses and saw them as coherent power structures that managed their objects despite changing historical contexts.

Drillable media: Jason Mittell's term for complex and engaging media forms that invite dedicated fan engagement (see Mittell in Jenkins et al. 2013).

Effervescence: Emile Durkheim's term for the intense emotional response that followers have when their heroes offer them attention. Also see **affect, totemism** and **symbolic economy**.

Egoboo: a derogatory term used in sci-fi fandom for the practice of aiming to enhance one's own reputation rather than give glory to the text and support the community. Also see **BNF**.

Emotional capital: industry terminology for a loyal consumer's investment or brand's potential for that investment. The term references Bourdieu's notion of cultural capital.

Empirical: involving observations from the field. Empirical researchers do their data gathering in the 'real world' outside of the academy.

Erotomania: a clinical delusion in which the patient believes, without rational cause, that someone (usually of higher social status) is in love with them.

Essentialism: the tendency to locate the meaning and significance of something *in the thing itself*, suggesting that it is a natural expression. An example would be folk song collector John Lomax's 1934 claim that the blue guitar player 'Leadbelly is a nigger to the core of his being' (Hamilton 2007, 92). While it is easy to see Lomax's claim as the product of racist ideologies circulating in society, the challenge is to spot more recent essentialist claims and use them to uncover the ideologies they promote. Essentialism hides the way that discourses and other frames of interpretation can shape understanding *before* acts of perception. As a rhetorical device, it is associated with deeply held notions of identity and processes of othering.

Ethnography: the study of human culture in the situation of its occurrence. It is practiced when the ethnographers immerse themselves in the experience of a particular cultural world.

Fan: a self-identified enthusiast, devotee or follower of a particular media genre, text, person or activity.

Fanagement: fan-focused management online akin to a revamped version of word-of-mouth advertising.

Fan base: the entire group of fans who support a particular person or text. This group can include closet fans who are not in the fan community.

Fanboy: a male fan marked out by his public enthusiasm. The term raises issues of both gender and maturity. It therefore stereotypes fans, but has also been 'rescued' by some as a proud self-designation.

Fan community: a socially organized group of fans who share one hero, text or genre and then network with each other.

Fandom: a way of identifying oneself on a deep level as being a fan and enacting that role (e.g. 'My fandom for manga cartoons'). I describe this as *personal* fandom; a shorthand for the fan community: 'Many fans feel freer in fandom than outside to express themselves, ask questions, and discuss alternative viewpoints' (Jenkins 2006, 85).

Fandom research: the entirety of academic scholarship that has taken fans and fandom as its object of study. Fandom research is older and larger than **fan studies** and can include Adorno's work on music listeners, pre-1990s fan research, articles in psychology journals and other such material.

Fanfic: a genre of fictional, often amateur writing created by fans that includes slash. Some subgenres are h/c (hurt/comfort stories), Mpreg (main character gets pregnant), deathfic (main character dies), curtainfic (characters do mundane tasks together, like buying curtains), episode fix, badfic (parodies), missing scene, AU (alternative universe), crossover (draws together characters from different series), fluff (light erotica that is low on plot), PWP (porn without plot) and kink (graphic, alternative sexual material). Also see **slash**.

Fangirl: a female fan, sometimes a fan of a BNF rather than simply of a celebrity, marked out by her public enthusiasm. Fangirl is also used as a verb ('she *fangirled* that writer'). The term raises issues of both gender and maturity. It therefore stereotypes fans, but has also been 'rescued' by some as a proud self-designation.

Fannish: typically, pertaining to fandom (e.g. 'That was a fannish thing to say').

Fanon: details or character readings contributed by members of the fan community that add to or delimit interpretations within the *meta-text*.

Fan-scholar: an expert from the fan community who gradually takes up the trappings of scholarly authority.

Fan studies: an ongoing tradition of sympathetic fandom research within cultural studies that was catalysed by Henry Jenkins' 1992 book *Textual Poachers*. Fan studies centrally aims to understand, recognize and represent fans in ways that are advantageous to their wider positioning in society. Such work has included, for example, questioning media representations, celebrating fan creativity and paying attention to practices like slash fiction writing, online campaigning and spoiling. Also see **fandom research**.

Fansubbing: video subtitling of foreign material by fans. Fansubbing has been facilitated by both the increasing globalization of popular culture and cheap video editing technology. For example, Anglo-American fans have 'fansubbed' a lot of Japanese manga cartoons. Fansubbers often dispute the meanings of translated words and which ones to leave in the original language.

Fanwank: a term of abuse for irrelevant continuity references thrown into stories specifically to please fans. Used as a verb it means the creation of scenarios (usually in fanfic) that account for continuity errors (see Hills 2010a, 58–9).

Fanzine: officially unauthorized, printed non-profit amateur publications created and circulated by fans to form communities and express fan interests. Before the internet took over some of the functions formerly filled by fanzines there was an extensive culture of fanzines. There are various subgenres too: letterzines, fictionzines.

Filk songs: songs, created by fans, that are primarily sung at fan conventions. Filking is the creation of filk songs (see Jenkins 1992, 250).

Focus group: a small, temporarily-assembled group of people interviewed by the researcher about their opinions, concerns or habits.

Folk culture: ordinary traditional practices like bee keeping, ale brewing and barn dancing that began before the era of mass production and remain outside of its commercial framework.

Franchise: an extensive corporate media property, usually based on a central narrative and fictional universe that contains a resonant social myth, begun in one medium (as a book or film, for example) and spun out across a range of different products and media outlets. *Star Wars*, *Doctor Who* and *Harry Potter* are classic examples. Franchises form meta-textual playgrounds for interested fans.

Game modding: the user-based reworking of personal computer games such as role-playing or real-time strategy challenges.

Genfic (sometimes '**gen**'): 'general interest' fanfic that does not dwell on romantic relationships between the characters.

Habitus: Pierre Bourdieu's term for a memory of learned pre-dispositions that allows its owner to display cultural capital and gain social status. Habitus comes from upbringing and education. Sarah Thornton (1995) updated the term to suggest that habitus resides not in the individual's head, but in the niche media of their cultural pursuit (in her case electronic dance magazines).

Heimat: the secure feeling of being at home in your own fandom (see Sandvoss 2005, 64). Also see **knowing field**.

Hegemony: Marxist Antonio Gramsci's idea that the public is led by alliances of ruling bodies (such as the monarchy, the church, corporations or charities) that come together to give ordinary people their desired cultural delights. This creates a process of *consented domination* that reduces the possibility of revolutionary change.

Het: a genre of fanfic focused on heterosexual relations between the main characters.

High culture: past culture that is selected by critics and educators to represent the greatest achievement of humanity or most sincere expression of the human spirit. Traditionally high culture has included opera, ballet and plays by William Shakespeare. The appreciation of high culture tends to entail a process of cultivation of one's faculties. This is opposed to mass or popular culture which is purported to be immediately accessible. However, popular culture has to involve a gradual or periodic process of social cultivation, for example, in getting audiences to hear rap or punk as music, or to accept camcorder footage as cinematic entertainment.

Hyperdiegesis: the process of continually constructing an extended imaginary world that forms a backdrop to the text.

Hyper-reality: a term that emerged from Jean Baudrillard's writing to describe a world in which mediated image and reputation precede and govern what we expect to find in real life.

Hysteria: an outdated clinical term which originally described 'emotionally excessive', anxious individuals, but was hijacked to describe live crowds of excited fans. Also see **mass culture**, **affect**, **contagion**, **effervescence** and **squee**.

Ideal type: a notion, associated with Max Weber, which draws attention to the way that any generalized construct can affirm a false truth by focusing attention on what is typical. For instance, the inevitable variety of personal identifications erased any generalization about how fans identify. Weber's notion points out the mistake of generalization: what is frequent is not all that there is, nor is it necessarily definitive.

Induction: the approach to study in which researchers, unencumbered by theory, observe patterns in the world from which they build new ideas. Also see **deduction**.

Imagined memory: a fan's conception of one of their star's early performances from a time and place before the performer was famous.

Interactivity: industry parlance for consumer participation in new media organized on industry terms.

Introjection: a term associated with Kleinian psychoanalysis that describes the way individuals use others as role models.

Knowing field: the idea that personal and collective fandom means occupying a terrain of 'emotional knowing' above a threshold level of affect.

Knowledge community: an idea that Henry Jenkins ascribes to Pierre

Lévy, here suggesting that fan bases operate to rapidly harness collective intelligence online.

Liminality: the idea that certain threshold spaces can operate under social rules that are in opposition to the norm.

Literaturisation: a term used by Matt Hills (2010a, 55) to describe the way that a fan phenomenon can suddenly become subject material for a range of popular publications (memoires, comedy confessionals, celebrity magazine pieces).

Literary biography: the genre of biography that reads its subject's life in relation to his/her work.

Lovemarks: industry terminology for brands passionately supported by loyal consumers.

Loyal: industry terminology for a fan of a particular media product.

Mass culture: mass produced capitalist commercial culture. The idea of mass culture has been used by capitalism's critics to describe the empty predictability that comes when creativity is reduced to making the templates for formulaic manufactured products.

Media active: a term used for anyone born roughly after 1970 who grew up in an environment of post-broadcasting media, where ordinary people could use devices like the video cassette recorder to collect and store media output.

Media cult: the popular term for a fan phenomenon based on a particular media product or famous person.

Media effects argument: a position that connects the consumption of controversial media material with an individual's socially detrimental actions. By placing blame on the media for 'copy-cat' violence, such arguments fail to extend agency and social responsibility to audience members. Instead they confuse distaste with social danger, call for censorship, and make media products convenient scapegoats for deep social problems.

Media literacy: the idea that viewers can be equipped as citizens with particular discursive resources to help them understand the media and use their understanding in a socially responsible way.

Meta-text: the meaningfully whole constellation of texts that encompasses one phenomenon. For example, a rock star's meta-text might include his/her music, publicity, endorsements and biography. Franchises are meta-textual phenomena. Crucially, the boundaries of the meta-text are created, disputed, shared and policed with each fan community. Also see **primary text, fanon.**

Methodology: an umbrella terms for the particular way in which the researcher critically justifies his/her investigative approach. It can involve making a reasoned choice of research philosophy (see 'objectivity') and research design: justifying the sample procedure for example, or saying why a case study or comparison was chosen. It can also include the self-conscious choice of particular research methods (like interviewing) and ethical decisions such as whether to make private data public.

Mimetic media: media that hold up a mirror to life. Usually the term refers to electronic media like television.

MMORPGs: Massively Multiplayer Online Roleplaying Games like World of Warcraft. Some, such as *The Lord of the Rings Online* and *Star Wars Galaxies*, have been based on existing franchises.

Monofan: somebody who, for now, is only a fan of one famous person or media text. Sometimes these people are known colloquially as '100%ers'.

MUDs: Multi-User Dungeons. They represented an early use of the internet for immersive role-playing games.

Mythology: a constellation of myths and ideas that surrounds at least one text and/or its maker.

Mythos: a set of explanations or beliefs derived from myth that express a particular understanding.

Narrative activism: Henry Jenkins' idea that fans can disrupt media spectacles as they unfold by influencing the behavior of their participants on-screen.

Neutrosemy: a term connected with Cornel Sandvoss's work that suggests fans create different meanings by defining the boundaries of their texts.

Object: in fandom, the specific person or text attracting a fan. The term derives from psychological theories of attachment; in research, the precise thing being studied.

Objectivity: the idea that a universally agreed knowledge can be built from a seemingly impartial form of scholarly investigation.

Other: a person or social group who gets cast as inscrutable, exotic and absolutely different. The social process of creating an other is called **othering**.

Parasocial interaction: the idea that broadcast performances, at worst, misleadingly invite fans to believe that they are in an intimate, two-way relationship to a famous stranger when actually alone in a world of fantasy. The idea offers fans limited **agency**, forgets that fandom involves a range of activities, and misleadingly restricts it to the private sphere. In contrast, **fan studies** has shown the fans are socially and culturally active and also

that celebrity following is only one part of what they do.

Paratext: items beyond a media text, such as reviews or trailers, that we meaningfully connect with to inform our readings.

Participatory culture: the idea that the distinction between active producers and passive consumers has been reduced or sometimes even erased as both are now actively engaged as players in the flow of new media. It does not entirely negate the power relations between and within the two groups, but it does reformulate them (Jenkins 2008, 3). Participation is shaped by cultural and social protocols. The idea implies a kind of utopianism, in that previous incarnations of the media (cinema, TV and radio) historically appeared to promote less active one way relationships between members of the mass audience and broadcast media.

Performance: the enactment of behaviour that is designed to create an emotional effect in others who, when collected, are called an audience. Performance can have a complex relationship to agency, textuality, ritual and reality. While it can be recorded, a performance must happen in a specific place and time. It also elicits counter-performances. Stars perform, fans counter-perform and fans can also perform for other fans. Attention to performance moves us away from individuals to think about social relations.

Personal fandom: the fannish identity and experience of an individual person. Also see **fandom**.

Polemic: a contentious argument, usually couched in essay form, that attempts to dispute the worth of opposing beliefs. Polemicists present controversial theses as intellectual provocations. They often use bias as an opening gambit and rhetorical tool.

Polysemy: the capacity for a text to openly invite a wide range of different interpretations. Polysemic texts can be read in very different ways by different audience members; less polysemic texts tend to engender fewer interpretations.

Popular culture: a complex, politicized term for culture that is meaningful to large sections of the ordinary public. Before the modern era, what we now consider as folk culture was a central part of popular culture. More recently, popular culture has come to denote the mass culture that is meaningfully accepted and taken to heart by the public. Although popular culture has traditionally been opposed to high culture, the distinction is increasingly disputed, not least since high culture has been commercially marketed. Popular culture is derived from the commercial culture that helps ordinary people find performances, myths and ideas that speak to their own identities. For example, the dystopian 1968 film *Planet of the Apes* became part of popular culture not because it was a major studio release, but because it showed that science and technology could not save society in the absence of grounding moral values.

Primary text: the text that is central to understanding why a celebrity or other fan phenomenon matters. For example, J. K. Rowling's first book, *Harry Potter and the Philosopher's Stone*, is a primary text of Harry Potter fandom. Also see **meta-text.**

Producerly: an adjective used in John Fiske's work to describe texts that lay themselves more open to audience appropriation.

Projection: a psychological process in which an individual's own emotions are disavowed and ascribed to the outside world. For example, a suicidal person may perceive that the planet is on the verge of catastrophe. Projection can mean seeing the world through an invisible prism of your early childhood learnings and unconsciously perceiving strangers in relation to the roles set by family members.

Public sphere: an unfettered space of discussion in the social world where ordinary individuals can come together to persuade each other in forums that are outside of government control and can have significant political consequences. Developed by Jürgen Habermas, the term public sphere generally refers to a space of free public discussion.

Qualitative research: research that uses language as data to decide its arguments. Qualitative researchers gather words from their respondents and look at their expressed meanings, thoughts, perspectives and beliefs.

Reading: the individual and collective process in which audience members make meaning from texts.

Reading formation: a constituency within the audience who share certain expectations of the text based on their particular 'diet' of media consumption.

Reductionism: mistaken acceptance of theories that only explain part of a phenomenon instead of a full explanation.

Ritual: behaviour that is regularly repeated for the purpose of comforting the participants.

RPG: Role-playing game that allows fans to immerse themselves in a fictional universe.

RPF: Real person fiction created by fans who write about actual stars and celebrities by putting them into unreal scenarios.

Scholar-fan: an academic who wears his or her fandom in public and primarily identifies as a fan.

Semiotics: an approach to research that analyses each object for signs of its meaning. The researcher's role is to decode how the text is communicating and what it is saying. He/she therefore studies its chain of signifiers (surface representations) and signifieds (associated meanings).

Shippers: fans who are much more interested in the triumphs and tribulations of romantic relationships than other aspects of the dramatic text.

Slash: a form of fiction created by fans that takes pairs of same sex (usually male) characters who are portrayed as heterosexual in their film and TV shows and then charts how they negotiate intimate relationships with each other. It is disputed whether, in terms of its content, slash – which is named after 'K/S' or 'Kirk/Spock' fiction based on *Star Trek* – is a form of feminine erotica or gay genre. For women, slash is an alternative universe in which male characters can discover the emotional playfulness, nurturing and sensitivity that they may lack in the real world.

Solicited and unsolicited data: these are opposite forms of raw research data. The first is summoned into existence by the investigation, for example, in fresh interview situations. The second consists or words or other information that is already recorded elsewhere (such as newspaper stories and Websites) from which the researcher simply finds quotes.

Spoiler: information usually related to plots or contest winners that, once known, ends the central mystery of a narrative.

Spoiling: the act of exposing a **spoiler**.

Spreadable media: social media that lever fan participation to propagate culture online (see Jenkins et al. 2013).

Squee: letting out a squeal of adoration. This word began as a term of abuse.

Squick: to 'gross out' a fanfic reader with alternative and explicit sexual material.

Subbing: see **fansubbing**.

Subject: the individual human being as discerned by theory or research.

Subject position: a role offered by the text that restrictively acts to orientate and position the individual reader. The idea emerged in film studies from the notion that texts and their meanings do cultural work by hailing the spectator.

Symbolic economy: the shared constellation of assumptions and *felt* relationships that undergirds fans' manifest responses to totemic figures. Also see **totemism**.

Synergy: a harmonious and lucrative relationship between media outlets and products based on mutual promotion.

Text: a meaningful set of codes.

Textual Determinism: the idea that what is in a text can determine its meaning, regardless of its viewers. Also see **reading** and **media effect arguments**.

Textual Poaching: a metaphor derived from Michel de Certeau's work and pursued by Jenkins (1992) to suggest that fans do not always follow the meanings intended by authors, but can instead appropriate texts for their own ends. Also see **textual determinism**.

Textuality: the ability to interpret anything as being a meaningful set of codes. If we confer textual status on to performances, personalities or events, we can read them as meaningful sets of codes.

Totem: a focus of religious attention. Also see **totemism**.

Totemism: the capacity for a star to acquire, guide and lead their fan base. In lay terms, a totemic star is one who has the charisma to magnetize a committed audience. Totemism is a term that emerges from Emile Durkheim's classic sociological work on religion.

Transmedia: literally 'between different media'. A trans-media story asks fans to examine different resources such as Websites, video games, films and comic books to find out the information necessary to forward the plot (see Jenkins 2008).

Unsolicited data: see **solicited and unsolicited data**.

Uses and gratifications research: a widely challenged paradigm of media studies research that had its heyday in the 1970s and suggested that the media seamlessly met universal human needs for information and advice. Uses and gratifications appeals to new researchers because it seems to reflect 'common sense' views about media consumption. Behind this, however, is the fact that those views have been ideologically fabricated by the media industry itself. The idea ignores the history, context and conflicts of media production and consumption.

Vernacular culture: the everyday folk culture of the ordinary people; things such as playing roots music that people did before and do outside of mass culture.

Vernacular theory: see **amateur theory.**

Vidders: fans who make video artworks to distribute to other fans, formerly by exchanging video cassettes but now usually via online sites like YouTube.

Virtual co-presence: the idea that instant, two way electronic communication lets us experience togetherness with geographically separated loved ones.

Web 2.0: a term coined by business analyst Tim O'Reilly to denote a new era of internet activity where users generate the content on social networking platforms.

Zapper: media industry terminology for a viewer who is more dedicated than a **casual** and less dedicated than a **fan**.

Notes

Chapter 1

1 'Kairos' is an ancient Greek word that refers to the supreme or opportune moment. It is also the title of an academic journal that focuses on rhetoric, technology and pedagogy.

2 The scholars that I am thinking of here are Ellis Cashmore and Cornel Sandvoss. Cashmore's *Sports Culture: An A-Z Guide* discusses sports fans and fanzines (2000, 118–23). Elsewhere he writes about media fans, for instance in *Celebrity Culture* (Cashmore 2006, 78–97). His book on David Beckham (2004) for Polity's *Celebrity* series effectively merges those two interests. Meanwhile, Cornel Sandvoss' *Fans: The Mirror of Consumption* (2005) evidently arose from an initial engagement with sports fandom, but thoroughly encompasses media fandom. Most other writers have tended to stick to one path only.

3 See Alderman (2002) for an academic study about Graceland graffiti as a form of audience participation.

4 Material on early Hollywood fandom is taken from Barbas (2001).

5 Wray still has fanfic online. For instance, 'What Ever Happened to Fay Wray?': http://tales-of-josan.livejournal.com/54335.html

6 Elihu Katz's extensive study of 7,000 letters to radio presenter Ted Malone found that fan mail writers saw him as 'an *unseen* friend whose loyalty one need not ever question' (1950/2012, 112–13; emphasis in original).

7 Taken from www.elvisinfonet.com/spotlight_mostcontroversialarticle.html

8 For more information on 'Uncle Forry' see the excellent Roadhouse Films DVD documentary, *Famous Monster* (MacDonald 2007).

9 As well as spawning several movie adaptions so far, *Star Trek* has been re-incarnated in four further live action series: *The Next Generation* (1987–94), *Deep Space Nine* (1993–9), *Voyager* (1995–2001) and *Enterprize* (2001–5). It quickly stimulated a culture of fan fiction writers who had included adult themes in their work by 1972 and pioneered slash writing in 1974 (Pugh 2005, 90–1).

10 For work on Beatlemania in its own era see Taylor (1966), Cooper (1968) and Davies (1969). More recent research includes Barbara Ehrenreich, Elizabeth Hess and Gloria Jabobs' (1992) interesting discussion of gender, and Ian Inglis' (2000) research on the Beatles in America. Sullivan (1987)

discusses Lennon's infamous 'more popular than Jesus' comment. Other Beatlemania research includes Muncie (2000), Berman, Lapidos and Bernstein (2008) and Millard (2012, 22–41).

11 As well as 1950s rock'n'roll and the subsequent blues revival, the counter-culture was influenced by the beatnik margin and folk protest movement.

12 Bowie, of course, effectively moved from one audience to the other.

13 The counterculture and sexual revolution had its own set of celebrity leaders and cult products. I am thinking here of people such as Timothy Leary, Alex Comfort and Linda Lovelace, star of the popular porn film *Deep Throat* (Damiano, 1972).

14 See Neda Ulaby's report for NPR, 'Vidder's Talk Back': www.npr.org/templates/story/story.php?storyId=101154811

15 Together with earlier fantasy franchises like *Xena: Warrior Princess* (1995–2001), *Buffy* marked the emergence of a new era of television fandom. Not only did its fans buy box sets, watch broadcasts and chat online. Their shows also seemed more in tune with female, gay and lesbian audiences. A new generation of fan studies' academics also had the tools and interests to report on these fan phenomena. For example, see Cathy Young's discussion 'What We Owe Xena': www.cathyyoung.net/features/whatweowexena.html. For *Buffy* scholarship see, for instance, Porter (2004), Williamson (2005), Keft-Kennedy (2008), Kirby-Diaz (2009) and Collier, Lamadue and Wooten (2009).

16 Jason Mittell (in Jenkins, Ford and Green 2013) calls such complex, apprenticeship shows 'drillable' media.

17 I am thinking here of Radiohead's 2007 album *In Rainbows* which was offered for whatever audiences wanted to pay – although a collectors version *was sold* to fans. Artists such as 50 Cent have also used their fans to road test songs online before release.

18 Far from the internet being a utopian space, its comment sections often seem full of critical comments structured around regressive ideologies. Consumer sovereignty is limited insofar that audiences are *already* steeped in particular discourses and follow specific ideologies.

19 For example, Giesler and Pohlmann (2003), Pugh (2005, 15–16) and Scott (2009) discuss fan cultures as non-commercial entities.

20 I am using the term 'cooler' as Marshall McLuhan might have done: not to signify 'hipper' but rather 'less frenetic and emotionally slower'. Cool passions can still run deep, however.

21 The conception of power here is essentially Foucaultian: power is everywhere because everyone holds some of it, but that does not mean that we all hold an equal amount.

22 Hills (2012) has discussed 'inter-fandom', noting how particular fan cultures can negatively stereotype others in a process that leads their participants away from certain objects and potentially towards other ones.

23 Cornel Sandvoss (2005a, 64) calls this *Heimat*: a 'sense of [emotional] security and stability' associated with *being where one belongs*.

24 I am borrowing this useful ethical tenet from Hills (2002).

Chapter 2

1 Joli Jensen's name was misspelled in the Lewis volume as 'Jenson'; I have used Professor Jensen's actual name here throughout, including the bibliography.

2 The comparison between 'excessive' (dedicated) fandom and masturbation appears in other slang terms such as 'fayonnaise', which is listed online in *The Urban Dictionary* as a kind of fannish equivalent to semen, that is, the materialized embodiment of inappropriate emotion: www.urbandictionary.com/define.php?term=fayonnaise. The masturbation metaphor also emphasizes the parasocial critique of fandom as an unreal and unrealized meeting with an object of desire.

3 The sheer amount of 'flaming' and 'trolling' online suggests that many users take perverse pleasure in insulting, criticizing, mocking, putting down and jokingly threatening complete strangers. Many use the space as an anonymous arena in which their critical process has no consequence except for propagating sarcastic entertainment. In some instances, though, online comments have been read seriously as inappropriately hateful or even dangerous public declarations. They also act to *police* those who depart from dominant values.

4 In other words, anti-fandom is connected with the display of cultural capital.

5 Films like *The Bachelor and the Bobbysoxer* (Reis 1947), *Almost Famous* (Crowe 2000), *Ghostworld* (Swigoff 2001) and *My Sucky Teen Romance* (Hagins 2011) have been celebrated as relatively positive towards their fan characters. Yet even ambiguous or bad taste comedies like *The Banger Sisters* (Dolman 2002) and *Fanboys* (Newman 2009) have their moments of redemption. Finally, films that feature a 'deranged fan' protagonist, such as *The King of Comedy* (Scorsese 1983), usually ask us how much we might empathize with him/her. Insofar that they constantly ask us to consider the world from the fan's perspective, such dramas are arguably *more* empathetic than documentaries like *Mondo Elvis* (Corboy 1984) or *Sound it Out* (Finlay 2011).

Chapter 3

1 In *Textual Poachers* Jenkins explained, 'Fans are poachers who get to keep what they take and use their plundered goods as the foundations for the construction of an alternative cultural community' (1992, 223).

2 I am thinking here, for example, of Manic Street Preachers' fans who criticized Ben Myers for his novelization *Richard* (2010), a tale of the mysterious disappearance of the band's guitarist Richey Edwards. If Richey had started as a fictional character, such fans might have discussed the book as 'character rape'.

3 See Jenkins (2006, 42 and 2008, 185).

4 There was a backlash, for instance, against *American Idol*'s 2007 season that took the form of a 'Vote for the Worst' campaign (Jenkins 2008, 91).

5 David Wall (2003) offers a case study of policing a celebrity image.

Chapter 4

1 From the BBC news story, 'Worshipping Celebrities Brings Success'. 13 August, 2003. http://news.bbc.co.uk/1/hi/health/3147343.stm

2 For other work on fandom as attachment see Cohen (2004).

3 See Giles (2009) for an overview of recent research. Also see Schmid and Klimmt (2011).

4 Perhaps Žižek is uncomfortable because he has been marketed as a celebrity himself and even been called 'the Elvis of cultural theory': the quote is used on the cover of his eponymous DVD documentary, *Žižek!* (2005) It suggests that the social theorist not only draws together diverse academic audiences and can give them what they want but also that his message is secondary to the pleasure of watching his thought unfold *almost for its own sake* as a public spectacle.

5 Because the mass culture paradigm already located fandom as a disturbance, it did not allow researchers to properly distinguish people who used their fandom to express an unconnected pathological disorder. However, it now seems clear that the woman who, famously, did not sleep with her husband because she 'loved' Barry Manilow (see Vermorel 1985/2011, 11–21) was notionally *using* extreme fandom to mask and compensate for her abnormally deep fear of intimacy. What was interesting about the case was that the example then became widely circulated as a classic example of extreme fandom.

6 Although researchers like Ferris and Harris (2011) have shown that fans *do* meet their idols on a more frequent basis than parasocial ideas suppose, it is also true that very famous people *cannot* for any length of time meet *all* their many, many fans on an equal, individual basis. They therefore have to find ways to manage the encounter.

7 Some groupies did the same thing in a different way. The 'plaster-casters' were two women from Chicago – Cynthia Albritton and her friend Dianne – who, in the wake of the free love movement, made casts of the erections of prominent rock performers like Jimi Hendrix. Their exploits are recorded in the documentary *Plaster Caster* (Everleth, 2001).

8 Warhol was, famously, a childhood fan of Shirley Temple and later he developed a fascination with author Truman Capote. His personal fandom has therefore become part of his story.

9 See MacKellar (2008) for one typology of different levels of fan dedication.

10 Schaeffer was shot by a mentally ill serial stalker who had previously menaced the child peace activist Samantha Smith. The 1990s Latin pop sensation Selena was shot by the president of her fan club after Selena accused her of embezzling money. Her 'fan' was not a stalker.

11 There is, perhaps, a class element here. For example, when fictional movie characters like Hannibal Lecter and (the talented) Mr Ripley act as aficionados who appreciate classical music, they reference their own social elitism, whereas media fandom can often tend to appear in representations of lower class monstrosity.

12 Taken from Kennedy (1997, online).

13 The interpretation of Chapman's motive as a quest for fame is similar to the notion portrayed in many Westerns like *The Shootist* (Seigel, 1976). It implies that fame or public reputation can be acquired by anyone who shoots down a famous gunslinger.

14 It has to be said that Hills is not referring to the Kleinian approaches here. They position individuals who project as *normal*, even if a fraction of their fantasies may be disturbingly abnormal.

Chapter 5

1 Contagion relates to ideas about the 'sacredness' of religious objects.

2 Argento is an auteur director of horror.

3 The acquisition of fan knowledge may sometimes indicate that one is primarily competing for recognition *within* the fan community.

4 Daniela Hairabedian's comment is taken from the *Daily Mail* news story 'Frightening strikes twice: Second bizarre Jacko statue unveiled . . . but this one sparks hate mail and death threats' which appeared 5 April 2011 (author unknown) and is available on the Website: www.dailymail. co.uk/news/article-1373681/Michael-Jackson-statue-Maria-von-Kohle r-Hackney-sparks-death-threats.html

5 Taken from the artist's page at the See Line gallery: http://seelinegallery. com/kohlerstatement.html

6 Also see Cavicchi (1998, 52 and 98).

7 This wave of new interest was signalled in several ways. For the first time in a decade the idea of having a national Elvis Presley Day was revived in Congress and gained the backing of 15 politicians. As a mark of Graceland's 'exceptional significance', the National Park Service placed the mansion on its Register of Historic Places. During the New York primary electoral campaign, the soon-to-be president Bill Clinton gave a saxophone rendition of 'Don't Be Cruel' in 1992 on the *Arsenio Hall* television chat show. Finally, when the United States postal service held an 'election' to decide upon the definitive version of their 1993 Elvis stamp, around ten million people voted.

8 To consider how social electricity is actualized in particular performances requires a focus on the immediate emotional, musical and semiotic dynamics through which individual spectators square their identities and concerns with those on stage. This issue of connection relates to dimensions of meaning as well as those of energy. I find it useful here to borrow Lawrence Grossberg's (1997, 160) discussion of affect and separate the libidinal and semiotic. The energizing loop of empowerment outlined by Durkheim appears 'libidinal' insofar that it is a form of energy that is invisible except through its manifestation in *meaningful* shared moments. Understanding this dimension of performance requires critical attention to the local semiotics (not energetics) of the event in question, the *way* that each spectator finds himself or herself *particularly interested* in the performer's music, identity and attitude. Although we can separate energetics and semiotics *for analytical purposes*, they are actually connected in reality.

9 A focus on the difference between live and recorded music has in some ways blinded us to their equivalence as ways to accrue social recognition by performing for an audience. Tours and recordings can both act as ways to build the artist's popularity, either by operating independently or by mutually selling each other.

10 The quote is taken from the BBC *Imagine* series documentary *Tom Jones: The Voice Exposed* (MacLaverty 2010).

11 I find it helps to visualize this threshold of conviction as the baseline on a bell-shaped graph of emotional intensity. It has to be crossed to enter into the knowing field, but any fan can also cross back again to a low intensity of emotion if his/her interest is waning.

Chapter 6

1 Taken from the Website www.immoralmarilyn.com

2 For an interesting list of fan fictions see http://fanlore.org/wiki/ Category:Tropes_%26_Genres

3 Published in the third issue of the Star Trek fanzine *Grup*, this section starts the first ever slash story. See: http://elvanesti.tumblr.com/post/2202911407 9/a-fragment-out-of-time-by-diane-marchant

4 There is some female-female slash (Jenkins 2006, 62).

5 For mention of H/C see Pugh (2005, 77), Sullivan in Thomas and O'Shea (2010, 126), and Zubernis and Larsen (2012, 90).

6 Crawford (2011) uses fan theory to study computer game players.

7 See Jenkins (1992, 220–1) and (2006, 62–4 and 77–9).

8 Quoted in Jenkins (2006, 78–9).

9 Much controversy surrounds one tricky rape scene in the *Blakes 7* story "Nearly Beloved/Rogue" and another from an episode called "Consequences" in *The Professionals* (1977–83) (see Jenkins 1992).

10 Catherine Johnson (2007, 15) uses the idea of diegsis to distinguish three types of merchandise: *diegetic* (replica props and costumes used in the show), *pseudo-diegetic* (part of the narrative universe, but not in the show) and *extra-diegetic* (about the series as a TV show: posters, episode guides).

11 Ironically, by the end of *High Fidelity*, the exhuberant Barry also uses his cultural capital to become smoking hot soul singer.

12 The *White Feather* Website can be found at www.whitefeatherexhibition.com/story.htm

13 Some elite fans just passed stories across to each other through the mail (Jenkins 1992, 158).

14 Joanne Garde-Hansen (2011, 127) views impersonation as an act of recreating a prosthetic memory. It could equally be viewed as celebrating/ paying tribute to past performances, or even as working in a niche genre or performance style. For more work on 'false' memories facilitated by the media, see Duffett (2003b) and Landsberg (2004).

Chapter 7

1 Zubernis and Larson's (2012) lively study of the series *Supernatural* (2005 onwards) also suggests that fanfic writers feel ashamed for imagining a slash relationship between the show's two male leads.

2 Bury (1998) offers a parallel example in which female fans of *The X-Files* (1993–2002) used their mailing list to create a space of shared pleasures and concerns that were devalued in wider society.

Chapter 8

1 Christine Scodari's (2007) work provides one case example of how fans have 'recycled, contested, and/or recreated' myths about the Beatles in the online realm.

2 See contributions by Bear (2010, 13) and Kowal (2010, 166) to the *Doctor Who* fandom book, *Chicks Who Dig Timelords* (Thomas and O'Shea 2010).

3 Genette (1997) sees very immediate secondary elements – such as author names, titles, dedication and prefaces – as classic paratexts. In media research, the term tends to be used more for things like advertisements, trailers and reviews.

4 Of course Sherlock has always had fans (called Sherlockians) and his phenomenon has been boosted by a BBC series updating his stories. See Pearson (2007) and Stein and Busse (2012).

5 Some examples are necessary here. Sony's collector imprint *Follow That Dream* releases limited edition book and CD pressings based on key moments in Elvis Presley's career. Also, Anchor Bay re-releases interesting, non-mainstream horror films in home playback formats.

6 For Landsberg (2004, 2), prosthetic memory 'emerges at the interface between a person and a historical narrative about the past, at an experiential site such as a movie theatre or museum. In this moment of contact, an experience occurs through which the person sutures himself or herself into larger history . . . the person does not simply apprehend a historical narrative, but takes on a more personal, deeply felt memory of a past event through which he/she did not live. The resulting prosthetic memory has the ability to shape that person's subjectivity and politics'. In other words, individuals are somehow *implanted* with 'false' memories that never happened to them. In contrast, the idea of 'imagined memories' locates such individuals as *desiring subjects* who *wish* they had been in the time and place where the events occurred.

7 'Real memory' is also, of course, a contradiction; all memories are invented by the ways in which the brain records, stores, recalls and interprets specific events.

8 See Cavicchi (1998, 173) and Fritsch (2010, 112).

Chapter 9

1 As unknown singer, Susan Boyle sang 'Cry Me a River' on a Scottish charity CD single made in 1999 by a West Lothian school. Charity singles are not *commercial* recordings in the usual sense of the term and only 1,000 copies were pressed.

2 Hellekson and Busse's (2006) edited volume contains a variety of examples of online fan performances studied from different perspectives.

3 This passage quotes from the first episode ('Love and Power') of the BBC documentary, *All Watched Over by Machines of Loving Grace* (Curtis 2011), where the words are credited to online poster Carmen Hermosillo. Further investigation, however, reveals them to be a paraphrase of the essay, 'Pandora's Vox: Community in Cyberspace' (see humdog 1996).

4 As Doss (1999, 12) notes, some Elvis fans also feel that their star could have been a member of their individual family. Their sense of filiation and pride positions Elvis as *their* man making good in the world of corporate media.

5 Matt Hills (2002a, 9) claimed that Henry Jenkins often ignored the factionalism within fan communities.

6 One example of this is that new fans in some fanfic communities have not obeyed community taboos against using real people as a basis for writing fictional scenarios (Jenkins 2006, 142).

Chapter 10

1 This was more apparent because the conference was staged at a university in Salford, a relatively poor urban area which has seen life expectancy rates remain considerably below the national average and unemployment levels reach as high as 50 per cent in the poorest parts. However, it is also true that Mark E. Smith is a widely-celebrated musician who plays upon his working-class background and inevitably evokes a sort of cross-class fascination.

2 Primitivism is the now-contested idea that particular races, societies or cultures are less 'advanced' in comparison to others. In modernity, the idea allowed Western society to see itself as relatively civilized and other cultures as uneducated, animalistic or savage. Hierarchical conceptions of human culture justified the colonial expansion of Europe across the rest of the planet. In their attempts to grasp the point of view of various 'native' cultures through immersion in their localities, early ethnographers like Bronislaw Malinowski had a complex relationship with this ongoing colonial project.

3 This charge applies most strongly to deductive researchers who either never encounter real fans or use only them to confirm pre-existing theories.

4 Springsteen fans' cries of 'Bruuuce!' at live music events, for example, have sometimes been misinterpreted as booing by outsiders who did not know any better (Cavicchi 1998, 27).

5 Neglected fan objects can include right-wing fictional texts, for example, such as the writings of Aryn Rand. However, this does not mean that fan studies are static: marginalized, young postgraduates have sometimes, for example, seized on the study of 'trash' culture as refuge and revenge against older generations of scholars (Hills 2002a, 59). However, only the right 'trash' is cool and only in the right circles. *It is the stubbornly 'uncool' forms of fandom that are perhaps the most interesting.*

6 Detailed autoethnographies – or less thoroughgoing autobiographic or anecdotal approaches – tend to be pursued either by feminists (who see the personal as political), media practitioners (who wish to reflect on production experience) and senior scholars (who, perhaps, have more experience at interpreting their lives in relation to theory, or, more cynically, are too busy to do wider research but still likely to get published). In terms of subject matter, Sarah Attfield (2011) for example, has argued that the approach has lent itself to discussing punk rock, because it prioritizes individual subjectivity over wider academic conformity.

Chapter 11

1 'Twihards' are the much-maligned fans of the vampire film franchise *Twilight*. For recent studies of *Twilight* fandom and responses to it see Click (2009), Click, Stevens Aubrey and Behm-Morawitz (2010), Larsson and Steiner (2011), Hills (2012) and his fellow contributors to Anne Morley's (2012) edited volume.

2 See Cavicchi (1998, 154).

3 Click (2007) explored the responses of Martha Stewart's fans as the television personality's image was scandalized.

4 Pleasures for fans as they age can include nostalgia, discussion, camaraderie and heritage tourism.

5 For histories of fandom see, for example, Barbas (2001), Coppa (2006), Young (2008) and Jenkins (2012b).

6 A flash mob is a crowd that assembles for a short time in public to collectively *perform* something such as a Michael Jackson dance routine.

7 Will Brooker (2002, 57) surmised that black and white focus groups of *Star Wars* fans would view the film in very different ways. Cavicchi (1998, 147–9) rather inconclusively discussed fans' perceptions of the (white) racial composition of Springsteen's audience. *Doctor Who* fan Martha Jones (2010, 173) referred to 'fans of color'. These and other studies hint at what could be an interesting discussion.

8 See Jenkins (2006, 164) and Hills (2002b).

9 Jenkins adds that activism has been facilitated by changes in media and technology. On one hand, media products which invite the audience to interactively 'participate' in the construction (and destruction) of celebrities are invitations to collective action. On the other, 'As the [online] community enlarges and reaction time shortens, fandom becomes much more effective as a platform for consumer activism' (Jenkins 2006, 141).

10 For example, to say, 'Yes – I am addicted', socially performs one's fandom in a way that implies: 'My fan object is *more* important to me than my individual autonomy'. The meaning of saying this is complex because it is so contradictory. Is it a shocked recognition of self-absence (possession), a voluntary act of self-negation (sacrifice), a way to cover-up something else (hidden choice), or all three?

11 In an increasingly public era, people who are *not* performers (in the traditional sense) are entering the spotlight through internet and press coverage. What do we call the audience members who find themselves passionately attached to politicians like Sarah Palin, regressive social movements or famous criminals? In 2011, Teresa Bystram formed a test case in the British media when she took her children across the country to attend the funeral of the rampage killer Raoul Moat. Bystram had never met Moat and she was sometimes labelled a 'fan' by the tabloid press (see, for example, Phillips 2011). Following the scandal of Bystram's Moat 'fandom', she was convicted of animal abuse in a case that prompted journalists to further question her sanity. Outlaws have often captured the popular imagination, but the extension of the term 'fan' to their followers indicates a more sinister estimation of the word. It reflects an era in which mediated relationships – and associated evaluations of public life *as performance* – have rapidly become the norm (also see Kingsepp 2010).

Bibliography

Abercrombie, Nicholas and Brian Longhurst. 1998. *Audiences: A Sociological Theory of Performance and Imagination*. London: Sage.

Adams Kelley, Jennifer. 2010. 'Rutle-ing the Doctor: My Long Life in *Doctor Who* Fandom'. In *Chicks Who Dig Timelords: A Celebration of Doctor Who by the Women Who Love It*, edited by Lynne Thomas and Tara O'Shea, 74–80. Des Moines: Mad Norwegian Press.

Adams, Rebecca and Robert Sardiello. 2000. *Deadhead Social Science*. Walnut Creek: Altimira.

Aden, Roger. 1999. *Popular Stories and Promised Lands: Fan Cultures and Symbolic Pilgrimages*. Tuscaloosa: University of Alabama Press.

Adorno, Theodor. 2001. 'On The Fetish-Character of Music and the Regression of Listening'. In *The Culture Industry: Selected Essays on Mass Culture*, edited by J. M. Bernstein, 29–60. New York: Routledge. (Original work published 1938)

Ahmed, Sarah. 2004. *The Cultural Politics of Emotion*. New York: Routledge.

Alberoni, Francesco. 2007. 'The Powerless Elite: Theory and Sociological Research on the Phenomenon of Stars'. In *Stardom and Celebrity: A Reader*, edited by Su Holmes and Sean Redmond, 65–77. London: Sage, 1960.

Alderman, Derek. 2002. 'Writing on the Graceland Wall: The Importance of Authorship in Pilgrimage Landscapes'. *Tourism Recreation Research* 27, 2: 27–33.

Aldred, Sophie. 2010. 'An Interview with Sophie Aldred'. In *Chicks Who Dig Timelords: A Celebration of Doctor Who by the Women Who Love It*, edited by Lynne Thomas and Tara O'Shea, 68–73. Des Moines: Mad Norwegian Press.

Alters, Diane. 2007. 'The Other Side of Fandom: Anti-Fans, Non-Fans, and the Hurts of History'. In *Fandom: Identities and Communities in a Mediated World*, edited by Jonathan Gray, Cornel Sandvoss and C. Lee Harrington, 344–56. New York: New York University Press.

Angelini, Sergio and Miles Booy. 2010. 'Members Only: Cult TV from Margins to Mainstream'. In *The Cult TV Book*, edited by Stacey Abbott, 19–27. London: IB Tauris.

Attfield, Sarah. 2011. 'Punk Rock and the Value of Autoethnographic Writing About Music'. *Portal* 8, 1: 1–11.

Atton, Chris. 2001. *Alternative Media: Culture, Representation and Identity*. Thousand Oaks, CA: Sage.

Bacon-Smith, Camille. 1991. *Enterprising Women: Television Fandom and the Creation of Popular Myth*. Philadelphia: University of Pennsylvania Press.

Barbas, Samantha. 2001. *Movie Crazy: Fans, Stars and the Cult of Celebrity*. New York: Palgrave.

Barfoot Christian, Elizabeth (ed.). 2011. *Rock Brands: Selling Sound in a Media-Saturated Culture.* Lanham: Lexington Books.

Barfoot Christian, Elizabeth and Dedria Givens-Caroll. 2011. 'When Death Goes Digital: Michael Jackson, Twenty-First Century Celebrity Death, and the Hero's Journey'. In *Rock Brands: Selling Sound in a Media-Saturated Culture*, edited by Elizabeth Barfoot-Christian, 325–38. Lanham: Lexington Books.

Barker, Martin. 1993. 'The Bill Clinton Fan Syndrome'. *Media, Culture and Society* 15: 669–73.

Barker, Martin and Kate Brooks. 1998. *Knowing Audiences: Judge Dredd – Its Friends, Fans and Foes.* Luton: University of Luton Press.

Barrowman, Carole. 2010. 'Time is Relative'. In *Chicks Who Dig Timelords: A Celebration of Doctor Who by the Women Who Love It*, edited by Lynne Thomas and Tara O'Shea, 18–22. Des Moines: Mad Norwegian Press.

Baym, Nancy. 1999. *Tune In, Log On: Fandom and Online Community.* Thousand Oaks, CA: Sage.

—. 2007. 'The New Shape of the Online Community: The Example of Swedish Independent Music Fandom'. *First Monday* 12, 8: http://firstmonday.org/htbin/cgiwrap/bin/ojs/index.php/fm/article/view/1978/1853/

—. 2010. *Personal Connections in the Digital Age.* Cambridge: Polity.

—. 2011. 'The Swedish Model: Balancing Markets and Gifts in the Music Industry'. *Popular Communication* 9, 1: 22–38.

Bear, Elizabeth. 2010. 'We'll Make Great Pets'. In *Chicks Who Dig Timelords: A Celebration of Doctor Who by the Women Who Love It*, edited by Lynne Thomas and Tara O'Shea, 12–17. Des Moines: Mad Norwegian Press.

Beer, David. 2008. 'Making Friends with Jarvis Cocker: Music Culture in the Context of Web 2.0'. *Cultural Sociology* 2, 2: 222–41.

Belk, Russell. 1995. *Collecting in a Consumer Society.* London: Routledge.

Benjamin, Walter. 2005 [1931]. 'Unpacking My Library'. In *Walter Benjamin: Selected Writings 1931–1934*, 486–93. Cambridge: Harvard University Press.

Bennett, Lucy. 2011. 'Music Fandom Online: REM Fans in Search of the Ultimate First Listen'. *New Media and Society* 14: 478–763. http://nms.sagepub.com/content/early/2011/12/11/1461444811422895.abstract

Berlin, Joey. 1996. *Toxic Fame.* Detroit: Visible Ink.

Berman, Gary, Mark Lapidos and Sid Bernstein. 2008. *We're Going to See the Beatles: An Oral History of Beatlemania as Told by the Fans Who Were There.* Solana Beach, CA: Santa Monica Press.

Boas, Gary. 2006. *Starstruck: Photographs from a Fan.* Los Angeles: Dilettante Press.

Boon, Susan and Christine Lomore. 2001. 'Admirer-celebrity Relationships among Young Adults: Explaining Perceptions of Celebrity Influence on Identity'. *Human Communication Research* 27: 432–65.

Booth, Paul. 2010. *Digital Fandom: New Media Studies.* New York: Peter Lang.

—. 2012. 'Saw Fandom and the Transgression of Fan Excess'. In *Transgression 2.0: Media, Culture and the Politics of a Digital Age*, edited by David Gunkle and Ted Gournelos, 69–84. New York: Continuum.

Bourdieu, Pierre. 1984. *Distinction: A Social Critique of the Judgement of Taste.* Cambridge, MA: Harvard University Press.

Bradford, K. Tempest. 2010. 'Martha Jones: Fangirl Blues'. In *Chicks Who Dig Timelords: A Celebration of Doctor Who by the Women Who Love It*, edited by Lynne Thomas and Tara O'Shea, 168–74. Des Moines: Mad Norwegian Press.

Braudy, Leo 1987. *The Frenzy of the Reknown: Fame and Its History*. Oxford: Oxford University Press.

Brooker, Will. 2002. *Using the Force: Creativity, Community and* Star Wars *Fans*. New York: Continuum.

—. 2007. 'A Sort of Homecoming: Fan Viewing and Symbolic Pilgrimage'. In *Fandom: Identities and Communities in a Mediated World*, edited by Jonathan Gray, Cornel Sandvoss and C. Lee Harrington, 149–64. New York: New York University Press.

Bukatman, Scott. 1994. 'X-Bodies (the Torment of a Mutant Superhero) '. *Uncontrollable Bodies: Testimonies of Identity and Culture*, edited by Rodney Sappington and Tyler Stallings, 93–129. Seattle: Bay Press.

Bury, Rhiannon. 1998. 'Waiting to X-Hale : A Study of Gender and Community on an All-Female *X-Files* Electronic Mailing List'. *Convergence* 4, 3: 59–83.

—. 2003. 'Stories for [Boys] Girls: Female Fans Read the X-Files'. *Popular Communication* 1, 4: 217–42.

Busse, Kristina and Karen Hellekson (eds). 2006. *Fan Fiction and Fan Communities in the Age of the Internet*. Jefferson: McFarland & Company.

Butler, Judith. 1999. *Gender Trouble*. New York: Routledge. (Original work published 1990)

Buxton, David. 1990. 'Rock Music, The Star System and the Rise of Consumerism'. In *On Record*, edited by Simon Frith and Andrew Goodwin, 366–77. London: Routledge.

Cashmore, Ellis. 2000. *Sports Culture: An A-Z Guide*. London: Routledge.

—. 2004. *Beckham*. Cambridge: Polity.

—. 2006. *Celebrity Culture*. Abingdon: Routledge.

Castles, John. 1997. 'Madonna: Mother of Mirrors'. *Cultural Studies* 11, 1: 113–18.

Caughey, John. 1978. 'Artificial Social Relations in Modern America'. *American Quarterly* 3, 1: 70–89.

—. 1984. *Imaginary Social Worlds: A Cultural Approach*. Nebraska: University of Nebraska Press.

Cavicchi, Daniel. 1998. *Tramps Like Us: Music and Meaning Among Springsteen Fans*. Oxford: Oxford University Press.

—. 2011. *Listening and Longing: Music Lovers in the Age of Barnum*. Middletown, CT: Wesleyan.

Chadwick, Vernon (ed.). 1997. *In Search of Elvis: Music, Race, Art, Religion*. Boulder: Westview Press.

Cherry, Brigid. 2002. 'Screaming for Release: Femininity and Horror Film Fandom in Britain'. In *British Horror Cinema*, Steve Chibnall and Julian Petley, 42–57. London: Routledge.

Christgau, Robert. 2005. 'Writing About Music is Writing First'. *Popular Music* 24: 15–42.

Church, David. 2009. 'Of Manias, Shit, and Blood: The Reception of Salò as a "Sick Film"'. *Participations* 6, 2: www.participations.org/Volume%206/Issue%202/church.htm

Cialdini, Robert. 2001. *Influence: Science and Practice*. Boston: Allyn & Bacon.

Click, Melissa. 2007. 'Untidy: Fan Response to the Soiling of Martha Stewart's Spotless Image'. In *Fandom: Identities and Communities in a Mediated World*, edited by J. Gray, C. Sandvoss and C. L. Harrington, 301–15. New York: New York University Press.

—. 2009. '"Rabid", "Obsessed", and "Frenzied": Understanding Twilight Fangirls and the Gendered Politics of Fandom'. *Flow TV*. http://flowtv. org/2009/12/rabid-obsessed-and-frenzied-understanding-twilight-fangirls-and-the-gendered-politics-of-fandom-melissa-click-university-of-missouri/

Click, Melissa, Jennifer Stevens Aubrey and Elizabeth Behm-Morawitz (eds). 2010. *Bitten by Twilight: Youth Culture, Media, and the Vampire Franchise*. New York: Peter Lang.

Clifford, James and George Marcus. 2010. *Writing Culture: The Poetics and Politics of Ethnography*. Berkeley: University of California Press. (Original work published 1985)

Cohen, Jonathan. 2004. 'Parasocial Breakup from Favourite Television Characters: The Role of Attachment Styles and Relationship Intensity'. *Journal of Social and Personal Relationships* 12, 2: 187–202.

Collins, Jim. 1995. *Architectures of Excess: Cultural Life in the Information Age*. London, Routledge.

Collier, Noelle, Christine Lamadue and H. Ray Wooten. 2009. '*Buffy the Vampire Slayer* and *Xena: Warrior Princess*: Reception of the Texts by a Sample of Lesbian Fans and Website Users', *Journal of Homosexuality* 56, 5: 575–609.

Cooper, Robert. 1968. 'Beatlemania: An Adolescent Contra-Culture'. MA Diss., McGill University.

Coppa, Francesca. 2006. 'A Brief History of Media Fandom'. In *Fan Fiction and Fan Communities in the Age of the Internet*, edited by Kristina Busse and Karen Hellekson, 41–60. Jefferson: McFarland & Company.

Couldry, Nick. 2000. *Inside Culture: Re-Imagining the Method of Cultural Studies*. London: Sage.

—. 2007a. 'Media Power: Some Hidden Dimensions'. In *Stardom and Celebrity: A Reader*, Su Holmes and Sean Redmond, 353–9. London: Sage.

—. 2007b. 'On the Set of The Sopranos: 'Inside'a Fan's Construction of Nearness'. In *Fandom: Identities and Communities in a Mediated World*, edited by Jonathan Gray, Cornel Sandvoss and C. Lee Harrington, 139–48. New York: New York University Press.

Crawford, William. 2011. *Video Gamers*. Abingdon: Routledge.

Cubbitt, Sean. 1991. *Timeshift: On Video Culture*. Abingdon: Routledge.

Davies, Evan. 1969. 'Psychological Characteristics of Beatle Mania'. *Journal of the History of Ideas* 30, 2: 273–80.

Davies, Helen. 2001. 'All Rock and Roll is Homoscial: The Representation of Women in the British Rock Press'. *Popular Music* 20, 3: 301–19.

Davisson, Amber and Paul Booth. 2007. 'Reconceptualizing Communication and Agency in Fan Activity: Proposal for a Projected Interactivity Model for Fan Studies'. *Texas Speech Communication Journal* 32, 1: 33–43.

DeAngelis, Michael. 2001. *Gay Fandom and Crossover Stardom: James Dean, Mel Gibson and Keanu Reeves*. Durham: Duke University Press.

De Kosnick, Abigail. 2013. 'Fandom as Free Labor'. In *Digital Labor: The Internet as Playground and Factory*, edited by Trebor Scholz, 98–111. Routledge, New York.

DeNora, Tia. 2000. *Music in Everyday Life*. Cambridge: Cambridge University Press.

Derecho, Abigail. 2006. 'Archontic Literature: A Definition, a History, and Several Theories of Fan Fiction'. In *Fan Fiction and Fan Communities in the Age of the Internet*, edited by Kristina Busse and Karen Hellekson, 61–78. Jefferson: McFarland.

Derrida, Jaques. 1976. *Of Grammatology*. Baltimore: Johns Hopkins University Press.

Dickins, Christa. 2010. 'Martha Jones: Fangirl Blues'. In *Chicks Who Dig Timelords: A Celebration of Doctor Who by the Women Who Love It*, edited by Lynne Thomas and Tara O'Shea, 175–81. Des Moines: Mad Norwegian Press.

Doherty, Thomas. 2002. *Teenagers and Teenpics*. Philadephia: Temple University Press.

Doss, Erika. 1999. *Elvis Culture: Fans, Faith and Image*. Kansas: University of Kansas Press.

Dittmer, Jason and Klaus Dodds. 2010. 'Popular Geopolitics Past and Future: Fandom, Identities and Audiences'. *Geopolitics* 13, 3: 437–57.

Duffett, Mark. 1999. 'Reading the Rock Biography: A Life without Theory'. Conference Paper, Robert Shelton Memorial Conference, IPM, Liverpool.

—. 2000a. 'Going Down like a Song: National Identity, Global Commerce and the Great Canadian Party'. *Popular Music* 19, 1: 1–11.

—. 2000b. 'Transcending Audience Generalizations: Consumerism Reconsidered in the Case of Elvis Presley Fans'. *Popular Music and Society* 24, 2: 75–92.

—. 2001. 'Caught in a Trap? Beyond Pop Theory's "Butch" Construction of Male Elvis Fans'. *Popular Music* 20, 3: 395–408.

—. 2002. 'Naturalizing the Webcast: Live Performance, Nostalgia and Paul McCartney's "Little Big Gig"'. *Convergence* 8, 1: 30–42.

—. 2003a. 'False Faith or False Comparison? A Critique of the Religious Interpretation of Elvis Fan Culture'. *Popular Music and Society* 26, 4: 513–22.

—. 2003b. 'Imagined Memories: Webcasting as a "Live" Technology and the case of "Little Big Gig"'. *Information, Communication and Society* 6, 3: 307–25.

—. 2004a. 'A "Strange Blooding in the Ways of Popular Culture?" *Party at the Palace* as Hegemonic Project'. *Popular Music and Society* 27, 4: 489–506.

—. 2004b. 'Matt Hills, *Fan Cultures* [review]'. *European Journal of Cultural Studies* 7, 2: 255.

—. 2004c. 'The Ballad of Mark Chapman'. *Kindamuzik* December. www. kindamuzik.net/features/article.shtml?id=8099

—. 2009. 'We are Interrupted by your Noise': Heckling and the Symbolic Economy of Popular Music Stardom'. *Popular Music and Society* 32, 1: 37–57.

—. 2010a. 'Average White Band: Kraftwerk and the Politics of Race'. In *Kraftwerk: Music Non-Stop*, edited by David Pattie and Sean Albiez, 194–213. London: Continuum Press.

—. 2010b. 'Michael Bertrand, Race, Rock and Elvis, and Louis Cantor, Dewey and Elvis [review]'. *Popular Music* 29, 1: 169–73.

—. 2010c. 'Sworn in: Today, Bill Grundy and the Sex Pistols'. In *Popular Music and Television in Britain*, edited by Ian Inglis, 85–104. Farnham: Ashgate.

— 2011a. 'Applying Durkheim to Elvis: What Starts Popular Music Fandom?' IASPM UK and Ireland Conference, Cardiff University School of Music, 2 September.

—. 2011b. 'Elvis Presley and Susan Boyle: Bodies of Controversy'. *Journal of Popular Music Studies* 23, 2: 166–88.

—. 2011c. 'Fear Nothing: Self-fashioning and Social Mobility in 50 Cent's *The 50th Law*'. *Popular Music and Society* 34, 5: 683–92.

Dugdale, Timothy. 2000. 'The Fan and (Auto) Biography: Writing the Self in the Stars'. *Journal of Mundane Behaviour* 1, 2: 143–69.

Dunscombe, Stephen. 1997. *Notes from Underground: Zines and the Politics of Alternative Culture*. London, Verso.

Dyer, Richard. 1986. *Stars*. London, BFI.

—. 2004. 'Judy Garland and Gay Men'. In *Heavenly Bodies: Film Stars and Society*, 137–91. London: Routledge.

Eastman, Jason. 2012. 'Southern Masculinity in American Rock Music'. *Landscapes: The Arts, Aesthetics, and Education* 10, 4: 271–86.

Easthope, Antony. 1992. *What a Man's Gotta Do: The Masculine Myth in Popular Culture*. London: Routledge.

Eco, Umberto. 1995. '*Casablanca*: Cult Movies and Inter-textual Collage'. In *Faith in Fakes: Travels in Hyperreality*, 197–212. London: Minerva.

Edelman, Lee. 2004. 'The Future is Kid Stuff'. In *No Future: Queer Theory and the Death Drive*, 1–32. London: Duke University Press.

Egan, Kate and Martin Barker. 2006. 'Rings around the World: Notes on the Challenges, Problems & Possibilities of International Audience Projects'. *Participations* 3, 2: www.participations.org/volume%203/issue%202%20 -%20special/3_02_eganbarker.htm

Ehrenreich, Barbara, Elizabeth Hess and Gloria Jabobs. 1992. 'Beatlemania: Girls Just Want To Have Fun'. In *The Adoring Audience: Fan Culture and Popular Media*, edited by Lisa Lewis, 84–106. London: Routledge.

Eisen, Johnathan. ed. 1970. *The Age of Rock 2: Sights and Sounds of the American Cultural Revolution*. New York: Vintage Books.

Elliot, Anthony. 1998. 'Celebrity and Political Psychology: Remembering Lennon'. *Political Psychology* 19, 4: 833–52.

—. 1999. *The Mourning of John Lennon*. Berkeley: University of California Press.

Falkenberg, Pamela. 1989. 'No Sanity Clause'. *Cultural Studies* 3, 3: 348–52.

Farrington, Holly. 2006. 'Narrating the Jazz Life: Three Approaches to Jazz Autobiograhy'. *Popular Music and Society* 29, 3: 375–86.

Fein, Robert and Bryan Vossekuil. 2008. 'Foreword'. In *Stalking, Threatening and Attacking Public Figures*, edited by J. Reid Meloy, Lorraine Sherridan and Jens Hoffman, ix–xi. New York: Oxford University Press.

Ferris, Kerry. 2001. 'Through a Glass, Darkly: The Dynamics of Fan-Celebrity Encounters'. *Symbolic Interaction* 24, 1: 25–47.

Ferris, Kerry and Scott Harris. 2011. *Stargazing: Celebrity, Fame and Social Interaction*. New York: Routledge.

Fiddy, Dick. 2010. 'The Cult of Cult TV?' In *The Cult TV Book*, edited by Stacey Abbott, 225–32. London: IB Tauris.

Fingeroth, Danny. 2008. *The Rough Guide to Graphic Novels*. London: Rough Guides.

Fish, Stanley. 1980. *There a Text in This Class?: The Authority of Interpretive Communities*. Cambridge: Harvard University Press.

Fisher, India. 2010. 'An Interview with India Fisher'. In *Chicks Who Dig Timelords: A Celebration of Doctor Who by the Women Who Love It*, edited by Lynne Thomas and Tara O'Shea, 51–4. Des Moines: Mad Norwegian Press.

Fiske, John. 1989. *Reading the Popular*. Boston: Unwin Hyman.

—. 1989. *Understanding Popular Culture*. Boston: Unwin Hyman.

—. 1990. 'Ethnosemiotics: Some Presonal Theoretical Reflections'. *Cultural Studies* 4, 1: 35–57.

—. 1991. 'Madonna'. In *Reading the Popular*, 95–114. London, Routledge.

—. 1993. 'The Cultural Economy of Fandom'. In *The Adoring Audience*, edited by Lisa Lewis, 30–49. London: Routledge.

Forster, Derek. 2004. '"Jump in the Pool": The Competitive Culture of *Survivor* Fan Networks'. In *Understanding Reality Television*, edited by Su Holmes and Deborah Jermyn, 270–89. London: Routledge.

France, Anthony. 2011. '"Stalker" Seized Madonna In Mansion'. *The Sun*. 14 March. http://www.thesun.co.uk/sol/homepage/news/3464949/Grzegorz-Matlok-is-seized-inside-Madonna-London-mansion.html

Freud, Sigmund, 2001. 'Remembering, Repeating and Working-Through (Further Recommendations on the Technique of Psycho-Analysis II)'. In *The Standard Edition of the Complete Psychological Works, Volume XII: Case Study of Schreber, Papers on Technique and Other Works*, edited by James Strachey, 147–56. London: Hogarth. (Original work published 1914)

Frith, Simon. 1992. 'The Cultural Study of Popular Music'. In *Cultural Studies*, edited by Lawrence Grossberg, Cary Nelson and Paula Treicheler, 174–81. London: Routledge.

—. 1996. 'Performance'. In *Performing Rites*, 203–25. Cambridge: Harvard University Press.

Frith, Simon and Andrew Goodwin (eds). 1990. *On Record: Rock, Pop and the Written Word*. London: Routledge.

Frith, Simon and Angela McRobbie. 1990. 'Rock and Sexuality'. In *On Record: Rock, Pop and the Written Word*, edited by Simon Frith and Andrew Goodwin, 371–89. London, Routledge.

Fritsch, Amy. 2010. 'Two Generations of Fan Girls in America'. In *Chicks Who Dig Timelords: A Celebration of Doctor Who by the Women Who Love It*, edited by Lynne Thomas and Tara O'Shea, 112–17. Des Moines: Mad Norwegian Press.

Garde-Hansen, Joanne. 2011. *Media and Memory*. Edinburgh: Edinburgh University Press.

Genette, Gérard. 1997. *Paratexts: Thresholds of Interpretation*. Cambridge: Cambridge University Press.

Giesler, Markus and Mali Pohlmann. 2003. 'The Antropology of File Sharing: Consuming Napster as Gift'. *Advances in Consumer Research* 30, edited by P. A. Keller and D. W. Brooks, 273–9. Provo, UT: Association for Consumer Research.

Giles, David. 2000. *Illusions of Immortality: A Psychology of Fame and Celebrity*. Basingstoke: Hampshire.

—. 2009. 'Parasocial Interaction: A Review of the Literature and Model for Future Research'. *Media Psychology* 4, 3: 279–305.

Goddard, Michael and Benjamin Halligan. 2010. *Mark E. Smith and the Fall: Art, Music and Politics*. Fanham: Ashgate.

Goffman, Erving. 1990. *The Presentation of Self in Everyday Life*. London: Penguin. (Original work published in 1959)

Gray, Jonathan. 2003. 'New Audiences, New Textualities: Anti-fans and Non-fans'. *International Journal of Cultural Studies* 6, 1: 64–81.

—. 2007a. 'Mommy, is that a Boy Text or a Girl Text?' *FlowTV* May 18, http://flowtv.org/?p=417

—. 2007b. 'The News: You Gotta Love It'. In *Fandom: Identities and Communities in a Mediated World*, edited by Jonathan Gray, Cornel Sandvoss and C. Lee Harrington, 75–87. New York: New York University Press.

—. 2010. *Show Sold Separately: Promos, Spoilers and Other Media Paratexts*. New York: New York University Press.

Gray, Jonathan, Cornel Sandvoss and C. Lee Harrington. 2007. 'Introduction: Why Study Fans?' In *Fandom: Identities and Communities in a Mediated World*, edited by Jonathan Gray, Cornel Sandvoss and C. Lee Harrington, 1–18. New York: New York University Press.

Gray, Jonathan, Cornel Sandvoss and C. Lee Harrington (eds). 2007. *Fandom: Identities and Communities in a Mediated World*. New York: New York University Press.

Gray, Jonathan and Jason Mittell. 2007. 'Speculation on Spoilers: Lost Fandom, Narrative Consumption and Rethinking Textuality'. *Participations* 4, 1: www.participations.org/Volume%204/Issue%201/4_01_graymittell.htm

Gray, Jonathan and Roberta Pearson. 2007. 'Gender and Fan Culture (Round Ten)'. *Live Journal* http://community.livejournal.com/fandebate/4100.html

Green, Lelia and Carmen Guinery. 2004. 'Harry Potter and Fan Fiction Phenomenon'. *Media/Culture* 7, 5: http://journal.media-culture.org.au/0411/14-green.php

Gregg, Melissa and Geregory Seigworth (eds). 2010. *The Affect Theory Reader*. Durham: Duke University Press.

Gregory, Georgina. 2012. 'Transgender Tribute Bands and the Subversion of Male Rites of Passage through the Performance of Heavy Metal Music'. *Journal of Cultural Research* 16, 1: 1–16.

Grossberg, Lawrence. 1992. 'Is There a Fan in the House? The Affective Sensibility of Fandom'. In *The Adoring Audience*, edited by Lisa Lewis, 50–65. London: Routledge.

—. 1997. 'Postmodernity and Affect: All Dressed and No Place to Go'. In *Dancing In Spite of Myself: Essays on Popular Culture*, 145–65. Durham: Duke University Press.

—. 2011. *Cultural Studies in the Future Tense*. Durham: Duke University Press.

Gunkel, David and Ted Gournelos (eds). 2012. *Transgression 2.0: Media, Culture and the Politics of a Digital Age*. New York: Continuum.

Gunnels

Gunnels, Jen. 2009. 'A Jedi Like My Father Before Me': Social Identity and the New York Comic Con'. *Tranformative Works and Cultures* 3: http://journal.transformativeworks.org/index.php/twc/article/view/161/110

Habermas, Jürgen. 2005. *The Structural Transformation of the Public Sphere.* Cambridge: Polity Press. (Original work published 1962)

Hajdu, David. 2008. *The Ten Cent Plague: The Great Comic-Book Scare and How It Changed America.* New York: Farrar, Strauss and Giroux.

Halberstam, Judith. 1998. *Female Masculinity.* Durham: Duke University Press.

Hall, Stuart. 1980. 'Encoding/decoding'. In *Culture, Media, Language: Working Papers in Cultural Studies, 1972–79*, edited by Centre for Contemporary Cultural Studies, 128–38. London: Hutchinson. (Original work published 1973)

Hancock Hinds, Mary. 2001. *Infinite Elvis: An Annotated Bibliography.* Chicago: Acapella Books.

Harrington, C. Lee and Denise Bielby. 2005. 'Introduction: New Directions in Fan Studies'. *American Behavioral Scientist* 48, 7: 799–800.

—. 2010. 'A Life Course Perspective on Fandom'. *International Journal of Cultural Studies* 13, 5: 429–50.

Harris, Cheryl (ed.). 1998. *Theorizing Fandom: Fans, Subculture, and Identity.* Cresskill: Hampton Press.

Hellinger, Bert. 2001. *Supporting Love: How Love Works in Couple Relationships.* Phoenix: Zeig, Tucker & Theisen.

Hermes, Joke. 1993. 'Media, Meaning and Everyday Life'. *Cultural Studies* 7, 3: 493–516.

Hertitz, Daniel. 2008. *The Star as Icon.* New York: Columbia University Press.

Hesmondhalgh, David. 2005. 'Producing Celebrity'. In *Understanding Media: Inside Celebrity*, edited by Jessica Evans and David Hesmondhalgh, 97–134. Maidenhead: Open University Press.

Hills, Matt. 2001. 'Intensities Interviews Henry Jenkins'. *Intensities* 2, 7 July: http://davidlavery.net/Intensities/PDF/Jenkins.pdf

—. 2002a. *Fan Cultures.* London: Routledge.

—. 2002b. 'Transcultural "Otaku": Japanese Representations of Fandom and Representations of Japan in Anime/Manga Fan Cultures'. Media in Transition 2 Globalization and Convergence Conference, 10–12 May http://web.mit.edu/cms/Events/mit2/Abstracts/MattHillspaper.pdf

—. 2003. '*Star Wars* in Fandom, Film Theory and the Museum: the Cultural Status of the Cult Blockbuster'. *Movie Blockbusters*, edited by Julian Stringer, 178–89. London: Routledge.

—. 2005a. 'Academic Textual Poachers: *Blade Runner* as Cult Canonical Movie'. In *The Blade Runner Experience: The Legacy of a Science Fiction Classic*, edited by Will Brooker, 124–41. London and New York: Wallflower.

—. 2005b. 'Patterns of Surprise: The "Aleatory Object" in Psychoanalytic Ethnography and Cyclic Fandom'. *American Behavioral Scientist* 48, 7: 801–21.

—. 2007a. 'Media Academics as Media Audiences'. In *Fandom: Identities and Communities in a Mediated World*, edited by Jonathan Gray, Cornel Sandvoss and C. Lee Harrington, 33–47. New York: New York University Press.

—. 2007b. 'Michael Jackson Fans on Trial?'Documenting'Emotivism and Fandom in Wacko About Jacko'. *Social Semiotics* 17, 4: 459–77.

—. 2010a. 'Subcultural Identity'. In *The Cult TV Book*, edited by Stacey Abbott, 233–8. London: IB Tauris.

—. 2010b. *Triumph of a Time Lord: Regenerating Doctor Who in the Twenty-first Century.* New York: IB Tauris.

—. 2012. '*Twilight* Fans Represented in Commercial Texts and Inter-Fandoms: Resisting and Repurposing Negative Fan Stereotypes'. In *Genre, Reception and Adaption in the* Twilight *Series*, edited by Anne Morey, 113–30. Farnham: Ashgate.

Hinerman, Stephen. 1992. 'I'll be Here for You: Fans, Fantasy and the Figure of Elvis'. In *The Adoring Audience*, edited by Lisa Lewis, 107–34. London, Routledge.

Hoffman, J. M. and L. P. Sheridan. 2005. 'The Stalking of Public Figures: Management and Intervention'. *Journal of Forensic Sciences* 50, 6: 1459–65.

Hoggart, Richard. 1957. *The Uses of Literacy: Aspects of Working Class Life with Special Reference to Publications and Entertainments.* London: Chatto and Windus.

Hollows, Joanne. 2003. 'The Masculinity of Cult'. In *Defining Cult Movies: The Cultural Politics of Oppositional Taste*, edited by Mark Jancovich Mark Jancovich, Antonio LázaroReboli, Julian Stringer and Andrew Willis 35–53. Manchester, Manchester University Press.

Homan, Shane (ed.). 2006. *Access All Eras: Tribute Bands and Global Pop Culture.* Maidenhead: Open University Press.

Horton, Donald and Richard Wohl. 1956. 'Mass Communication and Parasocial Interaction: Obervations on Intimacy at a Distance'. *Psychiatry* 19: 215–29.

humdog. 1996. 'pandora's vox: on community in cyberspace'. In *High Noon on the Electronic Frontier*, edited by Peter Ludlow, 437–44. Cambridge, MA: The Massachusetts Institute of Technology Press.

Inglis, Ian. 2000. '"The Beatles are Coming!" Conjecture and Conviction in the Myth of Kennedy, America and the Beatles'. *Popular Music and Society* 24, 2: 93–108.

Jancovich, Mark. 2002. 'Cult Fictions: Cult Movies, Subcultural Capital and the Production of Cultural Distinctions'. *Cultural Studies* 16, 2: 306–22.

Jancovich, Mark and Nathan Hunt. 2004. 'The Mainstream, Distinction and Cult TV'. In *Cult Television*, edited by Sara Gwellian-Jones and Roberta Pearson, 27–44. Minneapolis: University of Minnesotta Press.

Jenkins, Henry. 1992. '"Strangers No More, We Sing": Filking and the Social Construction of the Science Fiction Fan Community'. In *The Adoring Audience*, edited by Lisa Lewis, 208–36. New York: Routledge.

—. 1992. *Textual Poachers.* London, Routledge.

—. 1995a. 'Do You Enjoy Making Us Feel Stupid?: alt.tv.twinpeaks, the Trickster Author and Viewer Mastery'. In *Full of Secrets: Critical Approaches to Twin Peaks*, edited by David Lavery, 51–69. Detroit: Wayne State University Press.

—. 1995b. 'Out of the Closet and into the Universe'. In *Science Fiction Audiences: Watching Star Trek and Doctor Who*, edited by John Tulloch and Henry Jenkins, 237–66. London: Routledge.

—. 1996. 'A Conversation with Henry Jenkins'. In *Enterprize Zones: Critical Positions on Star Trek*, edited by Taylor Harrison Taylor Harrison, Sarah

Projansky, Kent Ono and Elyce Rae Helford. Boulder, CO: Westview Press. http://web.mit.edu/cms/People/henry3/harrison.html

—. 2005. 'Why Fiske Still Matters'. *Flow TV* 10 June. http://flowtv.org/?p=585

—. 2006. *Fans, Bloggers, Gamers*. New York: New York University Press.

—. 2008. *Convergence Culture: Where Old and New Media Collide*. New York: New York University Press.

—. 2007. 'Afterword: The Future of Fandom'. In *Fandom: Identities and Communities in a Mediated World*, edited by Jonathan Gray, Cornel Sandvoss and C. Lee Harrington, 357–64. New York: New York University Press.

—. 2010. 'Avatar Activism and Beyond'. Confessions of an Aca-Fan. http://henryjenkins.org/2010/09/avatar_activism_and_beyond.html

—. 2012a. 'Fandom 2.0: An Interview with Henry Jenkins'. In *Transgression 2.0: Media, Culture and the Politics of a Digital Age*, edited by Ted Gournelos and David Gunkel, 212–22. New York: Continuum.

—. 2012b. 'Superpowered Fans: The Many World of San-Diego's Comic-Con'. *Boom: A Journal of California* 2, 2: 22–36.

Jenkins, Henry, Sam Ford and Joshua Green (eds). 2013. *Spreadable Media: Creating Value and Meaning in a Networked Culture*. New York: New York University Press.

Jenkins, Henry and Sangita Shresthova. 2012. 'Up, Up, and Away! The Power and Potential of Fan Activism'. *Journal of Transformative Works and Cultures* 10: http://journal.transformativeworks.org/index.php/twc/article/view/435/305

Jensen, Joli. 1992. 'Fandom as Pathology'. In *The Adoring Audience*, edited by Lisa Lewis, 9–29. London, Routledge.

Johnson, Catherine. 2007. 'Tele-Branding in TVIII: The Network as Brand and the Programme as Brand'. *New Review of Film and Television Studies* 5, 1: 5–24.

Johnson, Derek. 2007. 'Fan-tagonism: Factions, Institutions, and Constitutive Hegemonies of Fandom'. In *Fandom: Identities and Communities in a Mediated World*, edited by Jonathan Gray, Cornel Sandvoss and C. Lee Harrington, 285–300. New York: New York University Press.

Kang, Helen. 2010. 'Adventures in Ocean-Crossing, Margin Skating and Feminist Engagement with *Doctor Who*'. In *Chicks Who Dig Timelords: A Celebration of Doctor Who by the Women Who Love It*, edited by Lynne Thomas and Tara O'Shea, 38–45. Des Moines: Mad Norwegian Press.

Kassabian, Anahid. 2004. 'Would You Like Some World Music with your Latte? Starbucks, Putumayo and Distributed Listening'. *Twentieth-Century Music* 1, 2: 209–23.

Katz, Elihu. 1950. 'The Happiness Game: A Content Radio Analysis of Radio Fan Mail'. MA Diss., Colombia University. Reprinted 2012 in *International Journal of Communication* 6: http://ijoc.org/ojs/index.php/ijoc/article/viewFile/1633/758

Katz, Elihu, Jay Blumler and Michael Gurevitch. 1973. 'Uses and Gratifications Research'. *The Public Opinion Quarterly* 37, 4: 509–23.

Kaveney, Roz. 2010. 'Gen, Slash, OT3s, and Crossover – The Varieties of Fan Fiction'. In *The Cult TV Book*, edited by Stacey Abbott, 243–7. London: IB Tauris.

Keft-Kennedy, Virginia. 2008. 'Fantasising Masculinity in *Buffyverse* Slash Fiction: Sexuality, Violence, and the Vampire'. *Nordic Journal of English Studies* 7, 1: 49–80.

Kennedy, Harlan. 1997. 'Cannes Film Festival 1997: The 50th International Film Festival'. www.americancinemapapers.com/files/cannes_1997.htm

Kennedy, N., M. McDonough, Brendan Kelly and German Berrios. 2002. 'Erotomania Revisited: Clinical Course and Treatment'. *Comprehensive Psychology* 43, 1: 1–6.

Kermode, Mark. 1997. 'I was a Teenage Horror Fan'. In *Ill Effects: The Media and TV Violence Debate*, edited by Martin Barker and Julian Petley, 57–66. London: Routledge.

Kingsepp, Eva. 2010. '"Nazi Fans" but not Neo-Nazis: The Cultural Community of 'WWII Fanatics'. In *Returning (to) Communities: Theory, Culture and Political Practice of the Communal*, edited by Stephan Herbrechter and Michael Higgins, 223–40. New York: Rodophi.

Kirby-Diaz, Mary. 2009. *Buffy and Angel Conquer the Internet*. Jefferson: McFarland.

Kowal, Mary. 2010. 'Traveling with the Doctor'. In *Chicks Who Dig Timelords: A Celebration of Doctor Who by the Women Who Love It*, edited by Lynne Thomas and Tara O'Shea, 164–7. Des Moines: Mad Norwegian Press.

Lamerichs, Nicolle. 2011. 'Stranger than Fiction: Fan Identity in Cosplay'. *Transformative Works and Cultures* 7: http://journal.transformativeworks.org/index.php/twc/article/view/246/230

Lancaster, Kurt. 2001. *Interacting with Babylon 5: Fan Performances in a Media Universe*. Austin: University of Texas Press.

Landsberg, Alison. 2004. *Prosthetic Memories: The Transformation of American Remembrance in an Age of Mass Culture*. New York: Columbia University Press.

Larsson, Mariah and Ann Steiner (eds). 2011. *Interdisciplinary Approaches to Twilight: Studies in Fiction, Media and a Contemporary Cultural Experience*. Lund, Sweden: Nordic Academic Press.

Lavery, David. 1995. *Full of Secrets: Critical Approaches to Twin Peaks*. Oakland: Wesleyan State University Press.

Lendrum, Robert. 2004. 'Queering Super-Manhood: The Gay Superhero in Contemporary Mainstream Comic Books'. *Journal for the Arts, Sciences, and Technology* 2, 2: 69–73.

Leonard, M. 1997. 'Rebel Girl, You are Queen of My World'. In *Sexing the Groove: Popular Music and Gender*, edited by Sheila Whiteley, 230–56. London: Routledge.

—. 1998. 'Paper Planes: Travelling the New Grrrl Geographies'. In *Cool Places: Geographies of Youth Cultures*, edited by Tracey Skelton and Gil Valentine, 102–21. London: Routledge.

Lewis, Lisa (ed.). 1992. *The Adoring Audience*. London: Routledge.

Lewis, Randy. 2011. 'Piracy Watchdog's Mild Bite'. *Los Angeles Times* 9 June. http://articles.latimes.com/2011/jun/09/entertainment/la-et-web-sheriff-20110609

Lipton, Mark. 2008. 'Queer Readings of Popular Culture: Searching to [Out] the Subtext'. In *Queer Youth Cultures*, edited by Susan Driver, 163–80. New York: State University of New York.

Löbert, Anja. 2008. 'Cliff Richard's Self-Presentation as a Redeemer'. *Popular Music* 27, 1: 77–97.

Longhurst, Brian. 1995. *Popular Music & Society*. Cambridge, Polity Press

Lumby, Catharine. 2007. 'Doing It For Themselves? Teenage Girls, Sexuality and Fame'. In *Stardom and Celebrity: A Reader*, edited by Su Holmes and Sean Redmond, 341–52. London: Sage.

Macdonald, Dwight. 1957. 'A Theory of Mass Culture'. In *Mass Culture: The Popular Arts in America*, edited by Bernard Rosenberg and David Manning White, 59–73. New York: MacMillan.

Mackellar, Joanne. 2006. 'Fanatics, Fans or Just Good Fun? Travel Behaviours and Motivations of the Fanatic'. *Journal of Vacation Marketing* 2, 3: 195–217.

—. 2008. 'Dabblers, Fans and Fanatics: Exploring Behavioural Segmentation at a Special Interest Event'. *Journal of Vacation Marketing* 15, 1: 5–24.

Maltby, John. Lynn McCutcheon, Diane Ashe and James Houran. 2001. 'The Self-Reported Psychological Wellbeing of Celebrity Worshippers'. *North American Journal of Psychology* 3: 441–52.

— 2003. 'A Cognitive Profile of Individuals Who Tend to Worship Celebrities'. *Journal of Psychology: Interdisciplinary and Applied* 137, 4: 309–22.

Maltby, John. Liza Day, Lynn McCutcheon, James Houron and Diane Ashe 2006. 'Extreme Celebrity Worship, Fantasy Proneness and Dissociation: Developing the Measurement and Understanding of Celebrity Worship within a Clinical Personality Context'. *Personality and Individual Differences* 40, 2: 273–83.

Marcus, Greil. 1999. *Dead Elvis: A Chronicle of Cultural Obsession*. Cambridge, MA: Harvard University Press.

Marshall, P. David. 1997. *Celebrity and Power: Fame and Contemporary Culture*. Minneapolis: University of Minnesota Press.

Mathijs, Ernest and Xavier Mendik (eds). 2008. *The Cult Film Reader*. Maidenhead: Open University Press.

McCloud, Sean. 2003. 'Popular Culture Fandoms, the Boundaries of Religious Studies and the Project of the Self'. *Culture and Religion* 4, 2: 187–206.

McCourt, Tom. 2005. 'Collecting Music in the Digital Realm'. *Popular Music and Society* 28, 2: 249–52.

McCourty, Tom and Patrick Burkart. 2007. 'Customer Relationship Management: Automating Fandom in Music Communities'. In *Fandom: Identities and Communities in a Mediated World*, edited by Jonathan Gray, Cornel Sandvoss and C. Lee Harrington, 261–70. New York: New York University Press.

McCranor Henderson, William. 1997. *I, Elvis: Confessions of a Counterfeit King*. New York: Boulevard.

McCutcheon, Lynn. Rense Lange and James Houron. 2002. 'Conceptualization and Measurement of Celebrity Worship'. *British Journal of Psychology* 93: 67–87.

McCutcheon, Lynn. John Maltby, James Houran, Rense Lange and Diane Ashe. 2002. 'Thou Shalt Worship No Other Gods – Unless They Are Celebrities'. *Personality and Individual Differences* 32, 7: 1157–72.

McGuire, Seanan. 2010. 'Mathematical Excellence: A Documentary'. In *Chicks Who Dig Timelords: A Celebration of Doctor Who by the Women Who Love*

It, edited by Lynne Thomas and Tara O'Shea, 118–21. Des Moines: Mad Norwegian Press.

McKay, Emily et al., 2011. 'No.1 The Godfather: Iggy Pop.' In *The World's Greatest Frontmen Ever* (supplement), New Musical Express, 21 February.

McQuail, Denis, Jay Blumler and J. Roger Brown. 1972. 'The Television Audience: a Revised Perspective'. In *Sociology of Mass Communications*, edited by Dennis McQuail, 5–65. London: Penguin Books.

Mead, Johanna. 2010. 'Costuming: More Productive Than Drugs, But Just as Expensive'. In *Chicks Who Dig Timelords: A Celebration of Doctor Who by the Women Who Love It*, edited by Lynne Thomas and Tara O'Shea, 55–61. Des Moines: Mad Norwegian Press.

Meloy, J. Reid, Lorraine Sherridan and Jens Hoffman. 2008. 'Public Figure Stalking, Threats and Attacks: The State of Science'. In *Stalking, Threatening and Attacking Public Figures*, edited by J. Reid Meloy, Lorraine Sherridan and Jens Hoffman, 3–36. New York: Oxford University Press.

Meyrowitz, Joshua. 1985. *No Sense of Place: The Impact of the Electronic Media on Social Behaviour*. Oxford University Press: New York.

Middleton, Richard. 1990. 'It's All Over Now: Popular Music and Mass Culture'. In *Studying Popular Music*, 34–63. Buckingham, Open University Press.

—. 2006. *Voicing the Popular: On the Subjects of Popular Music*. New York: Routledge.

Mihelich, John and John Papineau. 2005. 'Parrotheads in Margaritaville: Fan Practice, Oppositional Culture, and Embedded Cultural Resistance in Buffett Fandom'. *Journal of Popular Music Studies* 17, 2: 175–202.

Millard, André. 2012. *Beatlemania: Technology, Business and Teen Culture in Cold War America*. Baltimore: Johns Hopkins University Press.

Miller, D. A. 1991. 'Anal Rope'. In *Inside/Out: Lesbian Theories, Gay Theories*, edited by Diana Fuss, 119–141. New York: Routledge.

Monaco, Jeanette. 2010. 'Memory Work, Autoethnography and the Construction of a Fan-ethnography'. *Participations* 7, 1: www.participations. org/Volume%207/Issue%201/monaco.htm

Morley, Anne (ed.). 2012. *Genre, Reception and Adaption in the Twilight Series*. Farnham: Ashgate.

Morley, David. 1993. 'Active Audience Theory: Pitfalls and Pendulums'. *Journal of Communication Research* 43, 3: 13–19.

Mulvey, Laura. 1975. 'Visual Pleasure and Narrative Cinema'. *Screen* 16, 3: 6–18.

Muncie, John. 2000. 'The Beatles and the Spectacle of Youth'. In *The Beatle, Popular Music and Society: A Thousand Voices*, edited by Ian Inglis, 35–52. London: St Martin's Press.

Murray, Simone. 2004. 'Celebrating the Story the Way it is: Cultural Studies, Corporate Media and the Contested Utility of Fandom'. *Continuum* 18, 1: 7–25.

Myers, Ben. 2010. *Richard: The Mystery of the Manic Street Preachers*. London: Picador.

Myles, Liz. 2010. 'The Tea Lady'. In *Chicks Who Dig Timelords: A Celebration of Doctor Who by the Women Who Love It*, edited by Lynne Thomas and Tara O'Shea, 137–41. Des Moines: Mad Norwegian Press.

Negus, Keith. 1996. 'Popular Music and the Printed Word'. In *Popular Music in Theory*, 71–4. Cambridge: Polity Press.

Neumann, Iver B. Neumann. 2006. 'Pop Goes Religion: Harry Potter Meets Clifford Geertz'. *European Journal of Cultural Studies* 9, 1: 81–100.

Nightingale, Virginia. 1996. *Studying Audiences: The Shock of the Real*. London, Routledge.

Nikunen, Kaarina. 2007. 'The Intermedial Practices of Fandom'. *Nordicom Review* 28, 2: 111–28.

Nye, Jody Lynne. 2010. 'Hopelessly Devoted to *Who*'. In *Chicks Who Dig Timelords: A Celebration of Doctor Who by the Women Who Love It*, edited by Lynne Thomas and Tara O'Shea, 103–11. Des Moines: Mad Norwegian Press

Orman, Kate. 2010. 'If I Can't "Squee", I Don't Want to be Part of Your Revolution: Crone-ology of an Aging Fangirl'. In *Chicks Who Dig Timelords: A Celebration of Doctor Who by the Women Who Love It*, edited by Lynne Thomas and Tara O'Shea, 142–53. Des Moines: Mad Norwegian Press.

O'Shea, Tara. 2010. 'The Tea Lady'. In *Chicks Who Dig Timelords: A Celebration of Doctor Who by the Women Who Love It*, edited by Lynne Thomas and Tara O'Shea, 98–102. Des Moines: Mad Norwegian Press.

Parrish, Juli. 1996. *Inventing a Universe: Reading and Writing Internet Fan Fiction*. PhD Diss., University of Pittsburgh.

Pearce, Susan. 1992. *Museums, Objects and Collections: A Cultural Study*. Washington: Smithsonian Institution Scholarly Press.

Pearson, Roberta. 2007. 'Bachie, Bardies, Trekkies, and Sherlockians'. In *Fandom: Identities and Communities in a Mediated World*, edited by Jonathan Gray, Cornel Sandvoss and C. Lee Harrington, 98–109. New York: New York University Press.

Penley, Constance. 1991. 'Brownian motion: Women, Tactics, and Technology'. In *Technoculture*, edited by Contance Penley and Andrew Ross, 35–161. Minneapolis: University of Minnesota Press.

—. 1992. 'Feminism, Psychoanalysis, and the Study of Popular Culture'. In *Cultural Studies*, edited by Lawrence Grossberg, Cary Nelson and Paula A. Treichler, 479–500. New York: Routledge.

—. 1997. *NASA/Trek: Popular Science and Sex in America*. London: Verso.

Phillips, Rhodri. 2011. 'Raoul Moat Fan Kept 24 Pet Cats in Squalor'. *The Sun*. 21 November. www.thesun.co.uk/sol/homepage/news/3948091/Raoul-Moat-fan-kept-24-pet-cats-in-squalor.html

Phillips, Tom. 2010. 'Embracing the "Overly Confessional": Scholar-Fandom and Approaches to Personal Research'. *Flow* 13, 5: http://flowtv.org/2010/12/embracing-the-overly-confessional/

Porter, Nicole. 2004. *In Search of Slayer: Audience Negotiation of Buffy the Vampire Slayer*. MA Diss., Concordia University.

Pugh, Sheenagh. 2005. *The Democratic Genre: Fan Fiction in a Literary Context*. Bridgend: Seren.

Radway, Janice. 1984. 'The Ideal Romance: The Promise of Patriarchy'. In *Reading the Romance*, 119–56. London, Verso, 1987.

Reynolds, Simon. 2012. *Retromania: Pop Culture's Addiction to Its Own Past*. London: Faber and Faber.

Rhodes, Lisa. 2005. *Electric Lady Land: Women and Rock Culture*. Philadephia: University of Pennsylvania Press.

Ribes, Alberto. 2010. 'Theorizing Global Media Events: Cognition, Emotions and Performances'. *New Global Studies* 4, 3: 1–20.

Roberts, Karl. 2007. 'Relationship Attachment and the Behaviour of Fans towards Celebrities'. *Applied Psychology in Criminal Justice* 3, 1: 54–74.

Robey, Tim. 2012. '*Vertigo*: is Hitchcock's Thriller Really the Best Film Ever Made?' *The Daily Telegraph, Telegraph plus*, 3 August.

Robson, Hillary. 2010. 'Television and the Cult Audience: A Primer'. In *The Cult TV Book*, edited by Stacey Abbott, 209–20. London: IB Tauris.

Rodman, Gilbert. 1996. *Elvis after Elvis: The Posthumous Career of a Living Legend*. New York: Routledge.

Rojek, Chris. 2007. 'Celebrity and Religion'. In *Stardom and Celebrity: A Reader*, edited by Su Holmes and Sean Redmond, 171–80. London: Sage.

Rose, Lloyd. 2010. 'What's a Girl to Do?' In *Chicks Who Dig Timelords: A Celebration of Doctor Who by the Women Who Love It*, edited by Lynne Thomas and Tara O'Shea, 46–50. Des Moines: Mad Norwegian Press.

Rosenbaum, Jonathan. 1980. 'The Rocky Horror Picture Cult'. *Sight & Sound* Spring: 78–9.

Ruggiero, Thomas. 2000. 'Uses and Gratifications Theory in the 21st Century'. *Mass Communication & Society* 3, 1: 3–37

Sanderson, Jimmy and Pauline Cheong. 2010. 'Tweeting Prayers and Communicating Grief over Michael Jackson Online'. *Bulletin of Science, Technology & Society* 30, 5: 328–40.

Sandvoss, Cornel. 2005a. *Fans: The Mirror of Consumption*. Cambridge: Polity Press.

—. 2005b. 'One Dimensional Fan'. *American Behavioural Scientist* 48, 7: 822–39.

—. 2012. 'Enthusiasm, Trust and its Erosion in Mediated Politics: On fans of Obama and the Liberal Democrats'. *European Journal of Communication* 27, 1: 68–81.

Sandvoss, Cornel. Matt Hills, Christine Scodari and Rebecca Tushnet. 2007. 'Fan Texts: From Aesthetic to Legal Judgments'. In *Fandom: Identities and Communities in a Mediated World*, edited by Jonathan Gray, Cornel Sandvoss and C. Lee Harrington, 19–74. New York: New York University Press.

Sanjek, David. 2008. 'Fan's Notes: The Horror Film Fanzine'. In *The Cult Film Reader*, edited by Ernest Mathijs and Xavier Mendik, 419–28. Maidenhead: Open University Press.

Santino, Jack. 2009. 'The Ritualesque: Festival, Politics and Popular Culture'. *Western Folklore* 68, 1: 9–26.

Sarris, Andrew. 1962. 'Notes on the Auteur Theory in 1962'. Film Culture 27: 1–8.

Schmid, Hannah and Christoph Klimmt. 2011. 'A Magically Nice Guy: Parasocial Relationships with Harry Potter Across Different Cultures'. *International Communication Gazette* 73, 3: 252–69.

Schwichtenberg, Cathy. 1993. *The Madonna Connection: Representational Politics, Subcultural Identities and Cultural Theory*. Boulder, CO: Westview Press.

Scodari, Christine. 2007. 'Yoko in Cyberspace with Beatles Fans: Gender and the Recreation of Popular Mythology'. In *Fandom: Identities and Communities in a Mediated World*, edited by Jonathan Gray, Cornel Sandvoss and C. Lee Harrington, 48–59. New York: New York University Press.

Scott, Suzanne. 2009. 'Repackaging Fan Culture: The Regifting Economy of Ancilliary Content Models'. *Tranformative Works and Cultures* 3: http://journal.transformativeworks.org/index.php/twc/article/view/150/122

Seaman, William. 1992. 'Active Audience Theory: Pointless Populism'. *Media, Culture and Society* 14, 2: 301–11.

Seiter, Ellen. Hans Borchers, Gabriele Kreutzner, and Eva-Maria Warth. 1989. 'Don't Treat us Like we're So Stupid and Naive: Toward an Ethnography of Soap Opera Viewers'. In *Remote Control: Television, Audiences and Cultural Power*, 223–47. New York: Routledge.

Sheffield, Jessica and Merlo, Elsye. 2010. 'Biting Back: Twilight Anti-Fandom and the Rhetoric of Superiority'. In *Bitten by Twilight: Youth Culture, Media, and the Vampire Franchise*, edited by Melissa Click, Jeniffer Aubrey and Elizabeth Behm- Morawitz, 207–24. New York: Peter Lang.

Shuker, Roy. 1994. 'My Generation'. In *Understanding Popular Music*, 225–50. London, Routledge.

—. 2004. 'Beyond the'*High Fidelity*'Stereotype: Defining the (Contemporary), Record Collector'. *Popular Music* 23, 3: 311–30.

—. 2010. *Wax Trash and Vinyl Treasures: Record Collecting as Social Practice*. Fanham: Ashgate.

Sontag, Susan. 2001. 'Notes on "Camp"'. In *Against Interpretation and Other Essays*, 275–92. New York: Farrar, Strauss and Giroux.

Spigel, Lynn. 2001. *Welcome to the Dreamhouse*. Durham: Duke University Press.

Spitzberg, Brian and William Cupach. 2008. 'Fanning the Flames of Fandom: Celebrity Worship, Parasocial Interaction and Stalking'. In *Stalking, Threatening and Attacking Public Figures*, edited by J. Reid Meloy, Lorraine Sherridan and Jens Hoffman, 287–324. New York: Oxford University Press.

Stacey, Jackie. 1994. *Stargazing: Hollywood Cinema and Female Spectatorship*. London: Routledge.

Stanish, Deborah. 2010. 'My Fandom Regenerates'. In *Chicks Who Dig Timelords: A Celebration of Doctor Who by the Women Who Love It*, edited by Lynne Thomas and Tara O'Shea, 31–7. Des Moines: Mad Norwegian Press.

Stein, Louisa Ellen and Kristina Busse (eds). 2012. *Sherlock and Transmedia Fandom*. Jefferson, NC: McFarland.

Stevens Aubrey, Jennifer, Elizabeth Behm-Morawitz and Melissa A. Click. 2010. 'The Romanticization of Abstinence: Fan Response to Sexual Restraint in the *Twilight* Series'.*Transformative Works and Cultures* 5: http://journal.transformativeworks.org/index.php/twc/article/view/216/184

Stever, Gayle. 2009. 'Parasocial and Social Interaction with Celebrities: A Classification of Media Fans'. *Journal of Media Psychology* 14, 3: 1–7.

—. 2010. 'Fan Behavior and Lifespan Development Theory: Explaining Parasocial and Social Attachment to Celebrities'. *Journal of Adult Development* 18, 1: 1–7.

—. 2011. 'Celebrity Worship: Constructing a Critique'. *Journal of Applied Social Psychology* 41, 6: 1356–70.

Storey, John. 2009. *Cultural Theory and Popular Culture: An Introduction.* Harlow: Pearson Education.

Straw, Will. 1997. 'Sizing up Record Collections: Gender and Connoisseurship in Rock Music Culture'. In *Sexing the Groove: Popular Music and Gender,* edited by Sheila Whiteley, 3–17. London: Routledge.

Stromberg, Peter. 1990. 'Elvis Alive? The Ideology of Consumerism'. *Journal of Popular Culture* 24, 3: 11–19.

Sullivan, Caroline. 1999. *Bye Bye Baby: My Tragic Love Affair with the Bay City Rollers.* London: Bloomsbury.

Sullivan, Kathryn. 2010. 'The Fanzine Factor'. In *Chicks Who Dig Timelords: A Celebration of Doctor Who by the Women Who Love It,* edited by Lynne Thomas and Tara O'Shea, 122–31. Des Moines: Mad Norwegian Press.

Sullivan, Mark. 1987. '"More Popular Than Jesus": The Beatles and the Religious Far Right'. *Popular Music* 6, 3: 313–26.

Swiss, Thomas. 2005. 'That's me in the Spotlight: Rock Autobiographies'. *Popular Music* 24, 287–94.

Taylor, Anthony James William. 1966. 'Beatlemania: A Study in Adolescent Enthusiasm'. *British Journal of Social and Clinical Psychology* 5, 2: 81–8.

Théberg, Paul. 2005. 'Everyday Fandom: Fan Clubs, Blogging and the Quotidian Rhythms of the Internet'. *Canadian Journal of Communication* 30, 4: 485–502.

Thomas, Lyn. 2003. *Fans, Feminisms and the Quality Media.* London: Routledge.

Thomas, Lynne. 2010. 'Marrying Into the Tardis Tribe'. In *Chicks Who Dig Timelords: A Celebration of Doctor Who by the Women Who Love It,* edited by Lynne Thomas and Tara O'Shea, 81–6. Des Moines: Mad Norwegian Press.

Thomas, Lynne and Tara O'Shea (eds). 2010. *Chicks Who Dig Timelords: A Celebration of Doctor Who by the Women Who Love It.* Des Moines: Mad Norwegian Press.

Thornton, Sara. 1995. *Club Culture: Music, Media and Subcultural Capital.* Cambridge: Polity Press.

Tidhar, Lavie. 2012. *Osama: A Novel.* Oxford: Solaris Books.

Till, Rupert. 2010. *Pop Cult: Religion and Popular Music.* New York: Continuum.

Tudor, Andrew. 1997. 'Why Horror? The Peculiar Pleasures of a Popular Genre'. *Cultural Studies* 11, 3: 443–63.

Tulloch, John. 1995. 'We're Only a Speck in the Ocean: The Fans as a Powerless Elite'. In *Science Fiction Audiences: Watching Doctor Who and Star Trek,* edited by John Tulloch and Henry Jenkins, 144–72. New York: Routledge.

Turnbull, Sue. 2005. 'Moments of Inspiration: Performing *Spike*'. *European Journal of Cultural Studies* 8, 3: 367–73.

Turner, Kay (ed.). 1993. *I Dream of Madonna: Women's Dreams of the Goddess of Pop.* San Francisco: Collins.

Valente, Catherynne. 2010. 'Regeneration X'. In *Chicks Who Dig Timelords: A Celebration of Doctor Who by the Women Who Love It*, edited by Lynne Thomas and Tara O'Shea, 181–5. Des Moines: Mad Norwegian Press.

van Zoonen, Liesbet. 2005. *Entertaining the Citizen: When Politics and Popular Culture.* Lanham, MD: Rowman & Littlefield.

Verhoeven, Deb. 2009. *Jane Campion.* London: Routledge.

Vermorel, Fred. 1983. *Secret History of Kate Bush (and the Strange Art of Pop).* London: Omnibus Press.

—. 2000. 'Fantastic Voyeur: Lurking on the Dark Side of Biography'. *Village Voice Literary Supplement*, October. www.villagevoice.com/specials/vls/170/vermorel.shtml

—. 2006. *Addicted to Love: Kate Moss.* London: Omnibus Press.

—. 2008. 'Starlust: Love, Hate and Celebrity Fantasies. Obscenity Law Stops Fans From Thinking Aloud'. *The Register* 12 November. www.theregister.co.uk/2008/11/12/fred_vermorel_girls_aloud/print.html

—. 2011. *Starlust*. London: WH Allen. (Original work published 1985)

Vermorel, Fred and Judy Vermorel. 1989. *Fandemonium*. London: Omnibus Press.

—. 1990. 'Starlust'. In *On Record: Rock Pop and the Written Word*, edited by Simon Frith and Andrew Goodwin, 410–18. London: Routledge.

—. 1993. 'A Glimpse of the Fan Factory'. In *The Adoring Audience*, edited by Lisa Lewis, 191–207. London: Routledge.

Victor, Adam. 2008. *The Elvis Encyclopedia*. New York: Overlook Duckworth.

Vroomen, Laura. 2004. 'Kate Bush: Teen Pop and Older Female Fans'. In *Music Scenes: Local, Translocal and Virtual*, edited by Andy Bennett and Richard Peterson, 238–54. Nashville: Vanderbilt University Press.

Waksman, Steve. 2007. 'Grand Funk Live! Staging Rock in the Age of the Arena'. In *Listen Again: A Momentary History of Pop Music*, edited by Eric Weisbard, 157–71. Durham: Duke University Press.

—. 2011. 'Selling the Nightingale: PT Barnum, Jenny Lind and the Management of the American Crowd'. *Arts Marketing* 1, 2: 108–20.

Wall, David. 2003. 'Policing Elvis: Legal Action and the Shaping of Post-mortem Celebrity Culture as Contested Space'. *Entertainment Law* 2, 3: 35–69.

Wall, Tim. 2003. 'Collecting'. In *Studying Popular Music Culture*, 205–10. London: Arnold.

Warren, Louis. 2002. 'Buffalo Bill Meets Dracula: William F. Cody, Bram Stoker, and the Frontiers of Racial Decay'. *American Historical Review* 107, 4: www.historycooperative.org/journals/ahr/107.4/ah0402001124.html#REF14

Wells, Alan. 1988. 'Images of Popular Music Artists: Do Male and Female Audiences Have Different Views?'*Popular Music and Society* 12, 3: 1–18.

Whitcomb, Ian. 1972. *After the Ball: Pop Music from Rag to Rock*. London: Penguin.

Williams, Mary Elizabeth. 2010. 'Mark Chapman, Fame Monster'.*Salon* 17 September. www.salon.com/2010/09/17/mark_david_chapman_fame_monster/

Williams, Rebecca. 2011. '"This is the Night TV Died": Television Post-Object Fandom and the Demise of *The West Wing*'. *Popular Communication* 9, 4: 266–79.

Williamson, Milly. 2003. 'Fan Cultures by Matt Hills'. *Journal of Consumer Culture* 3, 1: 121–3.

—. 2005. *The Lure of the Vampire: Gender, Fiction and Fandom from Bram Stoker to Buffy.* London: Wallflower Press.

Wise, Sue. 1990. 'Sexing Elvis'. In *On Record: Rock, Pop, and the Written Word*, edited by Simon Frith and Andrew Goodwin, 390–8. London: Routledge.

Wood, Helen. 2004. 'What *Reading the Romance* Did for us'. *European Journal of Cultural Studies* 7, 2: 147–54.

Wood, Robin. 1979. 'Introduction'. *American Nightmare: Essays on the Horror Film*, edited by Andrew Britton, Andrew Britton, Richard Lippe, Tony Williams and Robin Wood. 7–11. Toronto: Festival of Festivals.

Young, Clive. 2008. *Homemade Hollywood: Fans behind the Camera.* New York: Continuum.

Zubernis, Lynn and Katherine Larson. *Fandom at the Crossroads: Celebration, Shame and Fan/Producer Relationships.* Newcastle upon Tyne: Cambridge Scholars.

Index